'Written with humour and humani[...]
convincing and urgent: we need to r[...]
lifestyle if we want to prevent ecol[...]

'Unsentimental, hugely enjoyable and full of fascinating details ... Stylishly written and deeply researched, Mance ... makes a powerful case in this important book, which calls for radical change to the way we eat, farm and manage wildlife in this human age' Gaia Vince, author of *Transcendence*

'*How to Love Animals* is compassionate, funny and utterly readable. What's more, Mance does something of enormous value: he surprises himself and the reader, too ... In marrying this openness with his clarity of vision, Mance offers a new window on the climate emergency' *i* Newspaper

'A whip-smart, thought-provoking and thrilling investigation into one of the most essential moral issues of our time. Eye-opening as well as moving, challenging as well as frequently amusing, *How to Love Animals* surprised and fascinated me' Lucy Jones, author of *Losing Eden*

'Persuasive ... wry and on occasion laugh-out-loud funny. Like all the best reporters, Mance possesses an open mind and a strong moral compass, he's thorough and game for anything and he's good at drawing people out ... After reading this thoughtful and galvanising book, I've realised that it's better to keep trying to live in a way that shows compassion and respect for animals, and to sometimes fail, than to give up altogether' *New Statesman*

'Smart, provocative and funny, this book also throws down a huge challenge to all of us. You'll never look at your dog – or a glass of milk – in the same way again' Helen Lewis, author of *Difficult Women*

'Mance's lively first book argues for a profound reassessment of humans' relationships with other species ... He is a skilful writer who never shies away from painful stories, and leavens even the grimmest episodes with humour. He also has a rare ability to couch strenuous ethical arguments in terms that are warmly familiar' *The Economist*

'Henry Mance believes that the bad things we do to animals are the result of our failure to think through the consequences of our actions. *How to Love Animals* will remedy that failure, in a highly readable, informative and entertaining manner' Peter Singer, author of *Animal Liberation*

'Intensely researched and carefully woven ... varied and fascinating, and at times even funny. Mance ... has a lively style; if the subject matter is heavy, his prose slips down effortlessly ... I was gripped and provoked' *Spectator*

'I would recommend it to anybody' Sheila Dillon, BBC The Food Programme

'Challenging, but also funny and refreshingly low in sanctimony, this book is no frothing polemic. It will doubtless alter many readers' understanding of the systems we all participate in and lead them to make different choices. For others, it should prompt the difficult moral reasoning that those of us who love animals but also profit from their suffering cravenly manage to avoid ... Mance is an amiable guide: curious and open-minded' *Financial Times*

'Entertaining and thought-provoking, even if you loathe vegan sausage rolls' Piers Morgan

HENRY MANCE

Henry Mance is the award-winning Chief Features Writer at the *Financial Times*. He has contributed to a number of other publications including *Tatler*, *GQ* and the *Radio Times*. He lives in London with his wife and two young daughters, plus their cat and various frogs.

HENRY MANCE

How to Love Animals

Animals

And Protect Our Planet

VINTAGE

1 3 5 7 9 10 8 6 4 2

Vintage is part of the Penguin Random House group of companies whose addresses can be found at global.penguinrandomhouse.com

Penguin
Random House
UK

Copyright © Henry Mance 2021

Henry Mance has asserted his right to be identified as the author of this Work in accordance with the Copyright, Designs and Patents Act 1988

First published in Vintage in 2022
First published in hardback by Jonathan Cape in 2021

penguin.co.uk/vintage

A CIP catalogue record for this book is available from the British Library

ISBN 9781529112146

Printed and bound in Great Britain by Clays Ltd, Elcograf S.p.A.

The authorised representative in the EEA is Penguin Random House Ireland, Morrison Chambers, 32 Nassau Street, Dublin D02 YH68

Penguin Random House is committed to a sustainable future for our business, our readers and our planet. This book is made from Forest Stewardship Council® certified paper.

MIX
Paper from
responsible sources
FSC
www.fsc.org   FSC® C018179

For Eliza, who once thought she was a 'very tarian',
and Cleo, who sometimes thinks she is a tiger.

CONTENTS

INTRODUCTION

Love is the extremely difficult realisation that something other than oneself is real. Love ... is the discovery of reality.
                                                                    Iris Murdoch

In order to maintain a semblance of purposeful behaviour on this earth you have to believe that things are right or wrong.
                                                                    Joan Didion

I saw the best minds of my generation destroyed by cat videos. Pets sliding across polished floors, jumping into boxes, failing to calculate the correct trajectory required to land on next-door's roof. This was the golden age of the Internet, before the anti-vaxxers and the anti-anti-fascists came along and ruined things.

The videos said something about us. We consider ourselves animal-lovers. We soak up wildlife documentaries and heart-warming stories of animal achievement. We warm to politicians who cuddle animals; their pets would be re-elected more easily than they would.

But our love of animals comes with self-doubt. We know that our society has moved in a different direction. If pressed, we will admit that most farm animals probably don't have good lives and that many wild animals are losing their habitats. We would prefer the situation were different, but it is the price of our affluence.

So we don't think about animals much. Even though they are the source of much of our food and clothing, even though they have been responsible for the rise and fall of human societies, and even though they will probably be here after we have gone, we don't dwell on their existence.

This feels like a human planet. Living an urban life, as most of the world's population now does, I can go an entire day noticing only a couple of animals. I pass by pigeons, flick at a fruit fly, gently remove my cat Crumble from the precise corner of the magazine I'm trying to read – and then carry on as before. Animals appear in clichéd metaphors and quirky logos, but not as beings who comprise the majority of sentient life. We are one species out of 500 or so primates, 6,400 mammals and, at our best estimate, 7–8 million animals. How often do we recognise it?

When we do think about animals, we break them down into species and groups: cows, dogs, foxes, elephants and so on. And we assign them places in society: cows go on plates, dogs on sofas, foxes in rubbish bins, elephants in zoos, and millions of wild animals stay out there, *somewhere*, hopefully on the next David Attenborough series. This ability to compartmentalise has been wonderfully helpful: it has allowed us to feed ourselves, to find companions and entertainment, and to keep ourselves safe from dangerous animals. It has stopped us having a philosophical debate every time we go for a sandwich. It has saved us from feeling guilty about our very existence.

But the compartments are fragile. In fact, they are now splitting into pieces. Almost daily we are confronted with new insights into our fellow creatures. Animals we have treated as food – particularly pigs and cows – are now understood to be mentally and socially complex. Animals we have historically treated as disposable – like wolves and beavers – turn out to be vital for our living world. Animals we treat as priceless – such as jaguars and orangutans – are rendered homeless by human progress.

The compartments say more about us than they say about the animals. The more that we love animals for their own sake, the more broken our compartments become. In the west, we overwhelmingly think it's wrong that some Japanese eat whales, some South Koreans eat dogs, and some Cambodians eat rats. But try to explain why it's OK to eat pigs and cows, and not whales and dogs, and you disappear down a philosophical rabbit warren – like the hitman in Quentin Tarantino's *Pulp Fiction* who argues that a dog cannot be a filthy animal, because 'a dog's got personality'. Pigs have personality too. So why is it OK to kill 1.5 billion pigs this year, but an outrage to slaughter a dog? Why is it OK to keep pigs in barren enclosures, but not dogs? Why is it morally wrong to hunt a dozen whales, but not to use fishing nets that entangle hundreds of dolphins?

Put simply, love for animals is one of western society's core values, and rational thinking is another. But the way we treat animals doesn't fit with either of these values; it is guided by tradition and inertia. No one would vote for the looming mass extinction of wild animals, certainly not the animals themselves. Goodness knows how we will explain it to the next generation. But it is happening on our watch. Charles Darwin concluded that blushing was the most human of all expressions – which is lucky, as we have plenty to blush about.

Before coronavirus hit, optimists would often say that this was the best time ever to be a human – that, if you could choose any time in history to be alive, it should be now. But what would other animals choose? If you were born as a non-human mammal today, there is a greater chance than ever before that you would be born in a factory farm, in cramped, unnatural conditions. In a large dairy farm, a cow produces perhaps four times as much milk as she would have done a century ago, but her life expectancy has actually fallen. As a wild animal today, you would likely have a greater risk than your preceding generations that your habitat is being destroyed – or that the climate is changing to something you can't adapt to. Wild animal populations have fallen two-thirds on average since 1970, according to the Living Planet Index. Because of the growth of animal trading, particularly in Asia, there's probably also as great a chance as ever that you would be taken from the wild and kept in cruel conditions. We might fancy the life of a dog in modern-day America, lazing on the sofa with organic biscuits and a whimsical Instagram account, but, if we were randomly reincarnated, we'd be at least twenty times more likely to end up as American factory chickens. Given the choice of any time, would an animal choose to be born now? I don't think so.

What would happen if we thought about animals – *all* animals? Would we change the way we source our food, the way we treat the natural world and the way we look at animals in zoos?

Like many people, I fell in love with animals because I thought they were beautiful. My family had a pet dog, and my parents took me to zoos. We'd watch the Grand National on TV, and I'd feel baffled that jockey-less horses were disqualified; wasn't it kind of interesting that they ran faster once the humans had fallen off? At university I was briefly vegetarian for environmental reasons, until I clicked the wrong option on a drop-down menu and ended up on a long-haul flight being served a meal of raw carrots. In my twenties I took up photography. I became obsessed with capturing the speed of hummingbirds, the detail on grasshoppers and other kinds of animal wonder. In the spirit of George Best, I spent 90 per cent of my money on camera lenses; the rest I just wasted.

Animals make the best photographs. Half a dozen silver fish, shimmering on the dock. A Bornean orangutan, dangling nonchalantly between trees. A young hippo, on a Colombian farm once owned by drugs lord Pablo Escobar, who, unlike me, did regard raw carrots as soul food. The closer you look at our fellow creatures, the more astonishing they become. On the boat back from one photography outing, watching puffins battling the North Sea wind to return to their nests, I overheard a small boy murmur earnestly to his parents: 'I love the puffins.' I love the puffins too, I thought. But what had I actually done for them, besides taking photos? Had my admiration made them any better off? Had I repaid the pleasure that they had given me? I was an animal-lover in theory, but perhaps not in practice.

We use the concept of love freely these days to refer to everything from our parents to placemats. Iris Murdoch thought love was a central concept in moral philosophy, a force that would take us beyond our own selfishness. Love, in her view, rested upon an ability to pay attention to other beings. This would lead us to consider their flourishing and act justly towards them. Although Murdoch had human love in mind, her notion transfers neatly to how we might treat other species. It invites us to see love not as something we profess, but as something we practise, by paying attention to other creatures' individuality and reflecting on our own biases.

I decided to put myself to the test. I wanted to know whether my love for animals was reflected in how I behaved, or whether – like my love for arthouse films – it was mainly theoretical. Marvelling at the wonders of the animal world on nature documentaries is all very well; I wanted to do something. I wanted to look beyond animals' physical beauty, and to understand their place in our world. I wanted to confront myself with the reality of farms and slaughterhouses, zoos and pet shops, oceans and forests. Was I treating animals fairly? If not, could I find a better way? This was the animal test. The experience would take me out of my bubble and, in various ways, has changed the way I live. I believe it can change how we all live.

But why should we treat animals fairly in the first place?

*

There's a famous psychology experiment where children are left in a room with one marshmallow each. The children are told that if they wait and don't eat it straight away, they will be given a second one. On average, preschool kids resist for less than ten minutes before eating it. It showcases a quintessentially human experience – our struggle to control our desires and plan for the future.

Except how quintessentially human is it? A comparable test was designed for chimpanzees, who were shown rewards, which would accumulate next to them, if they waited patiently. The chimpanzees performed roughly as well as children – some resisted for up to twenty minutes. They even used the same tactics as children, distracting themselves with toys so they didn't eat the treat. Meanwhile, an African grey parrot, told to 'wait' for a tastier nut, managed to withstand temptation for up to fifteen minutes. Such experiments suggest that at least some animals have a sense of the future – they can evaluate different options and exercise what in humans we happily call free will.

Over the years thinkers from Aristotle to Karl Marx have tried to identify things that only humans can do. We were once the tool-making species. Then Jane Goodall saw a wild chimpanzee shaping a stick to extract termites. It's now clear this was not a one-off: indeed there's a theory that cobras evolved to spit as a defence against tool-wielding primates. Other animals don't just use tools, they also make them. In recent experiments New Caledonian crows assembled tools out of multiple parts, in order to take food from a box. Using tools is something they seem to enjoy.

Other animals grasp mental concepts too. Kea, large parrots native to New Zealand, have an instinctive understanding of probability. Presented with two jars containing a mix of treats and non-treats, the birds chose not the jar with the most treats, but the one with the highest ratio of treats to non-treats. The kea also realised when the researcher selecting from the jars tipped the scales, by always picking treats. The size and shape of the birds' brains are much less limiting than humans once imagined. Some parrots and chimpanzees are capable of using words: after being taught the words 'green' and 'banana', a chimpanzee devised the phrase 'green banana' to refer to a cucumber. Prairie dogs have different alarm calls for coyotes, dogs, humans and red-tailed hawks. What's more, when presented with an object that they have never seen before, they independently come up with the same alarm call to describe it. Complex communication stretches beyond mammals. Bumblebees have a method for communicating to each other the location of nectar – effectively a form of dance inside the hive, which plays on the position of the sun. They can remember different locations over a number of days. Experimenters have even set up a form of 'bee football': in a task where bees receive sugar water for putting a ball in a hole, a bee who has never done the task before can find a more efficient route to the goal. This is a task that bees will never have experienced in the wild. Yet 'there seems to be some sort of appreciation of the desired outcome, rather than simply copying,' says Lars Chittka, a psychology professor at Queen Mary's, University of London. Spiders use all eight of their legs spinning webs, but regularly lose legs and still manage to spin similar webs. One interpretation is that they have a mental image of what they are trying to construct, and adapt their behaviour to the circumstances. Their brains may be small, but they may be more efficient at using what capacity they have.

We know, with some certainty, that some animals can recognise themselves in mirrors, a sign that they understand their own existence, itself a prerequisite for them understanding the emotions of fellow creatures. Animals can learn useful behaviours and pass them on: when foil-capped milk bottles were introduced in Britain, blue tits and great tits worked out how to peck them open, and the practice spread across the country. From this form of learning and imitation, the same species can develop different cultures. Because of their environment, or simply experimentation, one group of elephants or whales may do things differently to another group – echoing the way that one human society differs from another.

So other animals are smart, but what can they feel? We cannot get inside a gorilla's head, just like we cannot get inside another human's. We cannot ask them what they feel. What we can do is observe animals' behaviour and study their bodies, free from an assumption that they are limited beings. We can also try to dig into the rationale behind their behaviour, for example using tests that force animals to choose and therefore reveal their preferences. Humans experience pain through specialised nerve endings, a central nervous system and the neocortex part of the brain. Other mammals have similar structures. Birds have a part of the brain that seems to perform equivalent functions. What's more, when subjected to a painful stimulus, many animals will learn to avoid it – or will pay a cost to access pain relief, just as we will drag ourselves to a pharmacy when a headache gets bad enough.

The evidence now takes us most of the way to concluding that animals have emotions. When African elephants encounter one another after periods apart, they measure their greeting depending on whom they are greeting and how well they know them. 'I have no doubt even in my most scientifically rigorous moments that the elephants are experiencing joy when they find each other again,' wrote Cynthia Moss, one of the pioneering researchers into elephant behaviour. 'It may not be similar to human joy or even comparable, but it is elephantine joy and it plays a very important part in their whole social system.'

As recently as 1987, the *Oxford Companion to Animal Behaviour* stated that animals were 'restricted to just a few basic emotions': fear, joy, maybe anger. I had university contemporaries like that. But if grief is defined as acting differently following the passing of a relative, then African elephants can be said to grieve. In 2018 a baby orca died near British Columbia; her mother repeatedly dived down into water to retrieve her. It must have been clear to the mother that her calf was dead, nonetheless she carried her baby for at least seventeen days and 1,000 miles. Other orcas and dolphins have carried dead calves for up to a week. We do not know how widely such behaviour is found in the animal world, but maternal instinct is not even limited to mammals: some snakes have been seen to guard their young.

Fairness might seem the kind of complex calculation that is limited to humans. But there are logical reasons why other animals would have evolved to co-operate, rather than to risk resentment among their fellow animals. Some primates and dogs show an understanding of fairness – sharing food, for example. Indeed, we may not even be the only species willing to act altruistically towards members of other species: the researcher Joyce Poole documented how a female elephant stood guard next to a herder with a broken leg. (To be fair, the elephant was the one who had broken it, albeit accidentally.)

Can animals have mood swings? Humans respond differently to ambiguous stimuli, if they have received positive stimuli before – which is why people buy lottery tickets when they're having a good day. Similarly, pigs become more optimistic – eagerly exploring new objects, for example – if they are well housed with plenty of straw and space. Bees can act optimistically too.

Are animals individuals? Every pet-owner knows the answer. One of my favourite examples came from the Chinese artist Ai Weiwei, who said of the forty or so cats in his Beijing home: 'One knows how to open doors ... if I had never met this cat that could open doors, I wouldn't know that cats could open doors.' I have lived with several cats, only one of whom enjoyed playing fetch with scraps of paper thrown across the room. But they were all undoubtedly individuals.

In human psychology, personalities are sets of behaviour that remain stable over time, and which can be contrasted to the mean in the population. Some decades ago, observing great tits in the Netherlands and wild bighorn sheep in Canada, researchers started to realise that some individuals had equivalent sets of behaviour – they were, for example, bold or aggressive. The very word personality seems specifically human. Some scientists are so instinctively uncomfortable with the idea of animal personalities that they prefer absurd workarounds such as 'behavioural syndromes'. But individual variation is how evolution works.

'We think that humans are special. If you look at the biological underpinning of behaviour, we are just like many other mammals, and many other mammals have similar underlying systems to, for example, fish,' says Niels Dingemanse, a behavioural ecologist at Ludwig Maximilian University of Munich, and one of the pioneers of animal personality research. 'If we see that fish have exactly the same stress response system as humans, we say, that's amazing. It's not amazing. If there's an optimal way to evolve something, why would it not evolve in multiple species?'

The other essential part of closing the gap between ourselves and other animals is to understand that we are not as smart as we think. In a 1977 classic study, shoppers were asked which of four pairs of nylon tights was the best quality. Although all the pairs were identical, the shoppers were much more likely to say the pair on the far right was the best quality. When asked why, they talked about the tights' fabric; no one mentioned their position. We humans delude ourselves about our own instincts.

Many of us find it instinctively easy to accept similarities in intelligence, emotion and social relationships between humans and other mammals, but harder to extend the principle to fish, birds and insects, who look so different to us. Yet some traits and abilities may go further back in the evolutionary tree than we had imagined. In 2016 Todd Feinberg, a neurologist, and Jon Mallatt, an evolutionary biologist, proposed that it's not just humans who have a sense of experience, it's not even just mammals and birds – it is every animal with a backbone. Consciousness, they argue, has existed for at least 520 million years, long before the forests grew and mammals evolved. It has existed since the first fish-like vertebrates swam in the oceans of the Cambrian period.

Consciousness is the slipperiest of concepts; trying to pin it down is like trying to solve a jigsaw with the pieces the wrong way up. Suffice to say that consciousness involves an ability to bring together information from different senses, and to process information about the world and the animal's place within it. Feinberg and Mallatt note that fossil records show early vertebrates had high-definition eyes, whose images were then processed by a more sophisticated brain. They could form a picture of the world. The stimulus for this appears to have been the evolution of the first predators – worms that could eat other worms, at the bottom of the ocean; this created 'an arms race' for greater senses and processing power. Some invertebrates – including insects, crabs and octopuses – seem to have evolved consciousness separately from vertebrates. It means that there is such a thing as seeing the world as a crow, a cod or a crab. A few decades ago, this might have been a ludicrous idea.

Occasionally marketers organise match-ups between an Olympic swimmer and a shark, or a pacey sportsman and a cheetah. The humans lose, obviously. There are countless things that animals can do better than us: dogs can detect the presence of diseases, including coronavirus, and turtles can navigate thousands of miles (although they often get lost on the way, like humans with sat navs). This principle extends further. Birds, fish, reptiles and amphibians have receptors for ultraviolet light. Hummingbirds may be able to see colours that we cannot even imagine. Is it possible too that animals have experiences and emotions that we do not? Or that the intensity of their experiences might be stronger than ours?

Human superiority is not what we once thought. African elephants have many more neurons in their brains than we do; other mammals also share our brain structure. Fish, birds and insects have fewer neurons, and do not have a cerebral cortex, but their brains do appear to be capable of performing many analogous functions. Now we know that parrots and octopuses have developed intelligence, we can no longer judge animals by how genetically close they are to humans. One day, if or when humans are extinct, other species – perhaps descendants of rats or crows – may even evolve into ones that dominate the planet as we do today. To quote the American conservationist Aldo Leopold: humans 'are only fellow voyagers with other creatures in the odyssey of evolution'.

As a child, I remember how adults would dismiss Disney films for 'anthropomorphising' animals. For scientists, to anthropomorphise is to assume that, because an animal behaves in a similar way to us, it is acting on the same emotions as us. Like all assumptions, it is problematic. But Frans de Waal, a leading primatologist, says the greater risk is *not* to anthropomorphise. In terms of our capabilities and emotions, it makes most sense to see ourselves on a continuum with other animals. The fact that we can't tell definitely what emotions animals experience says more about the limitations of our scientific methods than it does about the limitations of their experience.

There are still some things that may be limited to humans. De Waal believes that (complex) language is the only 'uniquely human' capacity. Con Slobodchikoff, the behaviourist who has identified the different calls of prairie dogs, disagrees. There is, however, little evidence of animals communicating about something that happened yesterday. A sense of mortality may also be uniquely human; certainly our levels of self-awareness and future planning seem to go well beyond those documented in other animals. Feinberg and Mallatt point out that the form of consciousness that birds, fish and insects have is not as rich as humans' – it probably doesn't allow them to reflect on what they are feeling, for example.

Morally, however, the most significant distinction between humans and other animals is this: we have the power to determine other species' fate. We hold in our hands the life experiences of billions of animals – mammals, birds, fish, insects and so on – and the fate of millions of species. Sometime early in the twentieth century, humans passed the point where we had significant impacts over half of the earth's ice-free land. Through climate change, habitat destruction, and relentless exploitation of natural materials, we are the dominant force on the planet today. Scientists call this the Anthropocene, to distinguish it from previous eras. In practice, it means that wherever we look we can see our footprint: every species is reacting to our presence, our demand for resources, our pumping out of pollution, plastics and greenhouse gases. This is a human-shaped world. With power comes responsibility.

Treating animals well benefits us. Our water would not be clean, our carbon would not be sucked from the atmosphere, our coasts would not be protected from flooding – without the ecosystems of which other animals are a crucial part. Many of our crops would not grow, without insects and birds to pollinate them. Charles Darwin thought no species had 'played so important a part in the history of the world' as earthworms, who made agriculture possible. It feels silly to list what other animals offer us, because without them, we would have nothing at all. Anyone who thinks humans can set up self-sustaining colonies on Mars with no other species needs to spend some time with an ecology textbook – and a pet-owner.

But our ways of thinking struggle to accept the existence of other conscious beings. When I studied economics at university, nature was still treated as a subset of the economy, rather than vice versa. It was also taken for granted that the lives of animals could have no value in themselves. If we are prepared to pay for animals to exist – because we like watching them with binoculars, or because they pollinate our crops, for example – then fine. Otherwise their disappearance and suffering does not itself represent an economic loss. Not for the first time, economic theory falls short. If we accept that some animals are conscious, can suffer pain and have social relationships, we also have to accept that their lives have value. Jane Goodall once responded to the death of Flo, a wild chimpanzee she had known for eleven years, by saying: 'even if I had not arrived to record her history, to invade the privacy of that rugged terrain, Flo's life would have been, in and of itself, significant and worthwhile, filled with purpose, vigour, and love of life'.

There are other books about what animals can do for us. This book is about what we can do for animals. How we can take their experience of the world into account, as we relentlessly develop our own society.

We often shake our heads, and say how humans are confused or conflicted about other animals. This is a cop-out. Whether or not other animals have a sense of fairness, *we* certainly do, and we have the ability to act upon it. If we appreciate other animals – on holidays, in birthday cards and in wildlife documentaries – we can't cover our eyes and ears to farming and extinction.

*

For me, the change came when my daughters were born. They were soon completely surrounded by animals. There was a rabbit with impossibly floppy ears, a knitted panda fat enough to act as a doorstop, an owl that sung if you blew through its neck, a toucan in all the wrong colours, a giraffe with suckable rubber legs, a plastic octopus with no arms but a head to scoop up bathwater, and so on. It was Noah's Ark, Made in China edition. Every family assembles its own. Our toys had arrived one by one, as presents, loans and hand-me-downs. Natural hierarchies had been eliminated: the ladybird was as large as the lion; the cow as exotic as the zebra. Eliza and Cleo didn't care. To them, these animals were harmless and unharmed; they were protagonists in human life. I felt uneasy.

Children have been exposed to romanticised visions of animals for decades thanks to Rudyard Kipling, Beatrix Potter and Walt Disney. I promise you I'm not one of these pedants who point out that Peter Rabbit wouldn't wear a jacket, that Peppa Pig would be part of a litter, and that, if the Tiger really did come to tea, he would eat the little girl first. Of course, picture books mislead: most farms aren't small, bucolic places, and wolves and octopuses are not sinister. This never really bothered me.

What bothered me was the bigger picture. In children's stories, humans and other animals are interchangeable: Mickey Mouse, Winnie the Pooh, Paddington Bear, Peppa Pig – they are animals with as much character and moral value as any human. A child would be entitled to conclude – from all these books, videos and toys – that humans understand animals. Surely we adults had sussed out how to live alongside other animals, and would pass on this knowledge in due course. Surely we wouldn't be handing out ever increasing numbers of rubber Sophie the Giraffes without making sure that the numbers of actual giraffes are increasing too. If only. I have come across a good few weasels in Eliza's and Cleo's storybooks, but I'm not sure I've ever seen one in real life. I started to wonder how I would explain our relationship with animals to my children, and I realised I'd rather not.

For starters, humans have a record of hunting the biggest creatures they find out of existence: when our species arrived in Australia, other mammals – such as eight-metre-long lizards and 300-kilo kangaroos – started disappearing. We think of elephants, giraffes and rhinos as the definition of wildlife. But if past trends are any guide, those animals and all others of similar size may be gone in two centuries, leaving cows as the largest land mammals. Not for 45 million years will the biggest creature on earth have been so small. As I looked at my daughters' toy tigers, that seemed a strange prospect. I dreaded my daughters one day asking why species are going extinct. Just a few generations ago, our relationship with animals could be summarised as hierarchy and triumph. Now it brings guilt.

When it comes to animals, parenting books tell you how to keep your children safe around pets, but that's where they stop. They are understandably concerned with other stuff, like how not to go out of your mind on four hours' sleep. Animal books, on the other hand, tell you quite a lot about parenting. They bring home how formative those first moments are. Salmon return to the same stream where they were spawned. Albatrosses return to breed where they were born years earlier. In *Utopia*, published in 1516, Thomas More noted how newly hatched chickens seem to consider people who feed them 'as their mothers'. Subsequent research has shown that many birds will become emotionally attached to the first moving object they see. If a duckling sees a human, and follows that human for a while, they will stop following their natural mother. Whether dogs warm to humans also depends on their early weeks. Those first experiences are when we can most easily cross the species barrier.

Humans are different, but early on, we too determine what is normal for the next generation. We are forced to articulate our world as we have never done before. 'Are owls real or pretend?' Eliza asked me one day. 'Why did the dinosaurs stop having babies?' she asked a few days later. 'Why are there so many animals in the zoo?' asked Cleo. I tried to placate them with a photo of an eagle swooping into a lake: 'Is the fish sad when the bird eats it?' asked Eliza. Raising children can be a moment of renewal – a time to ask who we want to be on this planet. Or it can be a moment of inertia – when, even while worrying about the collapse of bee and other insect populations, we crew-cut the lawn to provide a tidy play area for our small humans.

Every parent notices that children want to explore the animal world. Toddlers are more captivated by live animals than toys. Animals' names are among the first words our babies learn. Their sounds are among the first noises. Over the years, people have seen introducing children to animals as part of their moral education. I wouldn't say that saving my daughters from a life of crime was my primary reason for teaching them about animals, but sure, it wouldn't hurt. But what should I be teaching?

*

We can mostly agree that some things don't fit with loving animals: bullfighting, beating dogs, and imprisoning bears in tiny cages in order to extract their bile for dubious medicinal benefits. These are stains on humanity. In many countries, there is no law against them. Even where there is a law, voiceless animals are never the police's priority. But these are not moral dilemmas, and if you're reading this book, you are probably already persuaded that testing cosmetics on a monkey is a bad idea. We don't need to engage our brains – we need to engage our bank accounts, and give to animal welfare organisations.

Similarly, in South Korea, there are thousands of dog-meat farms, where dogs are often kept alone in small metal cages before being electrocuted. The dogs on these farms – who include corgis, poodles and Labradors – are chronically stressed; because dogs are not legally considered livestock, they don't even have the same protections as chickens. But most South Koreans don't eat dogs, and dog-meat farming in South Korea will end.

I was interested in those questions where we hadn't made up our minds, or where we had made up our minds but were persistently failing to act accordingly. From the outset, I felt that treating animals fairly meant two things. I didn't want animals to suffer unnecessarily, although on reflection I wasn't sure what 'unnecessarily' meant here. I also didn't want animals to become extinct, or even to be reduced in number. My starting point was that we humans should make reasonable, maybe quite significant, adjustments to our lives to make this happen.

Things get tricky immediately. Should we kill rats to protect rare birds? Should we kill deer to allow forests to grow? Animal campaigners say no, conservationists say yes. It turns out that caring for individual animals and caring for species as a whole is a head-on, philosophical collision. 'Environmentalists cannot be animal liberationists. Animal liberationists cannot be environmentalists,' the American philosopher Mark Sagoff wrote in a 1984 essay. Sagoff's point is that environmentalists care about protecting ecological integrity, whereas animal liberationists care about reducing the suffering of animals. Animal liberationists, meanwhile, don't have much interest in species, because species don't have feelings – only individual animals do. You can't punch a species in the stomach, or deprive it of social interaction. We can assume that, when Lonesome George, the last Pinta Island tortoise from the Galapagos Islands, died in 2012, he didn't feel existential sadness about the end of his subspecies. If he did, we owe him an apology – other hybrids of the subspecies have now been found.

The divorce between environmentalists and animal activists has been accepted for decades, and it has practical consequences. Animal protection organisations – like People for the Ethical Treatment of Animals (PETA), which claims 6.5 million members and supporters, and the Royal Society for the Prevention of Cruelty to Animals (RSPCA) – focus on animals under human control, in farms and laboratories. Environmentalists – like the WWF and Greenpeace – focus on wild animals. Animal activists and conservationists fight, in particular, over whether it is right to cull animals for the sake of the environment.

These animals may be invasive species, or their populations may have increased rapidly because their natural predators have been extirpated. Conservationists also accept the apparent cruelness of nature – lions eating gazelles and so on – whereas animal activists often welcome attempts to save individual wild animals, for example by feeding them. The split hurts both sides: animal activists are open to accusations that they do not understand how the natural environment works, and conservationists risk alienating some of their most natural supporters, those who appreciate the inner lives of animals.

I explore these debates later in the book. But my overarching view is that the divide doesn't make sense. Without conservation, animal ethics is incomplete. PETA's slogan is: 'Animals are not ours to experiment on, eat, wear, use for entertainment or abuse in any other way.' That's a vision for how animals should *not* live. So how should animals live? The obvious answer is that they should live in places for which they have evolved, and where they are largely outside human control, like the national parks advocated by conservationists. Animals will sometimes suffer in the wild, but human existence can be miserable at times too, and we still think it's worth living. As for culling, conservation might look different if it took animal lives seriously – biologists might be less cavalier about killing animals to collect them as samples, for example – but it's also likely that sometimes the ecosystem will come ahead of individual animals. In Kosciuszko National Park, New South Wales, which includes the highest town in Australia, politicians have prevented the authorities from culling feral horses. As a result, one-fifth of the park's feral horses were predicted to starve to death every year instead. This shouldn't be anyone's idea of loving animals. There is no animal welfare, no animal ethics, without a functioning environment, and there are no functioning environments without plentiful animals.

The divide between animal activism and environmental ethics doesn't reflect how people think. Most animal-lovers I know want the best for individual animals, *and* for whole populations and species. We delight in videos of cats and tigers. We're outraged by monkeys kept in cages and monkeys losing their forests. We don't want orcas to be kept in SeaWorld, or to go extinct. At least in theory, we care what happens to animals, whether they are wild or domesticated. After all, both animal ethics and conservation are built on the same truth: that it's not just humans who experience the world and fill it with beauty, and that non-human lives are worth considering too. To love an individual animal almost invariably means to want the species to continue on the planet. Despite the historic divide, conservationists and animal activists agree on most issues. They want such far-reaching change that fighting each other seems counter-productive. They are like the two storybook mice who argue so fiercely about how a scrap of cheese is divided that they don't notice that a rat is making off with it.

So this book seeks to bring together animal ethics and environmentalism. It's about eliminating the unjustifiable suffering that humans cause animals. It's also about accepting that wild animals will suffer – just as they also experience joy (although in this book we will meet people who think that we may ultimately find a way of improving the conditions of wild animals, just like we have improved our own lives).

Caring for animals is not the same as enjoying spending time with them. The two often overlap. But not always. Joe Exotic, the eccentric, unorthodox Oklahoma animal-breeder who founded his own zoo and featured in the Netflix series *Tiger King*, obviously enjoys rolling around with tiger cubs, but his commitment to their welfare is pretty dubious. Peter Singer, an Australian philosopher, has dedicated much of his career to fighting animal cruelty, but to the amazement of many admirers, he doesn't particularly enjoy the company of animals. It's the difference between seeing other animals through our eyes, and trying to see ourselves through theirs.

When Singer launched the animal liberation movement in 1975, he argued that it would require more altruism than any previous liberation: humans wouldn't be standing up for other humans, but other species. Even so the species barrier, our bias against other animals, can be lowered. We surely do not want our prosperity to come at the expense of animal suffering – any more than we want it to come through sweatshops and child labour.

The task of treating animals fairly should come naturally to anyone who believes in our shared origins. But it doesn't always. Take Charles Darwin, who did more than anyone to shape our view of animals. He broke down the idea that humans were wholly different or superior to other species. It was the search for a common ancestor that led later researchers to study chimpanzees' behaviour, reviving the field of emotional similarities. Darwin also hated cruelty to animals, and, as a local magistrate, punished wrongdoers.

But he never articulated an ethos on how to live beside animals. 'You care for nothing but shooting, dogs, and rat-catching and you will be a disgrace to yourself and all your family,' his father told him, perhaps when he dropped out of medicine aged eighteen. Darwin didn't engage with critiques of shooting, which he loved, or with the nineteenth-century vegetarian movement. He ate meat; indeed he had no compunctions about eating some of the tortoises he encountered in the Galapagos, despite being told they were being hunted towards oblivion on the island and despite finding the meat mostly 'indifferent'. For Darwin, curiosity came first. He recalled how, on visiting an island that is now part of modern-day Chile, he spotted a fox of a very rare species: 'I was able, by quietly walking up behind, to knock him on the head with my geological hammer. This fox ... is now mounted in the museum of the Zoological Society.' Darwin also killed birds and lizards to find out what they ate, and defended vivisection – the cutting open of live animals in laboratories – as long as it was done for good reason. Like many people today, he was capable of pushing animal suffering to the back of his mind. 'It is a subject which makes me sick with horror, so I will not say another word about it, else I should not sleep to-night,' he wrote to a friend, about vivisection. Darwin also liked visiting London Zoo – and donated his collection of birds and mammals to it – even though some of its conditions at the time were depressing. A young orangutan called Jenny, who Darwin delighted in observing at the zoo in 1838 while researching animal emotions, died of illness within two years of arriving; her short life was not atypical. Darwin vehemently opposed slavery, but on animal welfare issues he was not visionary.

Darwinism became associated in the popular mind with brutal, amoral competition for survival. Its founder left it to subsequent generations to work out what his scientific discoveries meant for our relationship with other species.

The good news is that, when people find time to think about animals, they do often change their behaviour. One of Britain's most famous conservationists was Peter Scott, the son of the Antarctic explorer Captain Scott. Born in 1909, Scott was one of the co-founders of the WWF (he designed its famous panda logo, chosen partly because black-and-white was easier to photocopy). He was a bird-lover who inspired rafts of conservationists. But for much of his life, he enjoyed shooting birds: 'it was part of man's instinct to hunt; it was part of the birds' instinct to be hunted', he wrote. It never quite rang true that birds were instinctively adapted to muzzle-loaders, and in his forties, confronted with the reality of how effortless and brutal shooting was, Scott did a remarkable volte-face.

Similarly, John Mackey, the founder of Whole Foods, spent years running the supermarket chain as a vegetarian, before reflecting on whether he was actually comfortable eating eggs and milk, given the conditions on chicken and dairy farms. Before becoming vegan, 'I just looked the other way,' he later reflected. 'I think I didn't want to be fully conscious of it.'

In my experience, changing your views on animals is, no pun intended, a matter of evolution. It's a process that begins with unease. I remember bumping into a colleague just after he'd taken the family dog to be castrated. 'I sort of see the problem now,' he said. 'It's some serious *Handmaid's Tale* shit.' It's the uncomfortable realisation that we control what happens to other species.

Before I started researching this book, I was vegetarian with an unfocused love for nature. I am now a vegan, who supports hunting and fishing in certain circumstances, and who thinks we need to set aside large parts of the planet for other species. You might reach different conclusions. This book sometimes refers to what 'we' think. This isn't because all humans think the same. In fact, I've barely met a family where everyone agrees on animals. But we should all think about animals much more than we do today, and if we do, we will find there is a lot we will agree on.

The next chapter summarises how human attitudes towards animals have swung in the past centuries, up to the vegan wave of recent years. After that, I look at how humans justify killing animals today: farming, fishing, medical testing, and hunting. What does it really take to feed a world of 8 billion human omnivores? The second half of the book looks at the ways that we have tried to love animals. It takes me to San Francisco, Mongolia, Colombia, Indonesia and the British countryside – to talk to zoo-owners, conservation biologists, and pet-owners. At the end there are some practical suggestions for how we, as individuals and as societies, can build a world that is better not just for us but for other sentient beings. We appreciate some animals already. Now we need to follow through.

For me, this is a story of discovery and hope – of side channels that may yet become the main streams. 'The mind is a chaos of delight, out of which a world of future & more quiet pleasure will arise,' as Darwin wrote during his voyage on the *Beagle*. Our minds are what most set us apart from other animals. They are also what can most help us to find a balance with them.

I used to think most of what we are doing badly today was a deliberate choice – that we just didn't care enough for animal lives. I'm now convinced that it's really a failure to think through the consequences of our actions. We can live in a way that fits our basic love for other species. We can work out what animals can offer us and what responsibilities we owe to them. By thinking more often and more deeply about animals, we can start putting our minds at ease.

1. A BRIEF HISTORY OF HUMANS AND OTHER ANIMALS

Whenever people say, 'We mustn't be sentimental,' you can take it they are about to do something cruel. And if they add, 'We must be realistic,' they mean they are going to make money out of it.

Brigid Brophy

I used to assume that humans started off not caring about animals, then became gradually kinder over millennia. Not true. Our relationship with animals – or, to be precise, with *other* animals – has flitted about like a bee on a lavender bush.

We evolved alongside other animals. We started off being hunted by them, before we turned into hunters. The earliest known cave paintings, found in Indonesia and dated to 40,000 years ago, are of pigs and buffalos being hunted. Most of the paintings at Lascaux, France, which date from around 18,000 years ago, are also of animals, including a woolly rhinoceros. We did what no other animal species has done: we selectively bred other animals for food and companionship. (Cows, pigs, sheep and goats were all domesticated at least 8,000 years ago – cats and dogs too, although they probably played a more proactive role in joining human society.)

So it's hardly surprising that many early human societies saw a continuity of spirit between humans and other animals. In some ways, their world view aligns better with recent research into animal emotions and consciousness than ours does. They believed that humans and animals (and plants and inanimate objects) had souls and consciousness, and that animals even had separate human bodies. Some humans could temporarily transform into other animals; some other animals had shamanic powers. In creation stories, humans were often seen as having descended from other animals, or as having been helped by them. The mythology of the Kayapó, an indigenous group who still live in the Brazilian Amazon, has held that a rat directed humans towards maize. This would inevitably make one feel differently about rats. Such beliefs didn't stop people killing animals – far from it, these societies have relied on hunting. But in theory at least, they have also recognised a duty of respect and care.

Similar perspectives can be found today among many indigenous peoples from Canada to the Kalahari. It is premised partly on the belief that not respecting the animals will bring direct, negative consequences for humans. Strains of animist thinking filtered into Hindu and Buddhist thought and prepared the ground for the western vegetarian movement.

The ancient Egyptians buried mummified cats, dogs, crocodiles and other animals alongside people – some were loved pets, some were intended for food in the afterlife, some were offerings to the gods. This was no afterthought: archaeologists estimate that up to 70 million animals were bred as offerings, requiring industrial-scale rearing. However affluent humans have become, we have not wanted to be apart from animals. This is strong evidence that we have evolved with a predilection for them, that genes that have predisposed us to want at least some animals' company have proved advantageous.

Some ancient Greek thinkers, notably Pythagoras and Porphyry, embraced ethical vegetarianism. But they were marginal. For centuries, the established European view was that humans were fundamentally different from animals. This division became inextricably theological. In contrast to those cultures that saw animals as having enabled human existence, the Bible blamed a serpent for tempting Eve. It set down humans as separate from beasts, and uniquely capable of salvation; Thomas Aquinas said that God had created animals for humans to use. In the seventeenth century, the French philosopher René Descartes assured readers that animals lacked souls – their cries were just mechanical responses, like the striking of a clock. In the age before modern anaesthetics, this was most helpful to biological researchers. In one French laboratory, the researchers 'administered beatings to dogs with perfect indifference', recalled a startled observer called Nicolas Fontaine. 'They nailed poor animals up on boards by their four paws to vivisect them to see the circulation of the blood which was a great subject of conversation.'

Some European philosophers claimed the danger to humans was not disrespecting other animals, but *respecting* them. Descartes argued that, if people thought they had the same souls as 'brutes', they would believe that 'after this life we have nothing to hope for or fear, more than flies and ants'. The Dutch philosopher Benedictus de Spinoza worried that, if humans were friendly to animals, they would start thinking of themselves as animals – putting all civilisation at risk. (This being the seventeenth century, he blamed humans' growing softness for animals on 'womanly compassion'. It was Adam and Eve part two, except this time Eve had been beguiled by a pet dog rather than a wild snake.) In early modern England, even pretending to be another animal – for example, by dressing up as one in a performance – was taboo. Humans needed to demonstrate their distinctive moral status.

Descartes' attempt to dismiss other animals as soulless 'automata' could not survive contact with science. He knew that humans and 'brutes' had the same organs (although one of his English contemporaries, the writer Gervase Markham, reported not being able to find a horse brain, despite cutting into various skulls). Within 250 years, Darwin would show that humans and other animals not only had similar brains, but also common origins.

Humans could see animals had feelings, even when Descartes' philosophy told them otherwise. In 1667, the English scientist Robert Hooke cut open a live dog in front of an audience at the Royal Society. By his own account, Hooke 'cut off all the ribs' and 'opened the belly'. He then inserted bellows into the dog's lungs, in order to keep the dog alive and breathing. 'My design,' he recounted, 'was to make some enquiries into the nature of respiration.' The experiment was a success. But Hooke could not disregard the dog's suffering. He was so alarmed by the 'torture of the creature' that he declined to repeat the experiment.

Many other humans had stopped worrying that they were going to be attacked by animals, and that civilisation might collapse if they showed them basic compassion. We don't have records of all the countless moments of kinship between animals and humans, but we are told that Anne Boleyn loved her dog so much that, when the animal died, only King Henry VIII dared to break the news. In his brilliant 1983 book *Man and the Natural World*, the historian Keith Thomas showed how, in Britain, this wall between humans and other animals cracked over centuries. As people moved to towns, they began to see animals as companions rather than productive assets. (I asked Thomas what made him so sure that this was why attitudes shifted. He drew an analogy with his own childhood on a farm in Wales, in the 1930s and 40s, where dogs were never allowed in the house and where horses were beaten as they pulled wagons over soft ground during the corn harvest. 'There was absolutely no sentimentality,' he recalled.) From the seventeenth century, some travellers to India came back avowed vegetarians – spurring an early wave of interest. In other words, even when mainstream religion said that humans didn't need to consider animals' feelings, many Europeans wanted to.

The dawn of western animal rights is often dated back to the English philosopher Jeremy Bentham. Born in 1748, he was happy to eat meat, to wear sealskin boots, and to encourage his acquaintances to electrocute pigeons in the name of medical research. He wrote happily of 'turtle dinners', a fashionable meal in late-eighteenth-century England, which featured several courses made from turtles that had been shipped alive from the Caribbean. Yet in 1789 Bentham published perhaps the sentence most quoted by animal activists. The question was not 'Can they *reason*? nor, Can they *talk*? but, Can they *suffer*?'

This sentence loses some of its power when you realise that it was only a footnote. Modern animal activists might also want to overlook the fact that Bentham concluded that humans were justified in killing and eating animals, on the basis that the animals' death was 'speedier [and] less painful' than 'the inevitable course of nature'. (He added, somewhat debatably: 'they are never the worse for being dead'.) As a utilitarian, he was sceptical of even humans having natural rights.

Bentham's question nonetheless represented a shift in how people viewed animals. Yes, other animals might look, think and act differently to us. Yes, the Bible might suggest that humans had dominion over virtually every animal species. But Bentham compared the situation to slavery: just as black skin was no reason for a human to be tortured, so it 'may come one day to be recognised' that animals should not be tortured on account of their physical differences from humans. Their well-being had to be considered.

At the time, there were no effective laws anywhere in the world preventing animal cruelty. English people still gathered to watch a bull or a bear be tied to a post and attacked by dogs. The dogs used were specially bred to have jaws strong enough to lock on to a bull's nose; they are now known as bulldogs. (Accounts differ as to whether the bull ever stood a chance.) Torturing bulls was justified on culinary grounds: it was thought to thin their blood and so soften their meat. Bull-baiting even took place at at least one wedding. After the aristocracy turned their back on the pursuit, critics of baiting were derided as opponents of working-class fun.

Britain was the pacemaker of western animal activism, perhaps unsurprisingly given its status as the first industrial power and a pioneer of urbanisation. In the early nineteenth century, a distinguished but pompous lawyer called Thomas Erskine used his retirement to launch a crusade for animal welfare. Erskine was an unlikely reformer, given that, in his thirty years in Parliament, he hadn't proposed a single change to the law. He was also a famous egotist: those reporting his speeches joked that their printers ran out of the letter 'I'. But he seems to have loved animals almost as much as he loved himself: according to his biographer, he had pet dogs, a pet goose, a pet macaw and even two leeches that he thought had saved his life.

Erskine proposed a ban on cruel treatment of animals in 1809. His arguments came not from Bentham but from 'what we [parliamentarians] all of us are obliged to see every day in our lives': horses flogged to death, so that travellers could take unnecessary journeys and 'fill up the dreary blank in unoccupied life'. His approach bridged the old Christian world view and today's animal rights discourse. He didn't dispute the idea that God had given humans dominion over animals, and that some animals' characteristics were 'obviously constructed' for our use. But he also argued that God had given each animal 'organs and feelings for its own enjoyment and happiness', and that animals had almost every sense and emotion that humans did.

It seems remarkable that animal rights were taken seriously at a time when there were other concerns, the most outrageous being slavery. Britain had only abolished the slave trade in 1807; it had not yet freed those enslaved men and women who remained in its Caribbean colonies. In fact, the analogy with slavery – made by Bentham among others – may have helped to mobilise campaigners against animal cruelty. William Wilberforce, the leading British abolitionist, backed Erskine, whom he had also hired as a lawyer in a family dispute a few years earlier. Wilberforce argued that improving people's views of animal creation 'would create a sum of sensitive happiness almost impossible to calculate'.

Erskine's efforts were defeated, but in 1822 the British Parliament did ban cruelty to cattle, horses and other livestock. Individuals including Wilberforce set up the Society for the Prevention of Cruelty to Animals (later the RSPCA) to help enforce the Act. The society then lobbied, successfully, for a ban on cruelty to other animals. In 1835 bull-baiting, already unfashionable, became illegal. Rat-baiting, where a dog and up to 200 rats were placed in a pit, and people bet on how many rats would be killed, was still permitted. Fox-hunting also survived; animals didn't matter as much as the aristocracy. Indeed, many of the RSPCA's leading figures engaged in blood sports. The society didn't oppose fox-hunting until 1971.

In 1842, the term vegetarian was used for the first time in England, probably referring to a diet that we now call vegan. Advocates of the 'vegetable diet' spent more time talking about the benefits for humans – including a 'sweetness of temper' – rather than animals. Opponents mocked them as sexually impotent.

Animal activism gathered pace beyond Britain. Throughout the nineteenth century, one of the most persuasive arguments for penalising animal cruelty was that there was a link between cruelty to animals and cruelty to other humans. Previously animals were just property, so you could be punished for damaging someone else's animals, but not your own. The state of Maine passed the US's first animal welfare law in 1821 for anyone who 'cruelly beat any horse or cattle'; the punishment would be a fine of between $2 and $5 (in today's terms, roughly $45 to $110), or up to thirty days in jail. New York was close behind, and then in 1866–7 expanded its laws to apply to all living creatures, due largely to lobbying by the newly formed American Society for the Prevention of Cruelty to Animals. In 1868, the society, which like its British counterpart drew its support largely from the upper and middle classes, pushed the prosecution of a man for overloading a horse car.

The nineteenth century was the peak of human reliance on the horse – for travel, cargo, agriculture, warfare and sport. Horses were required to perform largely mechanical tasks, and were treated often as unfeeling machines. In a rare moment of like-mindedness, the English thought England was 'hell for horses', while the French thought similarly about France. Cruelty came through fashion, as well as from economic imperative: the tight bearing rein, which kept horses from lowering their heads and risked damaging their windpipes, was favoured by owners because it gave their animals an animated air. (Elevating looks over welfare is echoed in how we breed some pedigree dogs today.) Such reins were the target of *Black Beauty*, an 'Autobiography of a Horse ... translated from the original equine', which became a bestseller after it was published in 1877. Readers were prepared not just to take pity on animals, but to see the world from their perspective. So our closeness to horses had bred both cruelty and the anti-cruelty movement.

Horses were displaced by electricity, the combustion engine, machine guns, tanks, and even eventually by football. By the turn of the twentieth century, they were seen as dangerous and unsanitary: in Paris, they produced more than 2,000 tonnes of manure a day. No modern society could tolerate such an unrelenting flow of crap, at least until YouTube came along. Horses no longer fitted with the cities that they had helped to create. In western countries, they are now fewer in number, but better treated than ever in modern history – evidence that humans find it easier to love animals when they don't rely on them economically.

In other ways the nineteenth century still shapes how we treat animals. We could have tried to cut ourselves off from other animals, as we moved to cities. Instead pet-keeping and zoos were born in their modern form. In 1779, Vienna led the way by opening its imperial menagerie to the public. New zoos were founded in cities like London (1828), Amsterdam (1838) and Philadelphia (1874). The word 'domestication' appeared in England in the 1770s, followed a few decades later by *la domesticité* in France. By the nineteenth century, there was a new enthusiasm in both countries for creating breeds of dog and livestock. Animal activists set about trying to regulate cruelty, particularly vivisection. Slaughterhouses were hidden from view. The Victorian era also shaped our understanding of animals – most crucially, through Darwin's theory of evolution, which showed that we weren't so different from other species after all.

But the shift could have been so much greater. In 1871, twelve years after publishing *On the Origin of Species*, Darwin published *The Descent of Man*, in which he suggested that some social animals might have 'a sense of right and wrong', and that they certainly would acquire one, were they to become as intellectually developed as humans. A year later, in *The Expression of the Emotions in Man and Animals*, he made clear his belief, based on close observation, that animals' faces showcased their emotions. His thinking foreshadowed modern studies on what animals feel, and what states we should attribute to them. *The Expressions* had much less impact than *On the Origin of Species*. While our knowledge of one part of Darwin's legacy has spiralled into the field of genetics, comparative psychologists are still debating his key statements on animal emotions, says Alex Taylor, who heads the animal minds research group at the University of Auckland.

For much of the twentieth century, the dominant approach to animals was behaviourism, which held what mattered was animals' behaviour, not their internal states, and that this behaviour could be shaped by selectively giving them rewards. Behaviourism fell out of fashion in human psychology – if internal states didn't matter, what explained the words people spoke? Yet behaviourism remained our guiding approach to animals. It did not always underestimate animals' abilities – its standard-bearer, B. F. Skinner, spent the Second World War training pigeons to pilot bomber planes, a project that the US Air Force ultimately declined to pursue – but it did deter scientists from appreciating the fullness of animals' interior lives. Frans de Waal, the primate expert, recalls: 'As soon as you said, "my dog is jealous", they would say, "that's anthropomorphic". That was a killer – as soon as you were anthropomorphic, you were wrong.' Descartes, not Darwin, was in the ascendant, and that stopped us from taking animals seriously.

Gradually researchers broke the straitjacket with a new approach – ethology – that focused on how animals' behaviour responded to their senses, genes and experiences, rather than training. In the 1960s Jane Goodall travelled to the forests of Tanzania where she observed how complex and fraught social interactions between chimpanzees are. Goodall gave the chimpanzees names, and talked of them as friends. Cynthia Moss documented how African elephants live in structured, matriarchal societies; ivory poachers did not just kill individuals, they disrupted elephants' community and capacity for learning. De Waal identified that chimpanzees consoled each other in an analogous way to humans. He found that prairie voles did too. When a female vole was exposed to stress, her male partner's stress hormone levels would rise; when the two voles were united, the male would groom her intensively. The voles are monogamous, adorable, hamster-like creatures; we could all probably benefit from some of their close attention.

In 2012 a group of neuroscientists held a conference at the University of Cambridge and signed a grandly titled Cambridge Declaration on Consciousness – affirming that humans are not unique in possessing nervous systems that give rise to consciousness, but that such systems are present in 'all mammals and birds, and many other creatures, including octopuses'. Yet the delay in recognising animals' mental complexity means that our empathy has been playing catch-up.

Our ability to cause animal suffering spiralled. Although the nineteenth century saw the invention of the English word vegetarian, it also saw the growth in meat-eating in Europe, the US and beyond. In Japan, until the 1870s, the Buddhist ban on killing animals had largely kept meat (although not fish) off the menu. Then meat-eating became part of Emperor Meiji's drive to modernise Japan and rival the west. He let it be known that he regularly ate meat; his government declared that meat was important for good health, and actively promoted the domestic cattle industry. India too was changing: meat-eating had become associated with the British strength, and some, including briefly the young Mohandas Gandhi, would eat meat in the hope of emulating it.

Even as countries protected animals from cruelty, they allowed their hunters to cause bloodbaths. New breech-loading rifles made killing on land easier than ever. Bison were disappearing from the US, elephants from sub-Saharan Africa. Grenade harpoon cannons, patented in 1870 by the Norwegian former seal-trapper called Svend Foyn, made the same true at sea. Attached to a small steamship, the cannon meant even the largest animals in the world could be reliably killed. It seemed like progress at the time. Not long afterwards, the idea emerged that humans could cause the extinction of other animals.

The alarming effects of hunting, against a backdrop of increased interest in natural history and preventing animal cruelty, led to the modern conservation movement. There were already laws around game animals. In 1869 a Yorkshire MP named Christopher Sykes proposed that the principle be extended to seabirds. He argued ingeniously that, if the birds continued to disappear, humans would suffer – because the birds' cries helped merchant sailors navigate near the shore in foggy weather and their hovering over the water helped fishermen identify shoals of fish. The Sea Bird Preservation Act laid the basis for a closed season for hunting some birds.

From the beginning, conservation has attracted both hunters who want to harvest animals, and nature-lovers who believe that is sacrilege. Gun-toting Teddy Roosevelt realised that, without conservation, hunters would endanger their own long-term entertainment. Gun-hating John Muir revelled in landscapes and what he saw as wilderness. The US had created the world's first national park, Yellowstone, in 1872, so that people could enjoy the magnificent scenery and some bison could escape being hunted. Yellowstone had a dark side: the Native Americans who lived in the area were driven out. It would provide a model, good and bad, for national parks worldwide.

Human population and wealth kept rising – and so did the pressures on the animal world. Factory farming arrived a century ago. Chicken meat had been just a by-product from eggs. In the 1920s farmers in Delaware started breeding chickens for meat; they worked out that chickens could be kept indoors their whole lives if they were given vitamin D. Farms went from a few hundred chickens to tens of thousands. After the Second World War in particular, farmers started keeping pigs in metal cages and cows in sheds, in search of greater efficiency. Consumers eventually protested, but by then the practices had become ingrained and global.

In 1962 in *Silent Spring*, the US biologist Rachel Carson despaired of the devastation wrought by pesticides, and urged humans to find 'a reasonable accommodation between the insect hordes and ourselves'. *Silent Spring* is often cited as a landmark moment for environmentalism – the book that led to a ban on the insecticide DDT. But global insect populations have not recovered since its publication – in fact, they seem to have collapsed further. New pesticides cause unforeseen damage to bees. Worms are driven out by agricultural ploughing. Fireflies are confused by artificial light. All kinds of insects cannot survive ceaseless human expansion, pollution and exploitation of the natural world. Between 5 per cent and 10 per cent of insect species may have become extinct since the Industrial Revolution. We are only dimly aware of how many more are following them, and how our existence will be made harder by their absence.

If the modern environmental movement began in the US, influenced by Muir and Carson, the animal rights movement began in Britain, as the reality of industrial farming became clear. 'To us it seems incredible that the Greek philosophers should have scanned so deep into right and wrong and yet never *noticed* the immorality of slavery,' wrote the novelist and campaigner Brigid Brophy, in an essay in 1965. 'Perhaps 3,000 years from now it will seem equally incredible that we do not notice the immorality of our oppression of animals.' In France, Brigitte Bardot retired from acting at the age of thirty-eight, and dedicated herself to animal activism, declaring that she did not want to be 'part of the human species', so long as it was 'arrogant and bloodthirsty'. Animal activism became established as a progressive, countercultural cause, rather than as part of the puritanism of the nineteenth century.

In 1970 Richard Ryder, a British psychologist, tried to put animal rights in the context of women's rights and racial equality. He coined the term 'speciesism' to describe humans' moral disregard for other species. This spawned a new phase in animal activism – concerned less with incremental improvements in animal welfare, and more with assigning animals rights that could fundamentally question human practices. In 1975 Ryder's friend Peter Singer published the book *Animal Liberation*, which singled out the worst practices in farms and research laboratories, and argued that humans had a duty to take animals' interests into account. Tackling speciesism didn't mean treating humans and other animals equally; it meant recognising that other animals' suffering was comparable to humans'. (Singer, a utilitarian like Bentham, prefers to weigh up interests rather than commit to animal rights.) Among those inspired by Singer was Henry Spira, a labour activist who in 1979 organised a successful campaign to stop cats and dogs from New York pounds being used for medical research. *Animal Liberation* is probably the most influential book on animal cruelty ever. Yet worldwide meat production has tripled since it was published. This is the paradox: animals have worse prospects in the very time that we have supposedly being looking out for them.

*

The 2010s were perhaps the most important decade for animal activism since the 1970s. A rethink seems to have been brewing.

Veganuary, a campaign for people to try giving up meat, dairy, eggs and other animal products for the month of January, had launched in Britain in 2014. Food had steadily become more central to people's sense of identity: 'Once we liked the Beatles; now we eat beetles,' as the economist Tyler Cowen put it. The world tried veganism, perhaps because it had tried and discarded every other food regime. Between December 2015 and December 2016, Google searches for the word 'vegan' doubled. In 2020, 400,000 people signed up to Veganuary; it was the new, post-Christmas gym membership. Our new-found sensitivity to animals didn't stop there. Volkswagen finally stopped testing its diesel cars on monkeys. A few decades ago, Hollywood was focused on animals' dangers, through films such as *Jaws* and *Anaconda*. Now, after viewer complaints, the British reality show *[I'm a Celebrity ... Get Me Out of Here!]* wouldn't even allow contestants to eat live insects.

Something was changing. In 2015 one-third of Americans said animals should have the exact same rights as people to be free from harm and exploitation, up from a quarter in 2007. Women were almost twice as likely to say this as men, and Democrats were almost twice as likely as Republicans. In the Netherlands, animal activists had their own party entirely: the Party for the Animals, which campaigned against everything from the size of goldfish bowls to the set-up of the euro, won five seats in Parliament in 2017. 'The public already wants politicians to protect animals better, and when they don't, obviously there's a huge chance for a party like ours to step up,' its current leader Esther Ouwehand said.

As of 2016, only 2 per cent of British adults said they were vegetarian, with a further 1 per cent identifying as vegan. In the US, 5 per cent are vegetarian. In Spain, land of ham and fish, perhaps only 1.5 per cent of the population do not eat meat. Data is often sketchy, but it's almost certain that vegetarians make up less than one-tenth of the population in every western country. India, because of its Hindu and Jain heritage, remains the beacon for many vegetarians. The country's constitution calls on the state to take measures to prohibit the slaughter of cattle. Even so, almost three-quarters of Indians say they eat meat. The figure is probably higher: recent research suggested that many Indians falsely claimed in surveys to be vegetarian, reflecting cultural pressure.

Why has it taken us so long to rethink? There have always been animal-lovers. All the arguments that are made about vegetarianism and veganism today were, in some form, made in the nineteenth century – and often before that. Now, for the first time, they are being heard by the mainstream, even if only a tiny proportion of people have switched. Two things have changed. One is the climate crisis, which has forced people all over the world to recognise how precarious our future is and how destructive our way of living has been. I have worried about climate change all my adult life. In the past few years, it has moved from a political cause that I believe in to a visceral, daily reality – a realisation that we have already left it too late, that our future is under a shadow. The best salve for this anxiety is to go to protest marches and see how many people share it.

The other change is social media. As urbanisation has intensified since the nineteenth century, and particularly since horses disappeared from our streets, there's been a physical distance between us and animals. Social media has shrunk this. Perhaps those cat videos weren't actually a giant waste of time; perhaps they actually sensitised us. I watched pandas rolling down hills, and trying to catch their sneezes. The Internet has certainly made it easier for fringe causes to roll into the mainstream; this applies to animal rights as much as the alt-right. The publisher The Dodo, based in New York, has become the crack cocaine of cute animal videos such as 'Chicken Runs Out to See Her Human Sister Every Morning' and 'Dog Copies Every Single Yoga Pose His Dad Does'. Now one of the most popular publishers on Facebook, it relentlessly shows animals as individuals, bringers of joy, and above all beings with agency. That turns out to be something people want to watch, and want their friends to know that they're watching.

Barely a decade ago, animal activists struggled even to reach people sympathetic to their cause. When activists filmed unsettling footage in farms and slaughterhouses, broadcasters would refuse to air it. PETA, one of the most radical campaign groups, resorted to strapping TV screens onto its volunteers' torsos and sending them out onto the streets. Any normal pedestrian would run a mile. Each volunteer would only reach maybe a hundred people a day. Today PETA uploads its clips of abuse to Facebook, and receives hundreds of thousands of views within a couple of hours. The tactic isn't limited to activists: the British supermarket Iceland produced an advert about the plight of orangutans near palm-oil plantations. As a political statement, it couldn't air on British TV, but it gained more than 6 million views on YouTube. Being 'banned from television' was the selling point.

The comedy writer Charlie Brooker once said that Twitter will show you the worst thing that is happening anywhere in the world at this precise moment. Quite often the worst thing is a dead animal. In 2014 Copenhagen Zoo euthanised a healthy giraffe; an activist's tweet set off an international storm. The following year, an American dentist shot a lion in Zimbabwe with a compound bow, and the online backlash was so strong that the US Congress tightened rules on importing animal parts. It surely helped that, like Jane Goodall's chimpanzees, these creatures had names – the giraffe had been called Marius by his keepers, the lion had been called Cecil by wildlife researchers. When unprecedented bushfires tore across Australia in 2020, some of the most shared videos were not of bereft residents or burnt-out homes – but of dead kangaroos piled by the side of the road. More than 3 billion animals are estimated to have died in the fires, a figure that excluded frogs and insects; unlike humans, animals cannot be warned. Their deaths feel particularly brutal.

Social media is a blunt tool. The outrage we feel at animals being killed or animals dying can often be misplaced. In the case of Marius the giraffe, what did we think happens to zoo animals in the absence of predators? Did we think the animals just lived forever? Didn't we notice that the zoos weren't getting any bigger? We're concerned, but confused.

In 2020, going viral stopped being a metaphor. Coronavirus emerged in Wuhan, and seemed to spread rapidly at a wholesale market, where wild animals were kept in horrific conditions, along with conventional meat and seafood. The virus exposed our flawed relationship with animals. One stall at Hunan Seafood Wholesale Market advertised a hundred types of live animals, including civet cats. Visitors to other Asian markets have found live bats strung up by their wings, bloodied pangolins and chickens in cramped cages. At the time of writing, coronavirus is thought to have originated in bats, and crossed to humans, possibly via a pangolin. Whatever we learn about its origins will not change the reality that our unthinking treatment of animals has historically been, and will likely remain, the biggest source of pandemic risks. Experts told us of the risks of diseases spilling over from wild animals and factory farms – we just ignored them. 'There's no "I told you so," it's actually a feeling of "could I have shouted louder?",' said Kate Jones, a leading bat expert. If ever we think we could separate our experience of the world from animals', the pandemic reminds us otherwise.

Coronavirus also pulled back the curtain. In the weeks of lockdown, the meat and dairy industries choked up. Vats of milk were poured down the drain. Pigs needed to be 'depopulated', because farmers could not afford to feed them. One Iowa factory farm killed thousands of sows by blocking up the airways to their barns, and then turning up the heat till the pigs effectively cooked to death, over several hours. Millions of hens were killed by being sprayed with foam, similar to that used in fire extinguishers. This wasn't cruelty-free meat, it was meat-free cruelty.

More happily as we sat at home, animals ventured onto the streets. There were coyotes in San Francisco, beavers in Washington DC, and jackals in parks in Tel Aviv. It was an anthropause in the Anthropocene. Birds lowered the volume of their song, because they no longer needed to shout above our vehicles; they could allow themselves to sing at lower minimum frequencies, so that their song would carry further. In those first few weeks, we could imagine a world without humans trampling all over it, and it seemed almost pleasant. 'We are the virus. Nature is healing,' went an Internet meme.

For a brief moment, we were reminded that this planet isn't home only to humans. By withdrawing slightly, we could see the shape of our impact. Under lockdown, people reached out for the company of animals: the UK briefly had a shortage of puppies for adoption. Others tried virtual meet-ups for their dogs. We dialled alpacas and llamas into Zoom meetings. They were probably better at unmuting than a lot of humans.

In many ways, coronavirus shook us from our inertia. It showed that white-collar workers didn't have to work in offices. Church services didn't have to take place in churches. So many things that we thought were fixed could, in fact, be shifted. Could the way we treat animals be one of them? Food, farming and hunting – these have defined our cultures and sense of identity. Could we change them? In 2017, the fashion label Gucci had a reluctant change of mind on using fur, admitting that the fabric was 'a little bit outdated'. After coronavirus hit, its creative director Alessandro Michele had a full-on nature conversion, complaining that humans had 'made us lose our sisterhood with the butterflies, the flowers, the trees and the roots'.

Our approach to animals is a mishmash. It's like a drawer we keep shoving valuable things into, but which we never get round to tidying. Throughout our history with animals, nothing has been more influential than our search for food. If we are to rethink our relationship with other species, nothing will have more impact. So food is where we must begin.

PART I
KILLING ANIMALS

2. SLAUGHTERHOUSE RULES

What can you expect from a pig but a grunt?

Old English proverb

Forget the pig is an animal – treat him just like a machine in a factory.

Hog Farm Management journal, 1976

'Why don't you eat meat?' When I became vegetarian a few years ago, I soon dreaded this question. It often came accompanied by absurd logic: a man in my local café followed up by asking whether, were I to be stranded after a plane crash, I would refuse to eat the bodies of my fellow passengers. (I would have happily bitten him.) But I also felt that I didn't have a proper answer. Like many people who are eating less meat or no meat, I didn't carry out detailed research. I had made my decision after reading a few pages in Yuval Noah Harari's bestseller *Sapiens*, which concluded 'modern industrial agriculture might well be the greatest crime in history'; it was 2 January, and I couldn't think of a better New Year's resolution. After that, I took in headlines about climate change and the health dangers of red meat by osmosis. I had little idea about what farm animals' lives were like, or whether ethical farming could exist. Being a vegetarian doesn't make you an expert in anything except avoiding conversations about why you became a vegetarian. In Britain, where I grew up, the images of farming – in children's books, TV dramas, and supermarket ads – had always made it seem an honest, jolly profession. Almost everywhere I went, particularly the US, France and Colombia, livestock farmers were the heart of the national character. I wanted to find the reality. I had to start somewhere, so I decided to start at the bottom of the heap.

*

The first thing you learn about slaughterhouses is that it's easy to find work in one. There are jobs for which you need a CV, a reference or even a permanent address. There are jobs for which each online listing brings a deluge of applications. 'Abattoir ancillary worker' does not seem to be one of them. I call up the number on an online job ad, and am told to come down whenever is convenient.

I take the train an hour south-east of London, and walk a few hundred metres down a country lane. Birds sing in the trees. A train passes nearby. It seems like a nice place. Except here – in half a dozen rudimentary buildings – over 1,000 sheep and pigs are 'processed' each day. This is Forge Farm Meats, a medium-sized slaughterhouse a stone's throw from commuter land. I want to know what killing animals actually involves: the smell, the noise, the psychology. Anything that might help me to make up my mind.

I knock on the office door, and meet an affable middle-aged man who introduces himself as Steve. I had concocted an elaborate cover story about why I, someone who looks, sounds and acts exactly like a middle-class journalist, would want to work in a slaughterhouse. But I shouldn't have bothered. Steve doesn't ask why I want to work in an abattoir. He doesn't even ask my surname. 'There's no point me telling you about the job,' he says, getting up from his chair. 'It's better that you just give it a try. People say it's a bit in your face.' He pauses and corrects himself. 'It *is* a bit in your face.'

The online job ad said 'training provided'. Training turns out to mean a pair of white overalls, white rubber boots and a hairnet. Steve gives me those, opens the door to a one-storey metal building, and leads me on to the production line. I find myself standing beside a line of headless sheep.

This is all within four minutes of me showing up and knocking on Steve's office door. At a London office block, it would have taken me longer to get past reception. I don't know what would reassure me that the abattoir took animal welfare seriously, but the list might start with a visitors' log.

Inside, the sheep are hanging from a motorised track, and every metre or so, a man is removing a different part of their insides or outsides. In a windowless space no bigger than ten metres by ten metres, the animals go from things you would see in a field to things you would see on a supermarket shelf. Red is splattered everywhere. Almost as soon as I arrive, the man next to me loses control of his knife, and cuts off the skin from his knuckle, as if opening a boiled egg. He stares at the scarlet-and-white circle, the size of a small coin, which has now appeared on his finger. 'Oooh, that's a nasty one,' chips in a man one down, laughing.

I am placed in front of a machine called the puller. By the time the sheep arrive here, their necks have been slit, their heads and trotters cut off, and the skin on their front legs cut from their flesh. The puller has two clamps that grab the loose skin on the front legs, and then drag it down, taking the wool coat halfway off the body. 'Don't get your fingers caught,' says a colleague, unaware that I have already made it my life's mission. The puller brings me face to face with the sheep's severed neck. It also gives me a bird's eye view into the animal's thorax. Is that a lung or a kidney, I start wondering.

I have around twenty seconds to guide the sheep's loose skin into the clamps of the puller, and press the pedal that moves the clamps downwards, taking off the wool. After that, the line starts moving again, taking that sheep to the next station, and delivering me a new carcass. Twenty seconds is a lot when the process works smoothly. It's not so much when the skin isn't loose, or when the machine jams, or when the man before me on the line is still trying to cut the back trotters from the sheep. Or when the end of the loose skin rips off from the body, before the puller has finished its work. Which is all the time.

In these cases, you have to pull the wool off by hand. You grab as much skin as you can with a fist, and use your entire bodyweight to separate it from the muscle. The tear can be smooth. But sometimes it can be too smooth. If you manage to pull the wool right down from the back of the sheep, the severed neck will bounce back in response, and throw a red splatter over your cheeks. As Steve says, it *is* a bit in your face.

Here's something that strikes you about a slaughterhouse: it's so messy. I'd seen assembly lines before – car factories and newspaper printing presses on the TV news – and they'd looked so honed. This disassembly line is different. Even though the equipment is specifically designed for these animals, even though literally millions of animals have been killed and cut to pieces right here, nothing quite seems to fit. Fluids slosh on the floor, along with wool and unidentified bits of bodies. I now know that the English word 'shambles' was once a term for slaughterhouse; I should have guessed.

The abattoir is noisy too. There's the grinding of multiple machines, which means you have to shout to make anything heard. Kiss FM is on; half the time I can't even make out the tune. I can make out the distinctive noise of news bulletins, but not the time. The smell, meanwhile, is a thick slurry of stenches. I feel like I can also see it. I just keep pulling in the hope that, at some point, all the animals will be dead and disassembled, and we will be given a break.

My cover story is that I have been living abroad for many years and have struggled to get a job through lack of references. I get to deploy it once, in a break, when a friendly co-worker tries to make small talk.

'What job did you do before this, if you did anything?'

'I was abroad.'

'Prison?'

It's a fair assumption. Abattoirs can't really choose who they employ. In the US, some workers are Somali refugees, who will put up with even worse conditions than Mexican immigrants. In some parts of the UK, 90 per cent of slaughterhouse workers are European Union migrants. Agencies help to sort out national insurance numbers and accommodation. 'We have Polish, Russian, Lithuanian, Romanian, Portuguese and Spanish contact [*sic*] based in our UK office to offer continuous support,' says one British job ad from an agency called 360 Recruitment, in these pre-Brexit days. Another says that 'Communicative English would be an advantage.' In other words, it's not essential. At Forge Farm Meats, though, the other workers are mainly British.

The line of sheep comes to an end. The man with the cut knuckle indicates a box of woolly pouches. He picks up one of the pouches, and shows me how to squeeze a sheep's testicles from their sack. You're kidding, I think. I join in, and silently apologise to the sheep. Then I sweep the bits of wool, and faeces, and unidentifiable body parts from the floor into a metal bin. I wheel the bin to a skip outside, where the smell slaps me in the face like a playground bully. As I tip the bin's contents, I momentarily worry that I will end up in the skip with them. In my newspaper office, taking the dirty tea mugs to the kitchen almost merits a round of applause.

By this point, I've concluded I am not very good at working in an abattoir. But the foreman, Darren, is sympathetic. 'Don't worry. It's not always like that,' he says. 'They were shitty sheep.' I smile. I can't help feeling that, given everything the sheep have just been through, they probably don't deserve that final insult. Darren has 'True Love Sophie' tattooed on his upper right arm, and a topless woman on the forearm. I want to ask if they are the same woman.

On my second day, I realise that Darren was right: they were shitty sheep. There is a new batch of animals, of a different quality. Their fat tears away easily from the muscle; the puller briefly looks like a smooth piece of machinery. The line of sheep starts, and goes on and on. The morning shift at Forge Farm feels interminable. I sweat through my overalls almost immediately, which at least means I can't feel the animals' body fluids as they soak in. In US abattoirs, there are reports of workers wearing nappies because toilet breaks are so infrequent. I don't know what I'd do if I needed the toilet; to be honest, my mind is elsewhere. Hundreds of sheep go by. 'You get used to it,' says one man, who says he's been there eighteen years.

There's a vet at Forge Farm Meats; under British law, there has to be. She is the only woman I see on the site, and walks around wearing a hard hat. Her whole demeanour is awkward like a work-experience student. What kind of vet ends up in an abattoir, I think. The men treat her with jovial disdain and placate her with small gestures. 'Keep washing your hands,' I was told for the first time, about four hours into my shift, by a co-worker, when the vet was near.

I have found my bearings enough to see how the killing process works. The sheep are unloaded from a truck, led into a metal shed, and stunned with electrified tongs so that they cannot feel pain. They then have their throats slit and are hung on metal hooks on a motorised track. How did humans come to this, I think. As the sheep hang on the line, they do kick their untied front feet, often for thirty seconds, sometimes for more than a minute. It's just a spasm, and there's no pain or bleating. Anyway, in the abattoir, your duty is very much to the next person on the line – not to the animals. The animals won't be there tomorrow; your co-workers will.

Forge Farm Meats has been accused of cutting corners. In 2016, it was fined £8,000 for selling two West Sussex butchers goat meat, which turned out to be sheep. In 2017, an animal welfare charity, Animal Aid, said it had covertly filmed inside Forge Farm Meats, and found that workers had trodden on sheep and smacked one in the face. The company denied wrongdoing; a criminal prosecution collapsed.

In the UK, the most rudimentary abattoirs are disappearing: the number of red-meat abattoirs in the UK has fallen almost 90 per cent in the past fifty years. As in the US, the shift is to mega-slaughterhouses, which can process more animals at lower cost. In fact this trend worries animal welfare advocates like the Sustainable Food Trust. Fewer, bigger abattoirs means that animals face the stress of longer journeys – often over a hundred miles – when they 'go off-farm', as the industry euphemism has it. Adult sheep and cows can be legally transported for fourteen hours without a break, pigs and horses for twenty-four hours. One farmer told me that each of his sheep would lose around a kilo – 5 per cent of their body weight – on a four-hour journey to an abattoir, through dehydration and stress. The Sustainable Food Trust has called for the government to support small abattoirs by reducing regulation, although this risks allowing abuse.

The US's federal rules on transporting animals are laxer. The Twenty-Eight-Hour Law, enacted in 1906, means that animals can be transported for twenty-eight hours without being unloaded for food or water – a period in which a human airplane passenger will demand, at a guess, five meals, and a dozen drinks. It's barely enforced anyway.

Even journeys across the US can be dwarfed by the international trade in live animals. Australia exports more than 2 million sheep and cows a year, many on a 10,000-mile journey to the Middle East. On ships, common diseases include pneumonia and salmonellosis. Animals become covered in their excrement – so-called 'faecal jackets'. Legs are broken. Bodies are thrown overboard. Videos from inside one ship show animals apparently collapsing from lack of water. By law, it's acceptable for up to 2 per cent of the animals to die in transit. That can mean 2,000–3,000 animals arriving dead on a single ship. Occasionally, somewhere in the world, a ship carrying live animals capsizes. More than 14,000 sheep drowned in one incident off the coast of Romania in 2019. The EU has long refused to ban live animal exports.

In the afternoon, one of the men at Forge Farm announces we are going to 'do some grunters'. Sixty or so pigs have been delivered to a holding pen outside. 'Something different,' shrugs another man.

Pigs *are* different. They are highly social animals; their noises are not just grunts, but messages. Pigs do not just want food and safety. They want stimulus and company. They communicate with each other through sounds, and by gently touching each other's snouts and heads – 'nosing'. They prefer engaging with new objects to ones that they have engaged with days earlier, suggesting that they can remember what happened previously. They are playful, and given the chance will push around balls and carry sticks. They will run around and play-fight. They can tell the difference between humans who have fed them before and strangers. Pigs and dogs have both successfully used mirrors to locate objects. In some experiments, like manipulating a joystick to move a cursor on a screen, pigs have outperformed dogs; in others, including those reading human gestures, dogs do better.

Crucially, in the abattoir, pigs can smell blood. Their snouts are many times more sensitive than a human nose. So they can quite possibly sense what is going on. They are stressed as they are separated from the group. A common phenomenon, recounted by an American farmer called Bob Comis, is when all but one of the pigs have been killed, and the last pig realises they're alone, and occasionally flips out until they injure themselves. Pigs don't always comply with their own death. In the abattoir, instead of provoking empathy, this is more likely to lead to them being hit and kicked.

This afternoon the pigs do not go quietly. They squeal when they are crammed in the holding pen outside. They squeal when they are dragged inside. Their last moments seem to be stressful ones. Like the sheep, they are stunned electrically, which causes the equivalent of an epileptic seizure in humans. The animal goes rigid and stops breathing; rendered unconscious, they can then be killed. But electrical stunning relies on a slaughterhouse employee doing the job right on every animal, every day. In the chaos of the production line, that will never happen. Animals will be improperly stunned. Many abattoirs stun the pigs by pushing them into metal chambers filled 80 per cent with carbon dioxide. The gas effectively pushes the oxygen from the pigs' brains, rendering them brain dead. Compassion in World Farming, an animal welfare group, wants to ban the use of carbon dioxide, which it says causes 'a burning and then drowning-like sensation'. Pigs can take as long as thirty seconds to lose consciousness. On videos, they squeal as they are lowered into gas chambers. A lot of debates about farming assume that the killing itself is not the issue. But there is no painless method of mass killing – there is no way that an abattoir worker can click his fingers and end a life.

At Forge Farm Meats, the pigs come around the line, stunned and hanging from their back legs. I can see how my co-worker makes the final cut: the knife goes into the bottom of the animal's neck, and the liquid gushes out as if from a bath tap. If we were not a team of workers in uniforms, this would feel like an act of unforgiveable barbarism. As it is, I just feel numb, a little less human than when I arrived. The blood flows onto the metal below. It gushes out in such quantities that a screen has been put up to shield the floor. It reminds me of something airports use to stop suitcases falling off the carousel. Like the sheep, the pigs keep kicking after the cut. Ten seconds, twenty seconds – and longer. They are eventually taken down from their hooks, and placed in a bath and then onto a roller. They emerge almost hairless and a brighter shade of pink, as if made of rubber.

The puller is no use with the pigs. So instead I am given a blow-torch to run along their skins, to make the hair easier to scratch off. 'Too long and they turn green,' I am told. You have to torch both sides of the pig, and the easiest way is to grab the tail. It's a slippery task. I am constantly aware of the risk of blowtorching the men on each side of me. Both men look as if they could settle any labour dispute without the need for a tribunal.

Eventually I blowtorch the last pig, and sweep up trotters from the floor. I take off my apron, and start washing my hands like I've never washed them before. A young guy, who has been in the abattoir for a year and who has been chatting loudly about his gym sessions, asks me if I am going to keep working there. I try to shift the subject. 'What's the best job here?' I ask him. 'Depends what you're best at,' he replies. 'For me, it's gutting.'

*

Paul McCartney once said, 'If slaughterhouses had glass walls everyone would be a vegetarian.' At a guess, not many of my co-workers in Forge Farm Meats were vegetarians. It would be easy for me to say that working in an abattoir shocked me. It wouldn't quite be true. There's some satisfaction in the manual work, at least before you get bored by the monotony. Forge Farm Meats didn't feel very clean or very safe, and I'm not going to recommend that you work there. But there was camaraderie. When someone told you to fuck off and do your job properly, it at least came with the acknowledgement that you were on the same team.

My immediate reaction to the abattoir wasn't so much about the ethics or the legalities of the process. It was about power – our power over other animals. Animals would be fully functioning sentient beings one minute, and a collection of edible cuts ten minutes later. We were two dozen men without much in the way of qualifications and training, but we had the power to do that. We could do it free from any real oversight, or soul-searching. In the collective endeavour of the abattoir, any sense of individual responsibility is quickly suspended. It's certainly less easy to disdain Descartes for thinking animals were fundamentally different, or nineteenth-century carriage drivers for hard-driving their horses, when you see how readily we manipulate animals now. In the abattoir, love is a distant emotion.

I've never bought the idea that it's wrong to kill animals per se. It always seemed simplistic. Take the possibility of using animal tissues to save human lives. Pig blood vessels are already used for transplants. In the last few years, some countries including the US, Australia and New Zealand have lifted bans on research using animal organs. Scientists are now looking to take livers, lungs, kidneys and even brain cells from pigs, and place them into humans. In January 2022, in what was heralded as a major breakthrough, surgeons in Maryland transplanted a heart from a genetically engineered pig to a 57-year-old man with otherwise terminal cardiac problems. The operation seemed to go well. This raises ethical and practical issues, but it could be justifiable in principle, assuming you believe, as I do, that human lives are worth more than pig lives.

Yet there is a chasm between the careful, thoughtful trading of one life for another, and the mass-scale, thoughtless nature of modern agriculture. The UK kills 11 million pigs a year, Japan kills 16 million, Germany 57 million, and the US a whopping 125 million. In the US, an abattoir is allowed to kill up to 1,106 pigs an hour – one every three seconds – a limit that the Trump administration proposed removing in order to save the companies money. The US kills 33 million cows a year – four times the UK, Japan and Germany combined. For chickens, you need to go up an order of magnitude: 1 billion in the UK and 9 billion in the US, killed each year. When we say meat is cheap, what we really mean is that life is cheap.

Across the world, there is a single trend: when countries get rich, they eat more meat. The only question is how much more. On average, Brits eat eighty kilos of meat a year, Germans eat nearly ninety. The average American, meanwhile, consumes 124 kilos a year, three times the world average. Even Japan, traditionally fish-eating, has doubled its meat consumption per person over the past forty years; Emperor Meiji would presumably be delighted. To meet this demand, we have set up a system to process animals by the billion.

Because we shut this killing away, because we place abattoirs at the bottom of the list of desirable workplaces, abuse is inevitable. On

YouTube, you can see clips of British sheep trapped on the conveyor belt that is taking them to their death, and pigs being slammed with metal gates. You can see Belgian cows being rammed with sticks to move, slipping on the metal machinery, and seemingly trying to escape the barred enclosures. If this is what happens on a planet of animal-lovers, I wouldn't like to see a planet of animal-haters.

In the weeks after working at Forge Farm Meats, in restaurants and at friends' houses, I found myself almost shaking my head at the contrast between the nonchalance of the slaughterhouse and the subtlety of our table rituals. I realised that I had managed to work in an abattoir because I had treated it like a war zone. I had focused on surviving. But wars are only justifiable if they are essential, if there is some higher cause. Where was the higher cause for all the blood and the squeals, the testing of human psychology? Instead of asking people why they are vegetarian, shouldn't we instead ask what higher cause requires them to eat meat?

Some meat-eaters say that the animals need to be eaten for their own sake. After all, if pigs, cows and chickens weren't killed, they would not be bred either, and we would be depriving them of life. Is their unnatural death just the price of life? Wouldn't the animals be worse off if they never existed? Such questions take me back to a place almost as brutal and interminable as my shifts at Forge Farm Meats – my university philosophy tutorials. To cut a long, philosophical debate short, my answer is that we don't have a duty to bring animals into existence. Animals who don't exist today don't have an interest in existing tomorrow. If they did, we would have a duty to bring as many animals as possible into the world. Where would that duty stop? Would we have to populate every field with as many sheep and cows as possible? And presumably unborn humans would have an even stronger interest in existing than unborn animals. So are we all obliged to have more kids? Claiming we eat animals for their own sake is as disingenuous as the schoolmasters who claimed corporal punishment hurt them more than the children.

We definitely don't have a duty to bring animals into existence if they won't have good lives. No farm can provide a natural life; the concept is probably meaningless for a domesticated animal. The question is whether the farm can provide for the animal's evolved instincts. Wild boar tend to move in small groups; older males are loners. In the US, three-quarters of pigs are raised on farms with at least 5,000 other pigs.

The growth of factory pig farms, particularly in Iowa and Minnesota, has been remarkable: in 1992, the average US pig farm 'finished' 945 pigs a year; by 2009, it was more than 8,300. On these intensive farms, animals are deprived of space, and often of sunlight. Their surroundings are metallic; their natural ways of socialising and living are impossible. Many pigs are forced to live on slatted metal floors. They cannot root around in the ground, and the absence of this possibility seems to explain why they often bite each other's tails, causing pain and infections. To manage this, factory farms often amputate piglets' tails – even though this tail-docking is itself done without anaesthetic and seems to harm long-term welfare. The EU ordered in 2008 that routine tail-docking should be stopped, and instructed farmers to make sure that pigs had enriched surroundings instead. Years later, tail-docking remains routine on intensive pig farms in most EU countries, and a lack of enrichment remains common, because it's cheaper. Denmark and Germany, successful pork exporters, keep pigs in worse conditions than the UK and Sweden; low welfare can be a winning export strategy. In the US, tail-docking remains legal; farmers justify it on the basis that there's no other way to stop pigs biting each other, even though adding straw has been shown to be just as effective at reducing tail-biting. These painful procedures are not more effective, but they are cheaper, because there's no price paid for the animals' additional suffering.

Castration is also common, because the pork of uncastrated male pigs is strongly flavoured – a problem known as 'boar taint'. Some farms avoid this by killing the pigs young. But prosciutto is made from pigs killed at the age of more than nine months, after they've reached sexual maturity: if you eat Parma ham from a male pig, that pig will have been castrated, probably with painkillers but no anaesthetic. EU countries are moving towards banning castration without anaesthesia, although this does not address the long-term health effects.

Many pregnant sows are kept in 'gestation crates', barely bigger than their bodies, for their entire pregnancies. The 'crates' – cages seems a fairer word – stop the pigs from turning around; they stop them from moving much at all. Temple Grandin, one of the US's most celebrated experts in animal husbandry, described the metal crates as like 'asking a sow to live in an airline seat'. The pigs cannot carry out their natural activities such as foraging; they cannot exercise at all. They bite the bars; they injure themselves on the hard floors. Their muscles wither; their bones lose one-third of their strength. Sows can spend virtually their entire lives in crates, excluding a short period around the time of giving birth where they are transferred to 'farrowing crates', which have a space for piglets to feed.

The EU is in the process of ordering that sows are only kept in gestation crates for a maximum of a few weeks per pregnancy. In the US, the crates are still mainstream. Some companies have promised to go 'crate-free', but they have sneakily defined this to include sows that are kept for the first month of their pregnancy in crates. In total 'crate-free' sows could spend around 40 per cent of their lives in crates. Tyson, one of the world's largest producers, says that 80 per cent of its pork derives from sows kept in crates. Many of the remaining 20 per cent are also kept in crates, just not for the whole time. This is why they tell us not to look how the sausage is made.

Nearly half of the world's pigs are in China. Historically small farms have predominated, but now production is shifting to large units with several thousand pigs, often in gestation crates. In Europe, the public has protested against two- or three-storey pig farms, where pigs are even further removed from the soil they love to root around in. In China, twelve-storey breeding units are up and running, with more than 1,200 sows per storey, who will spend their whole life on one floor. One media report described these metallic multi-storey facilities, astonishingly, as 'hog hotels'. This doesn't make me want to eat pork – it makes me not want to go to a hotel.

Factory farms are the only way that the world can produce cheap meat on the scale that we demand it. Most meat-eaters don't defend factory-farming: chickens unable to walk, pigs in metal crates, cows kept in sheds year-round. They argue that there is a better farming, where the animals are happy right up to the point that they are dead (or perhaps till the moment they are transported for hours). When I got into conversations with people about vegetarianism, this is often where the conversation ended up. 'I try to only eat meat from good sources.' 'The animals have good lives.'

Perhaps there is a way to square the circle, to quieten the extremes. Or perhaps it was a mirage, too good to be true. I wanted to find out which. I went back on the job sites, and found an ad for an outdoor pig stockperson. A few days later, in the last of the autumn sun, I drive north-east from London, past Cambridge and the horseracing course at Newmarket, to the heart of Britain's pork industry.

*

The head office of the pig farm is in a small village, the type of place that has no shops or pubs, just a row of large houses and cars. I drive my car into the yard, and wait for the boss. Andy is a headmasterly type, lean and smart, with clean overalls and a puffed-out chest. 'What made you want to work in outdoor pigs?' he says. There are probably several right answers to this question, but I quickly decide that writing a book about whether people should eat meat isn't one of them.

Andy loves his job and loves his pigs, at least judging by how often he says he loves his job and loves his pigs. 'We love the animals, and they pay our wages,' he says earnestly, as we drive round the edge of the pens in his pick-up truck. He shakes his head at those landowners who just see the pigs as a 'break crop'. Pigs dig into the soil, eat up stray roots, and pump out rich manure. (Potato farmers see this as helpful, although the process of upturning the soil damages its long-term fertility.)

Andy stops the truck, and we step over the low electrified wire that borders the pens. The wire is low so as to be in the pigs' narrow field of view. The pigs approach curiously. They are pale pink, wide, and surprisingly determined to move.

I immediately remember my mum warning me as a kid that, if a pig bites you, they will not let go until they hit the bone. When I mention this to Andy, he seems genuinely perplexed. His pigs sniff and honk and generally express interest. There is no sign of aggression or even unpredictability. One sow sniffs his thigh and nuzzles his overalls pocket. 'Ninety per cent of them are great,' he says. He jokes that his staff give him more headaches than his animals.

British farms are seen as good for pigs, relative to what goes on elsewhere. Most pigs are kept outdoors, not in the indoor mega-units that are common in the US. Although castration of male piglets is not illegal, it is hardly practised.

Andy's farm is a breeding station, where piglets are born and then, after four weeks, sent elsewhere to be fattened up. The sows who have given birth – or who are heavily pregnant – are kept in individual huts with semicircular metal roofs, which resemble mini air-raid shelters.

I notice there is a disconcerting crunching sound – the pigs are chewing stones. It's almost surreal: each sow has a handful of large pebbles in her mouth. Experts are not sure why pigs do this. Andy thinks it's because the pigs are fed concentrated cereals once a day, but their natural behaviour is to chew all day. He is aware that chewing stones is a bit odd.

Andy is also aware that the farm – with its bare soil – doesn't look idyllic. He is planning for the pigs to live on grass, because that is what people expect to see. 'So if Mrs Housewife comes, and sees the pigs jumping around, she'll say – "yes, I love pork",' he tells me, sincerely. Later, when he gives me a trial as a stockperson, he reiterates his passion: 'I want you to love it.'

When animals were domesticated, their brains and teeth generally became smaller. But livestock's bodies have swollen. In the past few decades in particular, farmers have bred pigs to be big, fatty and to have more offspring. Wild boar usually breed once a year, with an average of five piglets. Domesticated pigs breed every five months, with more than twice as many piglets each time. Breeding sows are three times as heavy and have three times as many piglets every year as they did in the Middle Ages. We humans have steadily opted to have fewer offspring ourselves, while engineering our farm animals to have more and more. It's a strange form of love.

Farming is a numbers game. If the farm produces twenty-eight piglets per sow per year, Andy can relax; if not, the sums start to go fuzzy. A sow's gestation period is 143 days; the average litter is eleven piglets; each piglet is worth £16. Eleven piglets is right up against the limit: after sows have thirteen piglets, the survival rates drop off; the fifteenth piglet has only a 30 per cent chance of weaning. Every stage of the process is structured. The sows have their feeding and fertility ordered to maximise productivity; they are taken by truck to different parts of the farm every three weeks. When Andy describes it, he descends quickly into a jargon that I can't follow. 'It's a very efficient system, but it is a system,' he summarises, and I get that.

Reproduction on the farm is a procedure, in which the male and the female never touch each other. Pouches of boar semen have been delivered. On my first day we corral the sows, four at a time, into a small pen. I stand holding one of the pouches, and the liquid slowly runs down a tube placed inside the sow. The sows protest mildly. To get them in the mood, a hormonal black boar has been placed on the other side of the railing. Everything is mediated by humans. Whatever the pigs are doing, it isn't sex.

How do you judge a farm like this? Andy's piglets are raised to be assured by the RSPCA, meaning that they must conform to a set of welfare standards. The ninety-six-page standards for pigs specifies how much space a pig should have at a feeding trough (1.1 times shoulder width), how much bedded area a pig should have (half a square metre for a hundred-kilo pig), and how much straw a pregnant sow should have before giving birth (at least two kilos per forty-eight hours, to allow her to build a nest). Piglets can only be taken from their mothers after twenty-eight days, or after twenty-one days if they are being taken to thoroughly cleaned and disinfected housing. Farmers must take care to minimise bullying. This is the gold standard, the stuff that merits a premium price at the supermarket.

What the RSPCA's principles don't do is interfere with the general routine. Sows are artificially inseminated early and often. And as soon as their productivity drops off – or they become cumbersome and suffocate an uneconomical proportion of their piglets – they are sent to the slaughterhouse. Selecting which pigs are redundant is one of the most disliked jobs on the farm. Wild boars live up to fifteen years; pot-bellied pigs kept as pets have lived up to twenty-five. On the farm, a sow will typically first be impregnated at six months, and then will be culled after six litters, around the age of three. Her piglets will be killed at five or six months. If we humans were killed at a similar stage of our lives, we would be culled before we reached our fifth birthday. We want to believe our farm animals live well, but they hardly live at all.

Sows are now so large that they are prone to accidentally lie on – and kill – their own babies. (There's a metaphor about humans' own environmental impact here somewhere.) One of my jobs is to check the pig huts for these dead piglets, or as they are called 'overlays'. I spot one in the corner of a hut. As I reach for the body, I realise that two others are below in the straw – apparently smothered days beforehand. In another hut, one of the live pigs freezes on top of another deceased piglet, and I wonder if there is a sibling attachment. The piglets are roughly the size of human babies, with a similar skin tone and warmth. But after a day or two dead in the straw, colour and softness depart; the piglets turn grey and taut.

There was something gruesome about pulling dead piglets from the straw – their lives only recorded as a financial loss, their passing not noticed by their own mothers. I tossed the bodies in a foul-smelling, fly-ridden bin, and moved away. I could handle the disgusting nature of collecting the bodies, by clenching my nose and averting my eyes, but I couldn't digest the lack of meaning. Months later I emailed some European wild-boar experts to ask if wild sows ever suffocate their young. The simple answer is that we don't know, because wild boar have not been studied in the same way. But it seems unlikely, given that wild sows are smaller and have fewer piglets. They also have no permanent shelters. They create temporary nests in the woodland. Unlike pig huts, these nests do not have walls, reducing the chance of a piglet being unable to squeeze out.

In 1964 a Quaker writer called Ruth Harrison published *Animal Machines*, an indictment of early industrialised farming. It was not widely read, but fifteen years later British scientists came up with the idea that farm animals should have 'five freedoms' – from thirst, hunger and malnutrition; from discomfort and exposure; from pain, injury and disease; from fear and distress; and to express normal behaviour.

The five freedoms have shaped our view of good welfare. Before I spent time on a farm, they seemed like a fairly comprehensive checklist of what a good life would look like. But at the farm, I realised how inadequate they are. The problem with livestock farming goes far deeper than the shape of the huts, or the quantity of the food. It starts with the intensive breeding of animals for meat. Evolution by natural selection should condition animals *not* to be meat. In wild boar, it has promoted animals with guile, agility and speed. Our breeding has promoted the opposite characteristics – warping their biology, to the point where sows are so large they don't notice when they kill their own piglets.

While animals' biology has changed, their behavioural instincts remain largely the same. Like wild boar, pigs would – if given the choice – alternate between open and wooded ground. Wild sows keep their piglets with them for a year; we can assume that domesticated pigs might do the same, if they were allowed to. We are dragging these animals away from their evolved selves. Modern livestock farming degrades animal life; it removes the choice and the serendipity. What makes animals special – their ability to take decisions, to play and form relationships – are inconveniences on a farm. This is mere existence, not life.

I have seen farrowing crates briefly, at a farming school, and felt physically sick. I know that, if I visited a factory pig farm with hundreds of them, I'd be outraged. Even at this farm where the intentions are good, I have a nagging feeling. The pigs lack something fundamental. Their feed, their lifespans, their breeding patterns are totally controlled by humans. Their space to exercise their imagination and social behaviour is entirely prescribed. My section of the farm alone has more than 800 pigs; the chance of developing any understanding of their personalities and needs is nil. We don't eat dogs because they have personality. But wouldn't it be better to eat an animal that has had a real life, a chance to develop their personality, rather than one that has been reduced to obedience? There is no prospect of forming a relationship that offsets the brutality of the killing process. Cows, pigs and sheep may be less cognitively developed than us in some ways. They are still sentient creatures with needs and instincts. If there were another species able to subdue us, would we think it was fair for them to treat us in this way?

There's a *New Yorker* cartoon of a doctor's surgery, where the doctor tells a young pig: 'It's your ribs. I'm afraid they're delicious.' One day, we finish work at the farm around four in the afternoon, and I head to my uncle's house nearby. He cooks pork chops under the grill. On impulse, I decide to put myself to the test once more. I put my vegetarianism to one side. The pork has an almost bready texture, like a firm sponge, and it releases its juice when I bite into it. It does taste good, I think. But the taste lasts only a few seconds. And I wonder, is that it? Is that what we do all this for? That was the last time I ate meat, and I have never regretted leaving it behind.

*

There are people in the world for whom vegetarianism would be almost impossible. Buddhism preaches non-violence against animals, but in Tibet, where growing crops is a struggle, the Buddhist population mainly does eat meat, leaving the job of professional butchering to Muslims. I once asked a Mongolian Buddhist monk how he survived in a country with not much arable land, and he smiled and said if the killing took place out of your sight, maybe it wasn't such a sin. You can't say that Buddhist monks aren't pragmatic.

In rich countries today, however, most people could give up meat – if they were really opposed to modern animal farming. They have just decided not to. Some consumers (especially women, research suggests) have grown uncomfortable about red meat, and others have demanded better welfare standards for cows and pigs. But mostly we have developed new blind spots. We rely on the misconception that a blood-red steak involves more suffering than a pale chicken breast, let alone a fish fillet. In Europe a surprising number of declared vegetarians, perhaps a quarter, eat chicken at least once a week.

In the 1920s, the average American ate around 200 grams of chicken a year; now they eat 45 kilos. In Germany, the UK and the US, the average person eats more than twice as much chicken now as they did in 1980. This has not happened by discovering some unused source of chickens; it has relied instead on creating vast chicken farms where chickens are pushed to their biological limits. There are now two types of chickens: broilers, who are intended for meat, and laying hens, who produce eggs. Broilers are genetic freaks whose bodies grow faster than their legs or hearts can sustain. They have doubled in weight since the Second World War. Many simply collapse on the floor, or drop dead. The rest grow largely in indoor barns with no natural light, and where there are so many birds their intense suffering and deformities often go unnoticed. The conditions are cramped and unsanitary: the path to clean white meat is covered in faeces. Do the chickens notice each other's suffering? In one study, researchers watched how hens would react when they and their chicks were separately sprayed with discomforting puffs of air. The hens' heart rate increased more when their chicks were sprayed with air than when they themselves were. They clucked maternally. Their behaviour was at least consistent with empathy. Chickens are not pecking automatons. They have social hierarchies, good eyesight and different alarm calls for different predators.

There are more than 22 billion broiler chickens alive at any moment – probably making the chicken the most populous bird in the history of the world. Wild junglefowl live for several years, but broiler chickens, their domesticated relatives, are killed as young as five weeks. That is not much longer than the lifespan of a housefly. The birds are transported to abattoirs in cramped cages. The killing process is traumatic, with the chickens often hung upside down via metal shackles. UK law allows chickens to hang upside down for up to a minute before they are stunned or killed. In the US, more than half a million birds are improperly killed each year. Perhaps because they are birds, and not mammals, chickens seem to be the most prone of all livestock to abuse by tired, frustrated workers. Inspectors, both in the US and Europe, are unlikely to come calling, because their budgets have been slashed. As Peter Singer puts it: 'there's no doubt that the animal that we inflict the most suffering on globally is the chicken'.

Meat changes our whole relationship with animals. When people talk about their animals, they often mention their pets. But our imprint on the animal world is not found in the gravestones in the garden and the photos on our Facebook pages; it is found in the abattoirs and the farms. A typical person might have a few pets over the course of their lifetime. The average British person consumes around twenty chickens a year. If meat consumption remains at its current level, a British baby born today will – over the course of their life – eat the equivalent of five whole cows, twenty whole sheep, twenty-five whole pigs and 1,785 chickens. The death estimates don't include all the sick and prematurely killed animals who never make it to the abattoir, and which instead are tossed into bins. They don't include the chickens that stand unable to move in the barns for hours until a worker puts them out of their misery.

Meat-eating relies on cognitive dissonance. Whether we choose to eat a dog or a cow makes no difference to whether that animal suffers. But we convince ourselves it does. In one experiment, researchers told one group of Americans that kangaroos lived in Papua New Guinea, and another group that the kangaroos were eaten in Papua New Guinea, and then asked both groups whether the animals could feel pain. The second group, told that the animals were eaten, judged the kangaroos as less capable of feeling pain. The act of eating changes our minds. If you give someone a beef snack and ask them whether cows suffer pain, they are less likely to say yes than if you give them some nuts. If you overstate the intelligence of tapirs, wild animals who look somewhat similar to pigs, people say that tapirs deserve more moral concern; if you do the same with pigs, they don't. In other words, we don't want to eat animals because we underplay their suffering; we underplay their suffering because we want to eat them. This is the so-called 'meat paradox', whereby people who care about animals manage not to care about farm animals. The psychologist

Hank Rothgerber gave some meat-eaters a short text about a vegetarian, and other meat-eaters a short text about a gluten-free individual. The first group were more likely then to deny animals' mental abilities, suggesting that the mere act of reading about vegetarians prods omnivores into a defensive mode.

Giving up meat is not a new idea. Pythagoras, Leonardo da Vinci, Benjamin Franklin, Leo Tolstoy, George Bernard Shaw, Mohandas Gandhi, Mary Shelley, Adolf Hitler, Steve Jobs – all were, at least for some part of their life, vegetarian. Any list that includes Hitler obviously isn't ideal, and quite a few vegetarians would rather that the balance weren't so tilted towards oddballs. In the nineteenth century, when the word vegetarian was coined, it was synonymous with religious abstinence. Sylvester Graham, a Presbyterian preacher who co-founded the American Vegetarian Society in 1850, believed not only that meat was bad for the body – but that white flour, alcohol, coffee, tea, mustard, vinegar and pepper were too. You have to hope his followers didn't have many tastebuds. Gandhi, before travelling to London to study, promised his mother three things: he wouldn't eat meat, he wouldn't drink alcohol, and he wouldn't have sex with a woman who wasn't his wife. In the 1970s, the UK's best-known vegetarian restaurants were a chain with the self-ironising name of Cranks. Vegetarian is still interpreted as an absence – a denial of pleasure. You're a stickler – you're the person who can't join in.

In 1982, the year I was born, a journalist called Bruce Feirstein published a book called *Real Men Don't Eat Quiche*. It was a joke about contemporary masculinity, and became a runaway bestseller. Yet men do view meat differently. According to one study, when women are asked to justify why they eat meat, they try to dissociate their meals from animal suffering; men, in contrast, fall back on straightforward justifications, such as human superiority. Women are much more likely to take part in Veganuary. Ironically if you do have a thirst for old-school masculinity – the type that requires outlandish courage and an I-take-no-crap-from-anybody attitude – you'd be much better off complaining about the lack of vegetarian options in a restaurant, loudly.

There is also a political split. Conservatives are less likely to view vegetarians positively and to be vegetarian themselves. If they do become vegetarian, they are less likely to remain vegetarian, perhaps because they don't have vegetarian friends. I once interviewed Nigel Farage, the Brexit campaigner, over lunch, and he chose a chophouse in the City of London. When I ordered the goat's cheese, he nearly fell off his chair. In the US, meat-eating also differs along racial lines: non-whites are much more likely than whites to say they are cutting down on meat.

I grew up eating sausages and chicken breasts. As a teenager I had worked at a supermarket deli, once cutting the very top of my right thumb off in the slicer, in a bid for the thinnest possible Parma ham. I'd eaten snake and rabbit and boiled-alive lobster and not felt any compunction to change until years later. My wife and I got engaged after a cured meats (and wine) tasting session. When I went vegetarian, my friends quizzed me on what I was missing. Bacon, surely? Steak? In fact what I noticed most of all was a sense of relief. I could take satisfaction in my food – that my hunger was not another animal's suffering. Screw the meat paradox, this was the vegetarian paradox – that in cutting out meat, I had felt there were more things I wanted to eat, not fewer. Vegetarianism is a presence, not an absence.

'Just don't go vegan,' my wife Susie, herself a vegetarian, told me. 'It's divorceable.'

I had every intention of following that instruction, until I found out about the dairy industry.

*

If you are really concerned about animal welfare, you should almost certainly stop eating dairy before you stop eating beef. Many dairy cows have worse lives than beef cows. The person who finally convinced me of it was a Scottish dairy farmer called David Finlay.

Finlay is a chain-talker. Each sentence leads inexorably to the next. To interrupt is futile; in fact it seems cruel, given how much Finlay clearly wants to tell the story of his farm – and his cows. 'Ninety-nine per cent of farmers think it's a no-no, it's a gimmick, it's so far out of the box that it's not worth thinking about,' he says, when we first speak by phone. 'Even the organic guys are saying, "You're setting the bar a bit high."'

Finlay is a dairy farmer with a difference. A lean man with a strip of grey hair around a large bald patch, he is leading one of the most radical experiments in how to produce milk. He's doing so out of disgust at how dairy cows are treated, even on organic farms.

Cow's milk is the first animal food that most Europeans and Americans consume. When I was a kid, there was a TV advert in which a boy says he'd spoken to the footballer Ian Rush, then playing for Liverpool. 'He said if I don't drink lots of milk I'll only ever be good enough to play for Accrington Stanley,' the boy tells his sister. 'Accrington Stanley? Who are they?' replies his sister. '*Exactly*!' says the boy. There was another ad where a jovial milkman led a line of dancing glass milk bottles down the street, and tidied up the street while he delivered them. Around the same time, the US Got Milk? campaign launched, with a man unable to win $10,000 by responding correctly to a trivia question about Alexander Hamilton, because he had a mouthful of bread and no milk to wash it down with.

With tradition and marketing firepower, of course no one questioned how milk was produced. When I gave up meat, I didn't think twice about dairy. Like many vegetarians, I ate more of the stuff. Milk was fine, yoghurt was fine, and cheese was more than fine – it was delicious and essential. To be honest, I didn't really even associate dairy with death. At most restaurants, I knew what I would order before I opened the menu: goat's cheese.

But to start with – and this is obvious when you do think about it – drinking cow's milk is not innate. Lots of species eat other animals' *meat*. But humans are the only species to drink and process other animals' milk. (OK, some exceptions: in Mexico, researchers have spotted seabirds and feral cats stealing milk from elephant seals; the birds and cats also ate the seals' placentas. In French Polynesia, a bottlenose dolphin was seen suckling a persistent melon-headed whale, although the whale learnt to act like a dolphin. And throughout human history there are cases of women breastfeeding animals such as piglets and bears.) Milk is not generally a food for adults in the animal world: after weaning, most mammals produce less of the enzyme lactase, which is needed to digest the sugar in milk. It's only relatively recently in evolutionary terms – that is, within the past few thousand years – that many humans, particularly in Europe, developed the ability to produce lactase into adulthood. Even now two-thirds of humans, including those in much of east Asia, have an impaired ability to digest cow's milk as adults.

Another thing that is obvious when you think about it: cows produce milk after they have given birth. To keep producing milk, cows have to be regularly impregnated. Natural reproduction would limit the farmers' ability to control the genes. Instead it's done by artificial insemination. What happens to the calves? They are separated from their mothers. Given that cows, like us, are mammals and that the relationship between mother and offspring has evolved over hundreds of thousands of years because it helps the young to survive, of course the separation hurts. The mothers bellow for days at the loss of the calves. 'There is no question about this being an unpleasant experience for the cow and the calf,' says Dan Weary, a professor of animal welfare at the University of British Columbia.

In an attempt to minimise the suffering, dairy farms separate mothers and calves within twenty-four hours of birth – when it's assumed that no bond will have developed. Dairy calves are therefore separated from their mothers far earlier than piglets or lambs. In the US and Canada, more than three-quarters are separated at birth and reared individually in those first few days when they would naturally be learning from their mothers and getting to know other cows. But there is little evidence to suggest that separating calves early lessens the blow of separation. In fact, some studies suggest that separation has lasting effects on the calves' behaviour. Researchers in Austria placed one group of cows who had been reared by their mothers together with another group who had been separated within twenty-four hours and fed by an automatic milk dispenser. After their first twelve weeks, the cows were all treated the same – and integrated into a dairy herd. But two years later, cows reared by their mother were more active and more likely to explore.

Some dairy calves are killed immediately. Others are raised for beef and killed before their second birthday. If you are vegetarian, you are in effect propping up the meat industry by drinking milk and eating cheese. A few weeks earlier I had visited a dairy farm in England, part of an open day event encouraging shoppers to take pride in their food. My biggest concern had been the welfare of the mothers, who are housed in sheds and led onto large rotating milking machines twice a day.

'Did they show you the calves?' asks Wilma Finlay, David's wife, when I mention it. They hadn't. 'It's easy to show people around if you don't show them the calves.' Nobody, or virtually nobody, thinks about the separation of mother and calf when they buy milk in the supermarket. Wilma and David found that visitors to their farm did care. 'The commonest question was, why were the cows over there and the calves over there?' says Wilma. 'That's the biggest issue, especially for women.'

David's major objection to traditional dairy farming was different. When he grew up a cow might last eight to ten lactations, now she would be 'lucky' to see three. He hated how cows were quickly worn out by consecutive pregnancies, then killed. He hated the mastitis and lameness. Just as in humans, mastitis is a bacterial infection of the mammary gland. The cow's udder becomes inflamed. Vets rate severe mastitis as painful as a broken bone, yet painkillers are unevenly applied. The disease can be fatal; it can also lead farmers to cull the affected cow, because it affects the taste of the milk. Cows kept indoors are most susceptible. To extract more milk, farmers speed up the milking process to increase the flow rate, but this faster milking speed makes cows twelve times more likely to contract mastitis. Cows bred for higher milk production are also more susceptible. The same genes associated with higher milk production also correlate with poor health. Yet we continue to drive for more productivity. In the Middle Ages, a dairy cow might produce a litre or even three of milk a day (enough for the inhabitants of Reggio Emilia to devise Parmesan cheese). Now US farmers take an average of thirty litres a day, itself an increase of more than 30 per cent over the past two decades. The most intensive dairy farms, which have spread in the US, the UK, Germany, Denmark and beyond, extract sixty litres per day per cow.

Farms achieve efficiency by keeping cows permanently indoors, feeding them intensively, and depriving them of the rich social life that we know they would naturally develop. Cows are herd animals, and they seem to be divided between dominant and submissive animals. When unfamiliar cows are placed together, they behave more aggressively, show more signs of stress – and produce less milk. Being indoors also increases tension.

High-performance cows work far harder than most humans; in terms of their energy output, they are not too far behind Tour de France cyclists. A dairy cow today is, as one academic puts it, 'a milkbag on legs, and unstable legs at that'. When I had seen dairy cows, with their swollen undercarriages and ungainly gait, I had assumed this was a quirk of the species; but of course, it isn't. These are animals we have created, putting productivity ahead of compassion. Some cows are injected every fourteen days with a growth hormone called bovine somatotrophin (BST), which increases the risk of foot disorders. BST has been banned in much of the world, but remains licensed by the US Food and Drug administration.

In the US, up to half of dairy cows suffer lameness, including sole ulcers and foot rot. Sole ulcers – raw sores that can become infected – can be caused by spending hours standing in urine and manure, or in sawdust that is used for bedding. Concrete floors worsen foot problems. Stress and cramped conditions lead to lameness. Lame cattle arch their backs, and walk only in careful steps. The worst affected cows try not to walk at all. It's not loving animals to push their bodies past their limits like this.

The Finlay family have farmed 850 acres in south-west Scotland, barely a mile from the Irish Sea, since 1928. But David and Wilma are now doing two things differently. The first is to keep mothers and calves together for five months, rather than the standard twenty-four hours. A calf typically takes around ten litres of milk a day. Dairy cows have been bred to produce three times that, so this still leaves a surplus. The other thing that the Finlays do is to allow cows to graze outdoors as much as possible. This is increasingly unusual. At Britain's largest dairy farms, in Scotland, Wales and Northern Ireland, cows are kept indoors all year round, where they can be most efficiently fed, inspected and milked. Instead of producing 6,000 litres of milk a year for sale, each of the Finlays' cows now produces only about 4,000. But lameness and mastitis have fallen by at least three-quarters, and the cows also need 85 per cent less antibiotics.

The Finlays' experiment is not complete. They tried a variant of it previously in 2012 – long before the surge of interest in veganism – but gave up because the books wouldn't balance. 'It was traumatic financially,' says David.

This time the Finlays took out a bank loan, and didn't tell the bank their plans. They rethought their method: the mothers start calving as young as twenty-four months, compared to thirty-two months previously. The male calves are fattened up more quickly, and sold for meat as young as eight months, as 'rosé veal'. Even so the first year was 'pretty awful', and their experienced herdsman left. By the second year, things had improved. 'We can see it's going to work,' says David. 'We can claw our way back. We're not there yet.'

Part of the problem is that dairy products are not labelled in a way that makes shoppers think about the cows' welfare. There's organic milk, which in the UK means the cows have access to the outdoors and that farmers have been asked to reduce the number of male calves who are slaughtered at birth. But organic standards say nothing about when the mothers and calves are separated, and don't set limits on the prevalence of mastitis or lameness. They also don't generate a large premium for farmers. So the Finlays produce cheeses and ice cream that they can sell to specialist purveyors. The cheeses cost at least three times as much as standard supermarket packs.

A few days after our conversation, I see David presenting his meat to food buyers in London. It's a small fashionable restaurant near Old Street, the gentrifying heart of the capital's start-up scene. The buyers are sitting on benches at three long wooden tables. David is a fish out of water. He talks for too long, and in too much detail about his cows. Or perhaps it isn't too long, and it isn't too much detail, because what people want is a story that they can trust. Two years later, three-quarters of the Finlays' cheese sales are in London, 90 per cent are to women, and quite a few are to near-vegans. The Finlays are nearly breaking even – at least they were until the restaurants closed in the corona-virus lockdown, and the market for rosé veal dried up. But how many cheese-eaters are really prepared to pay premium prices, for what is now a staple?

There's one more problem. All animal foods are inefficient. When you consider pasture and crops grown for feed, animals currently account for 77 per cent of all the earth's agricultural land, but they pro-vide only 18 per cent of our calories and only 37 per cent of our protein. It requires twenty times more land to produce a gram of protein from cows and sheep than it does to produce it from pulses such as chick-peas and soyabeans. Dairy requires around four times more than pulses. It isn't as bad as beef, but it's less efficient than chicken and pork. Dairy cows also burp out methane emissions – through the fermentation in their guts, and their manure contains powerful greenhouse gases too. Taking a global average, a litre of milk creates greenhouse gas emis-sions equivalent to three kilos of carbon dioxide. A kilo of cheese produces twenty-one kilos of carbon dioxide equivalent, as much as driving a new (fossil-fuel) car 160 kilometres.

Bluntly, if you are worried about climate change, then going vege-tarian is not enough. It will reduce your food greenhouse gas emissions by around one third, estimate researchers at Johns Hopkins Univer-sity. In fact, a vegetarian diet with lots of dairy will create more emissions than a mainly vegetable diet with some meat. Worldwide, if everyone replaced just the dairy in their diets, food greenhouse gas emissions would fall by nearly a quarter, almost twice as much than if everyone cut out red meat.

Those dairy farms that are most conducive to animal welfare – i.e. that allow cows to graze – also tend to be those that produce the most greenhouse gases for each kilo of milk. The grazing land could other-wise be used to store carbon, for example through trees. There's no good option: if you want low carbon emissions, you broadly have to put dairy cows in sheds and feed them grain; if you put them in sheds, you are damaging their social patterns. There's no way that, at scale, dairy can pass the animal test.

*

So, no meat and no dairy. I'm down to eggs. Most meat chickens live terrible lives. Egg-laying hens must do better, right? If there is one animal welfare issue that western consumers are familiar with, it's battery hens. Many western consumers have shifted towards cage-free eggs, to avoid chickens having to endure cramped lives that remind us very much of prison.

But cage-free eggs are no panacea. Laying hens are now so big and heavy that, if they are kept free-range and allowed to move about, up to 86 per cent will fracture their keel bone – the bone to which their breast muscles bind. Even after the fractures heal, the chickens' movement is reduced and they suffer ongoing pain. Chickens are more likely to die early if they are kept in outside cages, because they may be attacked or smothered by their fellow birds. The smothering is thought to happen when the birds become nervous; the farm environment is so removed from the jungles for which these birds' psychology evolved. Every option has serious drawbacks: barn hens have high mortality and frequent keel bone fractures; free-range hens have high skin damage; and large, so-called furnished cages may not allow chickens to exhibit their natural behaviours, like dust-bathing. Mutilation is often necessary. In the EU, many laying hens have their beaks sliced off to prevent them pecking each other's feathers.

It's startling what we have created through intensive farming. All domesticated chickens are descended from junglefowl who lay up to one egg a month. Today's laying hens are generally engineered to produce almost one egg *a day*. At the age of around seventeen months, hens become less productive – and are culled. Billions of new hens are bred every year to replace them.

What horrified me most was something else. Every year several billion chickens don't experience drawn-out suffering. They don't experience very much at all – because at barely a day old, they are thrown into industrial grinders or gassed to death. These are the male chicks, born in the hatcheries intended for laying hens. The males aren't needed in the egg-laying process. They can't be profitably raised for meat, because they are the wrong breed, and fattening them up requires inefficient amounts of food. So they are killed. It doesn't matter whether the laying hens themselves go on to be free-range or organic: this is what happens to the males. Their bodies are sometimes just thrown away; other times they are ground up for pet food.

This instinctively feels like a system gone wrong. There is an ethical issue of whether it's right to bring animals into the world, only to kill them immediately. There is also a welfare issue of whether the animals suffer a painful death. But it also goes to the heart of how we see other animals. Can we be so callous about their existence? Can we say we love them if we dispose of them so unthinkingly?

I want to know if there's an alternative. I take a train to the Dutch university city of Leiden, walk under the tracks, over a canal and soon find myself in the biggest science park I have ever seen. There are neat rows of large office buildings. I make my way to the edge of the park, past a group of floodlit tennis courts and a sign about new vascularised cancer treatment, and there I meet Wouter Bruins, a floppy-haired entrepreneur in a hoodie. He leads me down sterile, corporate corridors to a small office with a few Ikea tables and a blown-up photo of a cornfield at sunrise. A placard announces that this is the headquarters of 'The Eggsperts'.

In 2011 Bruins was not an expert in anything. He was a biology student at Leiden University with no knowledge about the poultry industry, but a desire to start a company. 'I went out to a bunch of people and I said, "What do you do all day long? I would like to start a business somewhere so I'm looking for issues to solve. What can I solve?"' he recalls. 'People tend not to have a lot of people come by and ask that.'

Among those Bruins met was a friend of his parents who farmed chickens. 'He told me, "We're killing these chicks and I don't like it." A lot of people will tell you that the hatchery people don't care. They do care. They just have to do it.' For Bruins, that was the starting point. How could farmers avoid having to kill male chicks?

One route was to genetically modify chickens so that male eggs were identifiable from female eggs – for example, by inserting genetic sequencing for fluorescence. That could allow the males to be killed before they hatched. Bruins dismissed that approach: 'People will see fluorescence and think, "Did you put a jellyfish in a chicken? That's pretty bad."' Other GM options were possible – such as trying to breed laying hens that didn't lay male eggs at all. But Bruins and his partner thought this too would provoke public anger: 'We said no GMO.'

Instead they came up with a different solution. It turns out that male and female embryos have different levels of a particular metabolite, a substance involved in turning food into energy. Bruins' team found a way of distinguishing between male and female eggs, by taking a tiny sample from the egg, sealing it and then testing it.

The standard test is accurate in 98 to 99 per cent of cases. It is administered on the ninth day after the eggs have been laid, while the chicks are presumed not to feel pain. 'Around day eleven and a half, the brain stem closes. That's when you would expect the chick to start feeling something.' The male embryos can be disposed of before that point.

Others groups in Germany and Canada have been working on the same problem. Bruins' company, In Ovo, has spent around €6 million getting to this point. The process 'needs to be quick, the cost needs to be low, hatchability shouldn't suffer, and it should be something that hatchery employees actually like to work with. If you do that, then I'm pretty sure most hatcheries in the world will start using it.'

And if this happens, you'd be saving billions of chicks, I ask. 'Yeah.'

Bruins's worst-case scenario is that only the top of the market – producers of free-range eggs – insists on the technology. He is now trying to solve other problems. Broiler chickens are often born up to three days early. They are stuck in hot hatcheries, and under Dutch law, they do not have to be given food or water for their first sixty hours, although, after campaigning by animal welfare groups, there are plans to reduce this to thirty-six hours. In Ovo has developed an early feeding system, which is now being used in several countries, including the US. Bruins even allows himself to dream of welfare-friendly foie gras. 'It would be a really nice case. I think it's not that difficult to get an animal's liver fattened up without force-feeding it. It's a terrible thing to think about – but if people are going to eat foie gras, then let's do it in a good way, right? I don't know, we could microinject stuff that regulates their liver activity. It may be possible, but no one is thinking about it. Growing someone's liver is not that difficult.'

You get used to people trying to explain away the cruelty of farming. It's disorienting when someone like Bruins insists it can be changed. It's also baffling that it has taken a few entrepreneurs – several decades since factory chicken farming started – to sort this problem. 'There's something wrong with the system,' says Bruins. 'We're six, seven guys and we're growing to fifteen. We're one of the leading companies in solving the chick problem. It doesn't make sense.'

The end of male-chick culling is hopefully in sight. If it happens, it will be a triumph of ingenuity – for curious, restless individuals like Bruins who believe that there is always a solution somewhere. But even if male chicks are spared from death, egg production will have lots of squeamish sides. All chickens are vulnerable to new strains of bird flu, which necessitate mass culls. Caged hens live in cramped conditions, but at least their faeces can be cleaned away. Free-range hens, in contrast, are more much vulnerable to infections and early death.

People may be more willing to vote for animal welfare than to shop for it. In 2008 cage-free eggs had less than 10 per cent of the market in California. But 63 per cent of Californians voted for a law saying that all egg-laying hens should be able to turn around freely. This is the 'vote-buy gap': people will demand something at the ballot box that they weren't choosing at the supermarket. Voting for change has two advantages: it makes us stop and think about the reality of animals' lives, and it makes us feel part of a movement, to know that our restraint won't just lead to others being free-riders. It's often assumed that you can't force people to change how they eat. But people are willing to force themselves to change. The problem is that, until we are confronted and until there is a political choice, we are happy to pass by obliviously.

*

By now, it's clear to me that there are inspiring, ethical people – like David and Wilma Finlay, and Wouter Bruins – involved in animal farming. But I'm not convinced that this could add up to an ethical industry. There's the abuse, which is an unavoidable consequence of putting voiceless animals together with tired, poorly paid humans. Even if we could eliminate it, we would be left with the mutilation we inflict on animals. Painful procedures, which in some cases leave lasting impacts on animals' behaviour and stress levels, allow farmers to manage large herds and reduce costs. In most European countries, cows can be branded with hot irons, or their ears cut, in order to identify them; Germany is the only European country to have banned nose rings for cattle.

Welfare laws, across the world, have improved in recent years. It's right to celebrate moves such as the phasing out of pig gestation crates and battery eggs. But change is so slow, and involves so many procedures. And is it even enough?

Over the past decade, veterinarians have increasingly been going beyond the five freedoms and thinking instead about how to promote positive mental states among animals – an approach known as 'positive welfare'. While it's easy to ensure pigs aren't hungry, it's much harder to ensure they're happy. Is happiness even an appropriate concept? When scientists study human happiness, they can simply ask people how well they feel most of the time or how they rate their life, against the best and worst possible life that they can imagine. You can't do that with a pig (or to be fair a human baby). We are left with trying to infer positive experiences, working from physiological readings, such as heart rate and stress hormone level, or from behaviour. One possible proxy is whether animals show an optimistic bias in their decisions – bluntly, whether they expect positive outcomes.

I went to the world's oldest animal charity, the RSPCA. As its name suggests, it dates back to a time – 1824 – when cruelty was the lens. Today, if you see a mistreated dog or a wounded pigeon or a stranded seal, the RSPCA or one of its sister organisations around the world will try to help. If you are a British farmer like Andy who wants gold-level approval, you sign up to the RSPCA's welfare standards. One-quarter of British pig farms meet RSPCA's standards. Among dairy farmers, where consumer pressure for high standards has been much lower, take-up is just 1 per cent.

If anyone can reassure me that farm animals live good lives, it should be Marc Cooper, the man who writes the standards. He is optimistic that farmers want higher standards. Meat chicken farmers, for example, 'get sick and tired of going into the shed every day and culling twenty to thirty birds. They don't want to be doing that.' Still, only 1 per cent of the UK's chicken meat is currently produced to RSPCA standards. Cooper admits freely that the standards are limited by what farmers are willing to invest. The lack of knowledge is another limitation. 'Things like happiness – positive mental states – that's all new stuff ... That knowledge just isn't there yet,' he says.

I ask Cooper whether it's right to think that, in welfare terms, dairy is worse than beef. 'If you take averages – would you rather be a beef cow or a dairy cow? – I think beef cow would be a safer bet,' he says. 'An average dairy cow – it's not a great life. You're heavily milked, and you can be kept in systems that haven't been updated to keep pace with your genetics and growth and so on. The investment just hasn't gone into the buildings.'

A cow struggles to eat enough to match their milk production. 'It's got a genetic propensity to produce milk over maintaining its own body condition, which is why you see a lot of very, very thin dairy cows.' In other words, cows evolved to sacrifice their own health for their calves; now they sacrifice their own health for humans.

Our meeting ends, and I walk out past through the reception, with its cabinet of RSPCA-branded soft toys and RSPCA-branded vests used in sponsored runs. On the train back to London, I feel the most vegan I have ever felt. It's not just one thing – it's the accumulation. Working in a slaughterhouse made me feel that killing animals should be a considered process, not a conveyor belt. Working on a good pig farm made me feel that even healthy farm animals live pointless, artificial lives. Speaking to an ethical dairy farmer and an egg technologist brought home just how slow the food industry is in improving welfare. And meeting the RSPCA made me think that the scientific uncertainties were too great. Our relationship with animals should be so much more than this, I think.

Pigs, cows and sheep are among the few animals who have allowed themselves to be domesticated. They have tolerated being bred to produce quantities of meat, milk and wool that would be useless to their wild cousins. But they have retained many of their instincts, including the desire for social interaction. We don't know how they truly respond to artificial insemination, pregnancy after pregnancy, the breaking up of their family groups and so on. If we don't understand how animals feel after thousands of years of breeding them, we should err on the side of humility. Perhaps one day we will be able to breed livestock without those instincts – happy to be unmoving breathing machines. But we surely wouldn't want to. For humans, lives must have meaning. To watch animals accept their lives as machines would contradict that.

The relationship between meat-producers and vegans is often vitriolic. But there was one thing I noticed repeatedly when talking to people in the meat industry: the visceral dislike of animals dying unnecessarily. When coronavirus hit, American pig farmers suddenly could not get their animals to market. They could not just wait for the pandemic to pass: their pigs would become too big for the slaughterhouse equipment, and their cuts would be too big for the Styrofoam trays. And so pigs were killed however possible, and left to rot on compost piles. The sorrow and anger of the farmers was clear. I would hear it again, when farmers talked about having to cull their animals due to disease or regulations: the outrage of a life lived in vain. Millions of gallons of milk were poured down drains, and crates of eggs had to be smashed, as supply chains choked up. It all seemed so unnecessary.

What if the whole system is unnecessary? What if all the slaughterhouses and the farms – all the spurting blood and unidentified body parts – are not actually needed? That is exactly the case. Humans do not need to eat animal products. The American Dietetic Association said in 2009 that appropriately planned vegetarian and vegan diets are 'healthful, nutritionally adequate, and may provide health benefits in the prevention and treatment of certain diseases'. The World Health

Organization says that only 10–15 per cent of people's calories need to come from protein. On average, people are consuming 40 per cent more protein than they need to. In most EU countries, people eat more than twice the recommended amount of protein. Plant-based foods can provide all the essential amino acids. In 1898 the *British Medical Journal* assured its readers, with the arrogance of blissful ignorance: 'we have ... no intention of taking vegetarianism too seriously'. These days the same journal tells its readers that red meat consumption increases the risk of death from most major causes, including cancer and heart disease. At this party, latecomers are welcome.

I'm reluctant to make too many health claims about veganism: it feels beside the point, and anyway it depends what vegan food you eat. But, for humans as a whole, getting rid of livestock farms would have real benefits. Our taste for meat breeds disease. Coronavirus was linked to a Wuhan market where wild animals were kept in dreadful conditions. Some infectious disease outbreaks, like Ebola, have been reliably traced to hunting and eating wild animals. Others have come from deforestation – disrupting ecosystems and exposing ourselves to pathogens. Some westerners view all eating of wild mammals as barbaric, and want it to be banned. Why not start closer to home, by looking at our factory farms? Wherever animals are kept close together, diseases spread and mutate more easily. Wherever animals are under stress, diseases will take hold more easily. That the animals are often kept indoors is another aggravating factor.

Diseases have always spread across species. The 1918–19 pandemic, which killed tens of millions people worldwide, had an avian origin. The 2009 H1N1 swine flu pandemic, which was first detected in the US, killed between 151,700 and 575,400 people worldwide, the vast majority of them under sixty-five, according to the US Centers for Disease Control and Prevention. That strain of H1N1 continues to circulate and kills people every year. In 2020 coronavirus itself spread from humans to mink on European fur farms. In Denmark, the world's largest producer of mink skins, the animals were found to host a mutant strain of coronavirus that had infected some humans. Fearing that the mutated strain could jeopardise future vaccines, the Danish government ordered a cull of more than 15 million minks, who had been kept in small cages away from the lakes and rivers that they would instinctively seek. It seemed shocking, but we should no longer be surprised. Since 1940, more than half of all diseases that have crossed from animals to humans have been linked to intensive agriculture – including irrigation projects and factory farms. What if H5N1, a bird flu that has killed around half of the humans known to have contracted it, develops the ability to spread easily from human to human? Why are we so keen to find out? Even before coronavirus, zoonotic diseases had cost us more than $100 billion in recent decades. And people say vegan food is expensive.

We're in denial about this. In the middle of the coronavirus pandemic, the Trump administration declared slaughterhouses essential operations. Soon one in five American slaughterhouse workers was infected with coronavirus. The phrase 'meat-packing industry' had invoked a rather mundane image of meat being placed neatly into boxes. The reality is cramped workers and poor standards. Slaughterhouses are breeding grounds for disease, not just in the US, but also in Australia, Brazil and Germany, where migrant workers from eastern Europe operated in unsanitary conditions and lived seven or eight to an apartment provided by a subcontractor. A meat-industry executive in Germany told the *Financial Times* that the arrangements, now illegal, were 'modern-day slavery'. 'Meat is too cheap,' Germany's then agriculture minister, Julia Kloeckner, belatedly conceded.

Our farms undermine our own health in another way. Farmers have come to rely on antibiotics, giving them even to healthy animals. Of all antibiotics sold in the US, 80 per cent go to livestock. Humans also depend on most of these same drugs. But resistant bacteria develop in animals, and spread to humans. More than 35,000 people die in the US each year due to antibiotic-resistant bacteria, says the CDC. Because of a lack of federal monitoring, the true magnitude of the problem is still 'unknown', according to the Government Accountability Office. A world where antibiotics are no longer broadly effective is a nightmare scenario. The EU has banned antibiotics being used to promote growth, but the US has not.

One day I was reading my daughters a simplified version of 'How the Leopard Got His Spots', from Rudyard Kipling's *Just So Stories*. It tells how the giraffe and the zebra developed patterns that allowed them to hide in the forest, and how the leopard became jealous. At that point, a man helps the leopard, by placing black handprints all over him – the leopard's spots. 'Now you and I can hide in the shadows too,' the man tells the leopard.

What a lovely fantasy this is for children – the idea that humans have given animals their beauty. In fact, the farming industry tells us the complete opposite. We have meddled in evolution, in the most damaging way thinkable. We have taken animals adapted for the wild, and bred them to be unhealthy. Cows and chickens are so bloated that they would stand little chance against their wild ancestors' predators. Instead of asking how the leopard got his spots, perhaps we should ask how the cow got her mastitis and how the pig got his swollen body and the birds lost their habitat. I wouldn't read that to my kids. Storybooks imply that certain animals belong on farms. But no animal has evolved for the reality of modern farming. We have also created such a huge, inefficient system that it's not just farm animals who suffer – it's the wild animals who no longer have niches in which to live. We are distorting evolution not once, but twice.

In my mind, loving animals does not prevent humans from causing suffering to animals in all circumstances. I could accept some of the brutality of the abattoir and some of the meaninglessness of the farm, if they were necessary for organ transplants that save humans' lives. That isn't what is happening. Mostly, we don't have to eat meat, dairy or eggs. What we gain is completely out of proportion to what we take. As a way to produce calories and protein, factory farming is a sledgehammer to crack a nut. Given the intricate social lives of livestock, it's a sledgehammer that is also cracking a stained-glass window.

Everything I love about animals – their adaptations to their natural environment, their otherness to the human world, their speed and elegance – is curtailed or wiped out on modern farms. How could I be amazed by puffins, but indifferent to chickens? How can we give so much thought to our dogs, but so little to our pigs? How do we think our kids deserve milk, but that dairy calves deserve almost nothing? As children, we go to farm parks – small-scale, bucolic places that are nothing like farms. We learn to love animals and to accept modern farming. But if you really love animals, you can't accept modern farming.

If we lived in a vegan world, and someone said there was an alternative, which involved breeding and killing billions of animals, and denuding much of the world's surface of wildlife, I'm pretty sure that Silicon Valley's venture capitalists would pass. But we are tied to animal products by a weird circularity. Shoppers think that, if farmers and supermarkets sell meat, it must have been produced to decent conditions; farmers and supermarkets think that, if shoppers want to buy meat, then it has to be produced, however imperfectly. We struggle to imagine a different system – where we can feed ourselves and relate to animals, without breeding and killing them by the billion. I know that many of my friends have wanted to cut down on meat, but have found themselves going back to burgers and goat's cheese. Could I really claim that a vegan world was worth it?

3. THE WORLD WITHOUT MEAT

Vegetarians are the enemy of everything good and decent in the human spirit, an affront to all I stand for, the pure enjoyment of food.

Anthony Bourdain

Our world would have been a different and a duller place without the cow.

Neil MacGregor

'Isn't it wonderful?'

I hope he's not talking about the room. It's a complete mess. I can see piles of papers, a tennis racket cover, two children's dolls, six chefs' jackets. I always suspected that, at the most sophisticated restaurants, there was the most incredible chaos somewhere. At London's Gauthier Soho, that chaos is in the chef's fourth-floor office. 'Sorry,' the occupant shrugs charmingly as he invites me to sit down, 'but it's a working world.'

Alexis Gauthier is in his mid-forties, and undergoing the most jovial of midlife crises. Ambitious French chefs aspire to two things: their own restaurant and a Michelin star. By his late thirties, Gauthier had both. Then something changed. In 2016 he decided to stop eating animal produce. No meat, no fish, no dairy, no eggs. 'From one day to another, I said, "That's it." I removed it from my head.' Then he decided to turn his restaurant gradually vegan too. 'If I had been born in the 1920s, it would have been impossible,' he tells me. Gauthier is grinning – he grins a lot.

I arranged to meet Gauthier because I wanted to understand whether veganism could become widespread. We eat meat for lots of reasons – because our parents did, because we think it's normal and because we want the nutrition. But above all, for most people, giving up meat would mean sacrificing the pleasure of eating. Have you ever met someone who went vegan because of the taste?

Gauthier believes he has a duty to make vegan food 'as good if not better than eating animals'. 'In the end, if it's not delicious what I put in front of you, I think the egotistical *Homo sapiens* will just say, "Fine, I can live with the guilt." That's the problem,' he says. 'Of course we're not going to convince people to consider turning vegan by selling them a green salad and white tofu. Impossible!'

Gauthier was influenced by his uncle, a fruit seller in Avignon; he first became excited by cooking as a boy, making cakes for his sister. He trained as a chef in France, making endless meat stocks, and worked in Michelin-starred restaurants under famous chefs, before branching out on his own in London.

Gauthier Soho, his second restaurant, is located in a Georgian townhouse. We are sitting opposite each other in office chairs, far from the kitchen. Gauthier is wearing a checked shirt, jeans and trainers, not a sauce stain or a bead of sweat is visible. He is slim with a tightly trimmed grey beard. His light French accent is more a garnish than a gravy.

Three floors below us, the last diners are finishing lunch, and walking out of the black front door, above which Gauthier's name is spelled out in gold metal letters. 'What's the point,' he tells me, 'in having your own restaurant, with your name above the door, and bluffing your customers by not really doing something that's you?' That something is veganism.

'For a chef, this is like a dream. It's like being in Silicon Valley in 1979, and being at the beginning of the revolution,' he says. 'We'll be changing the world much more drastically than any politician, film-maker, or anybody like that.' He looks at my notepad. 'Or writers like you.' I think about taking offence, but Gauthier has a point.

There is rarely just one reason why people become vegetarian or vegan; more often, it's a combination of push and pull factors, a series of experiments. But whenever people are asked to explain any life choices – why they dropped out of university, why they slashed their boss's tyres – they tend to simplify the decision-making process.

In Gauthier's case, the long story is that he started eating more vegetables after being diagnosed with a fatty liver ('the classic French chef disease!'). He was then upset when animal rights activists protested outside his restaurant, because it served foie gras. The short story is that he then read a book, *Antispéciste*, by a French journalist named Aymeric Caron. (Perhaps writers do matter after all.) *Antispéciste* introduced him to the Cambridge Declaration on Consciousness. 'I can tell you that animals have feelings,' says Gauthier. 'I can tell you that we are intelligent enough not to have to inflict pain and suffering on any other living species on this planet.'

Is Gauthier an animal-lover? Not particularly. 'I think we need to leave them in peace – so is that an animal-lover or is that someone who doesn't care about animals? We have no right to decide when they live or when they die, that's all. That's really all. I don't want to kill a mosquito in the south of France with a spray.' It would be impolite to mention the can of fly spray on the shelf behind him.

Why don't more chefs worry about the animals they cook? 'If they are classically trained like me, a piece of beef or beautiful langoustines, it's not something that has lived and died. It's a tool for me to be able to express my creativity.' Even now the sight of meat doesn't provoke any particular reaction in him. 'In a kitchen you feel nothing. I resent the fact that I don't feel bad about seeing a dead pigeon in my kitchen.'

In the traditions of French cooking, veganism is not attractive – it is not even acceptable. Auguste Escoffier, a modernising chef, meticulously assembled traditional French recipes and published them in 1903 as *Le Guide Culinaire*; the book has become the bible of French cooking and most French chefs are literalist in their interpretation. 'You can't say, I'm doing a very good chicken stock, if you are not following Escoffier rules of chicken stock, OK?' says Gauthier. Until he turned vegan, he considered himself an Escoffier follower. 'I was just photocopying what I was taught, in the same way as a hundred years ago.'

Since giving vegetables pride of place, Gauthier Soho has lost its Michelin star. Gauthier exhales heavily when I raise this, and complains about Michelin inspectors' 'bias towards the traditional'. French gourmands, and indeed the French in general, are famously hostile to vegetarians. Anthony Bourdain, the straight-talking French-trained chef who laid bare the restaurant industry before his death in 2018, summed it up. As a head chef in New York in the 1990s, he would buy in $10,000 worth of meat a day; later, as a TV presenter, he ate everything – including the beating heart of a cobra. As a Bourdain-loving vegan, I now knew how the cobra must have felt. Veganism was even less compatible with Bourdain's palette – to him, vegans were the 'Hezbollah-like splinter-faction' of the vegetarian movement. 'I don't care what they tell you they're putting or not putting in your food at your favourite restaurant, chances are, you're eating a ton of butter,' he wrote.

I put this to Gauthier. 'I disagree totally with that because I was brought up on butter,' he says. 'More than anybody, I can tell you that butter is, yes, delicious. Fresh butter is delicious. In a pastry it's delicious, burnt butter is delicious, brown butter is even better, brown butter with Parmesan is – you never tasted nothing better. But on this planet there are so many other flavours that are as good, if not better, than butter!'

Delicious is quite possibly Gauthier's favourite word, and I admire his ability to use it multiple times in the same sentence. 'The deliciousness of the beef jus – it's delicious, I swear, it's delicious,' he says.

Possibly Gauthier's second favourite word is creativity. 'Being a vegan chef – being able to put your creativity at the service of delicious flavours ... '; 'It's creativity. It's all about being creative.' On the day of my visit, in mid-autumn, the £75 tasting menu includes dishes such as butternut squash roasted in saffron, with braised plantain, and cranberries with a yellow dandelion and pumpkin seed crumble.

In 2018, Gauthier made a vegan foie gras – the depth of flavour coming from cognac, the texture from toasted walnuts, the umami from soy sauce. He has also made a vegan goat's cheese, and is fixated on making an alternative to Saint-Nectaire, a semi-soft cow's cheese from central France.

Such imitations are only 'the first step of veganism as a chef', he emphasises. 'I don't want to serve fake beef, fake charcuterie ... I want to sell true combinations of ingredients ... This is the new planet I'm talking about.' (By contrast, 'in the French gastronomy, you are not allowed to bring strawberry as a starter. That would be against the law, and you go to jail for that.')

Gauthier Soho is not fully vegan, and still provides a couple of options for those customers who demand animal products. That creates the slightly odd situation where Gauthier can't eat some food from his own kitchen. 'But I can still cook it,' he points out. 'Like risotto for example. I've been doing it for so many years that I've got the technique but I can't taste it.'

The transition is 'a gamble', because customers do not see vegetables as value for money. 'When there is carrot, celeriac, truffle, tofu, and you are given the bill of £70, you can be as vegan as you want, you might come to the conclusion that it's a little bit dear.' At the same time, he feels confident that there is no competition at the top end of London restaurants. (In Paris, there is a three-star Michelin restaurant called Arpège, which specialises in vegetable dishes. But it also serves 'body to body': half a chicken stitched together with half a duck. Gauthier is adamant that the chef there, the legendary Alain Passard, 'doesn't consider the animals'.)

At least as of 2005, there were more ex-vegetarians in the US than vegetarians. A large proportion of vegetarians and vegans switch back. They hit a health problem, they get bored, life changes – and they start eating meat again. I wonder if the same could happen to Gauthier. 'Can you imagine?' he laughs. 'There is no chance, of course not. I'm not remotely excited to eat meat or fish. Not at all! I think the time we were eating animals, OK, it was a long time, but it's going to be like this' – he pinches his left thumb and forefinger together – 'on a massive scale of the human beings on this planet ... It's a compassionate revolution that is happening.'

I first tried being a vegan in 2018, when it became fashionable. I lasted less than twenty-four hours. Then I agreed to write a magazine article on it. The first day I turned vegan, I came home and I looked in the cupboards, and realised that I couldn't make a simple dinner. I couldn't have pasta and cheesy pesto. I couldn't make eggs. Most of my recipe books became immediately useless. 'Everyone has to know how to roast chicken, pork, beef, game, lamb: what to do with slabs of meat,' Nigella Lawson says in *How to Eat*. I missed the taste of cheese, the texture of cheese, the simplicity of cheese.

'Is humble pie vegan?' Susie helpfully wrote on the fridge, a few days after I switched.

To become a vegan midlife is to relearn to cook. It's like riding a motorbike – for a few weeks, maybe a few months, you swerve all over the place and everyone looks at you strangely. Then it just works. You cannot substitute precisely the tastes of meat and cheese – and I have yet to find a vegan cheese I would give as a present. But you learn to use spices more imaginatively than in most meat re- cipes. I've probably chopped more vegetables in the five years or so since I became a vegetarian than in the previous three decades; I've definitely eaten more celeriac. I gorged on all the things you're sup- posed to eat – broccoli, brown rice, curries. I've never understood why vegans are mocked for imitating meat products: meat-free saus- ages and burgers. This is the scaffolding of taste and texture and preparation that we have learnt throughout our lives; of course we will hold on to it.

'I would give up milk if I could, but I cannot,' said Gandhi, not exactly an amateur in self-control. Things have changed. I tried the new ranges of non-dairy products that previous generations of vegans would have died for – such as CoYo, a yoghurt made almost entirely from coconut milk. My search was half-successful, but one day I real- ised that I had stopped taking so much pleasure in eating. I always wanted to believe that vegan food could be as good as animal food. Gauthier is the first person I met who made me believe it.

He convinced me of this without actually giving me anything to eat. Perhaps it was because his entire trajectory is caught up with the importance of taste. Perhaps it was because he used the word 'delicious' so often. Mainly, however, it was the seriousness, the credibility. I have met stock-market shysters, and Silicon Valley hype merchants, and overblown thought leaders. Gauthier didn't sound like any of them.

I descended the stairs, past the empty dining room and onto the street below the large Gauthier lettering. And I thought to myself: this could actually happen. In my lifetime, eating animals might just become the exception.

*

Veganuary, when people agree to go vegan for a month, is now a worldwide phenomenon. It's been most popular in the UK, US and Germany. After that comes Argentina, which has the highest meat consumption per head in the world, and where a vegetarian meal translates as salad with your steak. South Africa is high on the list too. But the excited headlines about veganism over the past two years hide an inconvenient reality: the diet has been around for centuries, and it has spread like treacle. The latest vegan wave starts from a very low base. In Germany, between 2015 and 2020, the number of people eating meat every day fell from one in three to one in four, but the proportion of vegans and vegetarians has remained steady at 1 per cent and 5 per cent respectively.

The most common reason for signing up to Veganuary is health, followed by animals and then the environment. Clearly animal welfare concerns have not been enough to shake most meat-eaters; indeed, there is some evidence that people can simply block them out. When researchers asked a sample group of Oklahomans whether they wanted to know how pigs were raised, around one-third said no. A similar proportion, given a choice between looking at a blank screen and a photo of pregnant sows on a typical farm, chose the blank screen. The researchers called this 'wilful ignorance'.

People cling to the idea that they can eat only the best meat. It's a mirage: in the US, 75 per cent of consumers say they buy humane products – but only 1 per cent of livestock is raised on non-factory farms. Of those consumers who say animal welfare is very important to them, about half say that they consider it when buying meat. As a meat-eater, I remember how little control I had over most of the meat I ate, let alone the dairy. Americans eat 30 per cent of their calories outside the home, but 50 per cent of their meat. Add in the dinners at friends' houses and the ready meals from the supermarket – unpicking what meat has gone into these is nearly impossible. You would have to be prepared to order vegetarian without specific welfare assurances; it would require extraordinary self-discipline to change from meat-eater to vegan at every mealtime. You might be able to guess that Whole Foods and Chipotle Mexican Grill, with their zero gestation crate policies, come top of the Humane Society's rankings of US food companies. But who knew that Burger King is worse than Taco Bell, that Starbucks is worse than Dunkin' Donuts, and that the Hilton group is as bad as Walmart? And who says, let's cancel the suite at the Hilton, I hear the animal welfare standards are subpar? That is why when people say 'I eat only good meat', it is – in my experience – lip service at best. At worst it's wilful ignorance.

I'm confident that veganism isn't just a fad – too many young people are committed to it. But I worry it might remain a niche pursuit. The societal impact of veganism could be offset entirely by other people switching to, say, the inexplicable keto diet, which majors in dairy and meat. Veganism might be a sign of society fragmenting, rather than animal interests winning. Even in the US and Europe, consumption of animal products has gone up over recent decades. It may be plateauing now, at least on a per person basis, but it's surging in Asia and Africa. Total meat production fell worldwide in 2019, mainly because swine fever in China led to the death of one-fifth of the world's pigs. It fell slightly again in 2020, because of the pandemic. But the big picture is alarming. Our livestock already weighs fourteen times as much as all the world's wild mammals; chickens and other poultry weigh three times more than all the wild birds. Do we really value red meat fourteen times more than we value the wonder of wild mammals? The UN forecasts that global demand for meat will rise to 364 million metric tonnes by 2028. If it keeps rising at the same rate, it would be 400 million metric tonnes by 2035. That's more than the weight of all humans on earth; as a species, we are eating more than our body mass in animals every year. The World Resources Institute predicts that consumption of milk and meat will grow faster in the next three decades than it has in the past five. The number of animals living miserable lives will continue to increase. Where does that leave the so-called vegan revolution?

Our closest relatives – bonobos and chimpanzees – are largely vegetarian, although they do eat some meat (as well as insects like the termites for which Jane Goodall saw them fishing). If humans evolved to eat meat, which seems likely, it was not in the quantities that we eat it today. In developed countries, people eat three times as much as they did in the nineteenth century. Cow's milk is unnatural, and cheese is an acquired taste. Parmesan, like undigested food, contains butanoic acid, which is why the fine Italian cheese sometimes gives a tinge of vomit. There's a Sardinian sheep's cheese (now illegal) with live maggots in; don't tell me that taste isn't cultural. People learn to love such tastes, but even so they admit the strangeness. In France, Camembert is eaten in greater volumes than almost any other cheese, yet its smell remains synonymous with sweaty feet.

'Everyone starts life drinking milk. After that, it's all up for grabs,' as the food writer Bee Wilson put it. The reality is that nearly all children start eating meat before they are old enough to think otherwise: 'Thus,' argued the animal liberation philosopher Peter Singer, 'we never make a conscious, informed decision, free from the bias that accompanies any long-established habit, reinforced by all the pressures of social conformity, to eat animal flesh.' In her book *Meathooked*, the journalist Marta Zaraska finds several reasons why we find it so hard to go vegan. Meat has long been a widely available source of protein and vitamins; it forms a big part of our cultural life; its cost is now subsidised by government; and its flavours – of umami and fat – are hard to replicate. So the easiest way to transform the livestock industry would be to find another method of producing meat.

*

I am standing outside a Dutch train station, when the future of meat arrives wearing a leather jacket. Peter Verstrate is a grey-haired, world-weary fifty-nine-year old, who has spent most of his career in the traditional meat industry. But if his technology works well enough, there will be virtually no need for beef, chicken, pig or fish farms.

'If you can do the same thing in a more efficient way, usually people do it. That's what history shows,' says Verstrate, once we have settled down to talk over coffee and muffins. 'I've no doubt it's going to happen.'

The technology is stem-cell meat – also known as lab-grown, cultured or clean meat. I'd heard breathless news reports that this will replace traditional meat within a generation. Indeed few technologies hold more promise for transforming our relationship with animals. This is truly the have-your-cake-and-eat-it option. Excitement escalated in 2013, when Verstrate and his partner Mark Post presented a lab-grown hamburger on stage in London. The headline cost of the hamburger was astronomical: €250,000, courtesy of Google co-founder Sergey Brin. Verstrate admits that number, which included various set-up costs for the laboratory, was 'a gimmick'.

It was Brin's people who came up with the idea of the hamburger, because of its centrality to the American diet. Verstrate and Post's original plan was to serve a sausage, while the pig that had donated the initial stem cells ran around on stage. 'It's less practical to have a cow running around on stage. Also taking a cow on the train to London is not very practical,' says Verstrate. In any case, the source of the burger was already dead: to avoid bureaucracy, the team took stem cells from a slaughterhouse, rather than from a living cow.

In every revolution, promise and reality can be quite different things. The 2013 hamburger was a proof of concept. It had no blood, no fat, no flavour. 'It had a meaty texture. But it was completely neutral,' admits Verstrate, one of the handful of people who tasted it. It wasn't even animal-free. The cells had been raised on foetal bovine serum, which was harvested from pregnant cows. (It is a process that enrages animal campaigners: the cow is killed, her foetus is removed and kept alive, and the blood containing the nutrient-rich serum is taken from its beating heart.) The burger also had no path to mass production. The researchers had to cultivate each stem cell by hand. 'It was probably the least sustainable burger in the history of mankind,' says Verstrate. 'Which is quite funny.'

We are meeting several years after the London hamburger presentation, and what surprises me is how far stem-cell meat still has to go. Mosa Meat, the company that Verstrate and Post founded in 2016, wanted investors to put up €13.5 million. It raised barely half that. Brin could have supplied the whole amount: Google's parent company makes that much profit every four hours. But Brin had made clear his interest was only in the prototype. So the revolution is being pulled by a shoestring. Since 2013, no one else had tried a Mosa hamburger. The company has been working on replacing the myoglobin, the protein that makes beef red and is a key part of the taste. It is aiming to produce Hamburger 2.0, with the right fats and colouring, but no serum involved.

Mosa's ultimate goal is ambitious: to replicate the meat tissues that make expensive beef cuts. The company's best-case scenario is to become the Tesla of meat, a premium product that has more cachet than the real thing, before branching into the mass market. 'Meat and cars – what they have in common is that people, especially men I guess, want the real thing. Tesla changed that. And we want to change that for meat.'

We have already been waiting several generations. In 1932 Winston Churchill predicted that within fifty years, 'We shall escape the absurdity of growing a whole chicken in order to eat the breast or wing, by growing these parts separately under a suitable medium.' (One explanation is that Churchill was inspired by his contemporary Alexis Carrel, who won the Nobel Prize in medicine in 1912 for his work on organ transplants. Churchill also predicted that the 'climate would obey our orders', a forecast that has hit its own problems.)

The emergence of stem-cell meat has relied on developments in stem-cell research and tissue engineering. From the 1990s, researchers at Dutch universities started to identify stem cells that could be taken from animals. At the time Verstrate was working in a meat producer called Sara Lee. 'I shouldn't lie – I wasn't there with a troubled conscience,' he admits. One day in 2002, an old man turned up at his office out of the blue. It was Willem van Eelen, now recognised as the godfather of stem-cell meat. In his late teens Van Eelen was held in a Japanese prisoner-of-war camp in the Dutch East Indies (now Indonesia). There he was surrounded by starvation and abuse; and it was to these horrific scenes that he would later attribute his interest in producing meat without livestock farming. 'At first I thought he was crazy,' says Verstrate. 'But my wife is a biologist. She had been working with heart muscle tissue for medical purposes, in small amounts. I did remember looking through a microscope at the weekend, and you see the cells throbbing.' With that image in mind, Verstrate decided that Van Eelen might not be so left-field after all.

In 2006, a landmark UN report highlighted meat's environmental impact – concluding that it accounted for 30 per cent of the planet's land and 18 per cent of greenhouse gas emissions (subsequent studies have revised down the latter figure). Beef, sheep and goat's meat were, by far, the worst offenders. Meanwhile, animal rights activists also became interested in stem-cell meat: in 2008, PETA offered $1 million to whoever could design slaughter-free chicken meat at a competitive price within four years. The prize was too small, the time horizon too short (even with a two-year extension), and as many scientists predicted, the prize went unclaimed. Verstrate and Post's funding ran out, and their project almost died, until Sergey Brin temporarily stepped in. They have persevered, but fundamental issues remain.

Mosa should be able to grow meat-like fibres on an animal-free medium. The real question is, at what cost? 'Getting to €100 per burger – that's a huge step, but the effort is getting from €100 to €10 or €5 or €2.' The product has to be cheap enough to be served by McDonald's. That hinges on the medium in which the cells grow. Mosa still needs a technology that can break down cheap proteins and sugars into something that individual cells can process, a replacement for the cow's intestines. When these things are done, building a supply chain and gaining regulatory approval will take years. You won't be able to buy Mosa's meat until late 2022 at the earliest, and even then only in a few restaurants.

For a steak, the challenge will be harder, requiring, among other things, a channelling system to replicate the work of blood vessels in removing waste from the cells. Nonetheless, if the process works, it should also work for pork and chicken too, even fish. 'Anything that has muscles, you can grow it,' says Verstrate. 'We're doing beef because beef has by far the biggest environmental impact. There will be a generation at some point who will think it very illogical to do with animals what we've been doing the last 10,000 years, yeah ... We will perceive animals in the future more as living things that you don't eat or hurt or do whatever you want with.'

Perhaps Mosa's strongest competitor is Memphis Meats, which launched the world's first stem-cell meatball in 2016 and the first stem-cell chicken a year later. By 2019, it had raised $180 million from investors such as Bill Gates, Richard Branson and two of the US's largest meat sellers, Tyson Foods and Cargill. It plans to build a trial plant, effectively putting it one step ahead of Mosa, which has since raised $85 million more from investors itself.

Stem-cell meat could easily be seen as unnatural or inferior. In surveys, the proportion of people willing to actually eat it has ranged from 16 per cent to 65 per cent. Even the name can make a sizeable difference: 'clean meat' seems to be more appealing than 'Meat 2.0'; to me, 'slaughter-free' seems better than either. In 1995 an industry survey found that three-quarters of British people were open to eating genetically modified food. But two decades later, the spectre of 'Frankenstein foods' remains, and growing GM crops is banned in the UK. By contrast, today if you asked consumers if they would buy meat from livestock pumped full of antibiotics and kept in cramped conditions, they would probably say no. Verstrate points to the reaction of children when stem-cell meat is described to them: 'one of the first things kids ask is, can I eat my friend? They don't have any inhibitions. And yeah, you can.'

But this is all premature. Stem-cell meat is still just an intriguing prospect, not a cheap, alluring product. In December 2020, Singapore became the first country to give it safety approval – in the form of chicken, to make nuggets. I hope the commercial roll-out works. But I don't think the prospect of slaughter-free meat affects our choices now. We can give up meat today. And in California, you can give it up while having the taste of a burger.

*

'Who here likes wild animals?'

Pat Brown is not a natural children's entertainer, but at least he's trying. On a patch of green in Silicon Valley, he is hosting an event for families of his staff. He stands at the front of a small marquee, wearing a green jacket, jeans, and a T-shirt that reads 'Happy cows come from mad scientists'.

'I have a question for the children: who here loves to eat hot dogs and fish sticks and those things? Who here is glad we make those from dead animals? Nobody?'

A dozen children look on, a bit baffled. For Brown, these kids are the future, and the future is meatless. 'You can come and beat me up afterwards if I'm wrong. But I promise by the time you guys are adults, the meat you eat won't be coming from animals. That's my promise to you and I'm not even running for president.'

First, the reality. Brown is the founder of Impossible Foods, one of two Californian companies that have produced arguably the most convincing meat substitutes ever. The other is Beyond Meat. It gets confusing: both companies are founded by vegans called Brown, and both received investment from Bill Gates. Impossible Foods sells burgers and pork; Beyond Meat sells burgers, sausages and mince. This is not the promised land of stem-cell meat – this is here today.

Beyond Burger relies on pea protein and beetroot for a blood red effect. Impossible uses heme – a soy protein, made from genetically engineered yeast – which provides its own blood effect. Because the 'meats' contain around twenty other ingredients, some of them factory-produced, critics deride them as highly processed.

I first ate a Beyond Meat burger after being vegetarian for four years. It looked like just another veggie burger, its shape a little too regular. And then I took a bite, and it was – for a split second – like seeing in colour after an age in black and white. To me at least, it was so close to real meat that it made no difference. The Impossible Burger was just as good. If I had to choose between this and a conventional burger, and I didn't care about animals or the environment, I'd flip a coin.

Pat Brown doesn't want there to be a choice. He thinks livestock farming is an environmental disaster, and he wants to end it – all over the world – by 2035. This is what makes him so intriguing: he is one of the few people to envisage a world where we stop seeing animals as food. While the RSPCA and other campaigners talk about improving welfare standards, while Veganuary talks about personal choice, Brown is promising economic warfare. More than 2 million years ago our ancestors scavenged for meat from carcasses left by other animals. Later *Homo sapiens* learnt to hunt. About 11,000 years ago modern humans domesticated livestock. Even by Silicon Valley standards, to end 2 million years of human history within two decades is pretty audacious.

I thought of all the livestock farms I'd ever visited – the Welsh sheep farmers who had been on the hills for centuries, the Brazilian ranchers encroaching into the Amazon, the Mongolian herders who saw their horses as both family and food. In Brown's vision, their lives would all radically change. Veganism wouldn't be confined to Hollywood celebrities, hyper-rational activists, and January dieters; it would be for everyone, all the time. And it would have arrived largely by stealth, because meat-lovers switched to a product that tasted just like meat.

I was in Silicon Valley for work. When Brown finished his stand-up routine with the kids – to his relief, as much as theirs – we found a quiet spot in the marquee, and I asked him whether his vision is anything more than a gimmick.

'The problem we're trying to solve is an ongoing catastrophe. Climate change is an emergency, and the biodiversity meltdown is probably even more of an emergency,' he says, slightly robotically. There are other ways to cut the amount of greenhouse gases and deforestation produced by livestock. You can turn cows' manure into energy. You can reduce food waste: around one-third of food worldwide intended for humans never makes it to our plates. Replacing meat altogether would go further than anything else.

But by 2035? Is Brown for real? 'Part of it was – if we reach a point where we have a sufficient amount of profitability and we invest all those profits in fuelling growth, and you have sort of what amounts to an exponential growth. Second, there's the competitive dynamics between us and the current industry. Our economics are structurally better. Even though it's a highly commoditised industry – well, maybe partly because of that – they can't significantly lower their input costs. Land, water, fertiliser, pesticide, labour – we require less of all those things, by a lot.'

At the time we are talking, the US alone has more than 720,000 beef farms and more than 60,000 dairy farms, housing 95 million cows. The scale does not impress Brown. Sentimentality is not on his menu. He doesn't entertain doubt; it's simple economics.

'They're fragile, OK? They're low-margin. The beef industry, definitely in the US, is low single-digit margins. They have a two-and-a-half-year planning cycle, because that's how long it takes from conception to slaughter of the average cow – basically you have to predict demand two and a half years in advance. And we are growing fast. We've been way more than doubling every year, and I don't see any end point to that. Because our products get better all the time. We are constantly innovating – the cows stopped doing that a million years ago.'

This is the kind of simplistic statement that makes Brown, a respected scientist, as unpopular with the meat industry as an outbreak of foot-and-mouth disease. Cattle productivity *has* improved thanks to breeding and intensive agriculture. A hectare of pasture produces more than twice as much meat or milk as it did in the 1960s. Beef produced in Europe and the US has much lower greenhouse gas emissions than that from South America and sub-Saharan Africa. Pushed on this, Brown just says farmers have 'pretty close to maxed out' productivity. In fairness I have seen how increasing productivity takes a toll on animals' welfare, so it's not hard to believe. The efficiency has come partly by keeping animals indoors and feeding them grain. There is also a basic law of thermodynamics at work. As you go up the food chain, there is less and less energy available. Livestock uses energy to live. Chickens and pigs are more efficient at converting plants into meat than cows are. But nothing is as efficient as humans eating those plants in the first place. For each gram of protein, meat emits between two and fourteen times as much greenhouse gas as plant-based substitutes; it's even less competitive with tofu, peas and lentils.

Plant-based meat accounts for around 1 per cent of retail meat sales in the US. Impossible has less than 0.1 per cent of the market for ground beef. Brown's short-term aim is 20 per cent, which he describes as 'entirely doable'. At that point, he reckons, the beef industry will start to implode. Meat and dairy producers currently receive nearly $100 billion in new funding each year, from investment firms, pension funds, and banks such as Barclays and JPMorgan Chase. As plant-based meat catches on, 'their investors, their lenders, their insurers, their partners are going to basically say, "Oh this business is heading for the dustbin." It's going to be harder and harder for them to raise money, to find partners, etc. Because it will be seen as a dying industry.' This makes it clear: in Brown's vision, the transition is fairly brutal.

The global livestock market is worth $1.2 trillion a year, roughly the GDP of Mexico. This is what Impossible would have to replace – before it even gets round to milk, cheese and seafood. Pat Brown knows this, right? He nods. Could Impossible provide all of this? He shakes his head, and points to potential partnerships, where Impossible could license its technology.

Brown's aim is for Impossible to double its impact every year. This sounds reasonable, until you realise that Google hasn't managed to double its sales in a year since at least 2006, and Facebook has managed it only twice since 2007. Impossible Foods, Brown says, won't ever need to depend on a small number of crops. It can isolate proteins from spinach, romaine lettuce and alfalfa. Alfalfa performs particularly well: Brown's modelling showed it could produce all the protein humans need on 3 per cent of the world's land area. But he says the company doesn't use it, because the crop is grown by too few farms.

Perhaps because he is so certain of his cause, perhaps because he has delivered this message so many times, Brown is a difficult person to warm to. It takes a certain personality type to want to bulldoze an industry. Outside the marquee, the children – or rather, their parents

– want to take a photo with Brown, and so the plant-based prophet is dragged away. I wander off and fix myself an Impossible burger with vegan cheese, while the group chants: 'One ... Two ... Three ... Heme!'

I call an Uber to take me to the train station. The driver has never heard of the Impossible burger. The year 2035 seems awfully soon for the end of livestock farming. But that doesn't mean it's the wrong ambition.

*

In 2019 nearly 10 per cent of US dairy farms closed – on average, nine a day. The country's biggest milk producer, Dean Foods, filed for bankruptcy, followed by Borden Dairy, itself once the country's largest dairy company. Dean Foods and Borden Dairy put some of the blame on the rising popularity of milk alternatives, like almond and soy. In 1974 Richard Nixon washed down his final meal as president with a glass of milk. Since then, the quantity of liquid milk drunk by the average American has fallen 40 per cent, from 110 litres a year to 65 litres. The vegan-apocalypse has arrived.

Except it hasn't. Demand for cow's milk is still rising in the US. Since 1975, dairy consumption is up by a fifth. The decline of liquid milk has been more than compensated by the growth of cheese and yoghurts. (As a rule of thumb, you need about one litre of milk to make one hundred grams of cheese.) The vegans have got the blame, but the real problem for those dairy farms was that the industry is consolidating into a few corporate giants. Small and medium farms are in trouble whatever happens.

Giving up meat and dairy is often depicted as a radical path. It is actually less radical than keeping on our current trajectory. Pat Brown is right: raising one animal to feed another is incredibly inefficient. The world's population is growing, the developing world is getting richer. It's not at all clear where new supplies of meat, dairy and eggs will come from. If our systems don't change, then we will need nearly 600 million more hectares of cropland and pastureland in 2050 than we had in 2010, says the World Resources Institute, a Washington think tank. That's a land area bigger than the EU, converted from forests and other natural ecosystems that currently store carbon.

Either we stop eating so much meat, or we prepare ourselves for a truly dangerous rise in greenhouse gas emissions. We also face huge loss of animal life. A study by the Netherlands Environmental Assessment Agency concluded that 60 per cent of the recent loss of biodiversity – that is, of variety of living organisms – was due to food production. I don't want to tell my daughters that the reason we destroyed the natural world is because it tasted delicious. We have already warped evolution through factory farming; we will smash through it if we keep converting forests into agricultural land and heating the planet. This more than anything is why it doesn't make sense for animal activists and environmentalists to fight each other: because veganism should be top priority for both.

What would a world without meat look like? Most obviously, it wouldn't have beef farms, chicken farms, sheep farms, pig farms, and all the other farms that house billions of sentient beings and take up a sizeable chunk of the world's surface. The millions of hectares that are currently used to grow feed for animals – particularly in the US and Brazil – would instead be used to produce food for humans, or would be turned over to wildlife and carbon capture. If we replaced meat and dairy in our diets, we could reduce global farmland by around three-quarters. Perhaps some farms will become forests for tourists, or nature reserves, and provide jobs to farmers and their children, many of whom have no interest in farming anyway. This can be the basis for a conservation movement, as I discuss later in this book.

(There's another way to reduce even further the amount of agricultural land needed: vertical farming. This involves rows of crops grown on top of one another, in warehouses, under LED lights. The genius of this is that food can be grown all year round, whatever the climate, near to where people live. Infarm, a Berlin-based company that has raised more than $300 million in funding, says its vertical farms use 99 per cent less land – as well as 95 per cent less water, 90 per cent less transportation and 75 per cent less fertilisers than traditional agriculture. Because it's a controlled environment, there are no pesticides. Wheat yields could be up to *600* times greater in a ten-storey vertical farm than the current average on farms around the world. The problem is that the cost of building and powering such facilities is astronomical, compared to seeding a field and relying on the sun. At the moment, indoor farms struggle to make a profit growing high-value, low-nutrition lettuces and herbs. Wheat and other foods are a long way off.)

In a world without meat, abattoirs and meat-processing plants would disappear, although most people have never seen them and would never notice. I could imagine Forge Farm Meats becoming commuter housing: potential buyers would be squeamish at first, but within a few years, they'd be eagerly telling visitors, 'You'll never guess what this place used to be ... ' There'd probably be a craft-ale bar called the Puller.

There'd be more production of vegetables, beans and fruits, and factories for new food – such as stem-cell meat, or fermentation-based protein including the Impossible burger. Solar Foods, a Finnish company, uses hydrogen, solar power and bacteria as a pathway to flours. The success of such products hinges on cost and taste, and on clean hydrogen production. Tony Seba, a Silicon Valley author who is one of the few people to take Impossible Foods' 2035 vision seriously, suggests that fermented food will be less than half the price of animal products – saving the average American family $1,200 a year. In my local supermarket, Beyond Burgers – which use beet juice rather than fermentation – still cost almost twice the price per gram of any other burger. One limitation is that peas, favoured by Beyond, are more expensive than, say, soyabeans. But cheap vegan fast food is here. Impossible burgers are available in Burger King in the US; Beyond Meat nuggets are in KFC. The British bakery chain Greggs found its vegan sausage rolls were so successful that it ended up paying staff a one-off £300 bonus. Sometimes veganism is criticised as an elitist fad; sometimes it's criticised for pricing the poor out of meat. The reality is alternative protein that everyone can afford, providing they accept the concept and the taste.

Livestock has never been just meat. I once sat in a Mongolian herder's tent, drinking something that vaguely resembled tea, while he explained how he used every part of his animals – pointing to walls made of wool and ropes made of camel skin. Mongolian herders are completely ingenious: another former herder told me how, after slaughtering a sheep, he would take the half-digested grass from the stomach, salt it and give it to the other sheep in the winter.

In the west, we use carcasses for clothes, medicines and half a dozen other uses. Every conscientious western consumer knows the problem with animal fur, thanks largely to PETA's 'I'd Rather Go Naked Than Wear Fur' ad campaign, which started in 1990 and featured celebrities such as Tyra Banks and Dennis Rodman. Other animal clothing has gone unseen. I was aware that inside my warm jackets, duvets and pillows were real feathers. Yet I never really associated the soft white and grey feathers with the meat industry.

This is odd, given that the use of feathers in fashion – namely, hats – was the motivation for the creation of one of the world's first conservation organisations. Britain's Royal Society for the Protection of Birds dates back to 1889, founded by women alarmed at the use of feathers in hats. Its members committed to not wearing feathers from any birds not killed for food – 'the ostrich only excepted'. Those feathers were visible, the ones we use now aren't.

Today nearly all the feathers used in clothing are from geese and ducks killed in slaughterhouses. 'The day-old goslings are like children,' one farm manager reported. 'They imprint on you straight away, trying to integrate you into the fold.' Ducks and geese have evolved feathers that moult, partly to create warm nests. Like cow's milk, it's an adaptation intended to make their offspring's lives more pleasant – but which in our hands, becomes a reason for them to live short, deprived lives. Geese often die as young as eight weeks of age; they never reach sexual maturity. People who would never eat goose will happily wear goose-feather jackets. From the birds' point of view, there isn't much difference which body part you use; it's not like they've filled in organ donation forms. It's tempting to think that the birds were going to be killed for the meat anyway, so using the feathers doesn't affect what happens to them. The price paid for the feathers helps make the meat industry financially viable.

There is an even worse source of feathers. Some farms pluck the geese and ducks while they are still alive – so that the bird can regrow more feathers, and be plucked again. Animal activists summarise the process of live-plucking as like someone holding your head and pulling your hair out. For a duck, the stress of being handled by a human would be bad enough. Videos of duck farms show a horrific process.

With meat, we can at least buy local, in the hope of high standards. But 80 per cent of the world's down feathers come from China, where standards are often lower and the risks of non-compliance are substantial. China's growing appetite for duck meat links directly to our ability to buy warm coats. Even within the EU, Patagonia, the ethical outdoor brand, found that some feathers for its jackets were being sourced in Hungary from geese force-fed to produce foie gras. Geese and ducks are waterfowl but on farms they may have no access to water to swim in; their legs struggle under the strain of constant standing. We know little about where our meat comes from – we know even less about our leather. Clothing companies struggle to track their leather to the abattoir, let alone the farm.

Nothing illustrates the clothing blind spot better than Indian leather. The Hindu tradition holds that cows' happiness will allow humans to flourish; cows should not be slaughtered, but thanked for their milk. 'The central fact of Hinduism is cow protection ... Hinduism will live so long as there are Hindus to protect the cow,' said Gandhi, who also called cows the 'purest type of subhuman life' and 'the mother to millions of Indian mankind'. But Gandhi argued that Hindus could make use of cows when they died. Everyone knows India is the land of cow-induced traffic jams. But, as well as a large number of cows, India farms more (non-sacred) buffalos than the rest of the world put together, and is one of the world's biggest producers of leather.

India kills 21 million bovines – cows and buffalos – a year, a number six times more than Germany and not incomparable to the US's 33 million. Because cow slaughterhouses are banned in most Indian states, many cows must undertake gruelling walks to places where abattoirs are legal – or even to neighbouring Bangladesh. Bangladesh kills more buffalos than France kills cows. PETA has documented dead animals being skinned in front of live ones. In recent years, the government of Narendra Modi has cracked down on slaughterhouses. That would be welcome, if it weren't a) accentuating tensions between Hindu nationalists and the Muslims who operate the slaughterhouses, and b) worsening the problem by making the distances to slaughter even greater. The grim lesson of the Indian leather industry is that it's not enough to abstain from eating meat; we have to stop using animal products. A world without meat will require a thousand alternative products. The rise of fake fur and fake leather suggests it is possible.

A vegan world would have human winners and losers. If animal products were taken off the menu, the same corporate giants – Monsanto, Unilever, Tyson Foods – would probably still dominate the food industry. They have the ability to buy upstarts like Memphis Meats or Impossible Foods. They probably will do so anyway, just in case. Fast food chains like McDonald's would switch suppliers, but they would still offer fundamentally the same experience. In 2014 Hellmann's sued a producer of vegan mayonnaise, arguing that, by definition, mayonnaise had to contain egg. The case was settled, and these days Hellmann's sells its own vegan mayo, which it (correctly) claims has "the same great taste" as the original. Perhaps some traditional meat companies would struggle to evolve like this, just as the big American carmakers have failed to keep pace with the investment in electric vehicles. Some meat exporters, like Argentina, would do badly. Some countries that are dependent on feed imports, like China, would do better. Some countries, like Mongolia, have so little arable land that their food security would evaporate if they gave up livestock altogether. In Ethiopia, people rely on animals for their financial security. Throughout sub-Saharan Africa, the realities of building and maintaining fermentation facilities is much more complex than Pat Brown's franchise model allows. For now, it makes sense to talk about eliminating livestock farming in rich countries, where alternative sources of protein and work are assured. If Europe and the US can cut down on animal products, others will follow.

What about the animals themselves? We wouldn't need billions of sheep, pigs and cows, and so their populations would shrink. But these breeds were never meant to exist in their current form, and they are not adapted to the natural world. Our ecosystems mostly do not need these domesticated breeds. Stepping back from animal farming will make it easier for us to focus on animals who are adapted to the wild, not the mutants we have created to feed our appetites.

Human society has been marked by transitions: from whale oil to kerosene, from horses to motor cars, from fossil fuels to alternatives, from print newspapers to websites, and so on. Some of these proved swift (95 per cent of whale oil was replaced within thirty-five years); others were more drawn-out or frankly illusory (nuclear power has never taken over as some expected).

If meat disappears, it will disappear slowly – more slowly than we can justify. The industry is spread around the world; the investment to recreate the supply chain is huge; the product is caught up with cultural traditions; and even though the societal benefit of stem-cell meat may be large, the benefit to the individual consumer is limited. Producing stem-cell meat that tastes like, and costs the same as, farm-raised beef would be a triumph; it still wouldn't represent a leap like the one from horse to car. Although there is no farm cow, pig or chicken alive today that will still be producing food in 2035, the system – from abattoirs to refrigerated trucks to butchers' shops – is built to endure. And when powerful businesses run into problems, they beg, successfully, for government support. When US butter sales were hit by the rise of cheap margarine in the late nineteenth century, dairy-producing states including New York, followed by the federal government, placed bans or taxes on margarine. Until 1967 it was illegal to produce or sell yellow margarine in Wisconsin.

Nonetheless, the squeeze on animal products has begun. Supermarkets are calculating the carbon footprint of the products they sell. This should lead them to stock less beef and more plant-based alternatives. Governments should tax meat heavily, just as they tax tobacco today, on environmental grounds alone. If the Impossible burger were $1 cheaper than a regular hamburger, would we really choose suffering and pollution? But politically it's tough when so few individuals have opted out. Tobacco taxes were only raised in the 1980s and 90s in the US, once cigarette smoking had fallen one-fifth from its peak in the 1960s. And even at its height, fewer than half of US adults smoked;

more than 90 per cent eat meat. Governments should also withdraw subsidies for animal farming. The world's farmers receive $600 billion a year, with few environmental strings attached. But farm subsidies are so entrenched that it'd be easier to shove a dairy cow through the eye of a needle.

Lewis Bollard, an animal welfare specialist at Open Philanthropy, a charitable organisation with a utilitarian philosophy of trying to do the most good possible, argues that it's simpler for governments 'to appropriate more money than to take someone's money away'. So activists would do better to call for more subsidies for plant-based foods, rather than fewer subsidies for meat. The EU's Horizon 2020 innovation scheme has committed around $10 million a year to research into plant-based protein projects. As the plant-based options grow, they create their own supporters: Canada, the world's largest producer and exporter of dry peas, now has an agricultural industry with a reason to lobby for vegan alternatives.

Bollard compares the rise of plant-based food to the energy sector, where wind and solar became more competitive thanks to subsidies and innovation, while coal became more costly due to environmental regulations. 'Yes, it's going to require the innovation,' he says. 'It's also going to require a lot from the other side. How does factory farmed meat become less appealing? How is it forced to internalise a lot more of its costs?' One example of this comes from Cory Booker, a US senator for New Jersey. In 2020 Booker became the first vegan to make a serious run for the Democratic nomination for president. He had to make clear that he didn't think the government should tell people what to eat; he couldn't even say more Americans should go vegan. But he does want to put limits on factory farms. Why shouldn't the government ban the worst practices, the ones that consumers are barely aware of? Animals should have space to move around and socialise, and abattoir workers should not be exposed to unnecessary risk. These causes are supported not just by vegans but also by ethical, family farmers, who are already being squeezed by industrial operations. The 'vote-buy gap' – where Californians voted to mandate cage-free eggs, although they had chosen not to buy them – shows that people may be ready to act as citizens whatever their spending habits.

At some point, the economics of factory farms will break. In 2018 Californians voted to ban the sale of meat raised in gestation crates, from 2022. The ballot measure was worded tightly enough that the industry's 'cage-free' definition – where sows can still be kept in crates for 40 per cent of their lives – would not pass the test. Even if a compromise is found, the pork industry has to ask whether gestation crates will remain acceptable in five or ten years. 'The pork industry is building new facilities with gestation crates in. I think they're going to lose a lot of money on these,' says Bollard. Tyson Foods, which sells around $40 billion of meat a year, has livestock buildings and machines that are expected to last decades. In theory, these could end up stranded assets – rendered useless, with their owners left to bear the cost.

The Impossible burger won't kill the livestock industry, but various strategies might have the same effect. 'People always like the idea that there'll be one silver bullet,' says Bollard. 'Pat Brown maybe has the closest thing to a silver bullet of anyone. But personally I think we're talking a dozen different silver bullets.'

By giving up animal products as individuals, people create space for governments to act. In turn regulations raise public awareness of what meat involves. They prevent meat-producers from pumping out ever-cheaper animal products. We would not be having a vegan wave now, without the past campaigns against gestation crates and battery chickens. We should campaign for vegan meals to be available in schools and public buildings. Our actions, as consumers and citizens, could accelerate the end of meat.

*

Food defines who we are. One of the characteristics of animals is that they eat other organisms, unlike plants which make their own food. Consciousness itself, on Feinberg and Mallatt's theory, developed to help the first predators catch the first prey animals, and the first prey animals to escape. In a vegan world, humans would be an interesting type of animal – neither predator nor prey. Would it matter?

People sometimes assume that a vegan society would be more peaceful but also more judgemental. In my mind, a vegan world looks surprisingly similar to our current society. We are changing one set of products, potentially for very similar substitutes. Socially the change would be far less dramatic than, say, the invention of the automatic dishwasher and the rise of women in the workplace that it enabled. Those developments have changed the very nature of human inter-action. Going vegan doesn't change where you go, whom you talk to, and what you can say. There is no need for what's on your plate to af-fect mealtime conversation. If you want to act like a big swinging dick, you can do it just as easily over a vegan tasting menu as over a T-bone steak. You can still be a vegan and be a foodie; indeed, veganism is a logical extension of the idea that what is on your plate must resonate with who you are as a person. Changing your diet does not mean changing your personality. It just means thinking logically. If you want to tackle climate change, vegetarianism won't take you very far. If you care about animal welfare, milk and eggs should arguably be the first things you cut out, not the last.

We think that meat is part of our culture and our traditions; actu-ally it's food that's essential – and vegans still eat. Veganism has changed my experience of Christmas much less than the arrival of TV streaming has. Veganism can transform the lives of animals and the future of our planet, but, once you get used to a few new recipes, the impact on our own daily existence is barely noticeable.

For me, veganism was not love at first sight; but it was the only re-maining option. I now cook vegan meals that are healthier and, I would estimate, at least 90 per cent as tasty as anything with meat and dairy. I am not evangelical. With veganism, you need to pick your battles. Are you going to go all-out? What about honey? What about clothing? What about your children?

I don't force veganism on my (vegetarian) daughters, although I do try to accustom them to the taste of soy and oat milk, so that one day perhaps they might find the decision easier to take for themselves. There's a *Simpsons* episode where Lisa turns vegetarian and has to ex-plain to Homer that she can't eat bacon, ham or pork chop, because these all come from the same animal. 'Yeah, right, Lisa,' laughs Homer. 'A wonderful, magical animal.' My daughter Eliza has the opposite reaction: she knows there are some things I don't eat, and is keen to extend the boundaries. 'Are you allowed pasta? Are you allowed aubergine?' she asks. To me, this underlines how hard it is for children to connect the foods they eat with the animals in their storybooks.

Personally, I try to go more or less all-out. I have bought vegan shoes and a vegan wallet, although I maintain a weakness for slices of friends' non-vegan birthday cakes. One of my most vegan friends – who has been known to check food packets at friends' houses to ensure they are not feeding him traces of animal products – puts his veganism on hold when he goes abroad on holiday. 'Fifty weeks of the year as a vegan is sufficient,' he says. I find this pretty strange, but I don't think it's hypocrisy. What matters most is changing the system, changing what is normal, and you do that better by showing veganism to be a happy lifestyle, not a constant source of neurosis. It's less important to act with total purity than to show that veganism is actually doable. If you cook good vegan food, people will eat it; spoiler alert – they generally like it.

It took me several years to go from cutting down on meat to becoming a vegetarian, and several more years before I became a vegan. It is a process. But in my mind, it is the single most important step to loving animals. Nothing fails the animal test as clearly and on such a large scale as modern livestock farming. Nothing should unite conservationists and animal rights activists as completely. Watching nature documentaries and cat videos does nothing to help animals; giving up meat saves farm animals from suffering and creates space for wild animals.

The French philosopher Jacques Derrida reportedly once said something along the lines of, 'I am vegetarian in spirit.' I hear this a lot. It makes me think, as more people opt out of meat and dairy, more will jump on the bandwagon. I meet other people who are already giving up meat. There's one caveat though. 'I don't eat meat,' they sometimes say. 'I just eat fish.' So do fish count?

4. THE OCEAN ALWAYS LOSES

Consider, once more, the universal cannibalism of the sea; all whose creatures prey upon each other, carrying on eternal war since the world began.

Herman Melville, *Moby-Dick* (1851)

'You're not doing anything wrong!' yells Brian, my fishing instructor, as my hook lands in the lake a couple of metres away.

He's talking about the technique. I'm thinking about the ethics. Either way, I'm not convinced that everything is up to scratch.

I lift the green rod up until it is beside my ear like a phone, and then flick it more in hope than expectation. I am wearing protective glasses, just in case I manage to hook myself. The hook again lands in the water only a couple of metres away. I could have thrown a dictionary further. And it probably would have posed more of a threat to a fish.

It's a day of unrelenting drizzle, the kind that gives Scotland a bad reputation and its inhabitants a good sense of humour. This is the day that I have chosen to learn how to fish.

Fish pose a particular problem for the animal test. It's easy to be repelled by the suffering of a dairy cow or a laying hen. It's much harder with a cod or a tuna. They can't scream; their emotions remain hidden to us.

That is partly why fishing is not just an industry, it's a hobby. In the US, nearly 36 million adults fish – one-seventh of the population, or one-fifth in Alabama, Kentucky, Mississippi and Tennessee. They spend an average of thirteen days, and $1,290, a year. Angling was the UK's most popular participator sport twenty years ago. Around that time Jeremy Paxman, then Britain's most famous news presenter, wrote a book on his love of angling called *Fish, Fishing and the Meaning of Life* (his life, not the fish's). In it, he attacked animal rights campaigners who opposed angling as 'a new breed of puritans': 'They cannot bear the thought that people are enjoying themselves. Their case presupposes that fish feel pain like any warm-blooded creature.' Anglers still tend to believe that fish are not conscious and cannot feel pain. Although angling has fallen in popularity recently, it remains in Britain's top twenty most practised sports.

'It's not difficult at all! Anyone can learn it!' chirps Brian, who, unlike me, probably does not have a leaking left boot. He is a friendly, plump, red-cheeked man whose past clients include Bruce Willis. He has been fishing on this lake – pegged between a railway and some moorland – for over thirty years.

Somewhere in the water in front of us are rainbow trout, each weighing up to a few kilos. What the trout want is to eat and not be eaten. What Brian and I want is to trick them into nibbling onto the golden hook, and then to wrestle them back to the bank for a few seconds – maybe a minute – just long enough to feel the achievement and take a photo.

This is fly-fishing, so there is no bait, only a hook diguised as a fly. Instead it relies on placing the hook so close to the fish that it becomes irresistible. Brian teaches me to wait until the hook has settled, and then to pull the line in smoothly until the metal returns to the surface. Then we both hope for the line to tighten with the weight of a fish.

Cast, wait, pull, hope.

Cast, wait, pull, hope.

After half an hour in the rain, there is no luck. We are covered in water – and worse still, so are the fish.

Brian resorts to another technique, jerking the line intermittently. The movement, he hopes, might confuse the trout.

'We're trying to make the fish think!' he says.

Perhaps the fish aren't thinking enough, perhaps they're thinking too much, because there is still no action. The rain pours down.

I ask Brian if rainbow trout are cleverer than other—

At this moment, the line goes tight. A fish! An actual fish! I freeze in anticipation. Brian grabs the rod, and lifts it. The trout thrashes, then goes quiet. The fish appears again above the waterline two metres away, its body spasming and shimmering.

'Bring it in!' says Brian.

In my mind, the fish is already on the bank. But in three seconds, it has disappeared. The line goes dead. The hook is alone once more.

'We all lose fish,' says Brian. 'I lose fish.'

I keep casting. There's an easterly breeze off the North Sea, and the temperature can't be much above zero. My mind wanders. One more trout grasps at my line, then disappears never to be seen again. We give up, empty-handed. 'We should have had two,' says Brian. 'Normally even a beginner would get half a dozen.' The rain – more precisely the run-off from nearby fields – has made the water cloudy. 'May/June's nice,' says Brian. It's February. We trudge back to the wooden club-house, where my left boot is now so sodden that I can't pull it off.

For me, fishing was walking into a metaphor. It was tracing the ter-minology of everyday life back to its source – 'hooked', 'fishing expedition', 'fish where the fish are'. An angler truly never enters the same river twice, said Brian, because the earth may have shifted or a log may have floated down.

For Brian, fishing is an escape. During a tangent about Scottish in-dependence (he's in favour) and most politicians (he's against), he reflects on the divisiveness of modern life, and says: 'That's why we have fishing.' A licence on a nearby river costs £45 a year, which he sees as an absolute bargain. 'You cannae go for a drink with £45!'

Anglers have a code – about which animals to take, which equip-ment to use. At the lake, 'boobies' are banned, because they hook the fish so deeply that releasing the fish might be impossible. So too are double-hooks, which increase the angler's chances, but may mean the fish gets hooked through the eye as well as the mouth. Anglers are not allowed to take wild brown trout or to take only the biggest fish from the water. The best anglers see themselves as custodians of the natural world. After two hours standing by a lake, you do feel closer to nature. You attune to the geese and the swans and the wind.

Brian used to fish competitively, but now is bored by the one-upmanship. 'There's a lot of "I'm the best", "he's the best". I find it really irritating. If you're fishing in a river, the river's always going to win. At most it might loan itself to us for a day. It might allow us to catch two or three fish.'

'The river's always going to win' – it's a lovely phrase, but later on I realised it was a misleading one. It detracts from considering the fish as animals. We think we are up against a waterway; in fact we are the real force of nature. We take away too many fish, discharge too much pollution, and create too much damage.

The river and oceans are not always going to win. On current projections, they are going to lose, and so are their inhabitants.

*

Imagine if we killed pigs slowly and didn't stun them first.

Imagine if, when we did this, we unavoidably swept up squirrels, rabbits and wolves into the abattoir, and killed them too.

Imagine if we didn't count the number of pigs that we killed, and instead we just weighed them, as if they were crops.

Imagine if we tried to maximise this weight, even though that meant maximising death.

Imagine if, when we ordered chicken in a restaurant, the waiter served us a carcass with the head attached.

Imagine if we kept pigs as pets but hardly ever took them to the vets, because we couldn't tell when they were sick.

Imagine if we caught feral pigs and put them in zoos.

OK, enough of the John Lennon tribute act – my point is that we treat fish differently. Fishing boats sweep up huge quantities of 'by-catch', animals including sharks, dolphins and turtles who are not the target, but who are trapped in nets and on hooks. The UN Food and Agriculture Organization, the leading source of global food statistics, tallies up the number of livestock killed each year, but cannot even give an estimate for the number of fish, only how many million tonnes. Governments and even Greenpeace decline to say that there might be a limit to the number of fish being taken from the oceans in the long term, because jobs depend on fishing; they just argue about what the sustainable level is. Not even meat-packing giants like Tyson and Cargill boast about trying to slaughter as many livestock as ecologically possible. In restaurants, long since it was acceptable to bring a chicken's head to the table, it's still delightful to serve a whole fish – eyes and all. Oh, and aquariums rely on taking fish from the wild, in a way that zoos now largely regard as unethical. And we are destroying some of the best habitats for fish, such as coral reefs, through pollution and climate change. Because we care about fish less, there is much greater potential for harm to go unchecked.

Some animals are dehumanised; fish are de-*animalised*. The same applies to other sea creatures, including crabs and lobsters. The problem is that we don't know fish, we don't understand fish. Will McCallum, an oceans campaigner at Greenpeace, told me that a few years ago the group had asked British consumers to estimate the size of tuna: 'Most people thought they were the size of the tins.' The UK is associated worldwide with fish and chips, but most British consumers cannot identify a cod. To be honest, I can only confidently distinguish a cod from a herring because I have just checked on Google Images. There are almost as many described species of fish – more than 35,500 – as mammals, birds, amphibians and reptiles combined.

All this helps to explain why many people who call themselves vegetarians are not bothered about eating dead fish. After all, the Catholic Church held that the faithful could not eat meat on Fridays, out of respect for Christ, but fish was fine. On average, every human now eats twenty kilos of fish a year; even if you exclude China, which eats one-third of the world's fish, it's fifteen kilos. It's become so easy that we are callous: much of the fish caught is simply ground up to make feed for pigs or farmed fish. We act as if there will always be plenty more fish in the sea.

I pretty much gave up eating fish before I went vegetarian. My friends thought this was a case of confused priorities, like a heroin addict giving up gummy sweets. The truth is that I was alarmed by headlines about plummeting fish numbers. Between 1974 and 2015, the proportion of the world's fish stocks that were being overfished rose from 10 to 33 per cent. The worst affected areas include the Mediterranean and the south-east Pacific. Historical data on fish numbers is rarely available. One (disputed) estimate is that we have taken 90 per cent of large fish from the oceans. What's clear is that we have fished the apex predators, mid-level predators, and prey fish. We are even fishing the krill, crustaceans that are just a few centimetres long.

As fish populations come under strain, we have already seen the decline in birds from albatrosses to puffins. The largest study of the world's seabirds found that their populations declined 70 per cent between 1950 and 2010. Overfishing is a major reason. In the Antarctic, penguins feed partly on krill. Commercial krill fishing is affecting penguin populations as much as severe climatic events, even though the fishing is within scientifically set limits. One in every three species of marine mega-fauna – the biggest, most recognisable creatures in the oceans, including sharks, whales, turtles, penguins and octopuses – is at risk of extinction. Even if they survive in reduced numbers, their ability to nourish the ocean, for example by transporting nutrients, will be much diminished.

Fishing is careless to the point of negligence. Our oceans are filled with old nets and lines, abandoned because they have become caught or damaged. Such discarded fishing gear makes up nearly half of the Great Pacific Garbage Patch, the archipelago of debris that measures three times the size of France. Tens of thousands of seals and whales become entangled in fishing gear and other human debris every year, along with probably millions of turtles, birds and other animals. This is what we order when fish is on the menu.

For Europeans, and Brits in particular, Atlantic cod has been a staple, plentiful fish. But our appetite has proved too much. Stocks have been declining for decades, crashing and then recovering slightly. Whenever scientists become alarmed, governments yield to the fishing industry and don't take as much action as they should. Overall, at least one-third of the EU's fish stocks continue to be overfished, despite scientific advice. We subsidise this short-termism: the world's governments funnel $35 billion a year into the fishing industry, a large chunk of it to increase how many fish are taken. We cannot move our fishing elsewhere: while one-third of stocks are over-fished, nearly all of the remaining two-thirds are being fished to capacity (the mathematical optimum). Simply put, we cannot keep taking as much fish from the sea as we currently are.

In 1995, the marine biologist Daniel Pauly coined the term 'shifting baseline syndrome'. Each generation of fisheries scientists, he argues, fails to see the decline in fish populations, because they accept as a baseline the population numbers that existed at the start of their careers. 'We transform the world, but we don't remember it,' says Pauly. Two hundred years ago, the Gulf of Maine yielded perhaps ten times as much cod as it does today. Which fisheries plan takes that into account?

Overfishing is clearly a bad thing – and we need to fix it, by doing more research, setting quotas, tracking boats and creating marine protected areas (7 per cent of the oceans are protected, compared to 15 per cent of the land). Why don't we act? One answer is that we view fish as an inexhaustible resource. You can see how this idea came about. A single female cod can release a million eggs in a month. Water covers two-thirds of the world's surface – how could our appetite leave a lasting bite? We've now seen enough declines to know that fish are exhaustible. So perhaps there's an aggravating factor: we don't really care about fish. Overfishing is a question of computer models, not lives. I was as guilty as anyone else of de-animalising fish. Even when I stopped eating them, I wasn't really thinking about them as animals.

When I was in school, we read *Moby-Dick*. It's the classic statement of how the sea is different to land. The narrator Ishmael describes the sea not just as the 'foe' to man, but as 'a fiend to its own offspring'. He contrasts 'the universal cannibalism of the sea' to 'this green, gentle, and most docile earth', and wonders whether the sea might represent the worst side of our nature. The idea that the food chain is more savage underwater is absurd. But grenade harpoons hadn't been invented, and boats were occasionally rammed by whales, so Ishmael's attitude is partly understandable.

Moby-Dick is a gruesome read now, because we have extended our compassion to whales. Greenpeace started campaigning against whaling in earnest in 1975; an international ban on whaling was voted through just seven years later. Although Japan and some other countries twist the rules, several whale species have rebounded: the population of humpbacks, once fewer than 500, could return to its pre-whaling level within a decade. After the film *Blackfish* showed the horror of SeaWorld capturing orcas from the wild, the theme-park operator promised to stop using them in theatrical shows. Every time a whale washes up, the TV news goes into a frenzy. We'd rather think about stranded whales than stranded migrants.

The Save the Whales campaign grew out of an appreciation of the whales as animals. Yes, there were stark statistics about the looming extinction of blue whales and humpbacks, just as there are about over-fishing today. 'Every 20 Minutes a Whale Is Killed', said a Swiss anti-whaling petition in the 1970s. But Paul Spong, a New Zealander psychologist who became a leading Greenpeace activist, had worked with orcas at the Vancouver Aquarium. He played an orca Rolling Stones songs, and claimed the species was capable of pain, joy and complex social relationships. We didn't always care about whales, our fellow mammals, but we learnt to. Should we do the same with fish? We love fish for their colours, their speed and their shoaling. To love them as we do whales we have to believe that they are sentient beings. The first part of the animal test is to understand what, if anything, they feel.

*

Lynne Sneddon remembers her first fish. They were pet goldfish with names like Bow and Arrow, and they were happy companions until one day her cat scooped them out onto her bedroom carpet. 'The little shit,' she says of Gizmo the cat. 'I went mental.'

Sneddon, now a biologist at the University of Gothenburg, has dedicated her career to overturning our preconceptions of fish and challenging what she sees as the speciesism that prevents their full capabilities from being recognised. We meet at an aquarium outside Liverpool, where she has done part of her research.

'The problem with fish,' she tells me, as we stand by experimental tanks, 'is that we eat them, we farm them, we catch them, we use them as a hobby, we pay £15 to come here and look at them, and we do research on them. You have all these complicated things in people's heads.' Which image takes hold may depend on that first childhood experience. 'I saw fish as a pet – something beautiful – and I loved watching documentaries on marine biologists,' says Sneddon.

There is no shortcut to working out what is going on inside fishes' heads. Scientists define non-human animal pain as an aversive reaction associated with actual or threatened tissue damage. The challenge is to distinguish this from nociception – a reaction to a negative stimulus of the type that causes you to instantaneously withdraw your hand from a hot iron. Sneddon suggested that intrinsic to pain is that an animal's behaviour will swiftly change as a result – to reduce the pain and prevent damage. This change in behaviour would not occur if pain relief were administered.

Sneddon's first step was to show that fish were physically capable of perceiving negative stimuli. Mammals seem to process pain through the neocortex, the part of the brain associated with complex emotion which is found at the top of the human head. Fish do not have a neocortex, but neither do birds, even those like crows and parrots that have shown sophisticated learning. What mammals and birds do have are nociceptors – neurons that alert creatures to potentially damaging stimuli. Using a microscope, Sneddon found that fish too have nociceptors analogous to those in humans. By measuring electrical activity in nerve cells, Sneddon was then able to show that a rainbow trout (the same species that Brian and I had tried to fish in Scotland) processed noxious stimuli centrally. In other words, these were not unthinking reflexes.

There are other indications that fish feel pain. Sneddon's team applied noxious stimuli to trout then returned them to a tank. Their ventilation accelerated, and they took three hours to start feeding, rather than just one. These effects dissipated when painkillers were applied. Other researchers have found that goldfish will avoid an area of a tank where they have received electric shocks. Humans will take a trip to a pharmacy and pay money, in order to have pain relief; for serious pain relief, we will knowingly accept potential side effects. Sneddon and her fellow researchers placed zebrafish, small fish who are used in medical research, in a tank, where they could choose between a barren area and one decorated with gravel and a plant. The zebrafish preferred the decorated area. But when some fish were injected with acid, and pain-relievers were dissolved into the water of the barren area, the fish preferred the barren area. The principle of Occam's razor holds that the simplest explanation is usually the correct one. The simplest explanation for the zebrafish's behaviour is that they experienced pain equivalent to our own. If it looks like a duck, and quacks like a duck, it is probably a duck. After all, feeling pain would have an evolutionary advantage, allowing fish to avoid predators and other threats.

Certain species have already shown evidence of self-awareness. Damselfish – small reef fish – are eaten by trumpetfish – long fish related to seahorses. Researchers have shown that damselfish can distinguish trumpetfish by size: they ignore small trumpetfish, who cannot eat them, but closely watch larger ones. Moreover, smaller damselfish reacted more strongly to trumpetfish, suggesting an awareness of their own size.

In 2018 cleaner wrasse, the species famous for its role cleaning other fish of parasites, became the first fish to show arguable signs of recognising themselves in a mirror, joining orangutans, bottlenose dolphins and others. The fish had been injected with a dot of red dye on their head or throat, and placed in a tank with a mirror. On observing their reflection, some of the fish appeared to act strangely, and scrape their throats against the substrate of the tank. Primate expert Frans de Waal compared the wrasse's level of self-recognition to that of macaques.

Scientific research over the past two decades has suggested that fish are capable of complex thought and social interaction. Fish co-operate: on the Great Barrier Reef, rabbitfish work in pairs: one watches for predators, while another feeds head-down in the cracks in the coral, and then the two switch positions. They probably communicate to each other by flicking their fins. To us, fish are expressionless and noiseless. But various species of fish make noises to communicate:

some by grinding their teeth, others by rubbing their fins and heads together. When fish swim in shoals, they keep spaced from one another, through a mixture of sight, sound and detecting water pulses. That itself is likely to involve complex thought, as is the decision whether to assume a position near the front of the shoal, where risks and rewards are both higher.

'You can find an example of a fish doing any behaviour that a mammal can do,' says Sneddon. 'If I told you an elephant did this, you'd be like, yeah, of course. The minute it's a fish, it's questioned.'

Some scientists do think fish are fundamentally distinct. Todd Feinberg and Jon Mallatt, the theorists of early animal consciousness, have proposed that fish are conscious, like all other vertebrates, but they are not convinced that they feel pain. James D. Rose, a neuroscientist, has questioned both how fish nociceptors work, and how behavioural experiments have been performed. He and his collaborators have argued that there was no evolutionary advantage for fish to develop pain – they could not hide from predators, as they needed to seek food continuously.

Most recent scientific papers on the subject, however, have come down on the side of fish feeling pain. Given how much we have broadened our conception of what animals perceive, it seems a safe bet that we will discover more. If fish feel pain, then suddenly de-animalising them becomes hard. Humans and today's fish evolved from common ancestors, and our bodies still bear the hallmarks of this evolution. As the palaeontologist Neil Shubin wrote in his book *Your Inner Fish*, fish have two eyes, a skull and a backbone; they have four appendages, albeit fins rather than arms and legs; they have a bilaterally symmetrical body plan, just like we do. Faced with stress, fish and humans produce the same hormone, cortisol – whereas mice and rats produce a different hormone, corticosterone. The fact that fish are used in medical research is a strong indicator of how much we have in common. All of this helped me to narrow the gap between myself and fish. These were not floating crops. Their lives had value.

If fish feel pain, animal-lovers need to consider not just their numbers – but their experience of the world. Fishing with Brian was catch and release: if we had caught any fish, we wouldn't have killed them directly, but we would have taken them from their natural environment, inflicted stress and reduced their survival chances once in the water – for the sake of a photo and a feeling of achievement. There are other ways to find peace by a lake. Catch-and-release angling doesn't pass the animal test. But it's also not the main problem. Between 800 billion and 2.3 trillion wild caught fish are killed every year, according to the researcher Alison Mood. And they are not caught by me or even Brian.

*

You don't come to Galicia for the weather. Contrary to legend, the rain in Spain falls mainly here, on the north-western province, the part above Portugal. Galicia specialises in two things: pilgrims and fish. It has the biggest pilgrimage site in Europe, Santiago de Compostela. It also has Europe's biggest fishing port, Vigo. More than 300,000 pilgrims arrive every year; so do 600,000 tonnes of fish. The difference is that the Catholics come more or less voluntarily.

I came for the fish. I wanted to see how the EU's biggest fresh fish market looked in practice. I arrive at 6 a.m. at the market – a series of vast, football-field size halls at the dockside. Business has already been going for nearly two hours. It should be 4°C, to keep the fish fresh, but the port authorities had settled on 12°C, to keep the humans sane. Crates of fish lie on the concrete floors. There are tubs of sardines and anglerfish. There are skates, their insides already cleaned out. A handful of orange octopuses fit together in a crate; they seem to flow into each other, their bodies meeting in little pools of black ink – almost as if they are one big, rectangular jelly.

How do you kill an octopus, I ask the man? 'Like this,' he says, picking up one by the head, and turning it inside out, so a squeeze of black entrails flows onto the creature's arms. I decide it's not the moment to mention that octopuses make playful companions. Instead I ask if the ones over there – in another crate – are dead. No one is quite sure, but the consensus is that they probably are. Very much alive are European spider crabs: large, dark, orange and nobbly. They are mostly motionless, until an assistant grabs at a leg.

Further down the large shed, there are piles of blue sharks and shortfin mako sharks. Mako sharks are the fastest of all sharks – able to swim up to twenty miles per hour, or several times the speed of Olympic record-holders. They can grow over four metres in length, dive below 800 metres, and jump metres out of the water, to catch their prey. But here what matters is their weight – thirty kilos, forty kilos, fifty kilos.

The main events are a dozen or so swordfish. The biggest weighs 157 kilos. 'That's nothing,' says my guide, a port employee called Jesús. 'They go above 200.' It's so large that its sword has been cut to make it fit in the row. A label says it was captured in the north-east Atlantic.

The phrase 'fish out of water' is a bit unfair. To human eyes, the swordfish in particular look magnificent out of the water. Their size, their curves, their sheen. We can appreciate them here as we could perhaps never appreciate them in their natural habitat. We rarely see what's in the sea until we kill it.

I ask one trader how to judge the quality of the fish. 'Experience,' he sighs. 'Years.' Out of a mix of pity and boredom, he introduces himself as Paco and begins a brief tutorial. The most important thing, he explains, is to see how recently the fish had left the water. A boat may have been fishing for a week: the fish taken on day one might be worth half that taken on day two.

He pokes a swordfish in the eye, to test its sheen, pulls apart the gills, so I can see whether the flesh inside is black. He rubs the ice from its sides, so I can judge the skin. I think I have the hang of it, until Paco starts enthusiastically talking through the shape of swordfish bellies. Ah well, I think, I don't need 157 kilos of dead swordfish anyway.

Paco complains about the Chinese fishermen whose nets don't let young fish escape. He complains about plastics and climate change. He himself has been to sea only once. He pinches his neck. 'Your *cojones* are up here,' he says. 'The sea is very tough. You've got to be men with balls. On the ocean, the boat is just the shell of a nut.'

The auction begins – the numbers go downwards.

'Nine euros ... Eight ninety-five ... Eight ninety ... Eight eighty-five.'

Men with loudhailers read the prices with the emotional investment of parking wardens – this is not Sotheby's. But my favourite of the
auctioneers occasionally pauses, and looks up from his notepad with
the disappointment of a man who has just crashed his car into his living
room and stubbed his toe escaping from the wreckage. None of the
traders take much notice, but I admire the effort.

In these auctions, the price would fall to a level where a trader indicated interest. At this point the trader would inspect the fish properly
– flipping them over from one crate to another, looking for damage.
The advantage of counting downwards is that if the trader decides the
fish isn't worth what he's offered, the countdown resumes where it left
off. This happened multiple times – men putting their hands back in
their pockets. The disappointed auctioneer would look even more disappointed, as if, having already crashed his car and stubbed his toe, he
had also forgotten to defrost his dinner.

Vigo is a hub for fishing. Some of the fish have been brought via
Portugal, some from as far away as Ireland, by traders hoping for a
better price. Yet for Vigo, fresh fish is the tip of the iceberg. In the
1960s, a group of Galicians realised that the future of fishing was not
close to the crowded shore – but thousands of miles away, in the south
Atlantic. They formed part of a wave of 'factory trawlers' with onboard freezers and packing operations. Refrigeration was a tactic
learnt from the meat industry. It meant the fish could be packaged
and preserved straight away, and the boat could keep fishing for
weeks. Nearly everyone in Vigo knew someone who worked on that
first ship.

The company, Pescanova, negotiated deals to access the waters of
Argentina, Namibia, Mozambique and Angola. It became the largest
fishing company in the world, a title it held until the financial crisis,
when its tax filings were found to be as fishy as its core business, neces-
sitating a bout of emergency corporate surgery. Pescanova is still a
giant: along with twelve other companies, it catches more than one-
tenth of the fish taken from the world's oceans. Modern fishing is a
remarkable operation. Some seafood now arrives at port just as it will
arrive at the supermarket – frozen in cardboard packets. Some will be

transferred at sea to cargo vessels, so that the fishing boat can continue fishing for months on end.

Away from the market, along the shoreline, I walk up to huge freezer trawlers, which had recently returned from the Falkland Islands, swollen with 1,500 tonnes of squid. The boats feel almost mythical in scale. Certainly the port has its mythologies. The head of the port, an affable former politician called Enrique López Veiga, tells me that 'Sea people are ill-disciplined people, who want discipline.'

Vigo made me realise how little fishing is about fish. Livestock farmers know their animals and largely try to make allowances for them, within the confines of economics and tradition. Fishing centres on pulling animals out of the water, rather than rearing them. So there is less chance of any internal restraint. Vigo also showed me why we find it so hard to question the fishing industry. It's not just that we don't feel empathy for the fish. It's that fishing, even more than livestock farming, plays to a sense of human endeavour. We have been fishing for longer than we've been farming. Fresh fish, perhaps netted just a few hours earlier, connects us to a place. Frozen fish, which has been brought from half the world away, represents our struggle with the wild seas. Here we are, creatures evolved for the land who have managed to conquer the two-thirds of the earth's surface that is sea. We cannot walk on water, but we can live off it.

In Vigo, you can't question fishing – let alone become angry about it – without questioning the city itself. It is a great city – the coffee costs a third of the London price, and comes with a free slice of cake, and the Christmas lights are, at least according to the mayor, the envy of the world (they do include a four-storey silver tree). If we had never fished – if our ancestors had taken one look at the ocean and said, nope, not going back in there – Vigo would not exist as we know it today. Nor would thousands of other coastal cities, towns and villages – among them Amsterdam, Aberdeen and Aalborg – which were, at least at one stage in their history, metaphorically dragged out of the ocean.

Questioning livestock farming – that honest, salt-of-the-earth vocation – is hard enough. Questioning fishing is to question the commitment, and sacrifice, of sailors who have risked their lives at sea over the centuries to provide food. Fishing is not as dangerous as it once was, but from Scotland to Alaska, it is frequently named among the most dangerous professions. In the US, the fatality rate for commercial fishermen remains twenty-nine times that of the average job. About half of deaths are caused by boats sinking; many of the others by fishermen falling overboard without a life jacket. Worldwide, many fishing boats are staffed by poorly trained, poorly treated workers. The *New York Times* reporter Ian Urbina met a Cambodian man called Lang Long, who had been sold into forced labour in Thailand, kept at sea for three years, and chained by a metal collar on deck when he tried to escape. Lang Long's story is not uncommon: the fishing industry is a hive of exploitation and slavery.

On land, we felt more empathy for animals once they stopped being a regular threat to our existence. The ocean is still a threat to fishermen's existence – and that is why it makes it harder for them, and all of us, to empathise with fish.

I tried to shake off this cultural baggage, and process what I had seen at the port. Sharks can be caught in a variety of ways, but more than 90 per cent (by weight) of the shortfin mako caught in the Atlantic is caught on longlines. These huge fishing lines stretch some forty or fifty miles out into the ocean, with metal hooks spaced every three metres. They are left out for one to two days, sometimes with live fish impaled as bait. As the line is reeled in, the sharks' long bodies writhe until they are pulled out of the water and gripped with a metal noose. The sharks are hauled onto the boat and stabbed. This seemed much worse than an abattoir. Even when makos are released back into the water, one-third of them die. Sharks and rays are elasmobranches, a class of fish that diverged from the ancestors of so-called bony fish like trout and tuna more than 400 million years ago. We know little about how they experience pain. But assuming they do experience it, they face prolonged agony before they die. Hauling in the longlines takes hours. This was the likely fate of the mako sharks I had seen. We are not only hunting the cheetahs of the sea, we are doing so barbarically.

The only thing worse than fishermen catching mako sharks on longlines is fishermen *not* catching them on longlines – because it suggests that there aren't many left. Between 2015 and 2018, the weight of shortfin mako fished from the north Atlantic fell by a quarter. In 2018 the species was declared endangered. Sharks are the most endangered of all marine mega-fauna: a quarter of species are threatened with extinction. The great white shark and the whale shark are both on course to go extinct this century. Some humans love sharks, but human progress in general has not been their friend. News reports sometimes lure us to thinking that the biggest problem is the popularity of shark fin soup in Asia; in fact, the fishing of sharks for meat does more damage.

To the average human, sharks still represent danger. Watching cartoons with Eliza and Cleo, I can see the legacy of *Jaws*. The shark in *Jaws* kills six humans. In US history, sharks have, as far as we know, never killed more than five people in a single year. Maybe at some age my daughters will learn that sharks kill an average of four humans a year, whereas humans kill perhaps 100 million sharks a year. When the Save the Whales campaign began in the 1970s, killer whales were seen as dangerous to humans. Environmentalists rebranded the animals as orcas, a derivation of their scientific name.

Our fear of sharks may make it harder for us to care about them, but it is not why we fish them cruelly and excessively. No one made a thriller film about killer tuna, and tuna populations too have been grossly overfished. Bluefin tuna are often caught on longlines; their populations have also flirted with disaster. In fish-mad Japan, the first bluefin of the year is sold in an auction that serves as promotion for rich restaurateurs. In 2019 the price hit a record of $3.1 million for a 278-kilo fish. Even kilo for kilo, it was several times more than any trophy-hunter pays for a lion or elephant. Imagine such a publicity stunt for a cow or a pig – the closest I can think of is the White House's annual tradition of *sparing* a Thanksgiving turkey.

Humane slaughter is nowhere to be seen in most industrial fishing. With trawler boats, many fish are crushed to death as the net is dragged through the water. This death may take hours. If the net is brought to the surface from deep water, the effect of decompression may burst the fishes' bladders and pull their guts out through their mouths and anuses. (The standard-bearer of decompression is the blobfish: sometimes called the world's ugliest animals, they in fact only look like gelatinous blobs because they lose their shape when hauled more than 2,000 feet up from the ocean depths. It's not a fate you'd wish for your pet.) Those fish who get on the boat alive often struggle. Some are gutted. Others are simply left to suffocate. This is among the most lingering ways a fish could die. It could take hours. 'To me, the way we kill fish is just insane. It's reminiscent of how mammals were killed in the Middle Ages,' says Open Philanthropy's Lewis Bollard.

Three-quarters of Europeans now believe that fish feel pain, but this attitude has not yet shaped the industry. There are no regulations on how wild fish should be killed. If there were – for example, smaller trawler nets that reduced the amount of time that fish would be chased to exhaustion – the industry couldn't produce so much cheap fish. Only a handful of fishing boats in the world have electric stunners that knock the fish unconscious before they're killed, as is routine for livestock.

Japanese fishermen have put the most thought into how to kill fish humanely. The *ikejime* technique involves shoving a spike through the fish's brain, cutting across the gill arches and at the base of the tail, then folding the tail against the body and running a metal thread through the fish's spinal cord, to end the possibility of sensation being transferred. The fish is then left to bleed in an ice bath.

Ikejime can look horrific: in one YouTube video, I watched a tuna being hauled out of the water on the end of a metal hook, thrash on the deck, and then struggle plentifully as the spike is inserted into his head. 'He didn't like that one,' says the fisherman. *Ikejime* relies on a fisherman knowing where the fish's brain is.

Proponents of the technique argue that the meat tastes better, because the fish wriggles only briefly and therefore does not have a surge of lactic acid, and remains fresh for longer, because the blood is removed. The method is used for fish destined to be high-grade sushi. What struck me is how battered and bloody the bodies looked afterwards – their tails cut, maybe severed. Let's face it: most of the fish we are served have not been killed humanely. They suffered. When mighty whole fish are served in restaurants, it may well be because they were left to suffocate to death. What I had seen in Vigo was not some romantic, mythic contest of man and sea beast. It was a process of industrial killing, and I didn't want any part of it. But maybe the alternative way of catching fish was actually worse.

*

I'd heard of farmed salmon, farmed trout and farmed tilapia, the largely vegetarian African species that are among the most efficient at turning feed into meat. But I had no conception of what a fish farm looked like. Unlike livestock farms, fish farms did not appear in my storybooks as a child – and they didn't appear in my daughters' either. Maybe that's because, unlike actual farms, there is no bucolic past. No discerning western consumer likes to think of their fish being mass-produced in a concrete pond, or a sea cage.

Officially, for the first time in human history, aquaculture accounts for half of fish production. In reality, it is probably still short of that, because there's plenty of illegal ocean fishing that isn't included in government statistics. Still, the number of farmed fish is between 51 billion and 167 billion, and the number of decapods – such as shrimp, prawns and crabs – is between 255 billion and 605 billion. If there is suffering involved, it is of a different order to that even experienced by chickens, the most numerous livestock.

We turn to fish farms because the oceans cannot provide enough. The FAO estimates that catches have plateaued since the 1980s, at between 78 million tonnes and 86 million tonnes. The actual trend may be worse. According to a study led by marine biologist Daniel Pauly, we caught 50 per cent more fish from the oceans between 1950 and 2010 than the official statistics show. If that's right, it means catches have fallen sharply – and that fish stocks are in a worse state than is commonly thought.

For the fishing industry, fish farms are the future. For animal-conscious consumers, they are rather less helpful. This should not come as a surprise. Once you've seen the shortcomings of livestock farming, and the mental abilities of fish, it's a short leap to realising that fish farms will bring problems. More than 500 species of seafood are farmed worldwide. Recreating the ideal psychological and social conditions for each of them has not been a priority for the farming industry. Salmon's journey upriver to spawn is one of the most incredible feats in the natural world – a task of memory and endurance. And we decide instead to keep them in cages?

Salmon are raised in freshwater tanks then transported to offshore pens – cages and nets, which from above look like huge steel circles. They spend around three years in total in these barren environments, where they have little of the stimulation that they'd find in the wild. Most farms struggle with the basic challenge: keeping fish physically healthy. So that salmon grow quickly, farms selectively breed the fish, expose them to constant light, and feed them a concentrated diet. This feed turns their flesh grey, so they have to be fed a pigment to have the pink colour that shoppers expect. For reasons that aren't understood, the farms also cause irreversible hearing damage in the salmon: one study in Norway found 100 per cent of large fish were partially deaf.

Farmed salmon in Scotland and Norway are often covered in lesions. They face a particular problem of lice. The lice are crustaceans, less than two centimetres long. They attach themselves to the salmon and feed upon their mucus, skin and tissue. They occur naturally, but in congested fish farms, they spread with ease. In small numbers they cause stress and at times lasting damage. Hundreds of lice have been found on a single fish. Farmed salmon's skin is often so damaged that chunks of red flesh are visible. Wild salmon, migrating to spawn, can mingle with the lice and larvae and become infested. In Norway, some farms use cleaner wrasse to kill the lice; millions of these fish are then themselves killed along with salmon. Overall, at Scottish farms, around a quarter of salmon – more than 10 million a year – die prematurely due to various diseases. Their bodies, often diseased and deformed, pile up in dumpsters on the shore, an industrial-scale version of the bin where I placed dead piglets. When storms damage the offshore pens, tens of thousands of farmed salmon often escape: the Scottish government says that anglers may be able to identify farmed fish by their deformed fins, gill covers and snouts.

Even if fish farms sorted out their welfare problems, they would run up against the same problem as livestock farms: producing meat is inefficient. The fish have to be fed other (wild-caught) fish, or crops. There is no such thing as a free lunch. Scottish salmon farms take two and a half tonnes of wild fish for every tonne of salmon they produce, according to campaign group Feedback. We could eat some of that wild fish directly ourselves, get the same amount of omega-3 fatty acids, and leave more than half of the wild fish in the ocean.

If discerning consumers knew this is what fish farms were like, they would surely eat less fish. Yet in Vigo, I found that things were moving in the other direction. Instead of giving up on farming seafood, we are looking to subject more animals to it.

With other mammals, what we appreciate is their similarity to us. Even with fish, it's possible to see our evolutionary heritage. With octopuses, we have to appreciate the difference. You cannot help but marvel at creatures whose evolution diverged from our own more than 500 million years ago. Octopuses are so different to us that we can't even depict them properly. I once met an animator called Jason Deamer, who was the character art director of Pixar's film *Finding Dory*. 'You never realise until you draw an octopus 400 times how annoying it is to draw an octopus. Think graphically, right?' Deamer explained to me. 'When you get to about four [arms], you're running out of places to put them. Look at any drawing of an octopus that's not done in a clinical fashion, and you'll notice that most artists leave out some of the tentacles.' Sure enough, in *Finding Dory*, the octopus Hank ended up as a 'septopus'; his loss of an arm had to be written into the story. Of all the animals in my daughters' storybooks, none seemed so inaccurate as the red balloons-with-arms that passed for octopuses.

What few of us have realised until recently is that octopuses' number of arms is only the start of their glorious divergence. These arms contain most of the octopuses' 500 million neurons; in some octopuses, the arms regenerate. Octopuses, like cuttlefish, vary their skin colour for camouflage and to reflect their moods – a trait that puts into perspective humans' unique ability to blush. They can change colour in 30 milliseconds.

Octopuses are not fish; like squid and cuttlefish, they are cephalopods, a class of mollusc, a phylum that also includes snails. Octopuses are smart enough to eat all the crabs in a fisherman's cage and then slink to safety; they can disguise themselves with shells to avoid being caught by sharks. They can learn how to solve puzzles and remember the solution. In aquariums, they can be the creatures that keepers relate to most easily. They are capable of distinguishing between different humans.

Octopuses represent a different path to intelligence. They are often solitary – and can become cannibalistic when kept with other octopuses – yet enjoy being stroked by humans. They show intelligence but generally live only a year. We have much to learn about how octopuses' brains work, and how they perceive the world around them. If nothing else, we can watch the precision with which they hunt, sometimes in tandem with fish. They are playful and curious, show interest in new objects and watch humans intently. Octopuses have a sense of what other animals can see: the biologist David Scheel recounts how they hide behind an object, revealing only their eyes.

The last decade has helped to open our eyes to octopuses' abilities. In 2012 the Cambridge Declaration on Consciousness singled out octopuses among all invertebrates as having the biological basis for consciousness. In 2016 an octopus called Inky managed an improbable escape from New Zealand's National Aquarium, finding a long drainpipe that led to the ocean. There have been documentaries on the BBC and Netflix, and bestselling books like Peter Godfrey-Smith's *Other Minds: The Octopus and the Evolution of Intelligent Life*.

Yet this awakening has done little for octopuses. We should have so many questions about them. But the most common question that people seem to have right now is: how can I eat them? You can see horrifying online videos of octopuses being eaten alive – or being dismembered arm by arm, while still alive. The videos largely come from Asia, but there's nothing to stop restaurants in the US serving octopuses similarly. Sik Gaek, a Korean restaurant that opened in Queens, New York, in 2010, imports octopuses live from South Korea, keeps them in a tank at the front, before they are dished up live – or recently dismembered. The wriggling octopus arms are the attraction for diners. We would never be so callous with the life of a rat, and a common octopus has six times as many nerve cells as a rat.

Since the 1980s, catches of cephalopods have tripled to 4 million tonnes a year. Even countries that didn't traditionally eat octopus are doing so as consumers become more squeamish about eating livestock. An official report about octopus farming in Australia noted that appetite for octopus had multiplied, 'in parallel to a reduction in red and white meat consumption'.

For Galicians, octopus is culinary delight. But it has fallen off the menu of even some high-end restaurants because it is so expensive. In 2018, the wholesale price went up to €18 a kilo, because fishing boats struggled to find any. In early 2020, catches plunged 90 per cent. What if there were a stable supply of octopuses? What if octopus could be farmed like salmon?

This is what Ángel González is trying to do. González is a charismatic biologist in his early fifties, and when I met him on a Friday afternoon at his concrete block of a research lab, he was wrestling with a familiar problem: how can humans grow octopus larvae in tanks?

A female octopus may produce 200,000 larvae. In the wild, young octopuses live on the ocean current – they float a hundred metres out to sea, and their diet changes along the way. 'We know what they eat in the wild. What we aré trying to find out is what is going on in the larvae's stomach,' says González.

González, who is working with one of Vigo's major fishing firms, Armadora Pereira, is reluctant to say when farmed octopus could be served. 'It could be two, three or five years.' Another team is working with Pescanova, and hopes to have farmed octopus in shops by 2023. Whatever the date, it's a disaster in the making.

Octopuses appear wholly unsuited to farms. Their social lives are beyond our understanding. They want novelty; their habit of escape suggests they don't want to be in captivity. In *Other Minds*, Godfrey-Smith tells the story of Charles, a common octopus who refused to comply with the task of pulling a lever in return for food and instead 'spent much time with eyes above the surface of the water, directing a jet of water at any individual who approached the tank'. As for the killing process, there is evidence that octopuses do experience pain. In one experiment, they were given food if they attacked a white ball. When presented with a red ball, the octopuses attacked that too – but some were given an electrical shock. Some quickly stopped attacking the red ball. (Squid also show evidence of experiencing pain.)

González knows that octopuses are curious, marvellous creatures: he shows me a photo on his iPhone of where he found an octopus one morning – up on the doorframe. But he is ploughing on. Talking to him, I had the sinking feeling that octopus farming would indeed happen. I look outside at a large, windowless warehouse. Is that what an octopus farm will look like?

'Hopefully,' says González.

I ask if he worries about what the octopuses will experience. He points out that octopuses live short lives. 'They are animals. I'm not crying! We are researchers, we do care for the animals. In the end you are trying to make some benefit for society.'

My objection to González's research felt fundamental. It's not that octopuses shouldn't be farmed, I felt that they shouldn't be eaten at all. Food is not just about taste and nutrients; otherwise we might be willing to eat our deceased pets and relatives. There comes a point where we have to put our wonder at fellow living beings first. To me, loving octopuses means leaving them alone: every mouthful brings the dawn of octopus farming nearer. If we can't step back and put the idiosyncrasies of the octopus above the taste, then we can't call ourselves animal-lovers.

*

I had one final stop in Galicia. I drove across from Vigo to the neighbouring port of Bueu. In front of me in the harbour, a mechanical scoop – the size of the digger on a building site – transfers black-and-gold mussels from the back of fishing boats onto a lorry. A few seagulls squawk. Seagulls, in a rare evolutionary failing, can't open closed mussels, but can, and do, eat cracked ones. A crab scampers around.

I met Matías, a mussel farmer, on his boat.

'This is agriculture,' he says, holding up a mussel. 'It's just like a crop.'

Like oysters, clams, scallops and cockles, mussels are from a class of mollusc called bivalves. Don't eat anything with a face, some people say, which is actually a defensible starting point if, like Darwin, you see a link between facial expressions and basic emotions. Mussels do not appear to have faces. Up close their most noticeable features are a dozen threads – sometimes nicknamed beards – that emerge between their shell and attach them to rocks.

Mussels are a strange mix of the cultivated and the wild. They are not taken from the water in nets, or dredged like wild scallops, a technique that ruins the seabed. Here they grow in the mouth of the river – attached to large ropes, beneath huge wooden platforms. They are filter-feeders: they feed on plankton and other organic matter suspended in the water. They also clean the water of nitrogen from sewage and fertilisers.

Galicia produces more than 90 per cent of Spain's mussels; it's a family business, with each family tending to own one or two platforms. A few hundred metres out from the harbour were Matías's platforms, buoyed by steel containers, and anchored by a line to a couple of tons of cement.

Unlike fishing, with its mystique of danger and bravery, mussel-farming is easy. Matías showed me the tiny seed mussels – smaller than the nail on a little finger. He told me how he paddles in a small boat around the rocks to find them, and attaches them to the ropes on his raft. He unwinds the ropes into the water, and the mussels then grow. Little intervention is required. In the summer, Matías wanders topless around the rafts in the sunshine; his friends call him Tarzan of the Rafts. As the mussels grow, new ones emerge on the outside of the shell. A few are fine, but once they start multiplying, they risk overloading the whole line. Matías has learnt a trick from his father: to find a starfish, and to put it to work eating the baby mussels. Every summer, he paints the rafts with a form of tar, to prevent them becoming too slippery with algae.

Matías had hauled 5,000 kilos of mussels from the water that morning, and sold them for around €1 a kilo. He took a bag the size of a large rucksack, and we walked back to his flat for lunch. He steamed them in a frying pan with a dash of water and lemon, and soon they were popping open – their pink flesh turned orange. I ate my portion, not sure whether I should feel guilty or not.

I knew that crustaceans probably feel pain. In one experiment, hermit crabs were given an electric shock and then presented with a new shell, into which they could move. The crabs were much more likely to move to the shell if they had received a shock; they also spent less time inspecting it. The change in behaviour could be detected even if the new shell wasn't offered until a day after the shock. Evidence suggests lobsters survive for up to a minute while being boiled. It's not conclusive, but it's enough to give them the benefit of the doubt. In 2019 Switzerland banned live-boiling lobsters and other crustaceans, ordering cooks to seek a less painful death such as a knife through the head or chilling to dull the senses. It also mandated that they must be transported in their natural environment of water, rather than on ice.

Are mussels conscious? Do they feel pain? Is steaming them alive as cruel as boiling lobsters or crabs? Is transporting them on trucks heartless? Mussels are molluscs, like octopuses. But molluscs are a large, diverse phylum, with around 50,000 marine species known so far (and nearly 500 new ones identified every year). Octopuses and other cephalopods have developed large brains but mussels and other bivalves have not. In fact bivalves have no central nervous system, and so, as far as Feinberg and Mallatt's theory goes, no way of unifying sensory information – and no ability for consciousness or pain.

There's another reason to think that mussels don't feel pain: many bivalves are not free-moving. Robert Elwood, emeritus professor of biology at the Queen's University Belfast, whose work was instrumental in Switzerland banning the live boiling of crustaceans, points out that this means the evolutionary advantage of pain is limited – mussels and oysters cannot run away and hide, for example. Sustaining a neural system to process pain would require the animals to expend a lot of energy for little reason. 'I would wonder what they could gain from having a pain system that would offset the cost of having one,' says Elwood.

What mussels can do is close their shells, but simple reflex might be enough for that. In fact, the shells may be an alternative for pain. Bivalves, and barnacles, which have plates, 'seem to have taken a different evolutionary path with different ways to protect. In both, they simply shut down when disturbed and then open up again to resume feeding,' Elwood says. 'There is less need for pain in bivalves and barnacles than in squid and lobsters.' Octopuses, which have no physical protection against predators, have developed intelligence to survive. Bivalves are different.

Elwood's caveat is that not much research has been done on bivalves – or indeed barnacles – and so today's speculation may be overturned. PETA points out that mussels can slowly relocate, by reattaching their threads. 'We don't yet know whether oysters feel pain, but if they do, they represent a very large number of suffering animals,' it adds.

I think the likelihood is strong that bivalves don't feel pain. Bivalves are sustainable and, so far as we can see, cruelty-free. Mussels, clams and oysters – farmed, not dredged – may be the only seafood that a vegan can eat in good conscience.

(Prawns, who are crustaceans rather than fish or molluscs, show similar evidence to fish of experiencing pain. If acid is applied to their antennae, they react by flicking their tails immediately, then carrying out extended grooming of the antennae. But if an anaesthetic is applied to antennae before, the grooming is reduced.)

The good news is that oyster reefs are being restored in New York City, from Brooklyn to the Bronx, where they will have the additional benefit of protecting residents from storm damage. The UK's first offshore large-scale mussel farm has been built in Lyme Bay, Devon. Its chief limitation is how much people will eat. 'The mussels will grow pretty much anywhere,' says its co-founder, John Holmyard. He estimates that Britons eat only 10,000 tonnes of mussels a year – while the French eat fifteen times more, and the Spanish twenty-five times more.

Here is seafood that vegans can eat, confident that we aren't inflicting pain. It felt like a weird reprieve, like finding one remaining item on a wedding list that isn't either hideous or priced at £500.

There is another end to the spectrum – where inflicting even severe pain can be justified.

*

You expect animal research facilities to be sinister, nondescript places in the middle of nowhere – like landfill sites or Amazon warehouses. Some of them probably are. But others are bright, normal offices right under your nose.

In a basement of Guy's Hospital, near London Bridge, thousands of mice are waiting for their procedures. They are mostly white with red eyes and noses, and when the lid is taken from their box, they claw their way to the rim and try to perceive what lies beyond. They don't dare cross the threshold. You can guess that, in another world, they would be lovely pets.

The windowless facility has a strong musty smell. Its rooms hold a total of 7,500 boxes, stacked in racks of sixty. 'A lot of people say, it looks the same in every room,' says Stephen Woodley, who runs the facility. 'That's what we're going for – a clinical environment.'

Animal testing is perhaps the most toxic of all issues involving our relationship with other species – more divisive even than meat-eating or trophy-hunting. Gaining access to a lab is a test in itself, because the researchers know that a simple flap of publicity can trigger a hurricane of abusive letters and Internet posts. Some animal-lovers are outraged to learn, for example, that defects are induced in dogs in order to develop human medicines. For a time, as a student at Oxford, I would pass protestors against a new animal research lab almost daily. Their placards of damaged, deprived animals, particularly chimps in cages, stuck in the mind.

I myself once agreed to take part in medical tests when I was a student, answering an ad in a magazine offering a quick £2,000. I changed my mind when I realised I had no idea what I had signed up to. Unlike humans who take part in medical research, animals have no choice and they receive no benefit. They cannot give informed consent or back out at the last minute. We can chicken out, animals can't. At the end of the experiment, even if completely healthy, they are usually killed.

'I've had moments working with primates and you know it's the end of the study. I'll be honest, it just made you want to cry. I always felt they *knew*,' says Woodley, as he shows me around. 'Although I loved working with primates, I don't miss working with primates.'

British laboratories also tend to do little research on dogs, though Woodley fears that the work is simply being done in other countries, with laxer regulation. 'I think that's wrong,' he adds. He describes himself as someone who walks into a pet store and complains about animals who look terrible. Such an attitude is common among animal technicians, he says – 'You don't see many who aren't passionate about animals.'

In windowless laboratories like this, at least some research animals live much worse lives than farm animals. The justification is that the benefit to humans is potentially much greater. They don't suffer and die for our pleasure, but for our survival. They cannot be replaced by non-sentient beings, or at least that is the argument.

Woodley and I put on plastic aprons, hairnets and shoe covers, apply hand sanitiser, and cross the threshold into the research facility. The facility is focused on potential gene treatments for diseases including cancer. In the corridor I bump into James Arnold, a researcher, who insists that cancerous tumours are so complex that they cannot be simulated on chips or in Petri dishes. 'Replacing [animal testing] is going to be very difficult, at least in our lifetime.'

I didn't feel repulsed when I saw the mice. But I did feel sick when we turned into a small room, lined with tanks of frogs. Each tank was the size of two shoeboxes, and inside were eight xenopus – African clawed frogs. The tanks held nothing but water, frogs and eggs. No plants, no features, nothing that would simulate their native environment in pools and rivers of sub-Saharan Africa.

In the 1930s, scientists discovered that, if a drop of a pregnant woman's urine were injected into a xenopus, the frog would ovulate by the next day. This was the first mass pregnancy test, and it remained in use until the 1960s. Because of releases from laboratories and the pet trade, the frogs are now an invasive species in the USA, Japan, Chile, the UK, Italy and beyond. They may also have spread a deadly fungus that is killing amphibians worldwide. In the laboratories, they continue to be used because they produce lots of eggs that scientists can manipulate genetically.

Xenopus have odd, swollen bodies ('They're very difficult to pick up. It's a bar of soap, but it's moving,' explains Woodley), and they lie there in the water on top of each other, with their limbs stretched. Stickers indicated that many of the frogs had been there, in these barren conditions, for at least two years.

Woodley explained that some labs used fake lily pads. Real lily pads apparently 'cause problems for the filtration', and might not grow anyway, because of the lack of natural light. 'We're going to add some tunnels. In an ideal world, you'd have them in this big tank,' he adds, illustrating with his hands. We were obviously not in an ideal world.

Looking at the frogs in their tanks, I had virtually no idea of their experience of the world or whether their state felt like suffering. Anthropomorphising didn't feel much use. But research has found that an enriched environment can reduce the frogs' taste for cannibalism. There are mental processes of which we are unaware. The problem is that the thought afforded to primates and mice is not afforded to the frogs.

Finally, we headed over to see the fish. When people think of medical research, they don't think of fish. But zebrafish breed quickly, are cheaper than mice, and have equivalents of more than 80 per cent of the genes associated with human disease. They are tropical minnows, named for their dark blue and silver horizontal stripes (they still look as much like zebras as seahorses look like horses). Over the past decade they have become a fixture of medical experiments. In the UK, for every scientific procedure that takes place on a primate, there are 160 times more on fish. Zebrafish are more widely used in medical research than any other species except for mice. The data does not include zebrafish embryos under the age of five days, on which no legal restrictions are placed, because they are thought not to have the capacity for suffering.

This is a state-of-the-art facility, the largest standalone fish research unit in Europe. A robot works its way along the line of tanks, scanning the barcode on each one to ascertain the number and age of the fish inside, and then dispensing food. In each tank, between six and twelve zebrafish swim around in a couple of litres of water. Like the frog tanks, these are bare – except for a couple with small plastic green leaves.

The only other enrichment in the fish's environment is running water and live food. The lab manager, Bruno, shows me a video on his phone of a tank with a tube installed; the zebrafish decline to swim through the tube. 'They're just not interested!' he says; besides, he worries enrichment will prevent laboratory technicians from doing health checks.

In a typical experiment, zebrafish will be bred with genetic mutations to study the growth of cancers or muscle deformities. This allows scientists to work out which genes might facilitate, or inhibit, a disease, and test potential therapies and medicines. Most of the procedures are said to cause only 'mild' suffering, but around 40,000 are rated as moderate or severe. For a zebrafish, moderate suffering can be anything from swimming problems, resulting from having leukaemia induced (as soon as any problems are detected, the fish is killed), or the stress of hearing a loud sound intended to induce tinnitus. Severe suffering can arise when toxic substances or drugs are tested; in some cases, the law prevents the fish being humanely killed even when they are suffering – the researchers must use 'death as an endpoint'.

Because research labs are far from the public eye, abuse is possible. In 2019 activists obtained footage from a well-known laboratory in Hamburg, Germany, showing macaques being held in metal neck braces. Their cages had nothing for the monkeys to do or rest on – just metal bars. Several animals seem disturbed, even when not undergoing procedures – running round their cages. One, held in a neck brace, spun round repeatedly. Beagles lay in cages with blood on the floor. The laboratory was closed afterwards. As you read this, it's possible that other animals are enduring similar horrific conditions, due to poor research practices and a lack of inspections.

In at least some western countries, you can treat laboratory animals horrifically without breaking any rules. In early 2020, researchers at Harvard and São Paulo universities made news headlines with a study that suggested that stress did indeed cause hair to go grey. What went unreported was how the scientists reached this conclusion – by inflicting huge stress on mice. Some mice were restrained – that is, placed in small Perspex tubes barely longer than their own bodies – for four hours a day, for twenty days. Others were subjected to unpredictable stress – such as having their cage tilted, their bedding wet and lights switched on and off. A third group had injections of drugs that cause pain, along with some painkillers.

To inflict huge pain on mice in the possible hope of finding a treatment for grey hair is surely indefensible. Such experiments do have to pass ethical oversight committees. But two-thirds of the people who sit on such committees are themselves animal researchers, who unsurprisingly tend to say yes. Official studies have found that US oversight boards approve studies that do not meet federal standards. And federal standards are hardly stringent: they place no restrictions, for example, on the use of cephalopods in research. A laboratory of the University of Chicago is breeding thousands of squid, cuttlefish and octopuses, calling them 'the new kids on the block' of scientific research. One recent experiment at Johns Hopkins involved antisocial octopuses being given Ecstasy to see the effects on their behaviour (drugged octopuses, like drugged humans, touched each other more frequently). Octopuses' uniqueness make them fascinating subjects for research into sensation and limb regeneration. But that same uniqueness also makes it difficult for scientists to know how to treat them – and even whether anaesthetics will numb the pain to which the animals are subjected.

Standards are higher elsewhere. Cephalopods have been given the same protection as vertebrates in research since 1991 in Canada and since 2013 in the EU. The grey-hair experiment with mice would probably not have been allowed in the UK, where every experiment is assessed by an ethical review body and then by the Home Office, which balances the potential benefits against the likely harms. The UK prides itself on being strict. Chimpanzees and gorillas are not used in research; no animal testing is permitted for cosmetics. All animals, with limited exceptions such as fish larvae and fruit flies, are included in annual statistics published by the government.

What's surprising is how much of the public would like to go further. In 2001, 65 per cent of Americans said medical testing on animals was morally acceptable, and 26 per cent disagreed. By 2019, the split had tightened to 51 per cent to 44 per cent – animal testing is no more morally acceptable than wearing fur. Women are predominantly against, men are in favour. In the UK, only two-thirds of people accept the use of animals for medical research where there is no alternative. Because young people are more likely to oppose animal testing, there will probably soon be a majority against it. At the moment, there is almost nothing that individual consumers can do if they feel this way. To opt out of taking prescription medicines would be ridiculous. They might, however, want to opt out of cosmetic botox injections – some of which are still tested on mice, causing paralytic harm. Because botox is an injection, it is not included in the ban on testing cosmetics on animals.

Interestingly the RSPCA, which is not against livestock or fish farming, wants to phase out all animal research and testing. Penny Hawkins, the head of its research animals department, started working in the field in the 1990s, when most mice were housed in barren cages and seldom given adequate pain relief. Things have improved, but Hawkins argues that too many experiments that take place cannot be replicated – perhaps because of the barren laboratory conditions. 'It's poor quality science,' she says. 'It's a waste of animal lives.' She argues that too little investment is directed towards alternatives to animal research. Ultimately, those alternatives include focusing on health policy to reduce cancer rates, rather than overly relying on pharmaceuticals.

While Woodley emphasises the genetic differences between animals in labs and those outside, Hawkins argues the animals have exactly the same evolutionary needs as their wild counterparts. 'If you went to somebody's house and they had a pet like that what would you think?' Gravel – or even a picture of gravel – would benefit the fish, Hawkins suggests.

My visit to the lab underlined how easily we can disregard those species that are most different to us. The risks of animal research are particularly acute for fish, whose experience of the world is little understood and who rarely provoke empathy in most people. Researchers are emotionally driven to reduce the number of monkeys in their facilities; it's hard to be confident that they feel the same towards zebrafish.

Animals – collectively, if not individually – can benefit from animal experiments: stem-cell treatments are offered to horses, and chemotherapy to pets. For conditions where no animal drugs have been developed, some vets just use human medicines. But for fish, this silver lining falls flat: few fish are taken to the vet.

Taking animals' lives seriously would mean doing things differently. If animals are useful to research because they are biologically similar to humans, then we also must accept that they are emotionally similar – in needing stimulation and experiencing discomfort. Given the benefits we are deriving from these animals, it seems fair to err on the side of caution.

In 1959, two British scientists, Bill Russell and Rex Burch, came up with an approach to improve the lives of animals in research: replacement of animals where possible, reduction of the number of conscious animals used, and refinement of the methods to reduce suffering. The Three Rs, as the principles are known, have taken hold since. But they aren't enough. A broader approach, already contained in EU regulations, asks whether the research is truly necessary, and emphasises the need to give animals good lives in the laboratory. No animal should suffer severely for a long period of time. Scientists will be slow in embracing new methods, unless they are pushed.

I had seen live fish on wildlife documentaries and dead fish in markets. But it was perhaps in that London laboratory that I felt most connected to the fish – that I understood what we shared with them. Animal testing, when necessary for human health, does not require suspending one's love for animals; it means recognising our debt to them. We should find space to recognise the animals who have contributed towards our research. If medicine bottles listed the species on which the drug had been tested, we would surely feel a greater sense of responsibility.

*

In northern California, there is a tribe called the Winnemem Wintu. In the 1940s, the Shasta Dam was finished – at the time the second tallest concrete dam in the world – and 90 per cent of the tribe's ancestral lands were flooded. At least tens of thousands of Chinook salmon used to come each year up the McCloud River (also known by the tribe as the Winnemem Waywacket); since the dam was built, none have been able to make the journey.

The Winnemem Wintu have a prophecy: when there are no more salmon, there will be no more Winnemem Wintu. Given that the tribe currently numbers only 126, the prospect is not fanciful. The Winnemem Wintu creation story tells how the salmon gave their voices to humans, and so humans assumed a duty to speak for the salmon. The Winnemem Wintu believe that they failed in that duty by not preventing the Shasta Dam from being built. In 2010 a small group of Winnemem Wintu boarded a plane to New Zealand, where a batch of Chinook salmon had been successfully introduced a century earlier. There they apologised to the salmon and asked them to return to northern California. That alone was not expected to solve the matter, and it did not. The Winnemem Wintu raised more than $100,000 in crowdfunding for their plan to bring the salmon home, and California's Bureau of Reclamation has given hundreds of thousands of dollars more – to bring the salmon back from New Zealand, and to build a route round the dam that would allow the salmon to return. But at the same time, the bureau is planning to raise the Shasta Dam and flood the remainder of the Winnemem Wintu's ancestral lands.

For Pacific salmon in California, the prospects are bleak, even where dams are not a problem. The culprits include drought, overfishing, and farms (from almonds to marijuana) taking river water for irrigation. Even if those problems can be overcome, California's rivers are simply becoming too warm. The Winnemem Wintu's effort to preserve a relationship with the salmon seems doomed. But their desire to take responsibility for animals who might appear outside their control is a lesson.

The only sea or river creatures that we have really taken responsibility for are whales. Stopping whaling was possible partly because so few people relied on whale meat and oil, and partly because the number had fallen so much that there was no industry left. By the 1970s, just two countries, the Soviet Union and Japan, accounted for nearly 90 per cent of whale killings. Today, even if more people wanted to eat whales, they'd be quickly put off: the levels of mercury mean the meat is toxic.

Whaling often seems distant now. Galicia was once a centre of Spain's whaling industry, and campaigners sank two whaling boats there in 1980. In a museum old photos show men standing around carcasses on the shore, and women, with pink gloves and red aprons, hacking into huge pieces of flesh. In the ocean, the effects of our whaling past resonate more strongly. The hunting of great whales off Alaska left orcas in need of new sources of food; the orcas settled on sea otters. This triggered a cascade effect, because the otters no longer controlled the population of sea urchins that eat kelp forests. (A sea otter can eat 1,000 sea urchins a day.) We can only guess how overfishing will reverberate on land and sea.

The problem is that fishing is even harder to cut out than whaling. There are an estimated 3 billion people for whom fish is their primary source of protein. People in poorer countries, particularly in Africa and Asia, don't have another option. But soon climate change will squeeze the fish they have available. Warmer temperatures have already reduced the amount of fish that can be sustainably taken from the oceans, according to the Intergovernmental Panel on Climate Change. Fish populations are expected to fall in Latin America, Africa, India – and the south Pacific, which is among the world's most heavily fished regions. For those of us who live in the EU and US, this is a test. We can't keep taking so much wild fish from our own waters, because of overfishing. We also won't be able to keep importing so much from the tropics, because of climate change and local demand.

A world without fishing would come at a cost: it would mean that more agricultural land was needed to produce food for humans, and less available for wildlife. We have no precise way of weighing up different species like this. In practice we do decide that it's better to kill thousands of fish than one whale, even though the whale might yield the same weight of meat. There's an arbitrary element to this. What we can try to do is to tread lightly – leaving as many fish as possible in the sea, while returning as much farmland as possible to wildlife. The sea is not quite the fearsome domain it was in Herman Melville's time; nor is it a place that will always have plenty more fish for us.

We need a fishing industry that treats fish like animals who need to be killed humanely and not kept in barren enclosures. Fish farming is as hellish as livestock farming. Ethical wild fishing would find a way to kill fish with care. This might increase the cost of fish, but we could have cheaper meat too, if we didn't take any precautions when slaughtering livestock. Right now, the industry that produces most of our fish is cruel and wasteful. The only seafoods that consistently pass the animal test are farmed mussels, oysters and clams.

For all the damage it does, the fishing industry is still widely seen as more bucolic than brutal. One day it'll be taught as a masterclass of public relations. There's another way that people kill animals, which has the opposite problem. Hunting has a terrible reputation, but it may have a less brutal reality than we realise.

5. HOLIDAYS FOR PSYCHOPATHS

The man who does not like to see, hunt, photograph, or otherwise outwit birds or animals is hardly normal. He is supercivilised, and I for one do not know how to deal with him.
Aldo Leopold

It was a cold Monday afternoon in November when I first went to kill a deer. I'd made arrangements with a country estate. I laced up my walking boots and wondered whether I could really put a bullet through an animal.

This wasn't something I ever expected to do. As far as I remember, I had never killed a mammal or a bird, and never wanted to. I'd never flushed a guinea pig down the toilet as a child, or hit a fox with a car as a teenager. Whenever I found my cat Crumble toying with mice, I – like any limp-hearted liberal – tried UN-style humanitarian intervention. I had once shot a few clay pigeons, and even that just felt like a waste of pottery. Was hunting fair on animals? Absolutely not.

This probably all started with *Bambi*. The Disney film was just about my only childhood experience of hunting. It's the story of a young deer who frolics freely in the forest until a firearm intervenes. You don't actually see Bambi's mother being shot, but you do see the buck realising that the centre of his world has disappeared. 'Your mother can't be with you any more,' Bambi is told by his father – it's hard to imagine a crueller moment. It's also unmistakeably human: Disney animators drew inspiration from pictures of baby faces. I watched it with Eliza, aged three, but Susie insisted that we fast-forward through the scene. It was probably safest for all of us.

When *Bambi* was released in 1942, it outraged American hunters and lost money. The funny thing is that Walt Disney wanted it to be harsher: he wanted to show the hunter being burnt to death by a forest fire. You can imagine why this brutal karma didn't make the final cut of a kids' movie. Even so *Bambi* inspired animal activists, and seeped into the mainstream. 'I think that made me grow up thinking hunting isn't cool,' Paul McCartney has recalled. In 2018 a judge in Missouri ordered a deer poacher to watch *Bambi* at least once a month, while serving a year-long sentence, to realise the seriousness of his crime. *

Bambi's legacy must have stuck with me subliminally into my twenties and thirties. I cheered when the UK banned fox-hunting in 2004. Why would anyone dress up in a top hat and torture a fox, *often on a weekend*? When Cecil the lion was shot by an American dentist in 2015, the Internet exploded in fury at his agonising death. 'How is that fun?' vented the comedian Jimmy Kimmel, in one of the most shared clips. 'Is it that difficult for you to get an erection that you need to kill things that are stronger than you?' It wasn't difficult to pick a side. Thereafter, every so often my Twitter feed filled with revulsion at a new case of a trophy-hunter callously posing with a deer or a giraffe or an elephant.

Hunting was already a morality story before Facebook came along. But social media has never met a subject that it can't simplify further. Online the animal test for hunting was an open-and-shut case. Even hunting's supporters seem to have been losing the faith. Between 1996 and 2016, the number of American adults who hunted fell by 2.5 million – to fewer than 5 per cent of the population. On the east and west coasts, it's fewer than 3 per cent. More Americans go on birdwatching trips than go hunting. In Austria, a country with a strong hunting tradition, fewer than one in sixty people have a hunting licence; in Germany,

---

* *Bambi* also shaped our attitudes to forest fires, contributing to the practice of suppressing fires in the western US. Many land managers now argue this has been counter-productive, because it creates more flammable forests.

it's one in 240. A majority of British people favoured a ban on stag-hunting and fox-hunting as long ago as 1958; already by then, only one in five Brits lived in rural areas. In 2019, 85 per cent of the public said they backed a ban on trophy-hunting, which makes banning trophy-hunting more popular than drinking alcohol.

Hunting has come to symbolise human power over other species, and whether we are really prepared to restrain ourselves. In our society, where abattoirs, fish farms and medical testing laboratories are all out of sight, hunting is surprisingly visible, because hunters, unlike slaughterhouse operatives, post bloody photos of themselves on Instagram. The idea that killing animals for fun is immoral goes back centuries, including to the Puritans. Today little provokes an emotional response like a video of an elephant collapsing to his knees, fatally wounded, or a leopard, left lifeless on the ground. The Campaign to Ban Trophy Hunting says killing animals for pleasure is 'cruel, unnecessary, and has no place in a civilised society'. Ricky Gervais, the comedian, is even blunter: hunters are psychopaths. I guess that means that hunting tours are holidays for psychopaths.

But after working in an abattoir and on farms, I felt less comfortable on the bandwagon. Both farming and fishing had reminded me that some form of death was inevitable. What repulsed me about farming wasn't death so much as pointless lives. What repulsed me about fishing was the indiscriminate, inhumane methods. Was I against any human killing any animal? No – I was against humans thoughtlessly killing animals on a massive scale, especially if they'd been deprived of a good life first. Unlike animals on farms or in zoos, hunted animals live in the wild (with some exceptions). They could more easily have the lives for which they had evolved.

What's more, in theory, hunting had a rationale. Across the world, ecosystems are off-kilter. The US has too many feral horses, Italy has 2 million wild boar, and so on. This is largely our fault: we have killed some predators, spread invasive species, and built over natural habitats. If we don't cull animals now, we save the individuals but ruin the ecosystem. We have removed the predators – we have to replace them. We have interfered so much already that we can't step back. Hunting exposes us to the complexities of the natural world, and of the variations in how we treat it.

Once, when I lived in Colombia, the bus I was travelling in came to an abrupt halt. This was never a good sign. It generally meant that the bus driver had something better to do. I looked around, and wondered what misfortune had befallen us. Instead, I saw my fellow passengers pressed against the back window. We were in a wetland, rich in wildlife – maybe someone had seen a hummingbird. 'Divine!' said one passenger. 'So beautiful!' added another. Then I realised that they were taking pictures of a deer – a single white-tailed deer.

To me, this was baffling. Britain has a lot of deer, because our ancestors introduced new species for hunting and wiped out predators – lynx, wolves and bears. No one knows how many deer there are with any precision, but the number appears to be well above a million. Deer like to live on the fringes of the forest. In modern Britain, they have lots of suitable habitats, because agricultural subsidies now promote farms with trees and hedgerows, allowing the deer to browse and move around easily. I find deer beautiful, but they eat so much that other species cannot thrive.

The same has happened in the US. White-tailed deer were once wiped from much of the country, but there are now an estimated 30 million of them, largely free from predators. If that statistic doesn't bring it home, try this one: the country has nearly 2 million vehicle accidents a year involving animals – three-quarters of them involving deer. In Colombia, it's rare to see a deer. In the US, it isn't even rare to hit one: every year, one in every 150 drivers do. That costs more than $1 billion in damage, as well as perhaps 150 human lives. Scotland has around thirty deer-related road accidents a day.

Deer have a hefty effect on other species. In areas where they graze, there are around 40 per cent fewer insects above ground and half the number of spiders' webs. That's obvious when you think about it: the browsing deer eat the shrubs and saplings on which the spiders can spin their webs. There are also fewer places for songbirds to nest. When food becomes rare, the deer reduce the numbers of chipmunks and squirrels, by competing with them for food. After forest fires, deer can prevent regeneration: an experiment found that the diversity of trees reduced after a controlled fire, because the deer ate saplings such as oak.

I was an animal-loving vegan, but I wanted to live in the real world. I didn't believe the deer's existence should marginalise so many other species. Maybe someone had to kill the deer. What did it matter to Bambi if the person pulling the trigger took pleasure in it? What did it matter to the animals if the person pulling the trigger was ... me?

*

The Cornbury Park estate is an hour or so west of London, and advertises the opportunity to shoot surplus deer. I arrive at a set of stone buildings, where a man my age called Tom shows me into a small office. There are a dozen antlers on the wall, along with a poster that reads: 'VEGETARIAN: loose translation of old Indian word meaning BAD HUNTER'. This is not an ideal start.

As luck would have it, it is Armistice Day. I can't see a direct contradiction between remembering the sacrifice of human life in war, and trying to kill an innocent deer. Even so, I feel the timing could be better.

Tom has a few days' stubble and a few years' experience of rich city-dwellers who want to shoot deer in theory but maybe not in practice. 'See how you feel when you have a live deer in front of you,' he says. 'You might say you can't do it. You might be so excited that the barrel is going all over the place.' Note to self: don't be so nervous you can't pull the trigger, don't be so eager that you appear like a trainee serial killer. A balancing act.

'At the end of the day it's a living animal. Some people can shoot it and some people can't,' says Tom. 'There is absolutely no pressure.'

Well, there is a bit of pressure – in the form of a regular hunter called Peter, who has stopped by the office before heading on his own deer stalk. Peter is wearing a tweed flat cap, tweed jacket, tweed trousers – an outfit that I have only ever considered wearing as fancy dress. He swells with laddish bonhomie.

'I saw a buck out there with your name on it, Henry,' he says, pushing his iPhone towards me so I can see a blurry photo. 'You'll probably be able to shoot it from the car,' he winks. I make another mental note, to disregard anything Peter says.

Tom and I drive a cart to a small quarry, which serves as a shooting range. He pins a piece of paper with a target on one side of the quarry, and sets up a rifle on the other side. I push my cheek against the wooden stock and peer through the sight. This is it, I think, this is an actual gun. 'Take your time,' says Tom. 'And then pull the trigger.'

It cannot be overemphasised how pathetic it is to pull the trigger. 'It's quite lacklustre,' says Tom. Yes, it is. It takes less effort than cutting through a carrot, but it unleashes the force of a ceiling collapsing. Shooting a rifle is only a bit more physically strenuous than typing a query into Google. You personally kill an animal in the same sense that you personally search the Internet – the technology does the hard work.

Peter, meanwhile, has turned up and is wondering why his own bullets are going astray. He also complains of people on Facebook calling hunters 'pigs'.

We are ready to shoot at some live targets. Tom leads me off a path into some woodland. Three deer look up, and run away immediately. If they were thinking of returning, they presumably change their mind when I accidentally crunch a twig beneath my foot, and then can't stop myself from coughing. Stalking by foot has failed.

Instead we drive to a sitting position – a small wooden box on stilts overlooking an opening in the trees, like a narrow fairway. A couple of deer are grazing nearby. Tom says this is a good sign.

Two muntjac deer – their bodies low to the ground like large rodents – appear in the bracken twenty metres in front of us. Muntjac, originally from east Asia, were introduced to the UK in the nineteenth century; they are small animals so no one took much interest in hunting them until their numbers spiralled out of control a few decades ago. In front of me, one is chasing the other. Tom moves the gun into position. The larger of the two is a mother – and we can't shoot her in case she has a dependent fawn, who would starve. The smaller one is a legitimate target. We're not shooting Bambi's mother, we're shooting adolescent Bambi. I take a breath.

It is a principle of deer-hunting that you do not shoot to hit – you shoot to kill. This is a clear difference between hunting deer and hunting birds, where any hit is acceptable and where birds are often 'winged', meaning they will likely be caught by dogs or fly off to suffer elsewhere. No self-respecting deer-hunter is happy to see an injured animal run off into the forest, to a prolonged painful death. The target is a four-inch circle on the animal's chest. So we need the deer to 'broadside' – to present a clear shot. If the muntjac broadsides now, and if my shot is accurate, his or her pain should be momentary. But the deer remains in the bracken, little more than a brown shadow through the gun scope. The deer rustles off, unaware.

After this, nothing happens. No deer appear. In the treehouse, Tom and I sit next to each other in silence, connected only by the mist of old-school masculinity. Maybe this is what it felt like when fathers and sons hung out in the 1950s. Half an hour passes by, then another half an hour and we get no nearer to killing anything. If this were an abattoir, we would be going bankrupt. It is so numbingly cold that I wonder if I have fallen asleep and shot myself.

Eventually a deer appears in the distance. I size her up through the gun, her chest is in the crosshairs. In that moment, I feel much less than I thought I would. But the deer is too distant to guarantee a clean hit. She retreats into the forest, and I feel a pang of disappointment. 'If it had been fifty yards closer, we would have taken a look,' says Tom.

The cold bites, the sky darkens. Eventually, after nearly two hours in the hut, Tom has had enough. 'Better knock it on the head, or we'll lose the light.' Tom blames the cold, the rain, and the swirling wind, which he says gets up in the deer's nostrils and prevents them from settling down to graze. I nod.

He drives me back to the office, where I hand over a wad of notes. My afternoon of stalking plus instruction has cost £180, which feels sharp for the privilege of growing cold in a wooden box.

After saying goodbye to Tom, I am unable to book a taxi back to the station. So I trudge along a country path, lit only by moonlight. A deer moves in the bushes beside me, closer than any I saw with my gun.

In the pub, I start talking to a local man, who reveals he hates hunting animals – and the posh folk who do it. 'They're terrible people. Some of them,' he says. This strikes at a truth: in Britain, hunting is about class. More precisely, it's about an attitude of ownership – of dominance over the land and the other people who live on it. You can trace a line from the medieval kings who declared the deer forests off limits to commoners right through to the men who shoot on large estates today.

I realised that I hadn't found the gun or the possibility of killing hard to get used to. For me, the biggest obstacle to being a hunter was the feeling that I didn't really belong at the Cornbury Park estate, that these weren't my friends. In other words, it was nothing to do with the animals at all. Once I focused on the animals, I could see hunting without the baggage or the Instagram filter. It could be a functional activity – game management.

*

Why does hunting seem immoral? No animal-lover should relish the suffering and the loss of life. Nor should they relish the disappearance of animal abundance. We can be fairly confident that hunting played a significant role in wiping out large mammals, such as giant ground sloths the size of modern-day elephants, at the end of the last Ice Age. These creatures were so enormous, so fantastical that I still struggle to believe that humans ever existed alongside them.

As the imbalance between hunters and animals has grown, hunting has seemed less defensible. In the nineteenth century, gun technology soared and animal populations plummeted. In North America, hunters shot entire species into oblivion. Millions of bison were reduced to a few hundred. Passenger pigeons were once the most abundant bird on the continent, numbering in the billions and capable, according to Henry David Thoreau, of swallowing acorns whole. Uncontrolled hunting drove them to extinction in barely a century, the last bird dying in Cincinnati Zoo in 1914.

Meanwhile, imperialist Brits wandered round Africa blasting to pieces everything they could find. Roualeyn Gordon-Cumming – an

Old Etonian who toured southern Africa in the 1840s – boasted about his hunts in a way that can only be described as sadistic. He said of killing one rhino: 'I sent a bullet through his ribs to teach him manners.' Such adventurers were greeted as heroes. They saw themselves merely applying Darwin's theory of survival of the fittest. In reality their hunting had no justification except human entertainment. One hunter, Frederick Selous, was at least honest enough to act embarrassed, on the basis that large elephants were easier to hit than game animals in Britain.

But hunting wasn't always so wasteful. There was a time when humans were themselves at regular risk of being killed by all sorts of animals, and had yet to learn how to cultivate crops for food. The question of whether it was morally right to kill an animal presumably didn't arise initially. As human societies became more complex, hunter-gatherers developed intricate behaviours and beliefs around hunting. After all, among peoples such as the Yupik of Alaska, humans were not considered superior to animals, but as equals to them. The animals' deaths were rationalised as part of a relationship of respect, stewardship and sometimes reincarnation: Yupik mythology held that an animal presents themselves to be killed, and that their spirit gathers in the bladder, before moving on to another existence. Bladder feasts were held in winter to mark this.

Some of these beliefs and practices, including the bladder feasts, continue today. In Canada, some Chipewyans argue that animals cannot be killed without their consent; this assuages any human guilt in killing them, but also creates an obligation to kill them correctly, lest the animals refuse to give their consent in the future. Killing correctly has not always meant killing without suffering: the !Kung of the Kalahari killed animals with poisoned arrows; a wildebeest or a giraffe would take at least a day to die.

Hunter-gatherers ascribe intelligence, intentions and moods to animals. They also kill some animals who many western eco-tourists would regard as untouchable – in the Amazon, Yanomami kill monkeys, toucans and parrots; near the Kalahari, the !Kung kill giraffes and ostriches. In doing so, they challenge the way that we compartmentalise animals. We think some animals are too intelligent to be killed; hunter-gatherers may think all animals are intelligent and all can be killed. There are indigenous communities around the world for whom hunting remains vital, in areas from the Arctic to the Amazon, where agriculture has limited potential. But even in these places hunting is imperilled, partly because it clashes with the perceived needs of animals. Inuits are accused by animal rights campaigners and conservationists of brutally killing whales and seals, although Greenpeace now supports their whaling. The !Kung hunt less than they used to: they are subject to conservation restrictions, and some animals must be reserved for trophy-hunters. Canada's Łutsël K'é Dene First Nation used to find caribou 'everywhere and anywhere'; now they have temporarily stopped killing them, because the caribou's numbers have tumbled due to climate change and human activity.

In the nineteenth century, western hunters were confronted by the devastation their guns had wrought. Frederick Selous turned conservationist in the 1870s when he realised elephants were disappearing from southern Africa, partly due to his own actions. The western argument for ethical hunting coalesced around two ideas: respect for the animals by limiting their suffering, and appreciation of the healthy environment by protecting the ecological balance. Probably its two foremost advocates were Aldo Leopold and Selous's friend, Theodore Roosevelt.

Leopold, the great American conservationist, shot wolves, coyotes, deer and birds. For him, hunting was typically American – a reminder of how the country had been settled. Sportsmen had no audience, no leaders, 'no referee but the Almighty'. They, like bird-lovers, were motivated by 'the thrill to beauty' of America's landscape. He emphasised hunters' restraint – it could be as noble *not* to shoot an animal as to shoot one – and he himself often opted for a home-made bow and arrow over a reliable gun.

For Leopold hunting was not something to be excused. It was part of 'the biological basis of human nature'. It also bound people to the land. 'Every ground is a hunting ground, whether it lies between you and the curbstone, or in those illimitable woods where rolls the

Oregon,' he said. As many people as possible should hunt: Leopold complained that European hunting was limited to the upper classes, when it should be 'a poor man's right'. Today nine in ten American hunters are men, and 97 per cent are white. But unlike in the UK, hunting remains remarkably cross-class – roughly as popular with those who went to college as those who didn't, with those who earn $30,000 a year as those who earn more than $150,000.

The idea of a great conservationist also being an enthusiastic hunter does not really translate in the twenty-first century. Imagine David Attenborough dusting off his shotgun between BBC series, or Jane Goodall posing with a dead giraffe on Facebook. A century ago it was not uncontroversial either. John Muir, the other leading American conservationist of the era, wrote in 1903, 'Mr Roosevelt, when are you going to get beyond the boyishness of killing?' Teddy Roosevelt was famous for shooting everything he could. Mark Twain, who despite being a Republican considered Roosevelt the worst president in history, wrote a satire about him bravely hunting a bear who turns out to be a cow. But Roosevelt protected 230 million acres of land, a legacy that would not have been possible without the imperative of hunting. Today hunting and fishing licences – plus taxes on guns, ammunition, archery equipment, angling equipment and boat fuel – yield nearly 60 per cent of the budget of the state wildlife agencies that administer 464 million acres of America.

Roosevelt also inspired toy Teddy bears, after a cartoon showed him sparing a lassoed young bear on a hunting trip in Mississippi in 1902. The cartoon symbolised the hunter's ethic of restraint, although in reality the bear was unceremoniously knifed to death by a member of Roosevelt's entourage. What isn't in doubt is that, like Leopold, Roosevelt had an unusual appreciation of nature. He hated animal cruelty, loved natural history and as an adult buried his pets in a special graveyard.

Ethical hunters want to assure themselves that an individual animal has the chance to escape. It is considered unethical to poach deer by shining a spotlight so that the animals freeze on the spot; in the US it's also often illegal. Today some hunters – blessed with GPS, night vision and guns that can hit targets 500 metres away – sometimes wonder if they have too much of an advantage. This is as much a question of conscience as game management, but it underpins the ethos of restraint. To hunt ethically, it's not just what you kill, it's how you kill them.

So this is the blueprint for ethical hunting: hunting is a means to protect land and wild animal populations. It is also not bloodthirsty or easy. It is an appreciation of nature. The animals have a relatively painless death. On these terms, to truly understand *Bambi*, you would really need to know whether Bambi's mother was killed cleanly, whether the deer population was sustainable, and whether, without hunting, the land might otherwise be cleared for agriculture. OK, it doesn't sound like Netflix will be rushing for the rights.

I wanted to see whether Leopold and Roosevelt's legacy was alive. So I emailed a company called Diana Hunting Tours. It calls itself 'the world's largest hunting travel office'; critics call it shameful. Diana offers shoots on six continents – from musk ox in Greenland ($4,695 for three days) to big game in Zimbabwe ($14,495 for five days). It promises that all these hunts are 'ethically justifiable' and 'sustainable'; indeed, some hunts are even explicitly advertised as 'For the Sake of the Animals'. A few days later, I was signed up for a trip to Poland.

*

The holiday for psychopaths began at Berlin train station. Jens Høgh, a wiry man with a wiry beard and khaki trousers, was waiting for me under a large McDonald's sign.

It soon hit me that Jens was also the most enthusiastic hunter that I had ever met. On the six-hour drive from Berlin to our lodge in central Poland, he talked about hunting the whole way. Or at least I assume he did – I fell asleep for some of the journey.

A year earlier he had narrowly survived a pulmonary embolism – 'the doctor said, I don't understand how you are still alive' – and the experience had convinced him to dedicate his life to spreading a proper understanding of hunting. He talked about hunting wild boar near his home in Sweden, hunting a troublesome elephant in Zimbabwe, and hunting giraffes in Namibia. A giraffe, he argued, was just 'a lot of meat in a funny shape'.

In Jens's view, hunters had been unprepared for the backlash following the killing of Cecil the lion. They hadn't foreseen how a generation brought up on cute animal videos would view photos of hunters with dead creatures. 'It was an extremely closed community. Hunting organisations didn't used to communicate at all to non-hunters ... Two years ago every hunter would take trophy photos as a memento. Nobody thought about it. The only people who saw the photos were hunters. Now 99 per cent of the people who see the photos are not hunters. Hunters still take them but they are slowly learning not to post them on social media.'

So Jens was taking the fight to the anti-hunters. He had tried a stunt of auctioning big game to the highest bidder. He had written an open letter to celebrities opposed to hunting – Trevor Noah, Ricky Gervais, Kevin Pietersen – asking if they wanted to save a South African rhino (opening bid: $680,000). The response was 'just complete silence', said Jens, who seemed genuinely baffled.

Undeterred, Jens had then written to a larger group of animal-lovers – including Lewis Hamilton, Ed Sheeran and Boris Johnson's partner Carrie Symonds – saying they could save ten Namibian giraffes if they outbid hunters. Unsurprisingly, there was again no response. Jens saw this as proving his point: 'Nobody wants an old giraffe. Why should they? What would they do with it?' He went to Namibia as planned and with his group, shot the ten giraffes.

'I don't ask anyone to like hunting. But I ask people to accept it or find an alternative system. People have disliked hunting for as long as I can remember – so they have had time to find an alternative.'

Hunting was not exactly in Jens's blood. He grew up in Denmark, where his father, a mechanical engineer, bought a small plot of land in a spasm of rural nostalgia, but forbade his young son to hunt on it. Jens initially enjoyed taking photos of animals, but became curious about hunting after talking to an old man who did some farm work for his father. He waited for his father to leave the property, then borrowed his gun and taught himself to shoot deer. He was aged eleven; four years later, he was hunting legally.

'As soon as I got my licence, I was a poacher on my father's farm. My father likes to discuss things. So we had a lot of heated discussions,' recalled Jens. As his enthusiasm grew, his father's opposition hardened. At one point, Høgh senior even gave up eating all meat to try and prove his point. But to no avail. His son had caught the hunting bug.

Now forty-eight, Jens estimated that he has spent about 2,000 days hunting – the equivalent of five and a half years. 'It's much more a lifestyle than a sport,' he said. Thinking of hunting as a sport was 'very British and American'.

We were in Poland to meet a group of Swedish hunters, who had paid a sizeable sum for three days shooting wild boar and deer. It was a driven hunt: the hunters would stand in a fixed position, while beaters would walk with their dogs to harry the game towards the guns.

Boar numbers had an ecological impact, but they also brought health risks for livestock and humans. African swine fever was threatening to arrive in the area, and so the Polish government – which owns the nearly 10,000-hectare plot of fields and forest – wanted as many hogs as possible dead. There is some evidence that recreational hunting isn't particularly good at reducing populations: the pigs are good at learning to avoid hunters, and at escaping via nearby fields. Hunters want easy kills, so landowners have an incentive to ensure they are plentiful. But here the need to kill boar seems very real.

'They're everywhere!' said Hubert, the person in charge of organising the hunt. Hubert – a large man who carried a clipboard – expressed occasional disdain of 'eco-terrorists', the government and anyone else who purported to know more about managing the forest than he did.

Among Hubert's grievances at the time was the ban on shooting wolves, whose numbers were growing in Poland. 'It is easier to say you shot a beater by accident than you shot a wolf!' That reminded him that a beater had been killed in Poland three weeks earlier, by a bullet that probably ricocheted off a rock. I felt my survival chances were still better than the boars'.

On the first drive, I was put next to a man called Erland, who took off his camouflage rucksack and started marking out his position in the frozen leaves. We stood there in silence, waiting for the animals to arrive.

A sow appeared – much larger than I expected – fifty metres away. She hesitated behind a tree then trotted off. Six, seven young pigs followed her, now too far away for Erland to shoot. The man a hundred metres further down the line did try his luck. I wasn't prepared for the noise of the rifle shot. It thudded into my ears; goodness knows how the actual bullet feels.

There were two more bangs from the other direction followed by news, over the radio, that a boar had been shot. We strode across, and saw the carcass – a large grey pig, with the bloodied mouth of a boxer and a bullet hole between his eyes. The shot killed the animal but somehow he kept running, until the hunter, Per, fired another one into his chest. 'They don't realise they're dead for thirty seconds,' explained Jens. He showed me how to check the animal was dead by poking one of the open eyes.

Steam rose off the body. The boar had been slit open lengthwise, his internal organs removed, so as to protect the meat. A bloodied animal is never a pretty sight. But the wild boar was less gruesome than the bodies I had seen in the abattoir and on the farm. He looked like an animal that should actually exist – a well-proportioned, hairy hog, unlike his cousins that had been domesticated into miniature meat Zeppelins.

We moved on to the next drive, and the pattern repeated. We lined up, fifty metres apart down a track, and waited for the animals to appear.

The sky was blue, the leaves were frozen underfoot. We were surrounded by beech and oak trees. It wasn't particularly wild – you could hear chainsaws and traffic, and dirt tracks headed off in all directions. But there was plenty of time to consider the big questions. Questions that, in my case, included, why did I not put on a second pair of socks?

'Many people are getting into these driven hunts. There's a lot happening, a lot of excitement,' said Erland, as we waited by a tree trunk. It wasn't excitement like a football match or a decent conversation. It was a quiet, existential connection to the natural world. This was the world that I shut out every day, when, in that pre-coronavirus era, I went to work in an office. This was the world on which human existence depends. My senses – hearing, smell, vision – amplified; I felt more attentive to the forest even than I have done on a hike. Standing there, waiting for the animals, there was an immediacy, an understanding that lives have beginnings and ends and actions have consequences. Done right, hunting had meaning.

Perhaps hunting's greatest similarity to war is that it is mostly standing around, waiting. We heard a rustling in the trees, and a group of red stags appeared through the branches. One, two – ten of them, all with large antlers, and all strictly off limits at this point in the season. They jagged through the branches, and across into a nearby field, where their stride slackened, and their relief became almost visible.

We did a couple more drives. Each time a hunter shot a boar, Hubert would find a nearby twig, put half of it in the pig's mouth and give the other half to the hunter. This is a central European tradition known as 'the last bite'. Of course, in itself the twig meant nothing to the pig, but it did suggest a respect that is absent in much of the farm world.

In three hours, the eleven hunters shot only three boars. It made online dating look efficient. We certainly hadn't done much to reduce the population of wild boar or the spread of swine fever. To my surprise, the men were not agitated – those who hadn't shot anything didn't even seem bothered. The lack of guarantees was part of the process.

The carcasses had been brought back in a small green metal trailer. The leg of one boar was being used to hold open the belly of another, to help it cool down. When we returned to base, the boars were unloaded onto a bed of pines. One man posed for a photo next to his dead boar, another used his boot to reveal the prized tusk. The men were neither psychopaths nor animal activists. The scene was merry without being boisterous. It could have been the end of a village cricket match or the start of a wedding.

Back at the lodge, the group focused very much on the post-hunt. One man had placed a spoof plastic warning sign outside his bedroom:

'Drunken Men Crossing'. Another brought out a litre of lemon-flavoured vodka, and joined in singing Wham! songs. A third man soon remarked that any man who can understand women should win a Nobel prize and confessed that, when he wanted to express an emotion to his wife, he would find a relevant song and play it to her on his iPhone. A fourth man commented that 90 per cent of the best snipers in war are hunters – because they have 'crossed the line' already – a point that a fifth man quickly distanced himself from.

The hunters knew more about the forest than I did, and contributed more to maintaining it than I did. Three days' hunting would cost them more than £2,000 each; every boar killed would add maybe £800 to the cost, depending on the weight. Tony, a Liverpool fan who had shot one of the boars, said his favourite moment of the day was seeing the group of red stags run off into the countryside. Several of the men complained vigorously about British game-bird shooting and about hunters who put in little physical effort. 'That's shooting, that's not hunting. There's a big difference,' said one.

But there was pain on this hunt too. The next day the men had shots of Jagermeister at 6 a.m., and breakfast shortly afterwards. As the morning mist rose, we were in position above a dip in the forest. The beauty didn't last long. One of the hunters – who always seemed a shaky shot – managed to shoot a boar without killing it. The animal lay by the side of the track, writhing, with a dog locked onto its hind leg. Hubert walked over and cut the boar's neck. The body kept spasming – the back legs mimicking a now-impossible gallop, the head lowering as if to eat.

For me, the most disturbing moment of the hunt didn't involve blood. It was walking with the beaters, to drive the animals into the hunters' sights. It was then that I felt responsible for what was actually happening – wild animals were being pushed to their deaths. You could justify hunting as in the best interests of the population, but you were taking responsibility for the random choice of which individuals lived and died. We walked through the scrub, calling loudly, occasionally whooping. Then there was the scurry of feet, the crunch of leaves, and the approach of death. It didn't feel wrong necessarily, but it felt sombre.

Why do people hunt? Opponents suspect hunters have a dark psychological flaw. Researchers have tried analysing hunters' trophy photographs – the so-called grip-and-grin shots – for how genuine the smiles are. They have tried looking at evolutionary reasons for hunting. The results have been underwhelming. Is hunting a way to increase social standing or attractiveness to mates, a bit like pet-ownership? Among the Meriam people of Australia, successful hunters have more children and more partners than other men. Is hunting correlated with sociopathic tendencies, like a willingness to inflict pain on animals? If it is, we don't have the evidence.

What I can say is that the Swedish group didn't seem psychologically maladjusted. They weren't obsessed by cruelty or killing. Their justifications for hunting – that they liked the experience of the outdoors, that killing was ecologically necessary – were plausible enough.

It was very male. Studies of chimpanzee hunting show that males account for 70–98 per cent of animals killed. The gender bias is present in human hunting too, although hunting was rarely about brute force. (Even among hunter-gatherers, the hardest part of the hunt is often the tracking.) In the Kalahari, a !Kung man cannot marry until he has ritually killed a large male and female animal. Women are believed to be fatal to the hunt, and not in a good way. An arrow touched by a woman won't kill anything, nor will a man who has had sex with a woman the night before. Women, of course, do provide much of the !Kung's food, but vegetables, rather than meat. The anthropologist Lorna Marshall saw women dancing in praise after men returned home with a dead ostrich. 'I venture to say no women have been greeted in this manner when they returned with vegetables,' she noted in the 1970s. Several decades later, it still resonates. Yet hunting hasn't always been male-dominated. In burial sites from at least 7,000 years ago in the Americas, women make up two-fifths of people found buried with hunting tools. In western culture today, if hunting is ethical and sociable, it should become less macho.

I left Poland thinking that hunting was probably not for me. I have other pretexts for getting drunk. But I had felt closer to the land than I had for many months. I had listened and watched, as Leopold might have a century earlier.

I've developed a respect for hunting. There are sports, like rugby and American football, that I wouldn't want my children playing because they are fundamentally unsafe. There are sports, like boxing, that I think could easily be banned. And there are sports, like bullfighting, that are so bloodthirsty that I can't imagine anyone taking pleasure in them. Hunting – or at least what I've seen – is better than them. It feels necessary, restrained, connected.

In the car back to Berlin, Jens told me how being a hunter had helped him recover from his embolism. 'I am not afraid of the concept of death. I'm not afraid of anything,' he said.

For the hunters, killing the boars was not brutal – it was not even startling. 'You're just not supposed to feel that way in modern society. Death is meant to be evil and ugly,' said Jens. The *Bambi* mentality is to hope that death isn't inevitable. The hunters knew better.

*

If animals have the ability to feel pain, make decisions and build social relationships, then their deaths have meaning. The world loses a living being; the other boars lose a companion. I struggled to put myself in a boar's position. To imagine what a boar might have felt that morning. When hunters kill a female with young, they will also kill the young to avoid a more painful death from starvation. But even so, *something* must remain – someone must notice the absence.

There are people who believe that killing an animal is fundamentally wrong. No one has taken this further than Jains, members of a religion closely related to Hinduism, who state that every animal has a spiritual quality. Devout Jains are not just vegetarians or vegans – they don't eat potato, garlic or other root vegetables, because doing so prevents the plant from regrowing. They keep their food in airtight containers so it doesn't attract flies that they might be tempted to swat, and they do not travel by car so as to avoid squashing insects. To meet a Jain monk or nun outside India is rare, because they steer clear of any mechanised transport. But a couple of nuns were given special dispensation to study at London's School of Oriental and African Studies, and I went to visit one of them in their house, a building north of the city that used to act as a regional branch of the Football Association. The central heating was intense, the Christmas cards were still up in April, the place had a surreal vibe.

One nun, Pratibha, came in dressed in a white robe. 'I was a cat, I was a dog. There is no life form in the universe where we were not born,' she explained to me. 'We transmigrated so many times in so many life forms.'

Pratibha told me that a fellow Jain was in the process of fasting until death. He had decided his time had come, and would now abstain from food and contact with other humans. 'It could be two days or four days. Or fourteen days,' says Pratibha. 'He would not even respond back with his eye movement.' I struggled to contain my shock. We changed the topic on to factory farming and her hopes of moving towards spiritual liberation.

Ever since meeting Pratibha, I've been in awe of Jains' commitment. I also understood why fewer than 1 per cent of Indians follow the religion. Non-violence (*ahimsa*), in its purest form, would make participating in much of modern society impossible. Even the most devout Jains find themselves squashing insects; in reality, they accept that they can only do so much.

Jainism seemed an aspiration for kindness rather than a viable option for me. It didn't seem to respond to the ecological reality of a world dominated by humans. In the Netherlands, where the hunting of geese was banned, the authorities have been struggling with escalating numbers of the birds, who eat crops and cause risk to planes. They are now in the process of killing half a million geese – by gassing them; the hunting ban remains in force. Sometimes the only way not to kill any other animal is not to encounter any other animal, and this is precisely the world we want to avoid.

Gandhi, himself influenced by Jainism, distinguished between true *ahimsa* and blind fetish *ahimsa*: true non-violence might include, for example, killing animals to prevent them from starving. Maybe if we think of how ecosystems depend on population control, the possibilities for true non-violence become greater.

Hunting is not painless. I remembered the boar being chased in Poland, I saw one writhe on the ground before her throat was slit. I could accept that this was better than the boar not existing at all, because her forest was destroyed, or being torn to pieces by a wolf. But it still placed a responsibility on the hunter. Today Safari Club International, a hunting group, promotes alternative weapons like handguns and crossbows. Hunters are putting their own thirst for novelty above respect for the animals.

Killing has ripple effects. Among elephants, older animals have a social function. When old bulls were culled in Addo Elephant National Park, researchers found a subsequent outbreak of male mortality, broken tusks and puncture wounds. One male elephant tried to have sex with a rhino. Killing the old males had left a younger generation without male mentors.

Even animals who have evolved as prey may suffer more from hunting. After all, they haven't evolved to be hunted *by us*. Red deer and roe deer appear to be more stressed in areas with erratic human presence than they are in areas populated by their natural predators. Were the animals scared of us in Poland? I felt so. One boar hesitated, a younger one zigzagged away from the dogs. The red deer – which the hunters were legally unable to shoot – seemed delighted once they were away from us.

Animals seem to have a sophisticated perception of hunters. One woman told me that the red deer on her Scottish estate would come for food as soon as the hunting season ended in late October. 'They just know. They're ten to twelve years old. They just know the seasons.' I heard one story of a Swedish hunter who took a chainsaw in the forest, because – he believed – the moose had learnt not to be afraid of loggers. In Kenya, elephants have learnt to distinguish between Maasai men, who attack them with spears, and other locals, by the colour of their garments.

Even if killing helps the ecological balance, it probably also changes the animals. When Darwin visited the Galapagos, he noted that a gun was 'almost superfluous; for with the muzzle of one I pushed a hawk off the branch of a tree'. By hunting animals, we are selecting against those animals who trust us; we are encouraging species to fear us. Because hunters kill the biggest creatures, they may also be shifting the populations to become smaller. In Canada, there is a ban on shooting bears with cubs. As a result, mother bears have been found to stay with their cubs for an extra year, thereby protecting themselves.

The most sobering thought for me was a counterfactual: if a superspecies were to look at the planet, and decide to cull the species whose numbers were out of control, wouldn't the first species in the crosshairs be humans? Would we accept one of our neighbours being picked off on the way to the shops, for the sake of ecological balance? Until some monster IQ robot breaks free from Google's headquarters, we are the only ones with the guns. We are the only species who can think about ecosystems as a whole, and we have a responsibility to safeguard populations of wild animals.

Loving animals cannot mean imagining a fantasy land – without death, without suffering. It's about balancing our needs, with the welfare and abundance of animals. We don't need to hunt for food. If we value only deer and wild boar, we can leave these animals to multiply. But if we also value the broader life of the forest, then we need to control their numbers. If other people are willing to pay thousands of euros to control the populations of wild animals, then I'm not going to object on principle.

There is, however, an even better argument for hunting: that it protects the wild spaces in which animals can thrive.

*

Cecil the lion suffered a terrible end. If he'd been shot with a rifle in the chest, he might have died instantly. Instead his killer, Walter Palmer, used a compound bow, a much less accurate weapon. A decent hunter can kill an animal with a full-bore rifle from 300 yards; Palmer was said to trust himself with a compound bow up to a hundred yards. Whatever exactly happened, the dentist missed his spot. The lion spent many hours dying.

But the outcry around Cecil's death – the viral posts, the petitions, the demonstrations outside Walter Palmer's dental surgery in Minnesota – was slightly random. Cecil, who lived in Hwange National Park, wasn't the first lion hunted in the area: sixty-five lions were hunted between 1999 and 2015. Cecil had been collared by researchers. When an elephant with a similar collar was killed by hunters in Botswana in 2019, the attention was muted.

The Cecil outcry was also fuelled by a few misconceptions. Perhaps the most important one is that Cecil's death put the lion population in danger. It's easy to see why people would assume that. Lions, like most large mammals, are on an awful trajectory. They have lost 90 per cent of their historic range – to farmland and human settlements. This is not a problem of the distant past: between the release of Disney's original The Lion King in 1994 and the remake in 2019, the total number of wild lions roughly halved. (Still, great soundtrack.) But in southern Africa, where hunting takes place and where Cecil was shot, lion numbers are not falling. They are actually increasing. South Africa has 200,000 square kilometres of private hunting reserves – amounting to one-sixth of the country. Lions have fared much worse in Kenya, where hunting was banned in 1977.

When Jimmy Kimmel raged about the killing of Cecil, he flashed up the website of WildCRU – the research centre at the University of Oxford that had been tracking the lion – on the screen for viewers to donate. More than $1 million poured in; the website crashed. WildCRU has been studying the lion population in Hwange for more than twenty years. Kimmel's viewers might be surprised to know that it does not oppose hunting. Indeed in 2019 a WildCRU researcher, Amy Dickman, led a group of 128 scientists who stated publicly that trophy-hunting should not be banned. A ban, they argued, would jeopardise large areas of animal habitat; it would also cut off the income to local people, which gives them an alternative to killing wild animals.

Fewer than 200 wild lions a year are killed by trophy-hunters, judging by import-export records. Ultimately the biggest risk to many large mammals is not foreign hunters; it's local people seeing no economic benefit to having the animals there. Local people suffer the nuisance of living next to large mammals, which may eat their crops, kill their livestock and even attack their children. David Macdonald, head of WildCRU, points out that banning trophy-hunting does not mean lions aren't killed – in many cases, it probably means that they are killed by different people, namely farmers. Dickman, herself a vegetarian, points out that these killings do not appear on our social media feeds. Their best judgement is that trophy-hunting does work for conservation, in certain conditions.

Condition one is that hunters bring money. The landowner must gain enough to keep the land as natural habitat, and nearby communities must also see benefits. Hunting probably brings in more than $200 million a year for sub-Saharan African countries; Palmer reportedly paid $50,000 for the right to shoot a lion. Some of this goes to governments, some to hunting operators. Hunting parties, and their dollars, reach more remote areas than wildlife tourists. Whatever the downsides of machismo, it probably makes hunters agree to tolerate bumpy car rides and pesky tsetse flies. You have to laugh.

In Namibia, most community-run nature conservancies wouldn't be able to cover their operating costs without income from hunting, particularly elephant-hunting. Over the past twenty-five years, the elephant population has as much as tripled. Tourists and hunters deter poachers by funding park rangers and local communities, and by their very presence in remote areas. Many countries don't have the capacity to manage hunting, and to keep out illegal poachers. In Tanzania, the lion population has dwindled to the point where there are now few left to shoot in hunting reserves. If too many animals are shot, hunting becomes unsustainable.

How many animals are too many? It's hard to know what the lion population is and therefore what the right quota is. Some experts have proposed a rule of thumb – one lion a year per 2,000 square kilometres. In other words, you would need a hunting reserve nearly two and a half times the size of New York City to kill one lion per year. Because hunters are willing to pay so much to kill a lion, this would still give enough of an incentive for the land not to be used for farming. And it would sustain the lions, as well as all the other species that live on the land.

Hunting areas cover more land in sub-Saharan Africa than national parks do – 1.4 million square kilometres, which is twice the size of Texas. They make animals, and wild spaces, valuable to humans who might otherwise have little reason to protect them.

Shortly before I went hunting in Poland, I had found myself on a work trip to Mongolia, where the most expensive legal hunting prize is the Altai argali, a wild sheep with curved horns. Mongolia has fewer people, proportionally, than any other country on earth – five per square mile, compared to about ninety per square mile in the US, or more than 700 per square mile in the UK. This should leave plenty of space for other species. Much of the country is in fact grazing lands for livestock, and sadly Mongolians, who love hunting, have shot to pieces much of the wildlife. The skins and furs were an economic lifeline in the chaotic years after the collapse of the Soviet Union. Red deer used to graze on the edge of the capital city Ulan Bator – no longer. One man told me that he used to see wolves running alongside the road – no longer. Argali numbers also tumbled after the end of communism.

In recent years, Mongolia has tried to protect the argali by granting a small number of hunting licences, fewer than a hundred a year. Hunters will pay up to $150,000 for the privilege. I wondered whether the decimal point had got lost. Yes, the argali is the largest sheep on the planet. But it is still a sheep. Who would pay so much money to kill a sheep?

A Mongolian hunting tour operator called Tugso tried to give me a clue. 'Donald Trump Junior,' he told me. 'I cannot say if he is a customer or not. But here is a scan of his passport.'

Tugso turned his iPhone to show a photo of what looks very much like Donald Trump Junior's passport. 'Some of your royals, they come here too.' Tugso also mentioned that the 'sixth richest Russian' – name undisclosed – is a happy customer of his tour company. He added, philosophically: 'Not all rich persons is good persons.'

Hunting the argali is so expensive that just a few kills can make a big difference. On YouTube, you can see videos of American hunters on foot – and on horseback – approaching the animals, and then firing a single shot into their midriff. As one hunter recalled: 'Up close, I genuinely didn't understand wild sheep could get this big ... 400 pounds appeared to me, if anything, well on the conservative side.'

Nothing causes social media outrage like a picture of a large animal that has been hunted. Big animals are the most prestigious. When you think about it, that's slightly ridiculous – the bigger the animal, the easier the target. And when you are shooting a sheep from 200 yards away, size does not mean danger.

But Tugso argued that the large males – the ones with huge tusks or antlers – are the best animals to cull. The old argali might not survive the winter. 'We choose the oldest ram that will not survive next year,' he said. 'Instead of an old sheep dying, we kill them and get the money.' He produced a picture of a large horned argali on his iPhone. 'This one very, very curled. Excellent.'

How do people feel when they kill the argali, I asked Tugso? 'Some people waiting for their entire life, dreaming. So what can the emotion be? It's a dream hunt. One woman, she wasn't a hunter, her husband died. The trophy [list] wasn't finished. She taught herself to shoot. After she got the Gobi argali, she threw the ashes of her husband in the sky saying, I finished your dream.'

Argali hunting is a conservation success story. In 2003, there were only 161 argali in the Gulzat protected area, where hunting takes place. In 2010, when hunting was introduced, there were 724. Four years later, numbers had doubled to more than 1,500.

Tugso was satisfied with business. 'We already sold out for the next three years.'

A few months after we met, the US website ProPublica revealed that Donald Trump Junior had indeed shot an argali in Mongolia, and had only been given a hunting licence retrospectively. The story fitted into a pattern of the Trumps using their political leverage for favours: Donald Junior had jumped the queue for an argali licence. His trip to Mongolia also cost US taxpayers $77,000. A few months after that, it was revealed Walter Palmer, the dentist who killed Cecil, had himself paid to kill an argali.

But I couldn't help but feel the critics were missing the more benign side effect. By paying so much to kill sheep, Donald Trump Junior and Walter Palmer had actually become accidental conservationists.

*

At this point I would have been happy to conclude that hunting works, and that we should embrace it. If only it were so simple.

America's landscapes are dominated by white-tailed deer, to the expense of so much else. And the blame for this, paradoxically, rests on the hunters who kill them. Since the 1940s, game managers have worried about the explosion of deer populations. Forests were being cut down, opening the path to deer, while the deer's natural predators – wolves and cougars – had been hunted to extinction in the region. Aldo Leopold confronted this problem towards the end of his life. He understood that hunters, himself included, had disrupted the balance by purging wolves from much of America. 'I now suspect that just as a deer herd lives in mortal fear of its wolves, so does a mountain live in mortal fear of its deer,' he wrote.

Since Leopold's time, hunters have little interest in reducing deer populations. The more deer, the easier to shoot some – whatever the environmental damage. To control the deer population, you need to kill females (does) as well as males (bucks), and to allow more bucks to live beyond the age of two, so that some can become dominant males and structure the herd. But hunters want to shoot bucks – particularly those with big antlers – rather than does. Because hunters fund the state game commissions, they effectively decide what happens to the deer population. In the 1950s, a biologist at the Pennsylvania Game Commission called Roger Latham tried to push hunters to killing more does. Latham had built fenced enclosures to show how other life could flourish once deer were excluded from an area. No matter, he was fired from the commission. In the early 2000s, another biologist at the Pennsylvania Game Commission, Gary Alt, tried a similar policy. 'Hunters definitely want to see more deer than the habitat can sustain,' he complained. Alt urged hunters to 'stop looking at the deer and start looking at the habitat'. The resistance was so fierce that he started wearing a bulletproof vest to meetings with hunters; after some painful progress, he took early retirement. Across the United States, even though deer populations are effectively out of control, hunters have been unwilling to allow proper management; they have prioritised high deer numbers over a balanced environment.

Hunters' satisfaction is linked to the number of deer they see, not to the overall ecology, which is composed of lots of (less noticeable) insects, amphibians, birds and plants. Today some sportsmen buy corn to feed deer over the winter, further breaking the idea that hunting maintains a balanced ecosystem. American hunters are getting older: between 1996 and 2016, as the number of hunters overall dropped, the number of hunters over the age of sixty-five rose from 1 million to 1.6 million. They want easy targets.

'Hunters are creatures of habit,' says Donald Waller, an ecology professor at the University of Wisconsin. 'It's mostly old white guys with guns. Not moving as far from their pick-up trucks as they get older.'

In Alaska it's even more blatant. The legal aim of wildlife management is 'the achievement and maintenance in perpetuity of the ability to support a high level of human harvest of game'. In other words, screw other wildlife – we want to shoot deer. Hunters have lobbied for the right to cull brown bears, black bears and wolves, so that there are more moose and caribou available for shooting. Since the 1980s, the Alaskan Board of Game has granted their wish. Wolves have been snared, gassed and gunned down from the air, methods that don't fit with ethical hunting. Hunters could bait brown bears with doughnuts, kill wolves, coyotes and their cubs during the summer denning season, and go into black bear dens and use spotlights to locate and kill mothers and cubs. Alaska is the only place in the world where humans try to reduce brown bear populations over large areas of land: up to 900 bears are killed a year. The National Park Service asked repeatedly for its lands to be excluded from the predator control, saying maximising the number of game was 'incompatible' with its own legal duty to protect natural processes; the game board ignored it. In 2015, the Obama administration intervened to protect some federal lands. But six years later the Trump administration rolled back these restrictions. Hunting is justified when it helps to maintain the natural world; right now, in Alaska, it is designed to destroy it – and to put deer first.

Wisconsin actually found a way to reduce its deer numbers. In 1996, the Department of Natural Resources introduced an 'Earn a Buck' scheme, under which hunters had to kill an antlerless deer before they could kill an antlered one. It was the kind of sensible policy that brought down populations. But hunters disliked having to pass up a buck, simply because they hadn't killed a doe. In 2011, under pressure from disgruntled hunters, the state legislature – backed by governor Scott Walker – made Earn a Buck illegal. Wildlife officials tried to reinstate the rule in 2020, but hunters voted against it in an advisory referendum.

Waller, who himself took up deer-hunting after seeing the population rise steadily, struggles to contain his frustration. That frustration rests partly on the idea that the prospects of other species are worth more than that of individual deer. This is a question of values. But it seemed right to me that we should seek to restore a balance. In parts of Wisconsin, the current density is probably close to a hundred deer per square mile. Waller thinks it should be around ten to twenty, depending on the environment.

The best way to control burgeoning numbers of deer, says Waller, is to get people to hunt more like wolves. 'If we've eliminated predators across much of the landscape, we have a responsibility ourselves to become the predator.' That means killing not just those deer with the biggest antlers – i.e. the best trophies. He notes that, in areas managed by native Americans such as the Ojibway tribe, numbers of deer are lower, likely because of the greater tolerance of wolves and the willingness to shoot all kinds of deer. 'We should be shooting does, not bucks,' says Waller. 'We should have longer hunting seasons and ask hunters to shoot more than one deer.' But hunters won't agree.

An alternative would be to introduce wolves – or bears or cougars – to areas with too many deer. This could bring down numbers, although maybe not very quickly. It wouldn't actually reduce the deer suffering. The most terrifying moment in *Bambi*, the one I wasn't ready to fast-forward through, is not when the hunter shoots Bambi's mother

– it's when the dogs threaten to tear apart Bambi's mate. Introducing predators might not even reduce the need for culling. Some introduced predators, like wolves, have become a nuisance for farmers, because they feed on livestock, and therefore may themselves be killed. Wolves are not welcome in urban areas either. Some animals that are hunted today, like elephants, do not have predators.

Surgically sterilising female deer – a twenty-minute procedure where the ovaries are removed – is another option, particularly in suburban areas where shooting is not permitted. Animal rights activists prefer sterilisation to culling, because it doesn't take the life of an animal. But it's arguable that sterilisation, being an invasive, stressful procedure with potential long-term effects, is less ethical than culling. It's also expensive and time-consuming. If the US is really serious about reducing deer numbers, and managing its forests for the health of all species, it will need a mix of recreational hunters, deer sterilisation, and professional cullers. Anthony DeNicola, who has a PhD in controlling white-tailed deer and who is now hired by local US authorities to reduce their populations, says he regularly kills 150 deer in a night. 'A hunter has a good day if he kills a deer. I have a bad day if I don't kill every deer I see,' he says. DeNicola is hired in order to reduce traffic collisions and tick-borne disease. The overall health of the forest 'is usually given lip service', he says. 'People have no frickin' clue. They think, if it's green, it's good.'

America is not the only place where hunters have become the problem. In Scotland, the authorities said as long ago as 1959 that deer estates were not killing enough red deer. In 1963, the Red Deer Commission, which oversaw forestry, complained that few landowners had heeded its call, and that 'deer forests have suffered from too much emphasis on sporting values to the detriment of good management'. But paying hunters – many from West Germany and the US – wanted to kill stags, not hinds, and venison prices were too low. So there was no incentive for large estates to kill hinds. By 1986, Scotland had nearly twice as many hinds as stags, and the population has kept growing ever since. It's almost unbelievable: environmentalists have spent decades calling for more deer to be culled, while the hunting industry has dragged its feet. In Denmark, most goose-hunters are satisfied by killing one or two geese each time they hunt: overall they don't kill enough geese to manage the population.

Meanwhile, even though the US is largely overrun with deer, farms in several states now breed deer for hunters. Deer at these farms have tested positive for chronic wasting disease, a fatal condition which is related to bovine spongiform encephalopathy and which leads to dramatic weight loss in deer. Just when you think American deer management can't be any less rational, there's something else. In Texas, ranches have bred more than 1 million zebras, oryx and other non-native ungulates, for hunters to shoot. Hunters have caused deer overpopulation, and are now compounding it.

This is the problem: humans hunt the way they want to hunt, not the way the environment needs it. Once a management practice is established, it can become detached from any ecological needs. In England, fox-hunting was initially vermin control, but the sport became so popular that there weren't enough wild foxes to kill. Hunters had to breed and release more foxes. Sometimes hunts were stopped midway, so that the foxes could be killed another day – a practice that effectively increased the animal's suffering. (Even so, the irony is that the reason that foxes are not extinct in the UK, like wolves, lynx and bears, is that people enjoyed hunting them.)

Something similar happens with pheasant-shooting. The birds are often bred in cramped cages, before being released into the wild for rich people to shoot. At least 47 million farm-reared pheasants and partridges are released each year in the UK – their biomass is maybe twenty-five times that of any other bird in the country. Britain's released pheasants outweigh all the native wild birds put together. (And most people think there are too many seagulls.) This way, estates can guarantee to rich clients that they will shoot hundreds of birds in an afternoon, even if they are not very good hunters. It's like tipping lorryloads of greenhouse-grown strawberries onto a field and then organising a fruit-picking event. In grouse-shooting, the birds are wild, but carbon-rich peatland has to be burnt to promote the right plants for their nests. Clearly this is not restoring balance to the environment; it is creating imbalance. To make this more absurd, wood pigeons do such damage to crops that farmers pay specialist hunters to shoot thousands of them. These pigeons are agile, and can be shot for sport. But English hunters prefer the traditions of the pheasant and the grouse hunt.

In the Mediterranean, hunters shoot songbirds, whose populations are already in decline; not only that, but they lure the songbirds towards them by playing birdsong recordings. It's not population management – it's manufacturing death. The justification for destroying habitats and inflicting pain on animals simply doesn't exist – especially when pheasant meat isn't even popular. France is finally banning hunters from trapping songbirds by placing sticks covered in glue in the forests, a practice where birds become stuck and suffer agonising deaths.

In South Africa, some lions are bred in captivity so that there is a ready supply for foreign hunters. This 'canned hunting' is a cheaper alternative to hunting wild animals – it's the equivalent of factory farming. South Africa has recently classified thirty-three species of wild animals, including giraffes, cheetahs and lions, as farm animals, so that breeders can try to produce 'genetically superior' animals, i.e. ones that are more attractive to hunters. This doesn't just violate the spirit of hunting; there is a serious risk that the animals will breed with wild populations. Foreign hunters so far seem rightly repelled by South Africa's approach.

The idea that hunting is necessary is not easy to pin down. How many elephants are too many? Zimbabwe declared itself at full capacity in the 1990s – numbers have since doubled. Botswana banned elephant hunting in 2014, but then decided in 2019 that the population needed to be reduced, after a number of people were killed by elephants. Where the line is drawn is a judgement. In Botswana's case, part of the calculation was probably that the hunting ban hadn't been followed by an influx of peaceful tourists.

In Spain, the authorities allowed a couple of hundred wolves a year to be shot. The animals are hated by farmers, who complain they kill some livestock. But the case for hunting was weak. In one province where wolf numbers had been increasing, damage to livestock had been decreasing (likely because the wolves fed on wild animals instead). The money generated by hunting was pretty pitiful – a licence for killing a wolf cost about €3,500. In 2021, to the delight of conservationists, Spain banned wolf hunting.

In theory I find it easy to justify hunting. In practice, there is a lack of conclusive studies. Either the research hasn't been done, or it's been done only on particular areas with particular dynamics, or we don't know the counterfactual – that is, what would happen to the land if hunting were banned. A definitive answer, like an agile boar, keeps slipping out of view.

In this messy scenario, I side with those people who urge caution. Criticise, regulate and hopefully get rid of the pointless hunting – the pheasant- and grouse-shooting, the canned hunting. Push it from public lands and pressure private landowners not to allow it. Challenge the unsustainable practices of some hunters, for example by finding ways that non-hunters can pay a greater share of state authorities' budgets, and therefore have a louder voice. But leave the hunting that works with the ecology – that aims to manage populations and to pay for the protection of wild spaces. Banning this form of hunting might make us feel better, but it wouldn't reduce the killing or increase the abundance of animals.

*

Is it really OK to take pleasure in killing animals? For me, it remained weird. It was generally males killing males. It rested on the tenuous idea of a contest between humans and nature. I followed keen hunters on Instagram, and scrolled through their trophy photos – the grip-and-grin shots. I found them as simplistic and unconvincing as the anti-hunting posts. But honestly, I'm not sure I found hunters that much weirder than the birders who cross continents to tick off lists of hundreds of species.

In our minds, there are different types of hunting: hunting for subsistence, hunting for pleasure, hunting for trophies, hunting for population control. These distinctions aren't helpful. Even chimpanzees don't just hunt for food – it plays a social role. Hunting can be pleasurable and functional: for subsistence hunter-gatherers, hunts are social occasions, often filled with laughter and male bonding. Subsistence hunting is also not synonymous with the breadline. Anthropologists found that the Cuiva, nomads who lived around the border of Venezuela and Colombia, worked for less than twenty hours a week, spent fifteen to sixteen hours a day in their hammocks, and still each day had as much meat as five Big Macs. Their hunting didn't appear to even be particularly high-risk.

Hunting can be for subsistence and for trophies. The Yanomami keep hunting trophies in their kitchens – from monkey heads to armadillo bones. These trophies show triumph and ward off misfortune. Trophy animals can be used for food, and almost any mammal – including small muntjac deer – can be put on the wall as a trophy. When western hunters refer to 'magnificent animals', they are nearly always referring to old males. Are critics really saying that it's worse to kill older males than young females? Meanwhile, Maasai men in east Africa also hunt lions as trophies – as a rite of passage to signal their manliness.

In short, trophy-hunting is not a very useful term. What people mean by trophy-hunting isn't the trophy aspect at all – it's the idea of killing thoughtlessly, pushing animals to extinction, in the same way that Roualeyn Gordon-Cumming once did in Africa. Opponents call hunting 'the extinction industry'. But hunting today is, on paper, at least about licences and sustainable populations. It's right that we get outraged by killings like Cecil the lion's, which are not licensed. Yet in general the hatred of hunting is outdated. What matters is context. The world currently has as many as ten American dentists for every wild lion. So if every American dentist decides to shoot a lion, it's a problem. But if every American dentist decides to shoot a deer, it may be a solution. And if every American dentist shot ten deer, it might really give other species a chance.

Trophy-hunting has managed to mobilise celebrities, politicians and the public in favour of animals. But the outrage is disproportionate to whatever abuse there might be. If anyone wants to stop wasteful killing for pleasure, they should focus on farming. Meat-eating is killing for pleasure too – the pleasure of taste. Livestock farming is the real extinction industry. Eighty-five per cent of Britons oppose trophy-hunting, but fewer than 5 per cent are vegetarian. Those priorities are all wrong. (The poll question also failed to mention any conservation benefits.) Factory farming has all of the downsides of hunting – it causes individual animals to suffer, it drives species to extinction – and none of the upsides – it doesn't bring us close to the natural world, it doesn't restore ecological balance, it doesn't pay for the conservation of wild spaces. I would rather eat wild boar or venison than farmed meat or fish, and if I liked the taste and trusted the hunter, I would buy it. Give me a driven hunt over an abattoir any day.

When we're disconnected from nature, we risk seeing it as a series of individual triumphs and tragedies, like Bambi's mother or Cecil the lion. But if there is a major tragedy, it's that whole species can slim down or go extinct because of human activity. I could never expect my daughters to grow up in a world with Cecil the lion – Cecil was thirteen years old, and lions rarely live beyond fifteen in the wild. What I hoped is that they would grow up in a world with lots of wild lions. The real sadness is not that Cecil died. It's that his death didn't focus attention on what really matters: creating a part of this world where animal populations can thrive. Hunting means accepting there are times when we can kill an animal, even take pleasure in it. But done right, it is also a springboard to an understanding of other animals and a recognition of our place in the natural world.

Seeing hunting up close had prodded me to accept humans' dominance. It was uncomfortable: once I started seeing an animal as 'surplus' or 'killable', I saw justifications for the death of quite a lot of animals who I had thought of as almost sacred. Hedgehogs – whose survival is the subject of animal campaigns across the UK – have been culled in Scotland to protect sea-nesting birds. That is reality: to live alongside animals now means to kill them. We must think about how to cause as little suffering as possible.

I had seen people who were willing to spend a day in the fields and come home satisfied without killing anything, people who had a sense of environmental balance. Hunter-gatherers know animals intimately from their calls, footprints and their past behaviour. The Yanomami can use trails of urine to identify some animals and how recently they passed by. Rifle-holding hunters short-circuit some of that knowledge, but they know animals better than many of us. They are forced to think about animals' lives and minds.

The animal test had led me to give up all farmed livestock and animal clothing. It had led me to think that we should not farm fish, and that we should take far fewer from the seas. But there are circumstances in which humans are justified in killing animals – and hunting can be one of those. It can only be the beginning of our attempts to reconnect with the natural world. The second part of the animal test took me to those places where we aim to keep animals alive.

PART II
LOVING ANIMALS

6. THE ARK OF HISTORY

The zoo cannot but disappoint.

John Berger

'I've inherited a hypocrisy! Not a bureaucracy – a *hypocrisy*!'

Damian Aspinall has the confidence that comes with being very rich, very tall and quite good-looking. The hypocrisy he's referring to comes in the form of two zoos. Howletts and Port Lympne animal parks, in south-east England, were set up by his father, the maverick gambler John Aspinall, in the 1970s. By the time Aspinall Senior died in 2000, Aspinall Junior had decided that this form of keeping animals in captivity was a waste of money – and morally wrong.

'The only way I could justify taking over the parks was if I could find ways to get as many animals back into the wild,' he tells me.

So far, so Freudian. The Aspinalls are hardly the first family where the son is happily picking apart the father's legacy. What's different is the boldness of the son's vision. He has become perhaps the loudest opponent of zoos worldwide. It's like Donald Trump Junior launching a crusade against tax avoidance. Damian Aspinall wants to abolish zoos, even though he runs two of them.

We are meeting in his grand offices near London's Sloane Square. He sits under a framed Damien Hirst print; I'm opposite a handwritten birthday note from Pelé.

'If you take your kids to a zoo, you are telling them subconsciously that you can watch that tiger in a small cage. You can watch those poor elephants, you can watch the lions, and it's OK – because they're there for you, kids, those animals have got fewer rights than you. We can enslave them just so you can enjoy yourself. Isn't it time that we looked at ourselves as a species, and said, come on, we don't need to do that any more? We're polluting our children's minds.'

I must look anxious, because Aspinall moves to reassure me. 'I don't blame people – it's not their fault!' he says. 'They've been culturalised.'

The Aspinall philosophy – defended by both zoo-loving father and zoo-hating son – holds that all animals, or at least all mammals, are as valuable as humans. It holds too that humans can live harmoniously alongside even the fiercest species. Like posh Mowglis, the family has surrounded itself with tigers and apes. The house was full of them. John Aspinall, a dislikeable man who admired Hitler's view on eugenics, once said he'd rather leave his children with a gorilla than a social worker. Damian placed his first two babies with gorillas for a get-to-know-you session, although by the time the third came along, he decided not to risk an intervention by social services.

The results have sometimes been tragic. Five keepers were killed by tigers and elephants at Howletts and Port Lympne between 1975 and 2000. Animals who cause injuries in zoos are not always put down, so a chimpanzee who ripped off a two-year-old boy's arm in 1989 was able to bite off a twenty-five-year-old zoology student's thumb and index finger in 1994. There were other incidents. Damian's first wife, Louise, once needed fifteen stitches after being bitten by a tiger cub, although that wasn't why they divorced. His second wife, Victoria, received a gash above the eye from a wolf; the couple are still together.

In short, Aspinall's upbringing was mad, but it allowed him to conclude that zoos were not as good for animals as saving their natural habitat. 'When you go to a zoo, they'll tell you, "we're doing conservation, we're breeding animals and we're Ark-ing them from extinction",' he says. 'But what's the process of that? Where's the data? There are about ten mammal species that zoos can claim they've saved from extinction. Ten species!' His research says that – of about 850 mammal species held in European zoos – only forty-five are critically endangered, one notch from extinction, and only three of those have viable breeding populations. Animals in zoos are often hybrids – one species bred with another similar species, by accident (for example, because scientists hadn't yet distinguished between the two species) or for convenience. Others represent genetic bottlenecks, where the population descends from too few individuals. Hybrids occur in the wild too, but conservation practice holds that those born in captivity cannot be released.

'Bengali tigers – 100 per cent of Indian tigers in captivity are hybridised. They have *zero* conservation value. Zoos don't tell you that! ... If you've £10 million to build a tiger enclosure, is that money better spent in a zoo or in India or Sumatra? It's the dishonesty of the message that I find most disturbing.'

In Aspinall's vision, zoos should carefully consider whether a species should be in captivity. Those that can be conserved in the wild should be kept in the wild. Those already in captivity, which aren't at risk of imminent extinction, should be returned to the wild.

'A panel would say, this animal is actually rare now, so what do we do? Can we protect them in the wild? If it's impossible to protect them in the wild in any shape or form – which is *nonsense* – well, we might have to bring some of them into zoos. But none of that process happens.'

African elephants would not clear Aspinall's threshold. A generation of westerners have grown up expecting to see elephants in zoos, and knowing about the evils of ivory-poaching. The number of African elephants in the wild has fallen from roughly 650,000 in 2007 to 540,000 in 2016, partly because of continued poaching.

But Aspinall disagrees that zoos are the answer. 'There are half a million elephants left. They are being poached in some areas. But there are 20,000 elephants in reserves in South Africa, completely safe from poaching. So there's your bank of elephants to save them from extinction. So what possible reason is there for an elephant in captivity? None!' (This is without getting on to Botswana and Zimbabwe, where, as we saw in the last chapter, elephant populations have grown.)

Even the eastern black rhino – considered critically endangered – wouldn't pass the zoo test. The subspecies has been hunted for its horn, extinguished from countries like Sudan, South Sudan and Ethiopia, and since 1973 its population has fallen around 90 per cent. In 2002 there were fewer mature eastern black rhinos than members of the US Congress – 512. But numbers have increased a little since. 'Instead of wasting millions of pounds building rhino enclosures, and millions of pounds in salaries looking after those rhino enclosures all over the world, let's create four reserves – some in Tanzania, some in Kenya,' says Aspinall. 'Better climate, better diet.'

Ending zoos has proved a longer journey than Aspinall hoped. Some animals have died off or been moved ('When my father was alive we had thirty tigers. We've now got four'). Others have bred faster than they can be moved to the wild. So Aspinall still has around 1,400 animals, of eighty different species. That includes the world's largest collection of western lowland gorillas and a sizeable collection of black rhino. His zoos are like those shops that forever advertise their closing-down sale.

'We're chipping away,' he says. 'At any one time we probably have ten species that we're working on [relocating to the wild]. We're a small business. We can't work on fifty species. Where you send them is incredibly difficult.' When he took over Howletts and Port Lympne, the parks were losing as much as £4 million a year. They've done better recently, but still racked up nearly £1 million in losses the year before we meet.

Starting a programme to reintroduce endangered Javan gibbons to Indonesia took ten years. Aspinall also blames the zoo establishment for not supporting him. For endangered animals, the populations are managed across all zoos by someone known as a studbook keeper. 'I would say nine out of ten studbook keepers don't agree with animal reintroduction,' he complains. 'If they don't agree, you can't move the animal.'

When I discussed Aspinall's work with one zoo chief, he rolled his eyes, saying it cost a lot and achieved little for the species. 'It's easy for them to portray me as a mad, maverick, nutty person. My father was often portrayed that way,' sighs Aspinall.

His current hope is that zoos will be phased out within thirty years – that is, fifty years from when he first took over Howletts and Port Lympne. 'Why does it take twenty to thirty years to phase out? Because you can't euthanise animals.'

Before the coronavirus pandemic, and indeed since, US zoos attracted more visitors each year than the major American football, basketball, hockey and baseball leagues combined. Worldwide an estimated 700 million people went to zoos in 2008, the last time that the World Association of Zoos and Aquariums (WAZA) made a guesstimate. The current figure is probably higher, because not all zoos are WAZA members and because dozens of zoos have opened in China alone since 2008. If zoos and aquaria are defined as places that house animals and are open to the public, there are more than 2,300 worldwide, of which only 400 are accredited WAZA members, committed to particular standards. If you include farm parks and restaurants with animal enclosures, there may be 10,000, the campaign group Born Free says.

Aspinall's vision of phasing out zoos is not quite as ambitious as Impossible Foods' goal of eliminating livestock agriculture by 2035, but it's in the same bracket. Now in his sixties, he doesn't expect to be around to see it fulfilled.

When we meet, he is finalising the transfer of two cheetahs born in England to South Africa. He drove thousands of miles to identify a reserve for the cheetahs, and spent more than a year in negotiations with the South African government. 'We're semi-parents, but they're not domesticated – we can't make them pee or shit anywhere. Anyway, when cheetahs grow up, they go away from the parents.'

He sees his closeness to the animals as an advantage. 'If you like, I'm the brother, and my wife is the mother. When gorillas in the wild that we've released get sick, if they know us they'll come down to the river and we can feed them medicine. We'll go for walks with the cheetah, we'll show them around the valleys, and we'll show them where the antelope are ... Even if they don't learn to hunt that well, even if we have to supplementary feed them a bit, so what? Isn't it better that they're there, living free, with a female cheetah than stuck in a wildlife park?'

In various studies, captive-born animals have been less likely to survive reintroduction to the wild than wild-born animals relocated from other areas. Some of Aspinall's ventures have certainly not gone according to plan. Five of the ten western lowland gorillas released back to Gabon in 2014 were found dead, perhaps killed by the stress of being alongside a wild-born male. A black rhino named Zambezi died on a plane to Tanzania in 2019, although other rhinos have been successfully relocated. Aspinall spent years trying to introduce a pair of Javan gibbons into the wild for them to breed, but the female ran off with a wild gibbon, leaving the male bereft. 'What I've learnt is that it's always what you can't think of that is what they surprise you with.'

What happens if the cheetahs' reintroduction doesn't work?

'I won't stop. I'll say, what did we do wrong, and let's get the next two, and let's do that better. I will never give up with what I'm trying to achieve. Screw my reputation – my job is to rewild as many animals as I can. Every time I see an animal that I don't think needs to be in a cage, I'm not doing my job properly.'

*

My parents never handed me over to the gorillas like Aspinall's, but I was still a child of the zoo. Growing up in London, I went to the zoo, I joined the zoo, and I went to the zoo again. When I wasn't at the zoo, I was looking back at the pictures I had taken there.

I remember the elephants. I remember the giraffes' heads appearing over the fences. Most of all I remember a giant panda called Chia-Chia, and another called Ming Ming, who arrived shortly after my ninth birthday – my zoo-going prime. I never questioned any of it; it was bliss.

I thought I had been a pretty serious zoo-goer until I met my wife Susie, who it turned out had written the zoo a letter of congratulation when Chia-Chia successfully bred in Mexico and still had their reply. That is commitment.

At some point in my twenties, I fell out of love with zoos, and I wasn't sure why. Physically they were the same, yet emotionally their impact had changed. Susie and I made a pilgrimage to see two pandas at Edinburgh Zoo. Even though the zoo was nice enough, the experience was soulless, motionless. It was the conservation equivalent of a police line-up: does this animal look like the picture you saw in *National Geographic*?

So I avoided taking my daughters to the zoo. This wasn't easy. *Dear Zoo*, a children's book about a kid who writes to a zoo asking to be sent animals (and who receives them), has sold more than 8 million copies worldwide. Zoos try to put themselves on the side of the angels. The Zoological Society of London, which runs London Zoo, says: 'Our vision is a world where wildlife thrives.' San Diego – the world's most popular zoo, according to TripAdvisor – describes itself not really as a zoo at all, but as a 'a conservation organization committed to saving species around the world'. Paris Zoo calls itself 'a modern conservation site'.

We want to believe in zoos. We quickly forget unsavoury incidents. People were sad when Knut, a polar bear cub who became the star of Berlin Zoo, collapsed and drowned at just four years old, but it later emerged he had a rare auto-immune disease. People were outraged when, in 2014, Copenhagen Zoo culled a male giraffe, dissected him in front of visitors, and fed the pieces to the lions, but this was explained as a Danish thing. People were hooked when the Netflix show *Tiger King* showed the cruel, sinister reality of tiger-breeding, but the show focused on the US's roadside zoos – not on the august institutions that wealthy city-dwellers go to. If you wanted a better relationship with animals, step one was still to go to the zoo.

For me, rejecting zoos was also frankly inconvenient. Going to the zoo is an intensely normal thing to do with your kids – a walk-in storybook: 32 million people a year visit zoos in the UK and Ireland, equivalent to nearly half the population. Unlike them, I had to think of somewhere else to take my daughters on a sunny Saturday afternoon. Could I really not take them to the zoo in good conscience?

To start with, do any other species keep other species in captivity? The only example I could find was some herder ants, who feed on honeydew produced by aphids. In order to stop the aphid colony from flying away, the ants sometimes bite off the aphids' wings. The ants also excrete chemicals that tranquillise the aphids, again discouraging them from flying away. In return, the ants protect the aphids from predators. This aside, humans seem to be the only species that keeps other species in captivity.

Zoos might seem unnatural to us if it weren't for Noah's Ark. Here's a story, repeated at churches and many schools, where humans save animals by keeping them in captivity. The story of the great flood is found elsewhere – *The Epic of Gilgamesh* – but in the Christian version, Noah is told that God is about to flood the world, killing every living creature. Unsurprisingly the metaphor has spread through the conservation world. There was ARKive, an initiative to keep photos of every endangered species, and the Amphibian Ark, an effort to save endangered amphibians. There's a Noah's Ark Zoo in Somerset, west England, and one in Georgia, in the southern United States. London Zoo itself, located at the northern end of Regent's Park, was initially nicknamed the Ark in the Park.

When you visit a zoo, you don't see much about the history. Maybe that's because the one thing that everyone can agree on is that zoos' origin is not good. In fact their origin is very bad. You could go back over millennia to find examples of humans treating captive animals appallingly. The story that most shocked me dated back three centuries.

Augustus the Strong liked everything in excess. As ruler of Saxony and Poland, he collected art and palaces. When he died in 1733 – of alcohol poisoning, of course – he may have left more than 300 illegitimate children. He collected animals too, and had sponsored an expedition to North Africa to bring back specimens.

In the days before there were widespread paintings of exotic species, let alone wildlife documentaries, menageries like his must have been the most astounding places. For visitors, they were meeting zones between wilderness and civilisation. Not long before, people had wondered whether hippos were mythical creatures. Now, for the first time since the Roman era, you could see a rhino being paraded in Europe: one reached Lisbon in 1515, another reached London in 1684. What would it feel like, as an adult of the time, to see a rhino? What would it feel like *to be* the rhino?

For Augustus, seeing the animals wasn't enough. He was into what I suppose museum curators today call 'interactive exhibits'. In 1719, when his son married the daughter of the Holy Roman Emperor, Augustus treated the invited guests to a set-piece fight between lions, tigers, bulls, bears, boars and a monkey, while jams and refreshments were served. Everyone was interested – except the animals. One of the lions decided to lie down and sleep quietly, according to an account in a contemporary magazine, the *Mercure de France*.

Eventually Augustus the Strong became fed up, and shot all the remaining animals, apart from a lion that was strangled and another unspecified animal that bled to death. Bear that in mind next time you think the father-in-law has been a bit overbearing at the wedding. 'So ended those festivities, after which we moved on to the Italian theatre,' reported the *Mercure de France*, rather abruptly. At another event over which Augustus presided, more than 1,000 animals – mainly foxes and hares – were tossed high into the air (and to their eventual death).

The story of Augustus, which is not unique in its brutality, demonstrates how our ancestors could be absolutely indifferent to whether captive animals lived or died. Captivity didn't bring any moral responsibility. For owners of menageries, animals were creatures of whim: you could gawp at them or kill them. We had triumphed over wild animals; to the victor, the spoils.

Zoos were a variation on the theme of menageries. When they took hold in the nineteenth century, they weren't trying to save animals from disaster. Who would have looked at lions free on the African savannah in the 1840s and said, 'Quick, these will disappear unless we lock them up in the heart of London'? Zoos were instead an extension of the Enlightenment's search to collect, categorise and colonise the world.

Most accounts start with Paris as the first modern zoo. The French revolutionaries didn't like the opulence of Louis XVI's menagerie, so his animals were taken to a new home at the natural history museum. The conditions were so bad that most of the animals died within a year. An inauspicious start to the zoo era. Nonetheless, a zoo opened in London in 1828, followed by Berlin. New York's Central Park Zoo finally came in 1864.

Although zoos were different from the menageries that came before them, they ran up against some of the same issues. Their first problem was procuring the exotic animals whom their patrons wanted to see. This meant going into the wild, and killing vast numbers of their relatives so as to be able to take the babies.

Carl Hagenbeck, one of the most famous exotic-animal traders, sold thousands of lions, bears, elephants and other animals. The numbers slaughtered were multiples higher. Such bloodshed was kept from zoo visitors. The director of Bronx Zoo, William Hornaday, specifically told Hagenbeck not to mention that the capture of four young Indian rhinos had involved the death of forty adult ones. He justified the slaughter on the basis that the rhinos would benefit the world more in New York than 'running wild in the jungles of Nepal, seen only at rare intervals by a few ignorant natives'.

In one instance, the German colonial army set off to capture an elephant for Berlin Zoo. The men found a herd, built a fence around it so the animals couldn't escape, and shot all the adults. They were left with seven calves, of which three survived and one made it back to Berlin. 'We seemed so small, so insignificant when compared to the mighty animals in the mighty wild,' said Hans Dominik, the army captain involved, bizarrely. Our outrage at the wasteful hunting of the nineteenth century must also be directed at zoos.

The animals who survived may have wished they hadn't. An elephant seal transported by Hagenbeck went forty days without a bath or food. When animals arrived at the zoos, they found cramped cages or barren enclosures. The enclosures were designed so that visitors could surround the animals to gain the best possible view, a terrifying experience for creatures used to trying to escape predators. (This design nonetheless lived on, for example in Toronto Zoo, which opened in 1974.)

Zoos needed vast quantities of animals in the early days, because they couldn't keep them alive. London Zoo's big cats survived an average of two years. Its first gorilla died in 1887 after being fed cheese sandwiches, sausages and beer. Zoos weren't overly fussed by such premature ends, not least because many naturalists enjoyed working on dead animals. These weren't just teething troubles: in Paris, after the Second World War, most monkeys died within two years of captivity.

What was this all for? Historically 'the only time you see mass movement of animals is in time of empire', says Naomi Sykes, a professor of archaeology at Exeter University. Menageries had satisfied rich people's curiosity and search for prestige. Zoos came of age in the era of European empires. They showcased the fruits of imperialism. Alfred Russel Wallace is remembered as a naturalist and Frederick Selous as a hunter, but they both sent back specimens to the Natural History Museum. Shipping animals around was a sign of human power.

Colonialism relied on a sense of moral superiority. Zoos fitted snugly into this. Like colonisers themselves, zoologists could claim some noble, scientific purpose. London Zoo was supposedly the world's first scientific zoo, created by the Zoological Society of London. Initially visits were limited to the wealthy, but gradually they democratised, not least because the owners needed more entry fees.

The need for money led zoos down another, questionable path. London Zoo catered to animal-breeders, as well as scientists. Instead of saving wild animals, it would try to create domesticated ones. It offered subscribers animals for collections and hunting, and tried various cross-breeding schemes, including one with asses and zebus (cows from southern Asia with humped shoulders). Breeders could also pay the Zoological Society a stud fee for the services of a zebu or zebra to breed with their livestock. One domestication effort related to a brightly coloured pheasant called the Himalayan monal – its backers, including Queen Victoria, were keen to shoot the birds. More than 1,000 monals were collected from the wild, most died on the way back, only a few ever bred. Living throughout the Himalayas, the species today seems to be doing fine without London Zoo.

By the end of the nineteenth century zoos' hopes for domestication had been dashed. What remained was a willingness to play around with animals' natural state. Well into the twentieth century, seals were dressed as mermaids and donkeys painted with zebra stripes. Chimpanzees were taken to tea parties. (This was the inspiration for using chimps in adverts for tea, for which they were dressed in human clothing. PG Tips' chimpanzee-filled tea ads were the longest-running ad campaign on British television, lasting from 1956 until 2002. The trauma of performance and human handling meant that the last surviving chimp struggled to integrate into a zoo.)

Zoos saw themselves as different to circuses, but there was often a conduit between the two. In 1882 London Zoo sold its male elephant, Jumbo, to P. T. Barnum, the showman and circus entrepreneur, who shipped him to the US to perform. Barnum, who earlier in his career had exhibited a black man before becoming an abolitionist, was the type of morally flexible founder that circuses required. He knew an elephant was worth more in an American circus than in an English zoo. Jumbo was a commercial success, until, after three years in the circus, he was killed by a train in Ontario while being led to his wagon for transportation to the next venue. London Zoo was nonetheless happy to sell his mate, Alice, to the circus as a replacement. Barnum displayed the live female and the dead male together, until Alice too died in a fire in 1886.

Animals were disposable. In 1943, the keepers at Tokyo's Ueno Zoo killed twenty-seven animals. The slaughter was a wartime tactic by the government to show the need for sacrifice. Three elephants refused to eat poisoned food, so were starved to death instead. Afterwards, a memorial service was held in honour of the animal 'martyrs'; other zoos in the Japanese empire followed suit.

Ignorance was more widespread than evil. London Zoo held tea parties of baby mammals, separated from their parents. It allowed actual children to ride on a giant tortoise's back. Visitors were allowed to feed the animals – a practice not abandoned until the 1960s, when an African elephant died after falling over when reaching for a bun. The zoo's first scientific director, a zoologist called Edward Hindle, argued in 1950 that zoo animals didn't need large amounts of space, because in the wild their territories would be constrained by rivals and predators. 'Indeed, as a general rule, it is doubtful whether lack of space is a very serious consideration when providing suitable accommodation for animals,' he said. Hindle also thought that elephants and birds of prey were 'among the easiest to keep in menageries and generally live to a ripe old age'.

Perhaps the most influential zookeeper ever was Heini Hediger, director of Basel and Zurich zoos in the 1940s and 1950s. Hediger was in some ways a moderniser. He wrote books urging zoos to make animals' enclosures less barren (although many zoos ignored him). He decried how elephants were not given space to bathe, leading to their skin drying and their hair falling out. But even Hediger thought that it was 'important that elephants should become accustomed to being chained at night' – so that they learnt to be subdued. This has also turned out to be very wrong.

Zoos had other priorities than the animals. The first was attracting visitors. The day after the first giraffes arrived at London Zoo in 1836, more than 500 schoolchildren came to see them. But that novelty became ever harder to create. When the poet e. e. cummings complained in 1925 that zoos were 'poor, placid, colourless things', his real gripe was that they lacked the 'outrageous intensity' of circuses.

All the while, zookeepers seemed to believe that any animal – no matter how large, no matter what natural and social environment it had evolved in – could be kept in captivity. 'It only requires a few men with sufficient initiative and adequate funds at their disposal to make the keeping of whales a practical proposition in Europe,' said Hediger. Whales! All animal life could and should be mastered. David Attenborough's first television series, *Zoo Quest*, involved going round the world, and bringing back vast numbers of creatures – including lemurs from Madagascar, parrots from New Guinea, and armadillos from Paraguay – for examination at London Zoo. 'Most zoos assumed that there was an unlimited supply of exhibits in the wild,' Attenborough later recalled. Satisfying our curiosity is the spirit that has powered zoos for most of their existence.

If the best zoos were wrong, general practice was shocking. In 1973, an American collector called Peter Batten gave twenty-four mammals and birds to Gladys Porter Zoo in Texas. Just six weeks later, he discovered five of the animals were dead and six injured or mutilated by poor husbandry. He went on a tour of almost 200 American zoos, and concluded angrily that their 'animal husbandry was inept and in some cases nonexistent'.

If you told a child this history before taking them to the zoo, they would probably want to go somewhere else. Animals were harmed in the making of these institutions. That history doesn't necessarily mean that zoos can't be a good way of relating to animals today. But once you realise that their primary aims did not generally include the welfare and conservation of animals, and that things were indisputably bad until quite recently, it's easier to accept that things are still awry.

*

I assumed that, if there's one thing that zoos could guarantee, it would be a long life. But at least in the case of elephants, I was wrong. A paper in the journal *Science* reviewed the history of 786 zoo elephants, representing about half the global zoo population between 1960 and 2005. It compared them with nearly 4,000 elephants in Kenya and Myanmar. The results were eye-opening.

In zoos, African elephants had a median lifespan of 16.9 years. In a national park in Kenya, their median lifespan was fifty-six years, or around thirty-six years if human-caused deaths were taken into account.

In zoos, the median Asian elephant lived to the age of 18.9 years. In Myanmar's logging industry, where elephants have been used for labour, the median was nearly forty-two years. If elephants were living longer working in the logging industry than they were in zoos, then something seems seriously wrong.

'Overall,' concluded the researchers, 'bringing elephants into zoos profoundly affects their viability.' The study was published in 2008. If elephants' life expectancy has improved since, the Association of Zoos & Aquariums, the trade body of US zoos, could publish updated data. It hasn't done so. I emailed AZA multiple times asking why and it declined to explain. Instead it pointed me to more recent papers comparing the welfare of elephants in different zoo settings – that is, not comparing them to wild elephants. (One of those papers concluded that three-quarters of elephants in US zoos were overweight.)

Another study looked at how elephants spend their time in zoos. It found that, after feeding, the most commonly observed behaviour was activity not found in the wild, which appeared to serve no purpose. Elephants rock and sway. As many as 85 per cent of elephants in the US did this during the day; two-thirds did it at night. One possible explanation is that in zoos the elephants no longer need to search for food, as they would do in the wild. Biologists call this 'stereotypic behaviour', a strange name for behaviour which is the opposite of typical. Abnormal behaviour is also more common in elephants with foot diseases, which are often caused by hard zoo floors. Moreover, zoos used to chain animals at night, supposedly to avoid aggression. But the night is an important time for elephants to socialise: they sleep only two to four hours a night, and even then sometimes partly on top of one another. In zoos, many elephants are still locked up or placed in individual stalls. They are made to fit our schedule.

What about breeding? I seem to remember lots of photos in newspapers of baby elephants at the zoo, shyly rubbing against their mothers' legs. In fact, elephants also do not breed easily in zoos. Some females don't ovulate in captivity, and males have poor libido and low sperm count. The only way to maintain genetic diversity is to import more elephants or to ferry the existing elephants around the world.

In 2010 Janine Brown, an expert on elephant reproduction at Washington DC's National Zoo, predicted that all elephant species in North American zoos would die out in 'only a few decades', because of infertility. A team at Berlin's Leibniz Institute for Zoo and Wildlife Research, led by veterinarian Thomas Hildebrandt, pioneered a new method of artificial insemination. That's a pretty invasive procedure for animals as mentally complex as elephants. It also hasn't solved the problem. Some US zoos continue to bring in African elephants from the wild. Dallas Zoo, Omaha's Henry Doorly Zoo and Kansas' Sedgwick County Zoo imported eighteen elephants from Swaziland in 2016, where the wildlife service said they would otherwise have been culled. Zoos may be saving these elephants' lives, but they are subjecting them to long, stressful journeys and they are failing to establish self-perpetuating populations in the US. According to the Species360 database, there are now only around 150 African elephants and ninety-five Asian elephants in North American zoos. The efforts to ensure genetic diversity are ever more expensive and less defensible: in 2018 Melbourne Zoo flew an elephant called Ongard to Zoo Miami in a shipping container, at a cost of $500,000.

Why would elephants live shorter lives, breed less successfully, and perform unnatural behaviours in zoos? The zoo environment – so relaxing and natural for kids – involves various hazards. The elephants undergo long transfers between zoos, and often lose contact with their mothers. Wild elephants have complex family relationships – they live in matriarchal herds, with mothers, daughters and young (although there are differences between species, as you would expect given that Asian elephants are more closely related to extinct woolly mammoths than to African elephants). Without those relationships, their ability to breed drops off. Like humans, adult elephants find childcare easier when a grandparent is around. Among elephants in Myanmar's logging industry and in African parks, infant mortality is lower if the grandmother lives with the calf. In Myanmar, in the presence of a grandmother, females would also have more calves. In zoos, animals are shipped in and out, in line with breeding plans, financial reasons and space constraints. It's darkly ironic: zoos are built for families, just not the families of the animals who live there.

Most European and North American zoos, if they keep a male elephant, keep only one. So that bull has no opportunity to learn from other bulls. This partly reflects the idea that males are aggressive and naturally solitary. In fact bulls may become more aggressive when they are kept alone. And in the wild, males are often near herds and in groups of males. Adult bulls were within thirty metres of another elephant half of the time, one study found. They have social relationships that remain stable for years. Young bulls are even more dependent on company. Male elephants can wait until they are fifteen years old before they separate themselves from the family group, and spend time in all-male groups instead. Rather than this natural exploration and choosing of companions, elephants in zoos are liable to being lumped with whoever is available – and transferred to other zoos when space becomes too tight. Part of the reason some animals appear 'aggressive' or 'problematic' in zoos is probably that they can't choose their companions, or keep their distance from them; anyone who has shared a flat will empathise. Damian Aspinall's Howletts park at least keeps the animals together as a herd, bringing in males from time to time. It claims to have bred more elephants than any other zoo in the world, and more than all other British zoos put together. But even it is trying to manage complex relationships that humans don't fully understand.

This is the obvious reality of zoos: there's a lack of space. AZA, the US zoo association, recommends that an elephant be given a minimum of 500 square metres of outdoor space. In the wild, Asian elephants roam several hundred square *kilometres*. That is the difference between the size of a toilet cubicle and the size of several football pitches. Elephants' natural environment is also warmer than many of the zoos where they are kept in the US and Europe. Zoo elephants held at northern latitudes in colder weather have higher concentrations of stress hormones than those held closer to the temperatures where they have evolved.

Put simply, it has been hard for zoos to adjust their own physical limitations to the elephants' social and psychological needs. You can't provide an expansive elephant habitat and be conveniently located for the London Underground. We don't make animals suffer deliberately, like Augustus the Strong; we do it by a mixture of selfishness and ignorance, by overestimating our ability to provide wild animals with good homes. If this is love, it's the clumsiest variety.

Zoos are learning how to improve lives for their elephants: for example, the animals fare better when they can choose whether to be inside or outside, and they show lower stress levels when they have good relationships with their keepers. Zoos once tried to dominate elephants: 'we're part of the herd and we're the top part of the herd. Which is the way it should be,' a keeper at London Zoo told viewers of a 1994 BBC documentary. The European Association of Zoos and Aquaria has decided that all contact between keepers and elephants should take place through a protective barrier, so that humans have less of a dominant position and elephants acquire more autonomy, although zoos have until 2030 to implement this. But there is strong evidence that elephants cannot live as well in today's zoos as they do in the wild.

Georgia Mason, a biology professor at the University of Guelph, and one of the authors of the *Science* study on elephant longevity, believes that zoos could probably work out ways to keep elephants healthily, if they threw enough money at the problem. But she questions the value for money. 'Is it worth it? The tens of millions it takes to house elephants well, should that be better spent creating reserves in Sri Lanka? Or should it be better allocated to another species that has the potential to do fantastically well in captivity and is threatened in the wild?'

To me, the answer is fairly obvious. The elephant in the room is that elephants should not be in the room, they should not be in the small outdoor enclosure, they should not be in the zoo at all.

For Ron Kagan, director of Detroit Zoo, this was a gradual realisation. Kagan is an unusual figure in the zoo world. As a boy, he had two passions: motor racing and animals. He failed as a racing driver. 'I was about to say it's a silly story, but it's my story. So it is what it is,' he told me, when I reached him by phone.

In his early years working in zoos, Kagan saw elephants with behavioural problems. He visited Kenya and met Joyce Poole, who had done pioneering fieldwork researching the lives of male elephants at Amboseli National Park. 'I asked her, do you ever see problems with elephants in the wild – do you see foot problems, skin problems, do you see behavioural issues? She nicely but firmly said, "You foolish boy, of course we don't." And I needed to hear that, because I was struggling back then as I saw elephants in zoos with a lot of problems, and within the zoo world no one wanted to touch that.' On one occasion, an elephant arriving at the zoo 'screamed' while being unloaded.

Kagan's basic insight was that zoos had fallen behind pet-owners and farmers in understanding what animals wanted. And what those animals wanted, he surmised, was agency – freedom to take decisions, and control over meaningful aspects of their lives, such as whether to be close to humans or inside or outside.

'You could keep a man and a woman in a prison, and you could keep them healthy and alive for a very long time. That does not mean that their welfare would be good.'

Detroit Zoo increased the size of its elephant enclosure. But the city's winters are brutal, and elephants risk serious injury if they slip on the ice, so the zoo could not allow them to wander outdoors as they would like. In 2004 Kagan decided the zoo could no longer responsibly keep its two elephants – and announced he was shipping them off to a sanctuary in California. 'We can't create a proper matriarchal herd, and we can't change the climate, although it is changing. And we can't provide ten square miles or twenty or thirty or whatever. It just made no sense,' he recalls. The Association of Zoos & Aquariums, which has oversight over elephants in accredited US zoos, disagreed. It demanded Kagan send the two elephants to a zoo in Columbus, Ohio, where they would have no more space, no warmer climate, no soft ground and would be handled with bull hooks. Kagan sent the elephants to the sanctuary instead; AZA suspended him for three months.

Since then, other zoos have also closed their elephant exhibits – San Francisco Zoo, Alaska Zoo, London Zoo – but they have generally couched the decision in terms of their own facilities, rather than admitting the principle that we don't know how to care for elephants. London Zoo transferred its elephants to its sister safari park, Whipsnade. Safari parks are better in some ways – cheetahs wouldn't breed at London Zoo, but bred at Whipsnade, where they could be further away from lions – but they are not fundamentally different. At Whipsnade, the elephants still have just thirty acres: 0.12 square kilometres. Meanwhile, other zoos are clinging on to their elephants: Warsaw Zoo has experimented giving its herd medical marijuana, CBD, in an attempt to reduce their stress levels.

Are elephants the exception or the norm, when it comes to not being suited to zoos? Elephants' size and social nature do present particular problems. Most mammals live longer in captivity than in the wild, not least because of a lack of predators. Many, like lions, also breed well in zoos. But there are many others that don't, even though they have been kept by humans for hundreds of years. In American zoos, between 1970 and 2011, three-quarters of cheetahs died without having cubs. The species is vulnerable to extinction, but zoos can't help keep the populations up.

Zoos are so compressed that, if you look closely, you can't help but notice that something is off. Visitors to the zoo are unlikely to see giraffes and deer running. Going from exhibit to exhibit, we move around more than the animals do. In the wild, parrots spend most of their time flocking. In the early days at London Zoo, the birds were tied to posts so that visitors could admire them. That doesn't happen any more, but parrots are kept in aviaries a fraction of their natural range. Sea turtles dive up to 300 metres or more in the wild; no aquarium can replicate this. Polar bears have huge natural ranges, to which no zoo can ever come close.

If you've been to a zoo, you've probably seen animals behaving in a way that just doesn't look right. A giraffe licking a fence. A tiger pacing their enclosure. A bird plucking a lot of feathers. This is stereotypic behaviour, like the elephant rocking. What zoo-goers want is that animals can behave as they would in the wild. But zoos will never be able to mimic the wild. They put animals in artificial groups, and they fundamentally change how animals feed. Wild giraffes come and go frequently, rather than form defined units; they graze all day, rather than being fed at specified times. Zoos have often fed animals wrongly. Everyone knows that pandas eat only bamboo. But in the wild, pandas would eat other things, including scavenged meat. Bamboo alone is what they eat when their habitat is lost – it's 'essentially a famine diet', argues Naomi Sykes, who is studying the skeletons of dead zoo animals to understand how they have been fed over the years. Predators can't hunt in zoos, not least because we wouldn't want our kids to watch it. 'You don't release a live goat into a lion enclosure, but that would be the best thing for the lion,' says Sykes. At best big cats can be made to reach for their food. As for migratory species, they obviously can't migrate.

Then there's the human presence. Some species, such as red kangaroos, seem more vigilant as visitor numbers rise. Others, like orangutans, seem shy. Others, such as meerkats, seem to be unperturbed. We simply don't know how humans affect the well-being of most zoo species.

The coronavirus lockdown, however, gave us an indication that at least some rare animals do better when we are not there. Ying Ying and Le Le, two giant-panda cubs, had arrived at the Ocean Park amusement park in Hong Kong in 2007, a gift from the Chinese government to mark the tenth anniversary of the province's handover by the UK. The cubs came from China's famous Wolong Center, and had all the fanfare you would have expected – a farewell ceremony, bespoke cages, five handlers. 'We hope they will make babies soon,' said China's secretary of home affairs. More than 20,000 visitors came to see the pandas on their first day on display.

But the pandas showed no interest in mating. Ocean Park keepers tried to encourage them to mate for ten years, after the pandas became sexually mature. Then in late January 2020, the zoo was closed because of coronavirus. Weeks later, at the start of the breeding season, the pandas' behaviour changed: Ying Ying, the female, spent more time playing in the water, while Le Le, the male, searched for her scent. They mated for the first time, in early April. We don't know what exactly changed, but would it be surprising if the animals rather enjoyed not being inspected by hundreds of thousands of strangers?

Some zoologists have argued that animals don't need to be able to act as they do in the wild. Animals only walk and fly so far because they need to find food and avoid predators; in the zoo, they can do this without moving. 'I love it when I hear that, I love it! Because it's such a silly argument,' exclaimed Detroit Zoo's Ron Kagan, when I put this to him. 'If I say to you, Henry, I'm going to give you a lovely house and you're going to tell me what your five or six favourite foods are, and you're going to have these five or six fabulous foods, and you can just stay in the house, you don't need to walk around, I'll just feed you – obviously, anybody would go nuts.'

Detroit Zoo has decided to move out its large birds – eagles, vultures, flamingos. 'Most birds fly,' said Kagan. 'If a large bird can't fly, you are fundamentally compromising a large part of its life experience. I can't understand its language – I don't know if it's saying, I hate you, but I'm sure it's very frustrated.'

Kagan argues that there may be some species that do better in a zoo than in the wild. 'Penguins in the wild are just harassed by everything, if not killed by everything,' he says. 'And the penguins here have an incredible quality of life. I want to be able to say that about every single animal here. I don't feel confident saying that.'

Detroit wants to be a 'lifelong sanctuary' for such animals. Its annual visitor numbers had risen from 1 million to 1.4 million since the elephants left. Yet Kagan still feels that his message does not resonate with other zoos. 'I wish that I was part of a mainstream effort. But it is what it is.'

David Hancocks, a British-born architect who spent his career planning and directing zoos, tried to improve life for animals when he ran Woodland Park Zoo in Seattle. The zoo built new primate enclosures with living trees and shrubs to allow the animals to explore and climb. But Hancocks became disillusioned. 'It was obvious that other zoos weren't the slightest bit interested in doing what we had been doing. No one tried to do anything like this for more than ten years, when I prepared a concept design for gorillas at Melbourne Zoo,' he told me.

Although zoos do offer gorillas enrichment – that is, things to interact with – 'it's the sort of enrichment that people get in a retirement home.' Overall, 'the conditions the animals had in the 1960s are fundamentally no different to the conditions they have today.'

I've often wondered if animals are bored in captivity. For at least twenty hours a day, elephants must find things to do in their enclosure. To humans, captivity *looks* boring, but what we do we know? Georgia Mason and a fellow researcher, Becky Meagher, placed mink in cages – similar to those used by fur farms. Some of the cages had interactive features, such as a water trough and rubber dog toys; others didn't. When the researchers presented other stimuli to the mink, they found that those with bare cages were more responsive. Mason and Meagher concluded, using the typically cautious language of academia, that the animals' behaviour was 'consistent with boredom'. When we get bored at the zoo, we can just leave. The animals can't.

The field of animal welfare in zoos is a surprisingly new one. Some zoos aren't very interested. 'There are a lot of zoos that are awful and should be shut down,' the head of one well-regarded zoo told me. In the world of zoos, everyone admits there are bad zoos, but no one ever names them – beyond the most obvious examples. Zoo d'Amnéville in north-east France has three white Bengal tigers who take part in a nightly fire show in front of hundreds of spectators. It's still a member of WAZA.

Even the best zoos are beset with compromises and unknowns. Detroit keeps two polar bears, and allows visitors to walk below them through a passage, seeing them swim. Ron Kagan referred to penguins as one of the beneficiaries of captivity, but studies have shown that at least one species of penguin, the little penguin native to Australia and New Zealand, is bothered by zoo visitors. There's no evidence to say that all twenty-odd species of penguins would do better in zoos than in the natural environments for which they have evolved. Some zoo animals are said by their keepers to like the presence of visitors, but that could be partly because their captive surroundings would otherwise be so light on stimulation.

The very least we can do is stop keeping species in zoos, unless there is some pressing conservation need. But hold on: isn't every animal in the zoo already contributing to conservation?

*

When I spoke to zookeepers, I heard three basic self-justifications for their role. Number one: we educate people about wildlife. Number two: we conserve species – both through breeding programmes in the zoos and by raising funds for projects further afield. And number three, never quite as explicit: zoos now have to exist, because what else would we do with the hundreds of thousands of captive animals we have accumulated?

In other words, the argument is partly that some animals are being sacrificed for the sake of others. One hundred years ago, when species weren't so threatened with extinction and when zoo populations weren't so established, zoos may have been unjustifiable. Now, under this logic, we do need them. Maybe we should never have started collecting animals in captivity, but we can't stop.

The first argument, education, has been hard to test. Zoo visitors do seem to learn about animals, but not very much. In the largest ever survey, 5,661 people were given questionnaires about biodiversity when they arrived at a zoo, and then again when they left. The authors called the survey 'the most compelling evidence to date' of zoos' educational importance. But the actual results were underwhelming. The proportion of visitors that showed some understanding of how individuals could protect biodiversity rose from 51 per cent on arrival to 59 per cent on departure. A good documentary would surely have the same or greater effect. We don't need zoos to show us what a tiger or a rhino looks like; we have soft toys and television.

Seeing animals up close may actually backfire. In one study, people were shown photos of chimpanzees against a natural setting, and then asked to say whether the apes were endangered. Another group of people were shown the same photos, except now the chimps were alongside humans. The second group were one-third less likely to categorise chimps as endangered.

This instinctively makes sense – the more accessible the animals appear, the less plausible it is that they are disappearing. Take giraffes. They are the most visible animals in our zoos. At London Zoo, their enclosure can be seen from the road, so they act as a kind of free sample for passers-by wondering whether they want to pay the entry fee. As a result, they seem serene and unthreatened. In the early 1990s, when the zoo fell into financial difficulties and had to slim its selection, David Attenborough said: 'Who can imagine London Zoo without giraffes?' He was right. You can't imagine the zoo without giraffes, so you can't imagine the world without giraffes. Perhaps that's why it comes as such a surprise to realise that their numbers in the wild have dropped more than 40 per cent since 1985, and that some subspecies of giraffe are now in danger of extinction.

The second justification for zoos, that they conserve animals, has an immediate problem. If you want to release animals into the wild, it's normally better to take them from elsewhere in the wild, rather than breed them in captivity. In 1993 the government of Namibia wanted to save the country's critically endangered black rhinos. There were no rhinos in zoos in Namibia, so instead eleven rhinos were taken from national parks and moved to ranches. There are now an estimated 560 rhinos on private land. (The government remains the legal owner of these rhinos, but the landowners make money from selling licences to hunt them.)

There are some clear-cut examples of zoos saving animals. The Arabian oryx, a species of antelope, was extinct in the wild by 1972, mainly due to hunting. But conservationists had captured a small number of the animals, transferred them to zoos – starting with Phoenix Zoo, Arizona, chosen for its similar climate to the Arabian peninsula. These zoos bred a 'world herd' of oryx, then released individuals in countries such as Jordan and Oman. The black-footed ferret, America's only native ferret, was thought to be extinct, until a young male was found in Wyoming in 1981. More individuals were tracked down, bred, and taken to the National Zoo in Washington, which prepared for the species' release back into the prairies, Mexico and Canada. The California condor, whose story we'll come to later in this book, is another example. But these successes haven't happened very often. There are tens of thousands of endangered species. How many have been successfully bred and reintroduced to the wild by zoos? One group of researchers puts the total at seventeen, including the condor and the Mongolian Przewalski's horse; another group disputes that zoos were involved in three of these. Damian Aspinall is right to doubt zoos' track record.

Captive breeding is not what zoos are focused on. There are around 25,000 vertebrate species in zoos and wildlife centres worldwide (this includes subspecies and breeds, so is a slight overestimate). Only just over 700 of these are in managed breeding programmes. Of all the vertebrate species, subspecies and breeds in zoos, only about one in seven is threatened with extinction or near-threatened. Most programmes to reintroduce animals to the wild have not relied on zoos – they have taken animals from elsewhere in the wild, or from research centres and wildlife agencies.

The zoos' biggest contribution came with amphibians, and even with amphibians there is a dark side. In the late 1990s, biologists noticed that some frog populations were being devastated. The cause is now understood to be a chytrid fungus, which affects amphibians' skin; it originated in east Asia at the start of the twentieth century, then spread globally thanks probably to the trade in frogs as pets and for medical research. The fungus is one of the most devastating diseases for wildlife in history, hitting frogs, toads and salamanders almost everywhere in the world. US zoos may have facilitated the pathogen's spread, by lobbying against import restrictions on amphibians. They also didn't do much to save the amphibians affected – for example, building up reserve populations.

I thought that zoos would at least be an insurance policy – holding lots of animals, which could be bred for release one day if necessary. In 2011, three-quarters of the mammal, bird, amphibian and reptile species in zoos were not threatened. When you walk past meerkats, red kangaroos or brown bears, you are walking past animals in the lowest category of conservation priority. They are taking up space in zoos that could be used by threatened animals. Amphibians are small, breed well in captivity, and around 40 per cent of their species are threatened with extinction. But as of 2011, zoos held fewer than one in twenty of the known amphibian species, compared with one in four known mammals and birds. The species that could give the most conservation value per dollar spent are small, quick-breeders, such as invertebrates, amphibians and bats; there's no evidence that this is where zoos focus.

Even where zoos and aquariums hold a threatened species, generally they have fewer than fifty individuals in captivity. That is seen as a key threshold for breeding populations. The remaining California condors were bred from fewer than thirty individuals, but other species will require many more individuals to maintain genetic diversity. Even when zoos do hold fifty individuals of a threatened species, the animals will generally be split across several zoos, which may be too far away from each other for a joint breeding plan to be practical. In 2011, a group of researchers concluded: 'most zoo populations are not being managed at adequate population sizes, reproductive rates, genetic diversity levels, and projected long-term viability that would allow them to contribute positively to species conservation'. In other words, the insurance policy is full of holes.

The longer that animals stay in zoos, the less easy it is to release them into the wild. There is also a real risk that zoos semi-domesticate animals. They are likely to select animals for their docility, not what the animals' natural environment demands. A study on translocating (wild-born) brushtail possums in Australia is instructive: the brushtails most likely to survive were those who showed most fear of being held by humans. Captivity can deprive animals of the skills they need for the wild. Game birds in captivity lose some of the behaviours that allow them to avoid predators.

Zoos do spend money on conserving animals, both in zoos and in the field. In 2008, the roughly 300 zoos and aquariums that are affiliated to WAZA reported spending a total of $350 million on conservation. How much of this money is spent is not clear. The total amount puts these zoos in the top tier of conservation charities – behind The Nature Conservancy, ahead of WWF International. But for US zoos, it represents roughly 2–3 per cent of their income. Some zoos give nothing. Even conscientious zoos have to spend most of their revenue running the exhibits. ZSL, owner of London Zoo and Whipsnade, spent about £38 million in 2018/19 on its animal population. Ticket prices and memberships brought in only £36 million. So although ZSL did spend around £20 million on scientific research and conservation, this was largely covered by donations and government grants – not by the zoo itself. Showing people captive animals seems an inefficient way of raising money. Many charities would expect to spend £5 on projects for every £1 they spent on fundraising.

Indeed, the reason that London Zoo fell into financial difficulties in the 1990s is that it had relied on public subsidies. After they were withdrawn, there were even rumours that the zoo would have to slaughter some of its animals. There was an echo of this in the coronavirus outbreak. Neumünster Zoo in Germany admitted its plan, if cash ran really low, was to feed some animals to others, and euthanise the seals who needed fresh fish. Zoos' finances are fragile; they are not reliable money-spinners for conservation.

In 2019 I took a reporting trip for the *Financial Times* to Mongolia to highlight ZSL's role in tackling the illegal trade of wildlife. Mongolia is sandwiched between Russia and China: it once sold furs to Soviet Russia, now it sells animal parts for medicine and adornments in China. We saw a dead steppe eagle for sale in a city market. We heard how the zoo was teaching border customs officials and their sniffer dogs to detect wildlife. A few months earlier one dog had found that a Mongolian man travelling to China had four pieces of freshly killed deer tail cling-filmed to his stomach; his companion had three bear teeth stuffed in his sock. Another dog intercepted an incoming railway shipment of 49,000 bullets, almost certainly intended for illegal hunting. This is worthy work, but it doesn't require an amusement park of caged animals half the world away.

I feel bad dunking on zoos. They are full of friendly keepers and good intentions. They don't cause a fraction of the harm to individual animals that farms do. But they claim to occupy the high ground and to have a real purpose, and that's what we should judge them against.

The worst zoos are those barely regulated establishments, which are modern-day menageries. GW Zoo in Oklahoma, featured in Netflix's *Tiger King*, was a disaster in terms of welfare (and quite a lot else). Under its founder, Joseph Maldonado-Passage, aka Joe Exotic, the zoo allowed visitors to cuddle tiger cubs. The enclosures were small cages with little chance for the tigers to hide from visitors. Young cubs were separated from their mothers and shipped off to who knows where. There were unconfirmed allegations that those too big to cuddle were shot and buried.

If you watch the show, you notice that Joe Exotic and his friends who ran similar operations use the same justifications as well-respected zoo-owners. They talk about education. They talk about saving tigers ('the wild ... no longer exists', said one collector-cum-zookeeper). They complain that Carole Baskin, the tiger-lover whose feud with Joe Exotic is the centrepiece of the show, ran a sanctuary where the tigers were kept in worse conditions. There's a link between established zoos, with their best-laid plans, and Joe Exotic's desire to keep animals and visitors' desire to cuddle them. If you shout loudly that keeping exotic animals in captivity is a good idea, some people will slightly mishear. If you allow petting zoos of cows and sheep, some people will wonder why they can't do the same with other zoo animals too. The good zoos and bad zoos are part of the same system. We need to change the system.

Joe Exotic himself came to an even more dramatic conclusion when he experienced captivity first-hand. In 2020 he was sentenced to 22 years for hiring a hitman to kill Baskin. 'If I would have known twenty years ago what life inside a cage is like, I would never have had a zoo,' he told the journalist Mariana van Zeller from prison. 'It doesn't matter if it's a tiger or a gerbil: no animal belongs in a cage.'

*

Whisper it in church, but Noah was a bit of an amateur. He could never hope to fit all 8 million species on his Ark (even if he had time to fetch the polar bears, who appear without fail on my daughters' arks). He could never create sustainable populations from just two individuals of the species (this would also have been a problem for Adam and Eve). Plus his conservationist reputation was ruined a bit too, when he celebrated the end of the flood by eating some of the animals, and with God telling humans that they could now eat everything that 'lives and moves about' and that they should 'be fruitful and increase in number'.

But from Noah's point of view, we are the amateurs. He spent barely a year in his boat, before letting the animals free. If only zoos took the same, focused approach. It would stop them storing up animals without really defining what they will achieve.

In 1986 Michael Soulé, a Californian professor sometimes known as the father of conservation biology, came up with the concept of a 'demographic winter'. He argued that the human population would keep rising for centuries, leading to the devastation of tropical forests and the possible extinction of 2,000 large terrestrial mammal species. It would be zoos' job to keep captive populations of these mammals, until the human population had subsided. There was a catch: the 'demographic winter' would last for 500–1,000 years. Demographers now think that human population will plateau sometime this century, although the threats to tropical forests and to many species are almost as vivid as Soulé thought, not least due to climate change. Soulé put too much faith in zoos. Zoos were not, and are not, capable of holding genetically diverse species for a millennium. They can't even maintain populations of elephants for a few decades. They are caught in a bind, stuck with animals who aren't needed for conservation.

So even as a metaphor, Noah's Ark does not fit today's zoos. The zoos have kept individual animals in captivity for decades, and species for nearly two centuries. Release is a distant prospect. Zoos are weird retrofits onto the menageries that preceded them. They have tried to do too many things – to educate and entertain us, to inform scientists, to breed animals, to act as businesses. They have achieved remarkably little for animals.

You can't click your fingers and make zoos disappear. There are 1.7 million birds, 1.4 million mammals, 460,000 amphibians and 155,000 reptiles in zoos, aquariums and other facilities, according to Species360. (Who knows how many more are in roadside zoos.) A lot of these animals deserve better lives.

Some animals need to be rehomed in sanctuaries. Bronx Zoo now has just one Asian elephant, ironically called Happy. She arrived in the US from Thailand in the 1970s, along with six other young elephants, two of whom have ended up in circuses. In her early years, zoo-goers would ride on her back. Her enclosure is just 1.2 acres, the size of a small football pitch. Wild Asian elephants rarely experience temperatures below 15°C. Winter temperatures in the Bronx are regularly below zero. Happy has had no elephant company since another female elephant, Sammie, was euthanised in 2006.

In 2005, Happy became the first elephant to recognise herself in a mirror. A white paint cross was placed on one side of her head; when she then approached a full-length mirror, she repeatedly touched that spot on her head. That suggested a level of self-awareness that few non-human animals have shown. Now approaching her fiftieth birthday, she has survived longer than most elephants in zoos. But video clips show that her behaviour is abnormal – she swings her trunk from side to side and stands with one or two legs off the ground, perhaps to take the weight off diseased feet.

A campaign group called the Nonhuman Rights Project has been demanding Happy be now transferred to the Elephant Sanctuary in Tennessee. It claims that the elephant should be considered a legal person – because, like most humans, she can exercise freedom of choice. The argument is that the zoo isn't violating any statute, but the statutes themselves are wrong. Happy's case is supported by elephant experts Cynthia Moss and Joyce Poole, the latter suggesting that Happy's behaviour is likely to become more normal if she is moved to a spacious sanctuary.

'We're trying to create a social justice movement here,' says the Nonhuman Rights Project's founder Steven Wise, an energetic former Harvard law professor. His historical reference points are clear. He keeps 147 books on slavery and abolition in his office, and likes to quote Martin Luther King's phrase: 'The arc of the moral universe is long, but it bends toward justice.' The ark of animals, meanwhile, isn't bending at all. Bronx Zoo argues that Happy receives adequate care and might not survive the journey to a sanctuary. She doesn't get on with other elephants, but does have long-standing relationships with her keepers, the zoo claims. The Project denies that Happy is problematic: she has only ever been kept with four other elephants, two of whom she did get on with.

The idea that the problem lies with Happy, not her surroundings, would be more persuasive if she were the first 'problematic' elephant at Bronx Zoo. In the early 1900s, a male elephant called Gunda arrived from India. He was initially good tempered, giving children rides. But several years later, keepers reported that Gunda had become violent. He was kept in chains. Visitors complained about his treatment, and suggested a larger enclosure. In response, the zoo depicted the elephant like an insubordinate prisoner: 'It's now up to Gunda; Elephant's Chains Will Be Removed as Soon as He Becomes Safe,' ran a 1914 headline in the *New York Times*, citing the zoo's administrators. Gunda was out of luck. Less than a year later, he was shot dead, because he reportedly charged a keeper and had anyway become little use as an exhibit. 'It was a kindness to kill him,' explained William Hornaday, the zoo's director and coincidentally a keen taxidermist. Happy's state should make us wonder how far we've come.

New York judges have expressed sympathy with the Project's basic argument regarding Happy – and questioned how the law currently divides the world into 'persons' and 'things'. 'The Court agrees that Happy is not just a legal thing, or property. She is an intelligent, autonomous being who should be treated with respect and dignity, and who may be entitled to liberty,' wrote Justice Alison Tuitt in 2020. But she ruled, in line with precedent, that animals can't be legal persons because they can't have legal duties. The same precedent suggests that it's for politicians, not judges, to change the statute. Lobby groups of farmers, zoos and aquariums have warned that, if the Project's case is successful, "virtually *all* animals" who are currently kept in farms, zoos and homes could end up being freed. The legal battle continues. Meanwhile, the Nonhuman Rights Project's other 'clients' include chimpanzees and potentially soon orcas. If judges don't grant freedom to the animals, the movement may try to put the matter to public votes in California instead.

There are other ways that animals could be given a voice within our democracies. Sue Donaldson and Will Kymlicka, philosophers at Queen's University in Kingston, Ontario, argue that domesticated animals should be treated as co-citizens. These animals are members of our society, and democracies are founded on the principle that members of society should have a say in how the rules are made. Domesticated animals can't vote, but countries could therefore set up ombudspeople to look out for their interests or reserve seats in parliament for people to represent them. The real goal, argue Donaldson and Kymlicka, is to break our basic assumption that we can use animals in certain ways. They want domesticated animals to be able to choose how they interact with humans, and believe that animal sanctuaries could be places of experimentation for a more just future.

But even if all zoos were willing to give up their elephants to sanctuaries, the cost would be enormous. The Performing Animal Welfare Society (PAWS), where Detroit Zoo and Alaska Zoo sent their elephants when they closed their exhibits, says that caring for an elephant costs $70,000 a year. The Elephant Sanctuary in Tennessee, which has agreed to take Happy, costs even more. It offers five-star treatment for former zoo and performing elephants. No visitors are allowed, but on short videos you can see the elephants romping around on 2,700 acres of forests, lake and grassland (more than 2,000 times the size of Happy's current lodgings). If we wanted to provide sanctuary-style care for the nearly 250 elephants that are currently in US zoos, the running costs would be roughly $17 million a year (using PAWS's costs) or $85 million a year (using the Elephant Sanctuary's costs). And elephants can live to seventy and beyond. Europe has no elephant sanctuary at all.

Zoos, meanwhile, should stop hiding behind the vague, untestable promise of educating visitors. Their first promise should be to treat their animals well; that would also be the best education for visitors. In the Netherlands, Apenheul park allows primates to roam free with the visitors. Gorillas need to be separated from other primates, but the barrier is a water-filled moat, rather than walls or cages. The park closes for six months in the winter. This is a world away from zoos as we know them. This is what happens if you put the individual animal first. This kind of zoo passes the animal test.

'If we started again,' biologist Georgia Mason told me, 'we would have fewer species [in zoos]. There would be some kind of really smart triage – where you decide, OK, these animals don't need help; these animals do need help but zoos aren't the way to do it; and *these* animals need help and zoos are a good way to provide it.'

The zoos of the future would house only a few species that are close to extinction, are likely to breed well in captivity and for whom there is a reasonable prospect of reintroduction to the wild, because, say, land is being acquired and poachers are being excluded. Flying individual pandas around the world improved the Chinese government's image, but it did not provide optimal reproductive conditions for the pandas.

Today Detroit Zoo has 'only' 2,000 animals. 'Do you need to see 10,000? It's silly,' says Kagan. 'It's not all the old menagerie.' The animals are not easily seen either. 'Sometimes it will take you five or ten minutes to find the gorillas because you have to walk around the multi-acre facility. Some people get really upset, other people get it. We tell people there's an alternative – you can spent $1,500, go to Rwanda for two weeks, get bitten by a thousand mosquitoes, climb a mountain and you'll see gorillas for thirty minutes. I call it the McDonald's effect – people are so used to seeing things right away, and that's all they need. I need to see it, and then move on. That's not a meaningful experience. It's like a grocery store. There's really no great value in that.'

But Kagan thinks zoos can change people's expectations. 'The public, for the most part, if you explain stuff to them they'll go, oh, well, we didn't know and if that's the case, OK, make the changes. It won't be unanimous but we should believe in the public.' Look at it this way: if zoos can't convince visitors on this point, what hope do they have of educating people more broadly?

*

My resistance to going to a zoo crumbled in San Francisco.

We arrived on a cloudy weekday, when most kids were at school. A rhino with a horn shaved off butted around a large blue ball. A wolverine ran round disturbingly in a figure of eight. Penguin feeding would begin shortly. When a zoo is empty, you realise how much concrete there is – the wide walkways for families and buggies. For a place that prides itself on bringing you close to nature, it feels eerily unnatural.

If I'd seen one of these animals in the wild, I would have happily sat for hours watching them. But here in the zoo, surrounded by goodies, I felt impelled to keep moving. Eliza, Cleo and I wandered up to the western lowland gorilla enclosure, where half a dozen apes sat placidly ten metres from each other. Captivity has not always agreed with western lowland gorillas: I'd read that the apes have been found to pull out their own hair, a behaviour never seen in the wild. Some have been put on Prozac. Were these happy animals in front of us? Sad animals? In 2016 at Cincinnati Zoo, a western lowland gorilla called Harambe was shot dead after taking hold of a four-year-old boy who had entered his enclosure.

In San Francisco, such tragedy felt unthinkable. A young male gorilla sucked at a metal tap then rolled on his back while clutching his left foot. A silverback scratched at a rug. The enclosure was nice enough, but it felt weirdly out of context. A zoo worker tried her best, explaining that the gorillas' habitat was disappearing, partly because of mining for metals. 'If you do have any old cell phones, recycle them. That helps,' she said hopefully. 'I think we recycle old cell phone batteries at the zoo.'

'I want to go and see some different animals,' said Eliza, first requesting then demanding. A sign informed me that young gorillas have temper tantrums, 'just like human children'. It struck me that my daughter could tell me where she wanted to be; the gorillas couldn't. Zoo visits had been one of my happiest outings as a child. Now I feel like it was a mirage – that animals are suited to small enclosures with plentiful noises, that animals are abundant, accessible.

Zoos are reluctant to change, partly because they worry about losing visitors. 'What they do is exactly what they've been doing since

1828 – get hold of big, exotic, dangerous and, as they call them, charismatic megafauna,' says David Hancocks, the architect and former zoo designer. The term charismatic megafauna was first used in the mid-1980s to refer to those species – tigers, pandas, rhinos and so on – that adults around the world could name. It was hoped that these animals would marshal support for conservation in general. Nonetheless, one study at London Zoo found that a major factor in deciding how popular a species of zoo animal was with the public was how close the enclosure was to the entrance.

Hancocks argues that visitors themselves will actually drive zoos to treat animals better. 'If zoos don't choose to change, the public will do it for them,' he says. Certainly, the public got tired of animal circuses. They began to feel repulsed. Ringling Brothers, one of the successors to Barnum's circus, closed in 2017. Shortly before wild animal circuses were banned in England in 2020, there were fewer than thirty licensed animals. Animal welfare campaigners had targeted the circuses hard. But they had actually lost their legal cases against Ringling Brothers. And in Britain, MPs pointed out there was no scientific evidence that some species were unsuitable for circuses. It didn't matter: the public wasn't hanging around for the science. The circus had stopped being fun. Maybe zoos, in their current form, will stop being fun too. We don't need livestock for food any more, and we don't need exotic animals for entertainment. We have incredible documentaries, which show animals acting freely and naturally. One German circus has replaced live animals with holograms.

After coming back from San Francisco to the UK, I took my daughters to an aquarium, where hardly any of the species had conservation value and where we received a plastic badge for touching a starfish. In the penultimate room, a teenage girl sat on the floor dressed as a mermaid. Probably the most endangered feature was the aquarium's own business model.

Love requires us to watch and reflect. Zoos have taught us to be impatient, to expect animals to be visible on our terms. Frans de Waal, who has carried out pioneering studies in zoos, including the mirror test on Happy the elephant, once joked to me how adults would look at animals in enclosures, comment 'I could look at them all day', and then swiftly move on to the next exhibit. In Fuzhou, south-eastern China, a kangaroo was killed when visitors threw stones to make her move. Zoos need to be designed in a way that encourages people to sit and dwell, but there will always be limits to what they can offer.

The real joy of nature is not individual animals placed on show. It's how animals make decisions, interact as groups, and as species, form the natural world. It's about ecological processes, grandeur, a sense of our own insignificance. You can't get that at a zoo. Which partly explains the outrage at Copenhagen Zoo's decision in 2014 to cull Marius the giraffe. The zoo confuses us, by removing animals from their natural lives.

Zoos were once prisons for animals: cruel and uncomfortable. These days I agree with David Hancocks that zoos are more like care homes, laced with gnawing frustration. There's a basic truth here: humans are not as clever as we think. We are able to capture animals in the furthest corners of the world, to bring them across the globe and to keep them alive. But we can't replicate the environment and social dynamics of the wild. In the age of empire, zoos represented the breadth of our power over animals. Now they represent the limits of that power.

Aspinall tells people not to take their kids to zoos, but I took my kids to his. Port Lympne has trees, and enclosures where the animals can avoid being seen. My daughters and I spotted a tapir, almost by chance, resting at the edge of some woodland. A rhino appeared browsing several hundred metres away, further than I'd once seen one in the wild. This was not like taking part in an identity parade, it was almost like immersion. Some animals, such as the cheetah and the fishing cat, were nowhere to be seen. If you'd come all the way for them, tough. Eliza and Cleo found it just as exciting as any other day out, mainly because they had an ice cream. I learnt that day that kids do not need to see several hundred species or even the most exotic species up close.

What wild animals need, meanwhile, are spaces where they can live freely. For all the nice things about Port Lympne, some of the enclosures also seemed frankly too small. Aspinall is returning his animals to the wild slowly. But his forecast is pretty miserable. 'I think the inevitable slaughter of nature by man is unstoppable,' he told me. 'In fifty years, I think there will be pockets that will be protected – pockets of rhinos, pockets of gorillas, pockets of elephants. There will be little pockets. You just have to look at the rise of human population in some of these countries and it's inevitable what's going to happen.'

Was that really the best we could hope for? The thing about Noah is that, in the Bible's telling, he was blameless. Maybe we are not Noah. Maybe, to quote the nature writer Carl Safina, we are the flood.

7. NOTHING BUT FOOTPRINTS

Who has decided – who has the right to decide – for the countless legions of people who were not consulted that the supreme value is a world without insects, even though it be also a sterile world ungraced by the curving wing of a bird in flight?

Rachel Carson

Buy land, they're not making it anymore.

Mark Twain

Near the beginning of the Netflix series *Narcos*, a US drug enforcement agent flies from Miami to Bogotá, Colombia. From the plane he looks down on the Amazon rainforest, and seems unimpressed.

Like many things in *Narcos*, this is pretty annoying. The Amazon doesn't begin until a few hundred miles south of Bogotá, so if you see it en route from Miami, your pilot is lost. The Amazon is one of the most beautiful sights on earth, so even a cynical drugs cop would be impressed. From the air, you can see endless tree canopies and tea-coloured rivers, waves of clouds and the occasional rainbow. You can't help but think of the creatures who live away from our observation and oblivious to our existence – jaguars, toucans, snakes. A single acre of rainforest holds perhaps 6,000 insect species. 'A tree is a tree. How many more do you need to look at?' Ronald Reagan once said. He was wrong: scale matters. The bigger the forest, the greater the variety of species that is found in each acre.

But the most annoying thing is *Narcos*'s suggestion that what looks like animal habitat is in fact mostly cocaine laboratories. 'At 10,000 feet, Colombia was a paradise of untouched rainforest,' narrates the US agent. 'Things were different on the ground. Pablo [Escobar] and his partners built super-labs the size of small cities.' In other words – to save the rainforest, stop the drugs.

When I travelled to Colombia for the first time, as a postgraduate student in 2005, I had a similar idea. I'd read newspaper articles blaming deforestation on middle-class cocaine users. As well as being a human tragedy, Colombia's drug-fuelled war seemed bad for the environment. It was easy to point to examples why – from coca farms and cocaine labs, where chemicals were tipped into the forest, to oil spills, caused by guerrillas blowing up pipelines. We were the animal-lovers; they were the barbarians.

But gradually I had an uncomfortable realisation: the Colombian conflict, so horrific in human terms, was better for nature than the alternatives. The guerrillas, whatever their other sins, weren't dumb enough to cut down their own hiding places. (I remember being told of an escaped fighter, who, when asked what life was like in the insurgency, spoke of becoming sick of seeing nothing but the colour green. It's a problem he won't have in Bogotá.) War kept thousands of square kilometres of forest mostly off limits. International mining companies didn't want to invest when their employees might be kidnapped, and cattle ranchers were reluctant to colonise the Amazon, as they had in neighbouring Brazil.

Colombia's rainforests weren't protected in spite of the drugs war – they were protected partly *because* of the drugs war. Big businesses weren't interested in the rainforest, which freed the government to designate more than one-quarter of the country as indigenous people's territory and one-tenth as national parks. The parks and the indigenous reserves can overlap; together they cover most of the Colombian Amazon. Indigenous communities vary. In neighbouring Brazil, some have supported mining. But the Colombian experience is that many of these groups, particularly those whose societies weren't torn apart by disease and settlers in previous centuries, value the land in a fundamentally different way. Mountains, rivers and forests are the home of sacred beings; to damage them would be blasphemy. These communities don't want mining and forestry companies; they want to be able to live alongside the rainforest. Colombia as a whole has more bird species than any other country. During the three years that I lived there, I saw so many – hummingbirds, hoatzins, curassows – and not a gram of cocaine.

Since a peace agreement in 2016, however, times have changed in Colombia. Ranchers are arriving in the Amazon, and politicians are welcoming them. Palm oil plantations, vast monocultures, are replacing wild spaces. The trees are disappearing. Videos taken from the air now show light-green rectangles cut into the Amazon forest. Most of them are pasture for cattle. 'Cows are eating the Colombian Amazon,' as one of the country's best-known biologists, Brigitte Baptiste, put it. Grazing cattle is a way for people to take de facto ownership, quickly and cheaply, of land. In regions where the state is virtually absent, possession is nine-tenths of the law.

Intact rainforest is a hospitable place, just not for humans. It is full of spindly trees fighting for light, fleshy plants and lichens, columns of ants and the noise of birds and beetles. Rainforests cover about 6 per cent of the world's surface, but contain 80 per cent of the world's known terrestrial species. More fish species have been identified in the Amazon basin than in the north Atlantic ocean. I kayaked alongside pink river dolphins and heard the calls of monkeys, and fishermen's tales of the pirarucu, the giant, air-breathing fish. I spent mornings with my binoculars bouncing from one treetop to another. In the rainforest, the vegetation is so thick that, if you step just a few metres from the path, you may never find it again. But after the trees are cut down, you soon wouldn't know that they had ever been there. More often than not, there is just sodden pasture, barely more interesting than a lawn. Tens of metres of vegetation and life reduced to ten centimetres. This landscape works for humans, livestock, and not much else. Even if you allow an acre of Amazon to regrow for sixty years, it will still store less than half as much carbon as it did before. After twenty years, it will also have barely half as many tree species.

Colombia is just following the global trend. The amount of farmland on the planet has quadrupled in the last 200 years, and still the frontiers are being pushed back. Right now, farmland covers half the world's habitable land. On honeymoon in Borneo, I saw how palm oil plantations had cut into the forest, reducing orangutans to a few enclaves, where they were reliant on bananas left out by humans. Large-scale palm oil plantations destroy another 200,000 hectares of Indonesian primary forest every year. The sound of chainsaws was almost incessant; the rivers were choked with sediment from illegal mines, killing nearly all the fish. Animals don't just vanish when their habitat is lost – they are burnt to death in the clearing fires, or have to fight for food and territory in the habitat that remains. Some orangutans survive near the plantations, some are shot by farmers. Charities rescue a few, of which perhaps only one in five survives when released back into the forest.

The biggest obstacle to feeling like we live in harmony with other animals is the inescapable reality that they are disappearing from the planet. Agriculture covers more than one-third of the earth's ice-free surface. Through crops, livestock, deforestation, timber plantations and other activities, *Homo sapiens* consumes 25 per cent of the energy available for all animal species on earth. 'The animals may not be able to thank us for allowing them to live, and they certainly wouldn't do the same for us if the positions were reversed. But it's we, not they, who need life to have meaning,' the novelist Jonathan Franzen has written. I looked at the animals in my daughters' storybooks. Polar bears – vulnerable to extinction. Penguins and bees – many species decreasing in numbers. Lions – vulnerable to extinction, pushed from most of their range. I'd bet most children's bedrooms in North America and Europe have some kind of representation of a turtle, even if just in a storybook, but six out of seven sea-turtle species are endangered or vulnerable to extinction. High intelligence isn't enough to save animals. The kea, the New Zealand parrots who understand probability, are endangered because of introduced predators such as stoats and cats. The inquisitive birds are now also victims of well-meaning human intervention: they die from eating poisoned baits intended to kill mammalian predators, and by junk food fed to them directly by tourists. Even similarity to humans isn't enough to protect animals: all other great apes – orangutans, bonobos, chimpanzees and gorillas – are considered endangered or critically endangered.

I spent much of my life seeing extinction as an outlandish possibility. In school, the story of the dodo – extinguished from Mauritius in the seventeenth century – was taught as an exceptional example of human idiocy, not to be repeated. When I was about nine, I once thought about the possibility of elephants going extinct. And I remember thinking – it will never happen; if it gets really bad, the adults will take care of it. What else could they be doing that was more important?

But as of 2019, nearly 25 per cent of mammals and 13 per cent of birds are threatened with extinction. More than 200 known mammal species are classed as critically endangered – one notch from extinction in the wild, or total extinction. Extinction rates are already 'at least tens of hundreds of times higher than the average rate over the past 10 million years', according to the Intergovernmental Science-Policy Platform on Biodiversity and Ecosystem Services (IPBES). Risks are not arriving in dribs and drabs, but by the truckload: 1 million of the approximately 8 million animal and plant species on earth are threatened. This includes half a million terrestrial species that are 'committed to extinction' – which means that, in theory, they could survive if their habitats are restored, but on current trends they will go extinct. There's now the growing possibility that scientists will only recognise a species after it's gone extinct. The cryptic treehunter, a bird from north-east Brazil, was formally described in 2014, never seen again, and declared extinct five years later. Italian prime ministers have lasted longer. Conservation does help to slow the pace: the money spent between 1996 and 2008 reduced the extinction of mammals, birds and amphibians by somewhere over 20 per cent, according to one analysis; it saved up to twenty-five bird and mammal species from extinction in the past decade. But it's a Band-Aid on a wound that needs multiple stitches.

Andy Purvis, one of the leaders of the IPBES's work, points out that the species that humans previously pushed to extinction were 'intrinsically susceptible' – for example, flightless birds like the dodo, which were found only on particular islands – whereas now a wider range of species are threatened, on the mainland too. Since the 1970s, about 3 per cent of frog species have become extinct, many due to the invasive chytrid fungus that infects their skin. The fungus has created a cascade: as frogs disappear, so do the snakes who rely on them for food. Taking into account this disease and other threats, two of every five amphibian species are threatened with extinction. For millennia, Africa avoided the megafauna extinctions seen on other continents – because large animals evolved alongside humans and developed defences against our hunting. But defences developed against hunting can't save animals from changes in habitat and climate.

The list of species threatened by extinction is frankly numbing. The Christmas Island pipistrelle was last seen in 2009 and is now deemed extinct. The Vancouver Island marmot and the Philippine crocodile are on the brink, with fewer than 200 individuals left in the wild. But who, erm, knew they even existed? A lot of animals are insects, and a lot of insects are beetles. As I look through the International Union for Conservation of Nature (IUCN) Red List, humanity's best effort at tracking the status of animal and plant species, I could almost hear the voice of Marie Kondo. Do we really need more than 400,000 beetle species? Does each one spark joy? Would we be happy if all the world's species were safely moved to Australia, but then wiped out from the rest of the world? Obviously not.

There's another problem with focusing on extinction. Despite humanity's best efforts, it's very hard for an animal to go extinct. A species must first have been recognised by humans – and most species have not been. Its population must also have been assessed by humans – and nearly half of known fish species, for example, have not been. Often there must have been no recorded sightings of the species by humans in any of its ranges for thirty years. (Imagine having to wait until 2021 to say that the USSR had disappeared.) So species teeter on the brink: deemed possibly extinct, or extinct in the wild, meaning that, in the case of a snail, it might be confined to a plastic box in London Zoo. For most species, there will never be a moment where the last individual – the one who conservationists call the endling – dies, and the world stops, pays its respects and realises what has been lost.

I realise that what saddens me isn't precisely extinction, but the emptying of our planet. Species will rise and fall, but I hoped for a world where animal life as a whole should not be continually cut away by human existence. The Zoological Society of London's Living Planet Index shows territorial and fresh-water vertebrate populations fell 60 per cent on average between 1970 and 2014. This gauge is skewed by extreme changes in a few populations. But no conservationist doubts wild animals are in trouble. We just lack data, particularly in the tropics, to create a single gauge of animal abundance. A separate analysis of nearly 28,000 land vertebrate species found that one-third are declining in number and range. Even those at least risk of extinction are affected. Abundance and extinction are linked. Species are only viable with minimum populations, and those minimum populations generally depend on other species existing in viable numbers. 'You can't have abundance without diversity. You can't have diversity without abundance,' says Anthony Waldron, a conservationist at the University of Cambridge.

We can overcomplicate the reasons why animals are disappearing. Each species has particular threats, as does each corner of the world. But we can also put it simply: the major reason that terrestrial animals are falling in number is that their homes are disappearing. According to ZSL's index, for birds, mammals and reptiles, habitat loss has been more of a threat than hunting, pollution and climate change put together. 'If you wanted a single indicator for conservation, it would be the amount of additional land required for each new person on the planet,' says Waldron. 'You want that to go down to zero.' We are nowhere near that point.

In 2010 nearly every country in the world – except the US – pledged to at least halve, and where possible reduce to zero, the rate of natural habitat loss by 2020. Instead in 2016, 2017 and 2018, forests were lost at the fastest rate since the turn of the century. In 2019 a football pitch of forest disappeared every six seconds. (And that doesn't include those forests which remain standing, but which have lost much of their richness due to logging, grazing and fire.) The countries also committed to preventing the extinction of known threatened species – and improving their conservation status – within a decade. That goal wasn't met either. Nor were targets to eliminate harmful subsidies, to reduce pollution, and to respect indigenous practices for conserving nature. We are like customers in a pottery shop, who are apologising for the damage while continuing to smash items.

In Africa the ranges of lions, elephants and chimpanzees have been cut to pieces by roads and farmland. The forests of the Eastern Arc Mountains, in Tanzania and Kenya, have stood up to 30 million years and have hundreds of plants and animals that are found nowhere else on earth. More than half a million hectares of forest are lost every year, mainly to small farms growing maize. At least one-third of the species in the Eastern Arc Mountains are thought to have become extinct or highly endangered. A third of the forest is now fewer than 300 metres from the forest edge. Tropical species – largely insects – tend to occupy small ranges and niches, meaning they are particularly prone to disappearing if the land is turned to cropland or pasture, or if forests are exposed to desiccating winds at the edges.

Things are not getting better, especially in the tropics. New roads are being built through forests in Indonesia, the Congo Basin and the Amazon, where they act as vectors of deforestation. In the Brazilian Amazon, the right-wing government of Jair Bolsonaro has revived the idea that the forest is there to be exploited – or 'cleaned'. In 2019, fires swept through the forests at a rate of more than one football field a minute, the smoke blackening the skies of São Paulo, some 2,700 kilometres away. Bolsonaro simply denied there was a problem, calling deforestation data 'lies' and arguing that the Amazon could not burn because it's wet. When coronavirus distracted the world's attention the following year, his environment minister heralded an opportunity to 'move in the cattle'. In Bolsonaro's logic, the Amazon belongs to Brazil, not the world, and Brazil can destroy it if it wishes. But actually the choice is ours too: in 2019, Brazil again ranked as the world's biggest exporter of beef and the world's biggest exporter of soyabeans, mainly to fatten pigs in China and cows in Europe. In Mato Grosso, the biggest soya-producing state, nearly 300,000 hectares a year of forest and grasslands is being cleared. The culprits are not poor settlers, but industrial-scale operators – three-quarters of the clearance is done by farms ten times bigger than the average English farm.

'Take nothing but pictures, leave nothing but footprints,' runs the eco-conscious cliché. The world is becoming covered in human footprints – and tyre tracks and hoof marks. We are left with the pictures of the animals who lived there.

I once believed that peace and prosperity would make Colombia, and the world, a greener place. But I had to face up to a different prospect: that our model of human progress erodes wildness. It had always reassured me that there were some parts of the earth where we were leaving animals to live free, in their natural habitat. Isn't that the whole point of nature documentaries? That we appreciate why the animals should be free to exist somewhere? But the places where wildlife prevails tend to be those where humans do not – such as the Chernobyl exclusion zone. It isn't the drug lords and the guerrillas who are the big problem – it's us.

It's hard enough to perceive our impact on farm animals. The link between our behaviour and wild animals' fate seems tenuous. Aren't there still lions out there somewhere? Didn't we just see them on TV? But wild animals don't want our eyeballs, they want somewhere to live. How can we give it to them?

*

By 1990 Doug Tompkins had fallen out with his wife, Susie, who was also his business partner. He lost a boardroom battle, and decided to sell her his half of Esprit, the clothing company that they had founded in the 1960s, for around $150 million. He was always adventurous; now he was very rich too. He could have behaved like today's San Francisco multimillionaires – buy a vineyard, start angel investing and embrace intermittent fasting.

Instead Tompkins went to Chile, and spent $500,000 buying a 10,000-hectare cattle and sheep farm. It became the first piece in perhaps the most extraordinary private conservation effort that the world has seen. Tompkins had a small collection of impressionist art. He was also a mountaineer and an ecologist. He realised he could sell the art and buy thousands of hectares of land. He turned his back on consumer culture and focused on ecological restoration. In four years, he bought a fifth of one Chilean province.

Tompkins Conservation, run by Tompkins and his second wife Kris, the former chief executive of clothing company Patagonia, would go on to protect more than 800,000 hectares in Chile and Argentina, including wetlands, savannah, subarctic forest and rainforest. It would encourage the Chilean government to protect millions of hectares more. It's a turnaround from the time when Chile's military regime – like others in the region – was paying people to colonise new parts of the country and turn them into farmland. The protected areas are home to penguins, sea lions, condors, pumas, deer, monkeys and more.

Chile was pretty much the most favourable place for a foreign millionaire to buy huge amounts of land. It had relatively low population. Landowners wanted to sell their failing livestock farms. A law, passed in 1974 by the military regime of Augusto Pinochet, granted foreigners the same rights as Chileans.

Tompkins had a vision of paradise; he was also stubborn as hell. His biographer, Andrés Azócar, compares him to Steve Jobs; indeed, when Tompkins met Jobs in San Francisco, he laid into him about the negative impacts of technology. (Tompkins did not own a cell phone.) Like Jobs, he deeply cared about aesthetics, and micromanaged his projects obsessively.

He rubbed people up the wrong way. He negotiated hard for land, he didn't see the need to persuade local people of his project, and he took on established interests, including polluting salmon farms, which provided jobs. Some Chileans accused him of wanting to create a Jewish state, and others said he was splitting their country in two (his initial lands went across the south of Chile, from the Andes to the Pacific coast). Even Chilean environmentalists complained that his work made international donors think the country didn't need more funding. Kris did make efforts to win over the community, but she and Doug were never residents in Chile. It was not until the couple started donating their parks to the Chilean state that they became truly welcome.

Doug and Kris were not initially motivated by animals: they appreciated landscapes. When they bought farms, they sold the cattle and sheep, started controlled burns of the grasslands, and covered up roads. After about fifteen years, it became clear something more was needed. 'It wasn't enough to just have the land. The land had to be restored and functioning properly, and that in many cases implies bringing back the top predators and so on,' recalls Kris. 'That's how we got started in rewilding.' They sought to bring back native species: Andean condors, pumas and marsh deer. Giant anteaters have been reintroduced to the marshlands of north-east Argentina, from where they were extirpated last century by a mixture of hunting and cattle ranching. So have pampas deer and maned wolves. Releases of green-winged macaws were less successful. 'Most of them didn't know how to fly,' says Kris. 'You actually have to teach them how to fly, build their muscles up, teach them what kind of fruits they like.' Jaguars are next on the list. 'That's a ten-year programme just getting the individuals prepared who can be released.'

Doug Tompkins died after his kayak capsized in Chile in 2015. He was seventy-two. By this time, his and Kris's fortunes were largely spent. Their foundation's continuing work relies on funding from other sources, such as Hansjörg Wyss, a Swiss medical equipment billionaire who promised in 2018 to give $1 billion for nature conservation. (Wyss, too, was initially enthralled by grand landscapes, not wildlife.)

Even so, the $400 million that the Tompkins have spent on conservation and surrounding organic farms is not a lot by the super-rich's standards. Four French families pledged €400 million to rebuild the cathedral of Notre-Dame, after its roof and vaults burnt in 2019. Mohammed bin Salman, the crown prince of Saudi Arabia, spent $450 million on a Leonardo da Vinci painting of Jesus, *Salvator Mundi*. The lifeless painting measures 65.7 centimetres by 45.7 centimetres; I think Doug and Kris got more value for their money. Doug said that, if the 10,000 richest people on earth put most of their wealth and influence into saving wildness, the world could change overnight. There are 2,000 or so billionaires in the world; at most a handful have embraced the opportunity to save this world.

Why haven't more? 'One thing is people can't part with their money at all. They want it all to go to their kids, which is ridiculous,' says Kris Tompkins. 'There are too few people like Andrew Carnegie, who was very critical of his peers, that if you die with money in your pocket it's a sin. I tend to hold that same attitude. I don't, and may never, understand why families don't have the motto of "the more you get, the more you give". The accumulation of wealth is just astounding. A lot of people with money don't understand that giving it away in areas that are meaningful to you will bring you the greatest joy of your lifetime. Most people can't imagine that being the case.'

You don't have to have money. In Mongolia, I met a woman called Bayarjargal Agvaantseren, who had fallen in love with the snow leopards while working as a research assistant. Why the snow leopard? 'It's beautiful, it's so beautiful – and at the same time so secretive. So calm,' she explained over mint tea. She had never seen one of the leopards in the wild, but had seen enough on TV to be convinced that they were essential to Mongolia. Fewer than 7,000 snow leopards remain in the wild, and fewer than 1,000 are in Mongolia.

The land she had in mind was in the south of Mongolia, near the border with China. Mining companies were interested, and there was little public love for the snow leopard, which is best known in Mongolia for killing herders' livestock. For a decade, Agvaantseren worked with the local community and lobbied politicians relentlessly. Ultimately she convinced the government to create a 700,000-hectare reserve, and to cancel all the mining licences in the area. 'I'm sure there are probably people who lost lots of money. But we didn't have to deal with it because the government took the decision,' she told me. Even governments can put natural heritage above economic interest.

As Anthony Waldron of the University of Cambridge puts it: 'Conservation is not a battle of humans versus nature. It's a battle of conservationists versus non-conservationists.' And sometimes the conservationists win. Protecting land is a simple idea, and it works. Protected areas, though they are sometimes poorly managed and guarded, have been shown to reduce the rate of deforestation. Across the world, the number of species present is about 10 per cent higher in protected areas than in similar areas that aren't protected.

Yet, at the moment, we are heading in the wrong direction: all the land purchased by Doug and Kris Tompkins in three decades is equivalent to the amount of tropical rainforest cut down in three months in 2019.

To stop the bleeding dry of animal life, Edward O. Wilson, a Harvard biologist, has proposed that humans should set aside half the world's surface for conservation. The reasoning is partly psychological: 50 per cent is a goal that people can understand. It is biological too: island biogeography theory, which he co-authored, holds that half the land should sustain 85 per cent of the species. Half-Earth– as Wilson's proposal is known – would blow our current efforts out of the water. In 1982, the year I was born, the World Parks Congress set a target of 10 per cent of terrestrial lands to be protected. In 2010 the target was raised to 17 per cent by 2020, which was just about achieved. Half-Earth supporters now want the next target to be 30 per cent by 2030, followed by 50 per cent by 2050.

So far Chile and Mongolia have protected about one-fifth of their land – higher than the world average. Only a few countries, Namibia, Nepal and Bhutan, are close to or already past 50 per cent. In the US, it's just 12 per cent, a figure that includes national parks and wilderness areas, but not federal lands used for hunting and logging. All countries inflate their figures by counting some areas that are barely protected in reality. The UK does this even more than most. In theory, 26 per cent of its land is protected. But that includes areas where you can build houses, graze sheep, grow non-native trees, and burn moors for grouse-shooting. If you just count areas with some effective management plan, only 11 per cent of the country is protected, and most of that isn't in great shape. E. O. Wilson wants the focus to be on the most biodiverse areas, such as the forests of the Democratic Republic of Congo, the Atlantic forests of Brazil, and savannahs in Queensland, Australia.

Imagine, for every hectare of Yellowstone and Yosemite, finding three more to protect in the US. Imagine for every scrap of protected area we have in the world today – every national park we have visited, every nature reserve that we have hiked through – we would have to find another two. Imagine, for every Doug and Kris Tompkins, two or three more multimillionaires ready to invest hundreds of millions of dollars and several decades of their lives.

As of early 2021, fifty or so countries, including the UK and France, but not Australia, Brazil or Indonesia, had signed up to the goal of protecting 30 per cent of earth by 2030. The estimated cost is somewhere between $35 billion and $110 billion per year, not including the costs of managing existing parks. That's a lot less than the world spends on soft drinks each year. The cost of buying the land is relatively small, compared to the cost of managing the protected areas. If Half-Earth were about giving half the planet to other species for their own sake, it might seem a stretch. But conservationists argue that the costs would be outweighed by the benefits to humans, and that the parks represent an economic sector as important as those they displace. In South Africa, tourism contributes more to the economy than farming.

Deforestation is certainly bad for our health. Zoonotic diseases – those that cross to humans from other animals – are much more common in landscapes that have been transformed by humans than in nearby undisturbed ones. Transforming the natural world brings us into contact with new species, and therefore new pathogens, but it also changes the balance between animal species. When we degrade landscapes, such as tropical rainforests, the rodents, bats and songbirds who don't host spillover diseases tend to disappear, while those who do host such diseases tend to multiply. (The biggest reservoirs of spillover viruses are, of courses, domesticated animals, such as cows and pigs: twelve domesticated species have been found to host half of zoonotic viruses.) Our response to spillover viruses should therefore not be to love animals less, but to love the integrity of ecosystems more. There are more than half a million viruses in animals that could cross to humans. More than five new diseases appear in humans every year. We can't hope to keep track of them all, or to find vaccines for each one. We must stop creating the conditions in which they cross to humans: the trade in wild animals, and the expansion of the agricultural frontier. Doing these things is much cheaper than the economic catastrophe caused by coronavirus. Loving animals and ecosystems pays for itself. Take care of the pandas and the pandemics will take care of themselves (sort of).

Half-Earth does not mean wilderness. There is no such thing as pristine territory. We have changed the atmospheric carbon concentration everywhere, and so the temperature and the rainfall. Even much of the Amazon was fertilised with charcoals and farmed before Europeans arrived in South America. The river's banks once teemed with turtles, until the Europeans plundered their eggs. What we see today as virgin rainforest is partly human-made. Areas of animal abundance, such as the Amazon, have people living in them, who generally know much better how to conserve them than western conservationists do.

So this isn't about people versus other animals. But the costs of conservation can fall squarely on local people. When national parks first emerged, in the late nineteenth and twentieth centuries, they were quite often founded by kicking out the people who lived there. These local people had caused far less environmental damage than those who were evicting them. They lost their grazing lands and their hunting rights. They understood the local ecology, and were moved to areas with which they had no connection. They suffered from a mentality whereby conservationists put animals before local people. That mindset has lived on until recently: African Parks, a private conservation effort founded by the late Dutch philanthropist Paul van Vlissingen, takes control of African national parks and reinforces them with heavy security. In 2004 it signed a deal for two parks in southern Ethiopia, and said that the eviction of thousands of local people living there was not its problem. That was not an ethical response to a reality where many people in sub-Saharan Africa are poor and depend on land for their livelihoods. It also didn't work. African Parks terminated the contract after three years, saying that the government wouldn't agree to its solution for stopping local people from grazing livestock there. If your priority is animals, it's tempting to slip into a mindset of 'fortress conservation', where local people are seen as the problem.

Conservationists today do mostly try hard to work with communities. Protected areas are not, in general, bad for local people. Hunting

can bring revenues, and so can tourism. One study of the world's protected areas found that households living near parks with tourism are
17 per cent richer than similar households that lived far away. Young
children who grew up close to parks were also taller, showing better
nutrition. Tourism already funds the conservation of 20–30 per cent of
the remaining wild lions, African elephants, black rhinos and other
species, such as the wave albatross. Until coronavirus hit, eco-conscious
tourism had been growing quickly.

Yet tourism has limits. Tourists spent three times as much in national parks in North America as they do in national parks in Africa
and Latin America combined. To increase the number of wealthy
American and European tourists to the tropics, you'd have to fly thousands more people across the world unsustainably. If we want wild
spaces, we must pay local people to protect them. Environmental charities have tried giving cash to local people, in the hope that this will
reduce their need to cut down forests. In countries like Mexico and
Costa Rica, local people have been paid for not cutting down trees
and therefore maintaining ecosystem services – such as storing carbon
and mitigating floods. It's not failsafe: in a randomised trial in Sierra
Leone, cash payments actually accelerated rainforest clearance, at
least in the short-term. But it should work more often than not. If we
want the Amazon to exist, we have to ensure local people have a financial incentive to keep it standing, rather than log it illegally. That
bluntly means money has to flow from rich countries to poor countries
that contain the areas richest in animal life.

In 1996, nearly 400 members of the public in Cambridgeshire were
given information about the status of black rhinos in Namibia and
asked how much they would pay to protect the animals. After being
told that the rhino was only one of many endangered mammals, they
were still prepared to make a one-off donation of £15 on average to
protect it. This fell to nearly £13 if trophy-hunting were allowed. If
every British adult gave £13 to rhino conservation, that would generate
around £700 million. It would go a long way. Of course it isn't real.
WWF's UK arm receives only £35 million a year in donations. Only
one in eight Britons say they give regularly to 'conservation, the

environment or heritage' charities, fewer than half as many as give to animal welfare charities, such as dogs' homes and donkey sanctuaries. Britons don't want trophy-hunting to happen in Africa – but they're not providing an alternative source of income for local people.

Americans would pay $19 a year to protect sea turtles, $35 for seals and $20–40 for wolves. Sri Lankans would pay around $16 a year – a pretty incredible 1 per cent of their then average income – to protect elephants. In Orange County, California, in 2001, households were willing to pay $50–60 a year to protect all local endangered species. This money never comes through. (In the Orange County case, the researchers concluded that it would not be sufficient to fund the necessary land anyway.) You can blame the studies themselves – for starters, the people who will participate in a research group about the black rhino are definitely not a cross-section of the British population. But most of the blame is with ourselves: we do want animals to exist, we just don't pay for them.

In the 1980s, when conservation biology emerged as a discipline, the intrinsic value of animals and plants was a founding principle. Paradoxically, while ethologists and neuroscientists have revealed more about animals' rich emotional and social lives, a new school of conservationists have moved away from the idea that we should protect animals for their own sake. This new school of conservationists is sceptical about how far parks can be extended. They point out that the world does not have empty land. They estimate that protecting 50 per cent of the earth as parks would affect land that is home to perhaps 1 billion people. And so they suggest that we focus more on spaces which are shared by wild animals and humans. Most people want parks they can walk around – not parks that are off limits to humans, says Peter Kareiva, a biologist who was formerly chief scientist at the environmental NGO, The Nature Conservancy.

Some advocates of the new conservation school would like American national parks to be more like Britain's, which encompass houses and farms. But as the environmental writer George Monbiot has pointed out, British national parks are no model – because where they contain sheep, they contain precious little else. When grouse shoots take place, operators are suspected of poisoning and shooting buzzards, goshawks and other birds of prey, which may interfere with their business. This isn't a model that anyone should be imitating. Instead the focus should be the other way: public lands and waters in the US are currently, under their mixed use mandate, home to oil, gas and coal production. We need less extraction and more conservation.

We shouldn't give up so easily on arguing for conservation for animals' sake. People do love animals – hundreds of millions watch documentaries like *Blue Planet*, hundreds of millions of people keep pets. It's a shame that the terms that conservationists use to talk about nature are so disengaging. 'Biodiversity' – a concept to refer to the number of species, as well as the genetic diversity within species, and the divergence among them – means nothing to most people, and I say that as someone who briefly worked in a biodiversity think tank. 'Ecosystem services' – the term used to refer to the benefits humans derive from nature – sounds like the kind of unnecessary add-on that a software provider tries to sell you. The majesty of the living world – our emotional and moral connection to other species – remains the strongest card. We take pleasure from these animals' existence. We are saddened by their suffering. We want the chance to see them in the wild, and for our children to have the same. Is $20 too much? $100? If Sri Lankans can consider giving 1 per cent of their income, can't we?

Where is the land we would need to save? Of all the world's ice-free land, approximately half has very low or low human impact. That includes grazing land that could be turned over to conservation. The problem is that the low-impact half is the wrong half – it includes a lot of desert, tundra and boreal forest, and not very much temperate grassland or tropical dry forest. So as well as protecting more of this, we would need to restore some heavily impacted land.

Even proponents of Half-Earth don't imagine 50 per cent of the earth being cordoned off. But we have to face it: a lot of other animals do better when we're not around. In California, the sound of humans causes cougars to abandon carcasses, at least temporarily. Our lights confuse insects, who lay their eggs in the wrong places or die of exhaustion flapping around them. Our footprints on beaches can prevent plants from growing. Giant pandas were once found across China; studies show that they now try to avoid going within 500 metres of a hiking trail, or five kilometres of a major road. Grizzly bears stay away from roads that have just twenty vehicles per day on them. In tiger habitats, roads reduce the number of mammals by around one-fifth. The presence of tourists can also disturb animals: in Kenya, female cheetahs raised, on average, fewer than half as many cubs in high tourism areas, because safari vehicles interfered with their hunting for food. In New Zealand, sperm whales, which need to be on the surface to breathe, dive deep when tourist helicopters approach, while eco-tourism, like fishing, also increases the mortality of sea-lion pups. Animals' shyness is likely to reflect our past behaviour: less fearful animals, such as the fox that Charles Darwin hit with a hammer on the island of Chiloé, didn't last very long.

This is why remote places like Patagonia, like eastern Russia, like the Congolese forests matter so much. Those places are not wilderness, but they are wilder. The remoter they are, the less prone they are to destruction. In the Amazon, nearly all deforestation is in easy reach from roads and navigable rivers. Even benign visitors bring risks – the more tourists that go to Antarctica, the greater the chance of invasive species piggy-backing.

Is it worth the hassle to create large parks, rather than lots of small fragments? For the past decade, biologists have debated the most efficient way to fit conservation and agriculture together. Is it better for each farm to have a patch of woodland or fallow land ('land-sharing')? Or is it better to farm intensively over a bigger area, thereby freeing up one sizeable conservation area ('land-sparing')? Most of the research suggests that, at least in the tropics, wildlife does much better under land-sparing. It's better to have one big nature reserve than lots of small ones. Most animals just do better away from the disturbance of agriculture. Farming, at almost any intensity and whether it's organic or not, disrupts the delicate niches to which species have adapted. If you want to save animals, intensive farms, the ones that look terrible in drone footage, may be part of the solution. Better to have big palm oil plantations – for all its sins, it is an efficient crop, producing five times as much oil per hectare as coconut trees or sunflowers do – so long as you can ensure some remaining land is protected properly and the pollution is managed.

What we need is action. 'It's the doing. The opportunities are there,' says Kris Tompkins, when we speak after the first coronavirus lockdown. 'Did I think that globally people would stay in their houses for three months? No. And we did. This has shown me that, when pressed sufficiently, we can do a lot of stuff. And I'm no pie-in-the-sky, I'm generally a pessimist.'

*

Years ago, I became a bit obsessed by a video of a jaguar fighting an anaconda. At one point, the jaguar looks to be in serious trouble, but then the cat swerves, pounces and claws with majestic nonchalance. The anaconda goes limp; the jaguar loses interest. After a few dozen views, I dreamed of seeing a jaguar in the wild. Eventually I booked a trip to the Pantanal, the wetlands in the middle of South America, where tourists are almost guaranteed the chance to see one.

We left the lodge early in the morning, threw ourselves into a motorboat, and headed at full speed down the river. We hadn't got far before the engine cut out and the guide began frantically pointing. There by the edge of the river was a jaguar – her body bathed in the orange light of the dawn, her jaw ajar, her eyes and ears following our progress upstream. Further back, half-hidden in the bush, were her cubs.

For us tourists, it was the highlight of the trip, worth a thousand dollars. But late one evening, after a few drinks, someone from the reserve let slip that they sometimes shot jaguars too. These animals brought the tourists, but they often killed livestock. So some had to go. I had a similar experience in the Andes, when an old man – a lover of nature – opened his mountain shed to reveal the skin of a spectacled bear, an elusive species that is threatened with extinction.

This is the reality of wildness. Some of us love powerful animals from a distance, others have to face their effects close-up. Bringing back charismatic animals is a core part of rewilding, because without them the ecosystems are imbalanced – wolves' return to Yellowstone has helped to create smaller, more resilient deer herds.

In some contexts, we have become so unaccustomed to large wild animals that we misjudge the risks. Between 2008 and 2015, an average of 201 people a year were killed by animals in the US, nearly half of them by wasps, bees, hornets and dogs. We don't think of those creatures as risky, because we have accepted their importance. But we shudder at wolves, alligators and bears.

If you live on a farm in Brazil, Tanzania, or many other countries, you think of big cats not in terms of charisma – but in terms of costs and benefits. And the costs are not just economic. Kim Jacobsen, a Norwegian researcher, has surveyed how the presence of lions affects the well-being of people near Zimbabwe's Hwange National Park (where Cecil the lion lived.) Nearly 80 per cent of residents said there were no benefits to having lions nearby. Those who had lost cattle to lions were scarred by a lasting fear and anxiety. This emotional impact is hard to offset with money. In fact, Jacobsen's estimate is that it would take $5,800 to compensate the median person for the anxiety that the lions bring – hundreds of times more than the value of the lost livestock. A similar dynamic occurs in Jacobsen's native Norway, where farmers have strongly opposed the reintroduction of wolves, even though there's an insurance scheme for any direct financial losses. The wolves represent something more than lost livestock – they represent the imposition of a new set of values by people who live in cities. So a large proportion of Norway's wolves are killed illegally. Jacobsen's conclusion is that money alone will not convince local people to live alongside carnivores. Indeed some schemes that offer money may lead people to stop appreciating the animals for other reasons. Lions do have cultural value for some Zimbabweans, but this might be 'crowded out' if lions are just seen in transactional terms. Jacobsen suggests that conservationists work to assure people that predators actually pose a much lower risk to livestock than is assumed, and that there are ways of reducing it further.

A lot of the problems come because wild predators kill livestock. If we move away from meat-eating, then wolves will kill deer – not sheep or cows. If we work out how wild animals behave, we will find ways to adjust to their presence. In Kenya, hungry elephants have long trampled on farmers' crops. But elephants do not like being around honeybees, and one way to keep them out is to build fences with beehives. The honey is a bonus.

Sadly honey is not enough. Sub-Saharan Africa is getting richer and more populous – demand for food calories is expected to more than triple between 2010 and 2050, according to the World Resources Institute. That is great news for reducing hunger and malnutrition. Nevertheless, even if sub-Saharan Africa's crop yields increase and even if it continues to import much of its food, the continent will need another 100 million hectares of cropland and 150 million hectares of pastureland by 2050. That's three and a half times the size of Texas, or more than half the size of Africa's protected areas today. It's likely to come on those areas – primarily savannahs and forests – that are crucial for animal life. Populations of lions and other animals will continue on their downward trends; they will become reduced to a few well-protected parks.

There's another, better future: the extra calories are found, but less land is turned over to crops and pasture. That's by encouraging a shift away from meat, by paying for forests and savannahs to be protected, and by allowing some trophy-hunting and high-value tourism. Africa's national parks could have perhaps three times as many lions – if their prey weren't illegally killed for food ('bushmeat'), for example. That means finding billions of dollars to fund parks' managers properly.

Even then, it's hardly realistic that significant amounts of wild spaces won't be cut down. Many sub-Saharan African countries can already say that they protect more of their territory than European countries. So one response is to try to compensate for the wild spaces lost there within our own borders. It's amazing to know wildness exists somewhere around the world. It's even better to have it on our doorsteps.

*

'This is proper oak woodland!'

Merlin Hanbury-Tenison divides his farm into two parts. The first part is effectively a rainforest, in south-western England. The air is damp, the stream is clear and fast-flowing, and the branches all around us are coated with beard lichen.

We reach a clearing and a metal gate. 'What we've just walked through is what makes this area special,' says Hanbury-Tenison. 'And *this* ... ' he pauses, theatrically, 'is not.'

This is an enclosure for grazing sheep. There is grass, bracken and a couple of oak trees, although they are barely covered in lichen. The oaks also probably lack the fungal networks in the soil that allow the neighbouring rainforest to thrive. 'These trees are loners ... There's much less benefit to the environment.'

Hanbury-Tenison's plan is simple – to let the rainforest take over the whole farm. 'If we can take these fences down and get this wood, which is straining against it – like a crowd at a football match, pushing against the barriers – then that's the real potential,' he says.

In 2013 George Monbiot published the book *Feral*, which urged farmers, landowners and citizens to replace Rachel Carson's silent spring with 'a raucous summer' of wildness. Monbiot's vision was not a return to the environment of the past – whatever that might be – but a reduction of sheep and deer that would allow other species to thrive. The land would become alive once more with beavers, wolves and even elephants. He was quick to emphasise that this was 'not for the sake of wolves but for the sake of people', who could finally feel wildness again.

Feral helped to inspire a movement, to motivate those landowners who knew that the perceived beauty of the British countryside – ploughed fields, tidy hedgerows – was in fact a series of absences. No beavers, no lynx, too few birds and frogs. Even broad fields of bluebells, England's signature woodland beauty, testified to the absence of wild boar rooting around in the soil.

Hanbury-Tenison is one of the converts. He is getting to know the land properly for the first time. 'The more you learn, the more you feel ashamed,' he says. 'I used to walk through these woods and not really know whether I was looking at a hazel or a rowan, or an oak or a beech, especially in the winter when the leaves aren't out.'

Since his father bought the farm in 1960, the land has been through various reinventions in search of a profit. It started off with a few crops and types of livestock. It was turned over to farming red deer, then wild boar, until an outbreak of foot-and-mouth. Now the land is let to a tenant who farms mainly sheep. 'My tenant very much farms subsidies, not animals,' says Hanbury-Tenison.

Nearly half of England's farms would make a loss without public subsidies. (Agriculture is managed separately in Scotland and Wales, but the situation there is even worse. Most Scottish and Welsh farms would make a loss without subsidies; indeed one in five Welsh farms makes a loss even with subsidies.) The government has promised that, with the UK having left the European Union, public money will be directed to those who offer public goods, like carbon storage and bio-diversity, not just marketable products, like food. This idea promises a revolution in how the land is managed, without any Tompkins-style land purchases. If the subsidies are set right, farmers could become conservationists.

This would be a revolution. England represents an extreme of marginalising wildness. There are no large land predators. There is very little that approaches wilderness; even escaping from light pollution is a privilege. England is a densely populated country, dotted with towns and villages, and where agriculture accounts for two-thirds of the land. Large forests have been cut down for timber and farmland over centuries. Not until 1951 did the UK create its first national park. Some of the forests have grown back, and now cover 11 per cent of the country, up from 5 per cent a century ago. That is still lower than almost any European country. Moreover, much of the new forest is plantation, which suits animals less well, and the other habitats that are crucial to species, including heaths, grasslands and meadows, have not recovered. Only half of England's Sites of Special Scientific Interest – those places meant to be most valuable for wildlife – are in adequate condition. At least that's our best estimate. Half of sites haven't been examined in several years; Natural England, the body in charge of improving them, has had its funding cut by nearly three-quarters over the past decade. Even since 1970, there has been a depressing decline across Britain: animal abundance, the sheer number, has fallen by 13 per cent, and is probably falling further. Nearly half of birds and a quarter of terrestrial mammals present in Great Britain are at risk of disappearing from the islands.

In the tropics, land-sparing – separating agriculture and nature – is the best way to protect animal life. In Europe, too, the answer is probably not small, inefficient farms, that try to produce food and to help wildlife, but do neither job very well. But perhaps because farming has been widespread for many centuries on the continent, the species that survive today tend to be more tolerant of agriculture than those in the tropics. Studies in the UK and Poland have found that there are some bird species that thrive on farms, and which do badly under land-sparing. It's possible that, when these species are taken into account, the best option might be a middle way – with some nature reserves, some high-intensity farming and some wildlife-friendly farming. Even small scraps of land like Hanbury-Tenison's can have a role. These can be supported by farms that don't plough their soil and that cut down on pesticides, thereby providing corridors for insects, birds and mammals. Partly because these no-till farms can be more resilient to extreme weather, they don't necessarily have much lower yields – meaning that they don't require lots more land to produce the same amount of food.

For Hanbury-Tenison, who is in his mid-thirties, this is not just about nature healing itself – it's about nature healing people. He spent nine years in the British army, including three tours of Afghanistan, and then several years as a management consultant in London, pretending he understood more about business than he actually did. He was destined to inherit the family farm, but he didn't quite know what that meant. And then, suffering from mental health difficulties, he had an epiphany looking over this rainforest. He felt calm.

Throughout all of England's deforestation, the patch of trees on his land has stood intact. It escaped the axe or the chainsaw, because the slope was too steep and rocky. It forms a habitat so wild, so different that I keep having to remind myself that we are still in England. (In Hanbury-Tenison's mind, we aren't – we're in Cornwall.) This, I think, is what our country could look like if we took wild animals as seriously as we currently take meat.

Hanbury-Tenison started rewilding by uprooting a wire fence, and releasing a breeding pair of beavers into the stream. The beaver is the ambassador for rewilding in Britain. Driven to extinction in England for their fur and meat in the fourteenth century, the rodents have recently been released – some legally, some illegally from wildlife parks – into waterways. Each beaver might occupy a three-kilometre stretch of river. In England, there is a public complaint that beavers eat fish. Even James Dyson, the billionaire inventor who owns 35,000 acres of farmland, has echoed it. In reality beavers are vegetarians. Perhaps it's because C. S. Lewis depicted beavers frying fish (and drinking beer) in his *Chronicles of Narnia;* perhaps our love for meat means that we can't envisage other large mammals living without it. A long-term study found that beavers had no adverse effect on fish numbers, posed no health risks to humans, and reduced flood risks downstream by building dams. 'Beavers are 90 per cent good and 10 per cent bad, and the 10 per cent is relatively easy for us to deal with,' Alastair Driver, one of the advisers to that study, told me. The negative effects of beavers – for example, some localised flooding caused by their dams – can be mitigated by basic management, such as dismantling dams in some areas or installing 'beaver deceivers' that allow water to pass through the dams. In the worst case, some can be culled. 'Don't forget – we wiped them out once before,' says Driver. Indeed, one risk is that landowners will do it again: in 2019, one-fifth of Scotland's beaver population was legally culled.

Hanbury-Tenison wants to release more mammals: pine martens, water voles, Tamworth pigs, perhaps even bison. Each would have their role: the pine martens to control the grey squirrel, the pigs to mimic the earth-turning work of wild boar, the bison to rip out the gorse bushes. 'Bison! That sounds like the stuff of fairy tales,' he laughs. 'The idea is just to have a perimeter fence and everything else is just free-ranging.'

It's one thing to say that we should let nature take its course. Quickly you have to recognise the human decisions required. What species should humans introduce? What species should we try to extinguish? European bison are not popular with many British ecologists, who question whether the animals have been in the country since the last Ice Age, and argue that Longhorn cattle, descendants of once-native aurochs, are less likely to provoke public resistance. Hanbury-Tenison wants to control the more recent arrivals – grey squirrels, roe deer – but not to eliminate them. 'They have become part of this story,' he says. 'We have made such fundamental changes to the ecology of the UK, through introductions and eradications, that we have to continue to have some responsibility for trying to help nature get back to a more ethical position.' To love animals is not just to stand back and admire them. It necessarily starts from the acceptance that our lives are intertwined.

Turning inefficient, subsidised farms over to nature is exactly what we should be doing. The Knepp estate in West Sussex failed to turn a profit as an arable and beef farm, but has become Britain's most famous wild farming project, thanks to the book *Wilding* by its brilliantly named co-owner Isabella Tree. The estate is within easy driving distance of London and has industrial buildings, and since turning to nature, it has been able to balance the books by attracting day-trippers and renting out office space. Even then, Tree estimates that the value of the land has halved.

Hanbury-Tenison, with a mix of military planning and upper-class confidence, hopes that his own books will balance with green government subsidies. Yoga instructors could hold retreats, instead of taking their students to Morocco and Sri Lanka. Companies could bring their staff down for three-day off-site development meetings. (Hanbury-Tenison had brought some of his former colleagues down already. 'When they saw a cowpat, they thought someone should have picked it up ... I began to realise there's such a divide.' He pauses to pick up a clod of wet earth. 'It's about not being afraid of *this*! We're afraid of it!') In the summer, groups could scythe bracken, which Hanbury-Tenison describes as 'a wonderful group activity, incredibly meditative. It's like t'ai chi!' Moreover, he notes, employers wanted to provoke creativity

– and 'there's nothing more creative than a beaver!' He admits this pitch might need some finessing.

We walk through the farm. In another field, Hanbury-Tenison is trialling solar panels, a wind turbine and a wind fence. A couple of hives of Cornish bees are due to arrive shortly. The land is a Petri dish. And the experiments seem plausible. 'This is a three-, four-decades-long vision,' he says. 'My father is eighty-three. My dream is that, when I'm eighty-three, I can hand over this farm as both a financially sustainable and ecologically sustainable place – and without getting too hippy about it, spiritually sustainable, where I don't look at the fields and they're pockmarked like the Somme.'

Later I came across a short video on my phone of a beaver swimming through water and gnawing at a tree. I showed it to Eliza and Cleo, and felt it had given them a better sense of the natural world than any of our zoo visits.

Rewilding is now accepted as a concept in Britain, but it's still seen as a quirk – an aside to the main business of the countryside. In fact, it represents what so many of us value about the land – beauty and resilience, not to mention carbon storage, flood defences and the presence of lives beyond our own. To restore Britain's nature will require much more than a few farms. The land is there. Of all the land needed to produce food for the UK, both domestically and abroad, 85 per cent is used for livestock and livestock feed. With a move away from meat, we can free up much of this, without reducing our food security.

Rewilding could replace the unprofitable farms of Britain's uplands. It could go further too. East Anglia is one of the country's most productive agricultural areas – but its low-lying peat soils are eroding by one to two centimetres a year, throwing off carbon. 'At any reasonable carbon price, there would be no agriculture in the British fens whatsoever,' Dieter Helm, an Oxford economist who has advised the government's environment strategy, has warned. Peatlands cover 12 per cent of the UK, particularly wet parts of Scotland and northern England; they store more carbon than all the forests of the UK, Germany and France combined. They are also incredible habitats for insects. Yet we cut into them to fertilise our gardens: most compost sold in the UK is peat, even though good substitutes are available. Gardening with peat harms nature – the precise opposite of what most gardeners think they are doing, and want to be doing. Instead we can work to restore carbon to the soils, and wildlife to the land.

Rewilding Britain, an advocacy group, wants 1 million hectares of 'core' rewilding land by 2100, equivalent to about 5 per cent of the land. It also calls for a broader network extending to 30 per cent of the country. Today Britain has 1.8 million hectares of deer-stalking estates and 1.3 million hectares of grouse moors (some in national parks). There is land owned by the Ministry of Defence, by the Forestry Commission, and land by the side of road verges – all of which could be managed better to allow other species to thrive. The UK has an estimated 30,000 hectares of golf courses, while England has 20,000 hectares of car parks, which could support wildlife in urban areas. Household gardens, too, can provide havens for insects, birds, amphibians and small mammals – although it might require people to change their view of what a beautiful garden looks like.

Rewilding densely populated Britain is harder than rewilding Chile. A £3.4 million project in Wales called Summit to Sea was put on hold because local farmers complained about the threat to their livelihoods. Yet four out of five Britons say they support rewilding. The future of Britain's animal population is a political battle. We have to decide what we want our country to look like – whether we value more farming traditions, which produce inefficient food with public subsidies, or intact ecosystems, which can be the basis for tourism and human health.

Things become even more controversial with predators. Just over a third of the public want the reintroduction of lynxes or wolves, which were hunted off these islands centuries ago. Eurasian lynx – the species that once roamed Britain – weigh only as much as a Dalmatian and largely live off deer that they kill in the forest. They are present throughout Europe. They pose no threat to humans; the very few stories seem to have involved lynx with rabies, which no longer occurs in lynx in western Europe. You're more likely to be bothered by Lynx deodorant. The lynx might not even kill many sheep, because doing so would mean venturing into open fields. But lynx have large ranges: in south-eastern Norway, they are estimated to live at a density of around one per 300 square kilometres; to have a viable population requires a huge protected area, or several nearby forests with connecting forests and with tolerant farmers. Many landowners want to keep the door shut to predators.

Being an island, Britain is likely to remain behind continental Europe. Wolves have spread to the Netherlands and Belgium. For the first time since the Industrial Revolution, the French–Italian and German–Polish populations of wolves may soon be able to mix. The 1979 Bern Convention, signed by EU countries, places tight rules on the deliberate killing of wild animals. Wolves and lynx can be killed only where there is no other solution and where there is scientific evidence that it is appropriate to managing their population. Lynx are billed as a tourist attraction in Germany, although visitors need to have some imagination, because the cats are mostly too secretive to be seen.

Hanbury-Tenison's farm covers 330 acres; he is hopeful of convincing his neighbours to join him, creating an overall reserve of up to 1,000 acres. This would still not be big enough for lynx. The farm sits on the edge of Bodmin Moor. When I was ten, British newspapers became obsessed with sightings of a large cat on the moor. The Beast of Bodmin, as it became known, was never caught and never bothered humans. But there were dozens of sightings, a few grainy videos and multiple livestock carcasses. In other countries – like the US and Spain, which have always had bears and wolves respectively – this might not have been considered front-page news. In Britain, it caused a media frenzy. Experts identified the rogue creatures as leopards; they were probably wrong, they probably weren't even experts. Still, the furore forced an official investigation. A few years later it emerged that a circus trainer had probably released three pumas onto the moor, when her zoo had to shut down.

George Monbiot wondered if the Bodmin Moor sightings were fantasy, a part of 'an unexpressed wish for lives wilder and fiercer than those we now lead'. I think the hysteria was actually the opposite, a tendency for us to see danger in the traces of wildness. In Britain, we love animals who live far from us – lions, tigers, polar bears. We love imagining wild spaces like the Amazon that don't impinge upon us. If we make the case, we may learn to love the wild animals who live close to us too, and we may decide to turn over more land to them. After all, how can we expect Kenyans to live close to lions if we won't consider living close to lynx?

Unless we set aside 30 per cent of the planet or perhaps 50 per cent, the animal world will shrivel around us. We'll be the animal-lovers who wiped out animals. There is enough space for us and for wild animals to thrive – if we move away from livestock, farm crops better, and put our wallets where our animal-loving values are. It'd make a huge difference. It wouldn't, however, be enough on its own. Although habitat loss is the biggest threat to wild animals today, a greater threat has arrived: climate change.

*

On our honeymoon, Susie and I travelled to an island in Indonesia, surrounded by coral reefs. Most tourists went to scuba-dive. Susie doesn't dive and I was rusty, so we struck out alone – we put on goggles, wandered down to the beach and paddled to the reef a few metres offshore. Anyone who's snorkelled on a reef knows that moment when your goggles break the waterline, revealing in high definition the seabed of shells and sands.

Tropical reefs have the richness of the Amazon rainforest and the charisma of the African savannah. They cover 0.1 per cent of the ocean floor, yet host 830,000 plant and animal species, of which fewer than one in ten have been named. They provide fish with nooks and crannies, allowing the young in particular to shelter from predators such as sharks and octopuses. On each hour-long snorkel, we would see sleepy rays, fat sea cucumbers, grouchy porcupine fish. There were bright blue starfish lying on the bottom, a small shark, a couple of puffer fish, two cuttlefish, false clown anemone fish, clownfish, butterfly fish, parrotfish, cleaner wrasse, blue-spotted lagoon ray, Moorish idols, humbugs, triggerfish of different shapes and sizes, crocodile needlefish, a crayfish and on our last trip out a slightly lost great barracuda.

We would return to the hotel to try to compare what we had seen to a few old guidebooks.

We snorkelled so frequently over this small patch of reef for four days that it felt like ours. When we left Indonesia, we knew that we would probably never see the reef again. But I always imagined it would be there for someone – some other tourists, some other honeymooners. Maybe every eco-tourist has an experience like this, that by making a pilgrimage across the planet we are confirming ourselves as animal-lovers, we are confirming the existence of a world away from human micromanagement.

But I was naïve. Between a third and half of coral reefs have disappeared since the 1980s. In March 2016 surface water temperatures in the Great Barrier Reef rose 3°C above normal; millions of corals died. Previously, it was thought that the corals slowly starved, because the warmer water caused them to expel the algae with which they have a symbiotic relationship (and which give them their bright colours). But surveys found that half the bleached corals died within two weeks. 'They're literally cooked,' says Terry Hughes, director of the ARC Centre of Excellence for Coral Reef Studies, in Queensland. 'The temperatures were just too high for coral tissue.' The reef is viewable from space. The aliens must be wondering what we're up to.

Corals grow back slowly if at all. It takes years for bleached corals to become eroded, allowing larvae to start to take their place. By November 2016, coral cover across the 2,300-kilometre Great Barrier Reef had fallen 30 per cent. More than that, the mixture of corals had changed, with spectacular branching corals among the most affected. This catastrophic die-off only occurred for the first time in 1998. It is now almost an annual event. The Great Barrier Reef will never again look like it did even five years ago. The Intergovernmental Panel on Climate Change projects that, if global warming reaches 1.5°C, the world's coral reefs will decline by a further 70 to 90 per cent. At 2°C, 99 per cent of coral reefs disappear. In a few decades, there may be no reefs like the one Susie and I saw in Indonesia. We are not cutting the reefs down, but we might as well be. 'You can't regrow the Amazon if you don't do anything about logging,' says Hughes. 'We can't hope to regrow corals if we don't do anything about global warming.'

Coral reefs are often seen as a warning sign of what is to come. That's misleading: huge losses are already occurring now in other wild habitats. Off the coast of Tasmania, 90 per cent of kelp forests have disappeared since the 1960s. A marine heatwave killed most of the kelp forests in parts of northern California; warmer temperatures also seem to be making the forests more vulnerable to grazing by voracious sea urchins. Hughes prefers to call the reefs 'the poster child' of climate change. The results are likely to be most severe in the tropics, where species have evolved for smaller swings in temperatures. But no region is being spared. In Germany, where forestry and wood-based industries employ more people than the car industry, forests are under attack from bark beetles who can now survive the warmer winters. Bumblebee populations have collapsed in Europe and the US for various reasons. The bees' furry bodies are ill-suited to high temperatures; during heatwaves, 'It becomes a zero-sum game between keeping cool and gathering resources,' says Peter Soroye, a conservation biologist at the University of Ottawa. Put simply, the bees die of either heat or hunger. Bird and mammal populations are falling fastest in areas that are warming most. Animals' seasons may be out of sync with the plants on which they rely: hibernating animals may wake up before their food is available, migratory birds may no longer arrive when their food is on the trees.

Once we did experiments to judge the future – in aquariums, Antarctic scallops lost their ability to swim when the temperature increased by 2°C. Now we can barely keep up with what is happening already. Between the late 1970s and the early 2010s, the mass of insects in one section of a rainforest in Puerto Rico fell by 97 per cent. Numbers of birds, frogs and lizards, which feed on the insects, also declined. All things being equal, insect populations should have increased as their predators became scarcer. But all things were not equal: the mean maximum temperature had risen by 2°C since the 1970s. The insects and their predators could not survive. The forest itself may not be able to survive the century. In 2019, Australia had its hottest and driest year on record; wildfires swept across nearly 20 million hectares. When researchers visited burnt areas, they found that virtually no small, ground-dwelling animals had survived. In the state of New South Wales 5,000 koalas died.

But animals are mobile, right? Shouldn't they adapt better to rising temperatures than plants do? Not necessarily. What seems to matter are peak temperatures, and plants are often better able to withstand these than animals are – just as a pot plant can survive a day on a hot patio, so long as it has access to water.

Really the question is not whether animals or plants survive, but whether they both do. Ecosystems depend on animals, plants, insects and fungi. In Lopé National Park, in Gabon, a warm, drier climate has meant less fruit: in the 1980s, elephants used to find ripe fruit on one in ten trees; now it's fewer than one in fifty. Elephants are today thinner and less healthy. In ten years, will they still shape the forest as they once did? Elsewhere some insects will start appearing at the wrong time for migratory birds who feed on them. Some ecosystems will experience temperatures that don't currently exist on earth. Some habitats will cease to exist. The effects will depend on the interactions between pollinators and plants, plants and herbivores, prey and predators. 'We really don't know what happens,' says Alex Pigot, a biologist at University College London.

Pigot's models suggest that ecosystems will start to collapse this decade. He forecasts that in this century climate change will become an even greater cause of extinctions than the loss of natural habitat. 'Even if you've got a trickle of species going extinct because of climate change now, that's not a very good indication,' says Pigot. Like a highly infectious disease, 'the speed at which things can go from fine to really bad is really striking'.

Loving animals is therefore yet another reason to fight climate change. Nature can be brutal, but we are making it more so. We are forcing animals to live in conditions that they have not adapted for; the rate of change is so fast that they cannot adapt. So we need to switch to renewable energy, to keep forests and peatlands intact, to eat less meat and dairy, and to insulate our homes. Stop me if you've heard it before.

But maybe even that won't be enough. There is no precedent for a country becoming richer while its environmental footprint shrinks.

We are good at stopping using the worst pollutants, such as the CFCs that punctured the ozone layer. We are also good at moving pollution from rich countries to poorer countries, hence so many of our Amazon goods being made in Asia. We are good at finding replacements for animal products like whale oil, mink fur, and even meat. But until we stop using more and more of the planet's resources, we will always push animals to the edge. Underlying the problem is our affluence. At the start of the twentieth century, Americans spent more than 40 per cent of their income on food, now it's less than 10 per cent. Our remaining money has to be spent somewhere. The richest tenth of humanity, those earning more than $38,000 a year, were responsible for half the world's carbon emissions between 1990 and 2015, according to Oxfam and the Stockholm Environment Institute.

We think we live in a digital age – with paperless offices and minimalist home furnishings. But the amount of resources that the planet uses has risen roughly in line with economic growth. We use natural materials that we barely think of. The world digs up 50 billion tonnes of sand a year. It works out as eighteen kilos per person per day. This leaves tracts of the seabed uninhabitable, but we only notice shiny buildings. Leopold said that the oldest task in human history was 'to live on a piece of land without spoiling it.' Now we are living on one piece of land, while spoiling others. Only occasionally do we realise our reach: a friend remembers looking at a simple dinner he'd made, and realising the ingredients came from three continents.

Ignorance isn't much of an excuse, though. We know we consume a lot. The carpet ripped up, because we fancy a new colour. The clothes bought, because they were on sale. The long-haul flights taken, because we understandably want to see the amazing world we live in. There is no environmentally sustainable way to produce new clothing or to fly around the world. But we have focused on plastic bags, which aren't even the tip of the iceberg. Sometimes sustainability doesn't mean declining a carrier bag from a shop, it means not going to the shop in the first place. We own more stuff than our parents, we own more than we did last year. We have even less control over how our things are made – often in low-regulation countries, where clothing dyes run into rivers or factories are fuelled by coal – than how our meat is produced. This is how we can deny extinction and the loss of animal life, because it happens half the world away. We consume because we think we won't be judged for it, but sometimes I worry my daughters will judge me as exceedingly dim.

In his book *The World Without Us*, the science writer Alan Weisman envisaged what would happen if our species suddenly disappeared from the planet. The answer, in many ways, is that plants and animals would flourish; nature would break apart much of the infrastructure that we regard as permanent. Only a few aspects of our existence – such as the metals in the soils – would really stick around, as of course would our impact on the climate.

The idea of a world without us came into view during the coronavirus lockdown. For those who love animal life, it has become a darkly tempting prospect. You've heard the idea: there are too many humans, and only by reducing our numbers can we give animals the space to thrive. Doug Tompkins said he woke up every morning worrying about the 250,000 children that had been born that day. Today more than 350,000 babies are born each day, and the world's population grows 1 per cent a year. The UN forecasts our population will plateau at around 11 billion in 2100, but that 10 billion and 12 billion are plausible outcomes. Africa's population is projected to increase by 1.1 billion people by 2050, adding more people than currently live in Europe and North America combined. The rest of the world's population will increase by just under 800 million people. How can we find more space for other animals, if there are so many of us?

Arne Naess, one of the radical ecological thinkers who influenced Tompkins, said humans' cultural diversity and basic needs could be satisfied by a population of around 100 million. For Naess, reducing human population was a question of justice – humans have no right to crowd out other species, except where necessary for our vital needs. But this puts an individual human on the same level as a bear, bee or a bacterium. Biologist Reed Noss argued that humans should actually have a lower priority than non-humans, because 'our species is both more adaptable and more destructive than any other'.

Half-Earth's E. O. Wilson puts the ideal human population at 500 million. Jane Goodall pointed out that 500 years ago, when the human population was around 500 million, 'all these things we talk about wouldn't be a problem'. That would be equivalent to reducing humans' population to the current residents of South America. Ingrid Newkirk, the founder of animal rights group PETA, chose to be sterilised at the age of twenty-two. She has compared having children to buying a pedigree dog – a lifestyle choice through which 'we indulge our vanity'.

Maybe it's just because I have young kids, but this subject seems to bring out the worst instincts of the environmental movement – to suggest some humans are worth less than other animals, and to put preserving natural beauty for the wealthy above freedom for the poor. It allows animal-lovers to be thrown in the same bin as China's old one-child policy. Those concerned about population are rich, white and well-travelled; those who are having lots of children tend to be poor people of colour. In 2020 the WWF apologised for a promotional video, which called for the world to 'stabilise the human population as low as we fairly can' over footage of Asian crowds.

If you love animals, you should understand why humans want to have children. I had given up drinking cow's milk, partly because of the horror of breaking the link between bovine mother and child. I don't want elephants to live in zoos, partly because they can't create multi-generational herds. It would be a bit odd to say that the desire to have children, and live alongside them, is a disposable part of human existence. Also, even though I love animals, I don't want the human population to shrivel. Human society is brilliant. Why can't we love Twitter as well as turtles, Hollywood as well as hornbills? We do not need to wind the clock back to when New York was swampland and London was forest; we just need to find a better balance.

It's not offensive to question birth rates. More than 220 million women in developing countries don't want to get pregnant but don't have contraceptives. In Ethiopia, a woman with no schooling will have, on average, six children; a woman with twelve years of schooling will have fewer than two children. One trial in Kenya found that something as simple as cutting the cost of school uniforms reduced not only school dropout rates, but teenage marriage and childbirth too. If we refuse to talk about population growth, we are condemning some girls to grow up without education and without options other than to have more kids than they want to. And if people in rich countries want to have fewer kids, out of environmental guilt or sheer terror of the climate that awaits us, then I admire the sacrifice.

But the real problem is not how many births there are: it's how much the existing population already consumes. The average citizen of a rich country consumes between three and six times as much natural resources as the average citizen of a poor country. Martin Rees, the British astrophysicist, suggests that earth could sustain 20 billion people 'with a tolerable (albeit ascetic) quality of life' – starting with a vegan diet, little travel, and small apartments. He said this prospect is 'plainly improbable, and certainly not alluring'. It's certainly not happening.

Since 1970 the number of people on earth has doubled. The quantity of natural resources that the average person consumes has nearly doubled too. We like to blame China and India. But in absolute terms, the biggest increase has come from upper-middle-income and high-income countries. The average American produces a kilo of plastic waste every three days. When I lived in Colombia, I saw how the elite there aspired to own what North Americans and Europeans already did. They didn't feel much responsibility to restrain their own consumption, because they didn't feel rich compared to us.

One reason that animal activists get so worked up about hunting is that it seems so simple: whether or not someone loves animals can be boiled down to whether or not they pull the trigger. Yet to love animals truly, to find space for them in our world, touches all parts of our lives. A century ago, Leopold wrote that conservation would require a 'new kind of people' – a 'new kind of farmer, banker, voter, consumer'. He was right. We need to find a way of progressing while using less stuff. One vision involves less private wealth and more public assets, such as parks. To be honest, I don't know if it can work. But the first step is to recognise the depth of our current hole.

*

We don't believe in climate change. Of course we do in theory – we've seen the figures, we're not like the mad deniers on YouTube and Fox News. But if we believed, if we *truly* believed, we would act. We would be so terrified by the wildfires and heatwaves and hurricanes, not to mention the prospect of the unstable west Antarctic ice sheet collapsing, and raising sea levels several metres, that our response would be the defining feature of our politics. Instead humans have burnt more carbon dioxide into the atmosphere since the first United Nations summit to debate climate change in 1992 than they did before it.

We don't really believe that animals are disappearing and ecosystems are collapsing either. We have seen the headlines and graphs, we have seen photos of forests burning and rhinos looking lonely. We hear stories of coral reefs bleaching, and predictions that Amazonia is heading towards ecosystem collapse. Our world is a Jenga tower, with pieces being taken out at an accelerating pace. We laugh at those like Bolsonaro, who outright refuse to believe that biodiversity loss matters. Yet if we truly believed, we would do something – for our sake. When the Amazon burnt in 2020, the world's leaders offered $22 million, which the Brazilian government rejected. You can't even buy a decent goalkeeper with $22 million.

We were told that we were heading to the abyss. But how could we believe it when our existence never seemed fragile? We lived in a world of widening horizons – cheap airfares, cheap Chinese imports, free Google searches. Amazon's Jeff Bezos had put packages on our doorstep within hours, now he was promising to put humans on Mars within decades. Who were we to distrust him? Humans had always won. I wasn't deforesting the Amazon, I was just buying fridge-door-friendly yoghurt. At least until coronavirus came along, our progress seemed a one-way street.

Fragility is hard to process when you've enjoyed decades of cheap consumer goods, new technologies and relative political stability. People in poorer countries will be harder hit by climate change. But they may also find it easier to accept what's at stake. According to pollsters YouGov, 70 per cent of Indians say that climate change will have a great deal of impact on their lives, compared with fewer than 20 per cent of Britons, Germans and Scandinavians. People in the US and Europe are also far less likely than those in Asia to think that climate change will spark a new world war or the extinction of the human race.

Climate change and biodiversity loss are the two overarching crises of our time. They feed into one another: when forests and grasslands are protected, they host wildlife and store carbon; when they are destroyed, the wildlife is decimated and the carbon is released back into the atmosphere, where it accelerates the warming process, and leads other forests to die. Intact ecosystems sequester a lot of carbon. Forest elephants have been found to increase carbon uptake in African forests by trampling down slender trees and allowing larger hardwoods to grow. Without the elephants, the forests' biomass would shrink by 7 per cent. A team led by ecologist Fabio Berzaghi valued the elephants' contribution to carbon storage at $43 billion. The destruction of the Amazon, meanwhile, is reaching the point where the rainforest may collapse: there won't be enough trees to generate the rainfall on which other trees depend. The basin could become an emitter of carbon, rather than a store of it. It could become savannah, rather than forest. Its transformation would take animal life and our climate with it.

Tree-planting is in fashion with governments. I've taken part in tree-planting – and it was as good for my morale as it was bad for my spine. But we have to be realistic what it can achieve. New forests are not the same as old ones. They are less resilient to changing climates and forest fires than long-standing forests with many different species of tree. There's a Chinese saying that the best time to plant a tree was twenty years ago, the second best time is now. Well, the best time not to cut down the world's tropical forests was twenty years ago, the second best time is now.

A lot of our moral dilemmas with animals come because we are in fundamentally different positions. We have the ability to farm animals, hunt them, and put them in zoos. But with climate change and biodiversity, we are in the same boat in the long run. Overall climate change is very bad for us and very bad for wildlife. Overall biodiversity loss is very bad for us and very bad for wildlife.

Our children won't be able to grow up with the illusion that extinction isn't happening, or that animals are out there somewhere. They're going to realise that animals are being extirpated, and the adults have left it too late to save all of them. They're not going to inherit the same planet that we did. They will wonder what it was like to experience coral reefs and rainforests in the same awe-inspiring way that we have. Perhaps their loss will be diluted by new discoveries – up to 15,000 new species are named each year, and many are greeted with media headlines, such as 'New "mysterious" frog species discovered in India's Western Ghats'. But mostly I think their loss will be lessened only by action.

Conservation is very hard in practice, but it is simple in theory. Michael Soulé, the father of conservation biology, who died in 2020, said that even if no more scientific papers were published, humans knew what to do. We need to protect natural habitat, and, as a secondary issue, reintroduce missing species and tackle pollution. We also need to reduce carbon emissions dramatically.

Peter Soroye, who has studied the effect of heat on bees, is one of those who try to stay optimistic. On his website, he says: 'I like to call myself a conservation biologist, and I like to think that someday we humans will get our act together so I can call myself something else.' Terry Hughes, the Great Barrier Reef biologist, sees the next few decades as a 'climate gauntlet' – a time of intense risk that can nonetheless be overcome. Maybe it won't always be this hard to do right by other species. Maybe it's just a challenge that has fallen to our generations.

One of the few bits of good news is urbanisation. The number of people living in rural areas is projected to decrease – from 3.4 billion in 2020 to 3.1 billion in 2050. So although there will be more human mouths to feed, there could also be more potential to carve out parts of the world for nature.

When biologists evaluate whether a species is at risk of extinction, they estimate whether the population is rising or falling, and how widely it is spread across the planet. If humans were evaluated, we would be in the category of 'Least Concern'. Our population is rising on every corner of the planet. But that's misleading. Human extinction is not a ridiculous concept. In 1947, the organisation Bulletin of the Atomic Scientists created a Doomsday Clock in an attempt to illustrate how close humans were to destroying the world with technologies of our making. Humanity was four minutes to midnight in the early 1980s, when I was born. By 2020 the scientists had reduced the time remaining to a hundred seconds. We are beginning to understand multiple existential threats – climate change, runaway artificial intelligence, possible nuclear and biological warfare. Toby Ord, a philosopher at Oxford University, says that the chance of human extinction has gone from one in a hundred in the twentieth century to one in six now. We're playing Russian roulette with our species.

Coal miners once used canaries to detect the presence of invisible, life-threatening gases. Thousands – tens of thousands – of species are now playing a similar role. They can make us acknowledge our joint fragility – to understand that we too are animals evolved for one environment, now being thrust into another. We and other species are all on the same boat. The boat may or may not be the *Titanic*, and it may or may not be about to hit a (melting) iceberg. Let's slow down a little, just in case.

How do we face possible disaster? How do we process the fact that so much more needs to be done to shrink the human footprint? It is exhausting. Susie has banned me from starting off dinner conversations by mentioning a new record temperature over the Arctic. I expend a ridiculous amount of energy recycling plastic pots, something that has negligible impact on my environmental footprint. I sometimes lurch to extreme restraint – not opening a can of beer while watching the football. Other times, I resign myself – buying plastic-heavy presents for friends' children's birthdays.

It's sometimes said that the window for action is closing. That's wrong. We will have to act either way. We can act now, or we can act later – when more damage has been done to our lives, and when less of the natural world can be saved. Kris Tompkins says we are far past the point where individual action is 'an elective'. She's right. We can't call ourselves *Homo sapiens* and continue standing round like battery chickens, as if our fate were out of our hands. We can't call ourselves animal-lovers, if we don't intervene to save the natural world. We won't stop climate change and biodiversity loss as individuals. But we should at least act like we believe they are happening. There is a paradox that making local people richer is the only way for conservation to work, yet development itself is the biggest threat to conservation. We need to find a new ethic.

The best vision for what this new ethic might be comes from Peter Singer. 'The emphasis on frugality and a simple life,' he wrote in his book *Practical Ethics*, 'does not mean that an environmental ethic frowns on pleasure, but that the pleasures it values do not come from conspicuous consumption. They come, instead, from loving relationships; from being close to children and friends; from conversation; from sports and recreations that are in harmony with our environment instead of harmful to it; from food that is not based on the exploitation of sentient creatures and does not cost the earth; from creative activity and work of all kinds; and (with due care so as not to ruin precisely what is valued) from appreciating the unspoilt places in the world in which we live.'

My return flight from London to San Francisco, which I took for a work trip, created more greenhouse gas emissions than the average Brazilian does in a year. After coming home, I gave up flying – at least for a year. I had flown only once on holiday since the children were born. But work trips continued to pile up: in the space of twelve months, I travelled from London to Buenos Aires, San Francisco and Mongolia. These trips always had a justification, no one in the office raised an eyebrow, and if I hadn't done them someone else would have. I wanted to imagine a different system. I would rather not see the Amazon or the coral reefs again because doing so would contribute to their disappearance.

Individual action is not the opposite of collective action; it is the forerunner. By individually backing protected areas, we push our governments to do the same. By admiring wild animals, and paying to see them, we encourage local communities to accept reintroductions.

Our behaviour influences our neighbours. It also sends signals to those in power. Companies associate themselves with causes once their customers do. Politicians embrace difficult choices when they sense voters can handle them.

*

I've never liked protesting. I just feel ridiculous. Shouting in the middle of shopping streets. Signing up to simple slogans. Hoping to get arrested but not, you know, *arrested*. Perhaps I'm too English.

'Power to the animals! Animals got the power!' shouts a guy with a loudhailer, unpoetically, as we walk down the street. I can feel my inner cynicism bubbling. Until seagulls get the vote, or cows work on Wall Street, it's hard to see how animals have the power. We march on, a few hundred of us, towards one of Europe's largest meat markets. When Smithfield was founded eight centuries ago, it was outside London so that disease stayed in the suburbs. Even in the early Victorian era, it filled the city with animal life and death: Dickens himself describes 'a thick steam perpetually arising from the bodies of the cattle'. Animals were brought by train to London's railway stations, and then herded by road to Smithfield. Now all that activity has been pushed out of the city. Smithfield is just a wholesaler of dead chunks. Even that no longer really fits with the city's modern self-identity, and soon the meat market will be relocated, leaving a surrounding neighbourhood of trendy meat restaurants.

The peaceful occupation of Smithfield meat market is day one of Animal Rebellion. The group is an offshoot of the Extinction Rebellion climate change movement. Are the protestors here because of caged chickens or culled cows, beached whales or orphaned orangutans? Maybe all of the above.

You couldn't have asked for a gentler – or quirkier – group of protestors. I ask one of the organisers if she'll be camping out. She hesitates, then mutters: 'I have a cat.' A singer-songwriter named Giles performs what he hopes will be 'the first vegan number one' single. He claims it's big on Facebook.

A member of the Animal Liberation Front – the infamous group that sabotaged animal research laboratories in the 1980s and 90s – addresses the crowd about their relatively mellow tactics. 'I've been to fourteen prisons!' he starts off, unpromisingly. 'But movements move! Movements change! I don't know what's going to work. But as they say in Brazil, *put it on the pizza!*' They don't say that in Brazil, but the crowd appreciates the sentiment.

It gets dark and cold, and protestors pitch their pop-up tents on the concrete that runs through Smithfield. 'If only 5 per cent of those people download it … ' I overhear Giles the singer-songwriter explaining. Next to me in the crowd is a pensioner – she must be eighty – in an anorak with a pop-up tent on her back. 'I'm just here for the night,' she whispers. Then, as if shocked by her own rebelliousness, she adds: 'I normally go to bed at eight.' I bump into her the next morning, queuing for coffee. 'It was a great night,' she says. 'I didn't sleep at all.'

I don't sleep much either. I would like to pretend that I stayed up singing protest songs and sabotaging meat lockers. But in fact it's mainly because I have pitched my tent half over some sort of metal covering. Every time someone walks near the tent, there is a seesaw effect – and my buttocks are raised a few centimetres into the air. The struggle takes many forms.

Over the next two weeks, Animal Rebellion protestors target the offices of various companies that they say are making life worse for animals. They graffiti walls, stop the traffic, and disrupt London's biggest fish market. Two protestors lock themselves to a slaughterhouse truck, putting chains through their ear piercings. Just when morale is flagging, a protestor in a home-made broccoli costume is filmed being arrested and the clip goes viral online. Adding to the good spirits, the police's vegan chilli – served to all those arrested – is deemed 'very nice'. The protests culminate in a march down Park Lane, where people dress up as fruit and vegetables. I remember an organiser calling out, 'Does anyone want to be a pear?'

When I couldn't make the protests themselves, I followed the activities via the Telegram messaging app. The protestors' group was a comic mix of idealism and bureaucracy. Typical message: 'Can all fruit and veggie costumes please be promptly returned to the information desk?' There was a discussion on whether fish feel pain, which ended with the organisers asking protestors not to post a scientific article on social media for legal reasons. Change society, but go easy on the copyright.

So yes, at the time, Animal Rebellion felt a bit ridiculous. But when I stepped back, it didn't. The protestors believed that animals were worth taking seriously, for their own sake and for our own. They weren't deluded. They were the only wise ones among us. Their methods are imperfect – and the fetishising of being arrested would look strange in the light of the Black Lives Matter movement. Their views on hunting did not match up with my own. Nonetheless, their activism was so much better than nothing.

In Colombia, I used to be asked by some right-wingers why conservationists cared more about animals than they do about humans. This is nonsense. Conservationists recognise that humans are animals – that we too have evolved for this planet, and that we need to keep it liveable. They recognise that we feel a connection with other species, and sadness at their passing.

I tried to explain all of this, but actually what I should have said is that, if anyone puts animals before humans, it's not conservationists – it's pet-owners. Today, to love a pet is not to recognise that humans are animals, but to pretend that animals are almost humans. The animal test had pushed me to realise that society needed radical change. Could our relationship with pets point the way?

8. IT'S NOT ABOUT THE DOG

Idiots that we are, we have lost our link with nature even though we are part of it completely. All of this will end one day. What lessons will we learn? I'm eighty-three, I'm going to die. We die because we are born. The only things that matter in life are food and love, in that order, and also our little dog Ruby.

David Hockney

Be the person your dog thinks you are.

Unknown

'He's antisocial.'

I can understand why. Simba is a corgi in fancy dress. He has two antennae, each with a mini American football on the end. His front legs have sweatbands. Safe to assume this wasn't his idea. 'It's mainly for the humans,' says his owner, superfluously.

Welcome to CorgiCon San Francisco, where dogs are dressed ridiculously and then shoved together on a beach. Or perhaps just, welcome to California.

My first impression of CorgiCon is – it's glorious. Around me are people dressed as corgis, and corgis dressed as people. Eliza and I pass corgis dressed as a shark, a lifeguard, a snowman, a pilot, a horse with a cowboy on the back, a piñata and Chewbacca from *Star Wars* (the latter two are overweight). There is a corgi with a bandana, and a shirt reading: 'Bitches Love Me'. Another man wears his dog in a baby harness.

I was halfway through my three-month work stint in San Francisco. If you've spent years overdosing on stories about how different Silicon Valley is, the place feels sadly sober. Except for one thing: almost everyone is drunk on dogs. Marc Benioff, founder of software firm Salesforce, appointed his golden retriever as the company's 'chief love officer'. But this isn't just a billionaire thing. Americans are twice as likely as the French to own a dog. California takes dog-owning to extremes, and CorgiCon is one of many eye-opening results. The last time I saw a group of corgis, they were in a stately photo with Queen Elizabeth II. Now they're on a miniature wooden pirate ship, complete with three-cornered hats for the dogs.

'Is there a line for this?' says a woman, surprisingly normal given that she's attached to a corgi dressed as a clownfish.

'No, I think you just walk up and put them on there,' replies another woman, who equally surprisingly seems to understand what is happening.

The clownfish is duly onboarded.

Sand is not the ideal environment for dogs whose legs are no longer than ice lollies. But CorgiCon has been taking place on Ocean Beach, overlooking the Pacific, twice a year since 2014. 'That's like thirty-five dog years,' the organisers point out. It is now truly a fixture, possibly the world's largest gathering of corgis, although there is a rival event in Los Angeles. On the Facebook page, a woman called Savannah says she is flying specially from Boston, 2,700 miles away. Today for the first time the event has attracted more than 1,000 corgis, of both varieties, Pembroke Welsh and Cardigan Welsh.

There is nothing much to do here except be excited about dogs. Couples and families sit under parasols. It's an 'off-leash event', the canine equivalent of a swingers' party. A corgi careers towards a corgi-less woman. 'She sought you out!' says the dog's owner, joyfully. 'She said, I've got to say hi to this human!'

Photos, there are lots of photos. A few humans have signs advertising their dogs' Instagram accounts. One man balances a dog biscuit on top of his iPhone to entice his dogs to pose. 'We're going to have to settle for *one* dog looking in the right direction,' he sighs to his partner.

A dozen merchandise stalls have been set up. It's $6 for a CorgiCon sticker, $15 for two corgi wine glasses, $25 for a 'Hoomin' baseball cap. The queue is long. Next to me, a couple consider buying a corgi cushion, but decide against it, on the basis that they already have one. You can buy dog sunglasses, with a special foam bridge so they perch away from the dog's nose, and corgi socks – four for $14. You would struggle to believe that corgis were once fearless cattle-herders.

Eliza and I pass a stall offering dog 'cigars' and dog 'beer'. It turns out to be attached to San Francisco's premier dog restaurant, a former hub for illegal gambling that now prides itself on its 'Yappy Hour' and dog birthday parties.

At around 1 p.m., the crowd gathers round to watch the most energetic corgis try a small obstacle course. One of the volunteers starts to demonstrate the course, imitating a dog. 'That's not a corgi!' shouts out a teenager. 'I can't believe this is our entertainment,' laughs his friend, who, in a country with more liberal alcohol laws, would be drunk in a bar.

Outsiders are welcome at CorgiCon; indeed, they are fundamental to the joke. A beagle has been fitted with cardboard panels, reading 'in-CORGI-nito'. He looks unfazed. 'He grew up with two corgis,' explains his owner. 'So he thinks he's a corgi.' A couple of French bulldogs, one grey, one sandy brown, exchange greetings almost too excitedly – like world leaders pretending to like each other at a G20 summit. They rise from all fours to almost hug in mid-air. It's not even clear that corgis prefer being with other corgis. But it seems to me that corgi-owners prefer being with other corgi-owners.

I push Eliza along the beach in her buggy, the only thing worse adapted to the sand than the corgis' legs, and we start talking to a retired woman called Cathy and her corgi whose name is Penny – actually it's Penelope, well, to be completely honest, it's *Lady Penelope*. Lady Penelope is arthritic, but she has apparently enjoyed her day at Corgi-Con. 'She comes for the people. She loves people.' We talk about politics and England, but mainly about dogs, because everyone loves dogs, right?

At first, it felt a bit unnatural to take pets seriously: aren't they just cute distractions from the real world? What do they have to do with the injustices of abattoirs and deforestation? In fact, pets matter. They are the exception to how we treat animals. We push slaughterhouses to the back of our minds. We delay turning to the destruction of forests and coral reefs on which wild animals depend. But for domestic dogs and cats, we're always on emotional speed-dial. They expose the central lie of animal farming, that animals are just animals and that their needs are simple. They also show what happens when we love animals too much. The Egyptians treated cats as almost divine; in practice, we take things further. One of Virginia Woolf's characters suggested that loving dogs was a peculiarly female condition. I've seen more men pick up dog poo than change nappies.

Not long ago, old dogs were often taken out and shot, and excess kittens were drowned. Only recently have some animals – like rabbits, pigs and rats – become widely accepted as pets. Culture and tradition, which are the obstacles to changing our views on meat, dairy and so much else, don't remain the same forever.

So is this companionship a model for how we should approach other species? At CorgiCon, I felt like I had shown my elder daughter what carefree coexistence between humans and other animals could look like. We have created a category of animals whose worth is emotional, not economic. We align our happiness with their happiness, and so we open the door to a deeper, more harmonious relationship with other species. That's the theory. Is it too good to be true?

*

Humans' relationship with dogs began at least 15,000 years ago, and perhaps as long as 40,000. This is when archaeological evidence first shows wolves living alongside humans. Archaeologists have long debated whether we domesticated wolves, or wolves domesticated us. Did our ancestors capture and breed wolves for their hunting skills and companionship, killing the more aggressive offspring? Or did wolves sidle their way into human societies, appreciating the safety and food that we offered? One theory is that wolves came to feast on human faeces. It's plausible. Cats started living alongside humans, sometime after the start of agriculture, probably because grain fields attracted colonies of rodents for them to eat. This process is often described as self-domestication, but Greger Larson, an archaeologist at the University of Oxford, says there's no such thing. Domestication is a series of pushes and pulls, where two species gradually learn to depend on one another. In other words, humans, cats and dogs were not forced into this relationship but neither did they foresee where things would end up.

Some argue that we shouldn't breed pets at all. Gary Francione, an American law professor, and his partner have adopted several rescue dogs, whom they love dearly. But Francione would rather the dogs didn't exist in the first place. He says: 'As much as I enjoy living with dogs, were there only two dogs remaining in the world, I would not be in favor of breeding them so that we could have more "pets" and thus perpetuate their property status.'

Francione's sweeping argument is that animals have a right to live free from our control. He also has a more concrete point: dogs have been created for 'a world in which they simply do not fit', and however well we treat them, we can't meet their needs. This stance is arresting, because many pet-owners make such efforts to promote their pets' happiness.

George Orwell, who had a poodle called Marx, thought that a soft spot for animals was an English disorder. He couldn't fathom why his countrymen, still living amid post-Second World War debris and rationing, spent money on dogs and cats. The 'animal cult runs right through the nation and is probably bound up with the decay of agriculture and the dwindled birth rate', Orwell despaired in 1947. The war itself had led to a massacre of pets: in London alone 400,000 dogs and cats, a quarter of the population, were killed in a week in September 1939, as their owners anticipated the hardships to come. In the war years, humans appreciated perhaps more than ever before the company of those animals who remained.

Today Orwell would find that the animal cult is global (and that he is best remembered for telling a human story through animals). In the

UK, half of households have at least one pet. In the US, the proportion is even higher – rising over recent decades to two-thirds, according to the American Pet Products Association. Counting dogs, cats, birds and fish, the country has two pets for every three people.

It's not just how many pets we keep; it's how much money, time and emotional energy we invest in them. I am counting myself here. Nearly half of the photos on my phone are of my cat Crumble, or at least they were until my daughters were born. Nearly half of my evenings on the sofa end with her flopped over my shoulder. She is lying between my arms as I write this, and I feel guilty as I disturb her legs with each keystroke. I have to remind myself that my friends are not as interested in my cat as I am; I almost forgive them.

For most pet-owners, gone are the days when you would leave a dog outside overnight, or – as former presidential nominee Mitt Romney amazingly confessed to – strap them on a roof rack for a twelve-hour car journey. Humans take our own cutting-edge medicine, from chemotherapy to titanium prosthetics, and buy it for dogs and cats. Dog DNA tests sell for $200, and will tell your dog's heritage, although the tests' own pedigree is questionable. Japanese architects have experimented with architecture for dogs, including a folded wooden slope so that dachshunds can walk up to a platform and sunbathe next to their humans.

It sometimes seems that every benefit given to humans will eventually be extended to pets. In 1995, a former advertising salesman from Missouri called Greg Miller started selling Neuticles – prosthetic testicles, which he claims help desexed dogs and cats regain their self-esteem. These silicone implants sell at up to $499 a pair, or $689 for an exact replica (insertion not included), and the company claims that, without them, 'neuter-hesitant pet-owners' would not be willing to neuter their dogs. Neuticles are effectively banned in some countries, including Britain, where the vets' regulator decided they do not benefit the animals and are therefore unethical. Miller also sells stain remover for dogs' 'unmentionables' and implants to straighten dogs' ears. God bless America, and late-stage capitalism. Miller claims to be a millionaire.

Trouble became a millionaire in 2007, which must have been an unusual experience for a Maltese dog. He travelled by stretch limo, and due to kidnapping threats, his security costs reached $100,000 a year. Trouble's wealth was inherited from Leona Helmsley, the New York property entrepreneur known as the Queen of Mean. In her will, she left a $12 million trust for her pet, rather than her own family. Eventually after a protracted legal battle, a judge ruled that Helmsley's generosity was excessive, and reduced the dog's inheritance to a mere $2 million.

Humans kept pets before we domesticated livestock, and wealthy Europeans kept pets through the Middle Ages, but mass pet-keeping in its modern form didn't arrive until the nineteenth century. This is also when many breeds emerged, along with specialist dog food. Our love for dogs predates our scientific studies of their intelligence – only in the past two decades have scientists taken a serious interest in how dogs think. Orwell was right: it cannot be coincidence that, just as Europeans and Americans started moving to cities, and became removed from farming, they turned sharply to pets as a way of maintaining contact with animals. In farming communities, it's more natural to view dogs and cats as part of an economic reality. I was once in a village in north-western Colombia, where a woman hacked her cat to death with a machete because the cat killed one of her chickens. For her, it was an easy decision; for the US citizen I was travelling with, it was one of the worst things he'd ever witnessed. Yet the notion of pet-owning is widespread. In the Amazon, if the Matsigenka tribe hunt animals with young, they adopt the young as pets. When these animals grow up, they are released into the forest, but the Matsigenka avoid hunting them. Once an animal has become a loved pet, there's little going back.

One of the most amazing demonstrations of dogs' power comes from a wolf. A lactating wolf was given four wolf pups and four malamute puppies to nurture. She spent more time playing with the puppies, washed them more frequently, and showed more distress when one of them was missing. Even wolves think dogs are cuter.

Some people have distinguished pets from other domesticated animals by their lack of practical utility. I think that misses the point. We do expect something in exchange – pet-owning isn't altruism towards animals. Many humans believe that they receive benefits from owning a pet. If dogs and cats were a sure-fire way to improve mental and physical health, that might justify keeping them – even at significant cost to their welfare. Owning a dog gives people a rhythm of daily walks: Californians with dogs walk, on average, nineteen minutes a day more than those without dogs. Dog-owners have a lower risk of heart disease. They also live longer, possibly as a result. In the US, 36 per cent of dog-owning households say they are very happy, twice the number as households with just cats (although only slightly above those with no pets). It'd be irresponsible for researchers to say you should adopt a dog for your health, but that doesn't stop would-be adopters thinking it. Nonetheless, the evidence isn't all one-way. In San Francisco, sociologist Leslie Irvine found that homeless people were less likely to commit crimes if they had a pet dog – but they were also prone to drinking more alcohol and less likely to find suitable accommodation. Even service animals, which are trained and mostly dogs, are not definitively beneficial for humans; they seem to bring some psychological benefits, but also require the humans to accept significant training and often unwanted human attention. That is why the Department of Veterans Affairs stalled on offering them to military veterans, despite lobbying at one stage from Donald Trump's daughter-in-law.

Under the 1986 Air Carrier Access Act, the US has created a legal category of service animals to allow people with disabilities or poor mental health to fly on airplanes without distress. Pet-owners embraced – i.e. abused – the category in order to take their dogs, miniature horses and monkeys on board for free. A 300-pound pot bellied pig called Charlotte was reported to have 'relieved more than just stress' while travelling first class from Philadelphia to Seattle. But attempts to stop pet-owners from bending the rules proved unsuccessful. A new category of emotional support animals was born. In 2020, after several incidents of attacks and urination, Delta started demanding that its passengers produce a letter vouching for their support animal's behaviour. The airline also made it clear that turkeys and gliding possums were not eligible support animals. Is it really right to put an animal in such a foreign and stressful environment to achieve a moderate reduction in human stress, which might have been possible with a stuffed animal? Some airlines, including Delta, now only allow qualified service dogs onboard.

We will always find complex explanations when the simple fact is that we like having animals around. In the nineteenth century, parents bought their children pets in the hope of warding them, boys in particular, against cruel behaviour. When I was young, parents would buy dogs and cats to teach their kids about death. This idea always struck me as misguided, because pets mean so much to us. The New Zealander musician Lorde was so upset after her dog, Pearl, died that she delayed the release of her next album. 'He was instrumental to the discovery that was taking place,' she explained, adding that the loss was 'indescribably painful'. We humanise our dogs, and they humanise us.

Is the nature of our society in some way incompatible with pets' needs? If wolves could have known – as long as 40,000 years ago – what they were signing up for, would they have thought domestication was a good idea?

In London, when I grew up, pets were mostly part of people's private lives – an emotional Achilles heel that you discovered only when you visited someone's home. In San Francisco, dogs aren't seen as private and slightly infantile. They are part of people's public personas. The weather and the outdoors help. The more you take your dog out with you – rather than, say, leaving them on your flat roof to bark at potential intruders – the more it's logical to have one who expresses your identity. A dog becomes another way to show who you are to other people. And unlike with children, you can choose. Of course, all this is easier for people with disposable income, who have already sated any desire to show their personality through clothes, cars and pointlessly addictive step-counters. Rich households are more likely to own dogs, and the ultra-rich are much more likely to love dogs than cats.

So Californians have made remarkable efforts to incorporate dogs into their lives. They make weekend plans that revolve around their dogs – such as going for a Starbucks' puppuccino, a shudder-inducing marketing term for whipped cream in a paper cup. 'I don't have kids, so this is my kids. This is what we do. We take them to have puppuccinos and pup cones,' as a vet called Wailani Sung explained it to me. (Pumpkin spiced lattes for dogs are also an option.) Californians describe themselves as 'dog mom' or 'dog dad' on Twitter. They pose with their pets on Instagram and Facebook. Indeed, the demands of social media have created a whole range of subsidiary products: on Amazon, you can buy Chewy Vuitton toys – the 'handbags every woman wants for your pups to rule their social media following in style'. (If you want the genuine article, Louis Vuitton sells dogs carriers for $3,050.) The pets became a vehicle not just for superficiality, but for politics. After the killing of George Floyd in Minneapolis, I received a dog enthusiasts' newsletter, dedicated to 'the 8-to-10 dogs that have spoken out about Black Lives Matter to their Instagram fans'. It's as if pets, like the daemons in Philip Pullman's trilogy *His Dark Materials*, represent our true selves.

Some Tinder users in California who don't have their own animals have been caught posing with other people's dogs in order to make their profile pictures more adorable. This tactic, labelled dog-fishing, is deceptive. But it is also logical. Pet-owning, like hunting, may be a way of signalling one's fitness to possible mates. John Bradshaw, a British biologist and expert in cat and dog behaviour, theorises that our fondness for pets dates back tens of thousands of years to a time when young girls' ability to care for animals would have acted as a proxy for child-rearing. Girls most genetically disposed to pets would therefore have been more likely to be selected for marriage, a fact that might explain why women express greater sympathy for animals than men. The dynamic is more complicated now. When I look back, I realise that, soon after I started dating one girlfriend, I found myself with a new interest in cats and pandas. We are now married. (It's lucky Susie was the original cat-lover: research from Colorado State University concluded that a woman finds a man more neurotic, less open and less dateable if shown a picture of him holding a cat.) Dog-owning has become a shorthand for common humanity. 'Trump is the first president without a dog in the White

House in over a century', ran a pro-Biden ad in 2020. 'Choose your humans wisely.'

Meanwhile Silicon Valley, with its herds of young software engineers, has become a pioneer of dogs in the workplace. Google declared that affection for dogs was 'an integral facet of our corporate culture', and encouraged dog-owning employees to bring in their animals. Countless other tech firms followed suit. Cat-owners were not so lucky. Google explained: 'We like cats, but we're a dog company, so as a general rule we feel cats visiting our offices would be fairly stressed out.' If there haven't been discrimination suits in twenty years' time, the lawyers aren't working hard enough.

My own experience of dogs in offices is that the humans spend quite a lot of time attending to their animals, not their co-workers. Elizabeth Holmes, who founded the doomed blood-testing start-up Theranos, tried to use her husky to inspire colleagues – but ended up infuriating them when he left hairs in the laboratory. In the words of *Vanity Fair*, the dog 'urinated and defecated at will' throughout the company headquarters, although given the fundamental problems with Theranos's technology it's unlikely the poor thing caused any damage. Overall, workers are more co-operative and attentive during group tasks when dogs are present. Some forward-thinking companies, such as Scottish brewer BrewDog, offer a week's 'pawternity leave' to employees when they adopt a pet.

Shortly before I arrived in San Francisco, the city was hit by an 'innovative dog experience'. Doggy Style Inc. to give the experience its full name, proclaimed: 'In a city with more dogs than children, for many of us dogs ARE our children.' It promised to combine the benefits of a private members' club with the loving convenience of a dog day centre. Members would be able to browse a boutique and gallery, while their dog mingled with friends. The premium membership involved fees of up to $25,500 a year – more than California's minimum wage. In return, customers would receive a free doggy birthday party for up to twelve dogs and a mural of their dog painted by a local artist. Doggy Style Inc. was greeted with howls of outrage, from those who reasonably saw it as gentrification gone mad. It was a sign of absurd inequality in a city where 8,000 people were sleeping on the streets or in shelters. By the end of the year, Doggy Style Inc.'s founders announced they were 'Currently Re-Branding Our Business Concept' – Silicon Valley-speak for financial disaster.

My own view is that Doggy Style Inc. was just ahead of its time, because its basic diagnosis – that the social lives of dogs and their humans are merging – is right. If San Francisco seems to have a disproportionate number of 'no dogs' signs, that's presumably because otherwise everyone would bring theirs. California has a class of events that wouldn't exist if it weren't for the animals, including the World Dog Surfing Championships, a World's Ugliest Dog Competition (held to help promote tourism to wine country), and Splash Dogs, a semi-serious competition where dogs jump as far as possible into a tub of water (held to promote the state fair in Sacramento).

Imagine if our love for other species led us to anything like these investments.

*

OK, so you've never been dog surfing, and you've never been to Corgi-Con. You've never taken your dog to luxury day care, or even to the office. Your pet doesn't have an Instagram profile, and they're not in your will. You're just a normal loving dog-owner. There's nothing bizarre about that, is there?

This is where things became slightly strange for me. I set out thinking that pet-ownership represents a life raft to the broader animal world. Instead the evidence told me that we have fallen overboard.

In one study, researchers produced a fictional newspaper article about a beating in Boston, varying one detail – whether the victim was a human infant, a puppy, an adult dog or an adult human. University undergraduates were then asked to read the article and express their empathy with the victim. Human babies and puppies received the most empathy, followed by adult dogs. Adult humans came last. I usually celebrate each hole being punched in the species barrier, but I feel a bit ambivalent about this one. The explanation is presumably that we think adult humans should be able to take care of themselves. But it's still odd to place other species ahead of our own.

A quarter of dog-owners say that dogs are smarter than most people. That view is, to be polite, not supported by current science. While we underestimate many animals, the risk with dogs is that we *overestimate* their emotional understanding. Dogs probably don't feel guilt, however much we think we perceive it, argues Alexandra Horo-witz, who runs a research unit at Columbia University into dog–human relations. We seem to expect more of pets than of humans. Friends will fade away, partners will leave. Pets, in our idealised world, will never let us down.

Then there's the money. Americans spend more than $100 billion a year caring for their pets – north of $1,100 per pet-owning household. That is nearly twice as much as they spend on overseas aid, eight times more than they gave to environmental and animal charities, and seven times as much as they spent on ads for the 2020 presidential and congressional elections. (I always knew American politics was under-funded.) Per head, it is multiples of the next biggest spenders on pets, Brits.

Does this arrangement work for dogs? Studies show that dogs – particularly those socialised to humans when young – can find human company valuable. They have learnt to rely on humans to make deci-sions for them. If a human provides a cue as to where an object is hidden, the dog will generally follow that – rather than trying to figure it out for themselves. The stronger a dog's relationship with their human, the worse their ability to solve a problem independently.

So there can be a partnership between dogs and their owners. But the side effects of dog-owning go deep. It starts with where the ani-mals come from. At last count there are nearly 200,000 breeding dogs in the US, producing 2 million puppies a year. Undercover inves-tigations into puppy mills have found that infections, diarrhoea and poor veterinary care are common. Puppies are often transported large distances in trucks to their point of sale. Breeders argue that otherwise there would not be enough dogs to meet demand. Mean-while, in shelters, 670,000 dogs a year are euthanised, many of them because they can't find homes. Humans and dogs are not like wild symbiotic species that help each other, but live independently. We are very much in charge.

Breeding is the thorniest part of our dog obsession. People often buy pedigree puppies, because they have an idea of what a good dog looks like. Due to human intervention, no species has so much diversity of form as *Canis lupus familiaris*. This breeding was originally for physical tasks – hunting, sheep-farming, racing, et cetera. In the Victorian era, dogs became less valued for their abilities and more for their appearance. There's an old joke that a camel is a horse designed by committee. Dogs today were designed by committees of enthusiasts, who had little idea what they were aiming for. The results were so remarkable that they inspired Francis Galton, a cousin of Charles Darwin and one of the founders of eugenics, to wonder if the same could be done for people. If you could create dogs and horses suited for a particular task, it would be 'quite practicable to produce a highly gifted race of men by judicious marriages during several consecutive generations', he suggested in 1869. Given how appalling we now find humans' dalliance with eugenics, it's strange we are so keen on the canine equivalent.

Today we don't need dogs to perform physical tasks, and most dog-owners have no interest in competitions. Greyhound racing, which was Florida's top spectator sport in the 1970s, has fallen off the map. Greyhounds were bred in cramped facilities, suffered racing injuries, and were often euthanised when they became too old. Attendances at greyhound races in Britain totalled 50 million a year in 1945; before the pandemic, they were barely 1 million. All the tracks in London have closed; near my home, one is now a supermarket car park. In Emeryville, across the bay in San Francisco, I found that the site that housed the world's first dog track with a mechanised lure is now the headquarters of Peet's coffee. Two blocks away is Pixar Studios, which creates dogs as we prefer to see them. I wouldn't be surprised if horse racing vanished similarly, as people's tolerance for broken legs and euthanised animals decreases. Stopping the use of animals for our entertainment, for racing or circuses, should free us up to put their values first.

But with dogs, we continue to demand certain aesthetics and therefore we continue to breed dogs who are frankly unhealthy. The more we identify with pets, the more choosy we become about how they look. Like Victorian gentlemen, we want their appearance to say something about us. We want to bask in the glow of the pit bull's power or the Chihuahua's cuteness. This is a false love, because we are not really focused on the animals' flourishing, but on ourselves.

My own relationship with dogs began when I was two. That was when my family bought a Norfolk terrier. I loved him deeply and I still remember him fondly as the source of my strongest Internet passwords. (So he'll have to remain anonymous.) From middle age he struggled to walk, and was in obvious discomfort going up or down steps. This was no coincidence: according to the Orthopedic Foundation for Animals in the US, which keeps records of dog health, one in three Norfolk terriers has abnormal hips. Dogs with abnormal hips are liable to develop hip osteoarthritis, causing pain when they move; Norfolks are also vulnerable to loose knee joints. At the time, my dog's ill health seemed merely unfortunate. But when I think back on the pain he must have suffered, I feel angry – at the breeder who sold him to us, at the breeders who went before, and at the norms that made such breeding socially acceptable. Why didn't my parents, or any Norfolk-terrier buyers, do any research?

I was inclined to disregard this childhood experience: Norfolks are a relatively unpopular breed with a small gene pool that might feed abnormalities. I was prepared to imagine, in the US, where pet-owning had been taken to its furthest point, the most popular breeds would be much healthier. I was wrong. As of 2019 America's most popular dog breeds were Labrador retrievers, German shepherds and golden retrievers. To date the proportion of dogs with abnormal hips has been: 12 per cent for Labradors, and 20 per cent for both German shepherds and golden retrievers. There is some evidence that the dogs' proneness to hip problems has reduced, but even if the proportions are halved, they are shocking.

French bulldogs are America's fourth most popular breed, followed by bulldogs, the breed from which they were spun off in the nineteenth century. Bulldogs predate the nineteenth-century boom in dog-breeding. They were created for bull-baiting – the barbaric pursuit where people would gather to watch a bull be tied to a post and attacked by dogs. After bull-baiting was banned in Britain in 1835, the dogs lived on as national emblems, albeit altered significantly by Victorian breeding. I'm not quite sure why a country would want to be associated with a deformed, torturing breed – but I suppose that, unlike the Welsh dragon and the Scottish unicorn, British bulldogs do actually exist, and unlike the English lion, they did even originate in the country. Anyway, the dogs are now among the country's ten most popular breeds. French bulldogs have been in Britain's top three breeds since 2014.

It turns out that dogs created to torture bulls are not exactly healthy themselves. The bulldogs were bred with shorter jaws to produce more powerful bites. But this also created narrow airways, so bulldogs and French bulldogs – like other brachycephalic, or flat-faced, breeds – are now prone to breathing difficulties. Enlarged heads also lead to birthing problems: French bulldogs are sixteen times more likely than cross-breeds to suffer difficult births, which puts their lives and their puppies' lives in danger. They are more likely to need caesareans – we have created animals who depend on our continued intervention. In America, 30 per cent of French bulldogs, and a whopping 71 per cent of bulldogs, have abnormal hips. Brachycephalic dogs are more likely to suffer other disorders that don't seem to be linked to their skulls – such as umbilical hernias. To top it off, the breeding can also spoil dogs' social interaction: flat faces may make it harder to signal via facial expressions.

There isn't much evidence that we are getting better at selecting breeds. In 2008 the BBC broadcast a documentary exposing problems with cavalier King Charles spaniels (a breed featured in the series *Sex and the City*) and West Highland terriers. This reduced demand for those dogs in Britain, but led people to switch to French bulldogs, demand for which rose almost thirtyfold in the next ten years. In other words, people just move from one problematic breed to another. A similar exposé now on flat-faced dogs might push people towards dachshunds, who have limb problems. The UK's Royal Veterinary College wants people to fall in love 'with dog-shaped dogs', but is wary about naming good breeds, because a sudden surge in demand might lead to a rise in unscrupulous breeders.

Meanwhile, the desire for new dogs – with new abilities – is creating new problems. The idea of designer dogs, which combine the best of two breeds, captured the public mood in the late twentieth century. An Australian guide-dog trainer called Wally Conron crossed a Labrador retriever with a poodle in 1989, in the hope of creating a suitable pet for someone with an allergy to dog hair. But puppy breeders seized on his creation, and the demand for the dogs, from a small pool, soon led to genetic problems. By 2014, as the Labradoodle became one of the most popular dogs in the world, Conron said he regretted ever having created it. 'I find that the biggest majority are either crazy or have a hereditary problem,' he said. When his concerns were put to the head of the Australian Labradoodle Club of America, she shrugged: 'All dogs are crazy.'

I find it maddening that we invest so much time and energy in our dogs, but we still put our aesthetic desires over the dogs' health. If our happiness really is aligned with our pets' happiness, why don't we choose better breeds? We choose dogs who look cute, who look like babies, and indeed who look like us. Another explanation is that would-be owners don't know the risks. When I searched on the website of the American Kennel Club, the country's register of pure-bred dogs, I found that French bulldogs are described as a 'bright, affectionate' breed that 'city folk from Paris to Peoria swear by'. The AKC mentions the dogs' large, erect 'bat ears' and 'smooth, brilliant coat', concluding that they are 'completely irresistible'. Health problems aren't mentioned.

Many owners may be able to fool themselves. More than 60 per cent of owners say their flat-faced dog is healthier than average for the breed; only 7 per cent say their dog is less healthy than the average. Dan O'Neill, a former vet and now a lecturer at the UK's Royal Veterinary College, who was one of the authors of that survey, says that some owners almost welcome the prospect of a dog who needs plenty of care:

'A lot of people want a dog that needs them.' In California I met Dan and Amy – owners of a French bulldog, and world champion surfdog, Cherie – who had accepted the cost, because they liked the appearance. 'You're basically buying a vet a summer home when you buy a French bulldog,' joked Dan, a friendly, self-aware man, who works in marketing and looks like Andre Agassi.

Dogs' vet bills should be seen in this context. We are often paying to compensate for our selfish choices. Flat-faced dogs can require surgery to remove soft tissue from their airways, or to cut off folds in the skin. If these were breeds of farm animals – valued in economic terms – they would be phased out. In places where dogs are allowed to breed freely, the populations revert from breeds to a sandy brown, lanky mongrel. But among the posh breeders and buyers of major cities, dogs' reproduction remains controlled by humans. 'The dogs' health problems are actually human problems,' as O'Neill puts it.

Overall, dogs are likely to be healthier than they were thirty years ago, says O'Neill, because of the rise of animal medicine. Some dog disorders are becoming apparent only because dogs are living longer. But the problems are not limited to physical health. A study of more than 13,000 pet dogs in Finland found that three-quarters had some form of anxiety disorder. One in six showed compulsive behaviour, such as biting themselves or chasing their tails.

Dogs are required to live in vastly different societies to the ones they entered. Most humans now don't live in the countryside, and don't herd or hunt animals. With dogs, behavioural issues appear to be more frequent in urban areas, where opportunities to run free are often minimal. Researchers at the University of Helsinki found that dogs who live in cities are more fearful of strangers than those who live in rural areas; the reasons are not clear, although the noise and bustle of city life would be obvious contenders. (Happily for CorgiCon-goers, the same study found Pembroke Welsh corgis to be the least fearful breed.) Californians want to bring dogs into their public lives – but this often treats the dog as an accessory, rather than thinking whether he or she actually benefits. 'There's a lot of pressure on people to do things with our dogs and also to have dogs do fun things,' says Wailani Sung, the vet of the puppuccinos.

We shouldn't assume that dogs experience novel entertainment in the same way we do; we should focus on meeting the needs that we know they do have – including exercise, stimulation and company.

Many dog-owners, even those with regular dogwalkers, leave their animals alone for hours while they go to work. Dogs are highly social animals. For many hours while I've been writing this book, I've been able to hear the terrier next door howling with what I can only assume is loneliness. When lockdown started, people around the world adopted dogs. Britain pretty much ran out of puppies. What happens when these people go back to work? Dogs generally live for at least a decade. We take advantage of dogs' voicelessness. We are selective. We notice how excited the dogs are to see us at the end of the day, not how anxious they might have been when we were away.

Alexandra Horowitz, of Columbia University, has questioned whether we should be able to keep dogs at all. She asks whether we can accept dogs *as dogs* – with their inclinations to have sex and eat faeces, which can prove embarrassing for their owners. At the moment, we desex dogs and cats, even though this disrupts their sex lives and bodily functioning. Desexed dogs and cats have been found to live longer, perhaps because they don't roam so far from the home and die in traffic accidents, but the lack of hormones such as testosterone and oestrogen that are produced in the gonads has knock-on effects on the animals' health. Desexed dogs are more likely to be obese. Back in 1994, a study found most Australian dog owners would not desex their dog if they had not already done so. Years later, less debilitating procedures such as vasectomies are still shunned, partly because we haven't thought about them.

When our pets don't fit, we give them up. Susie and I went to a cat rescue centre once in Colombia, where most animals, through no fault of their own, had no hope of leaving. These are animals whom we created, and we have found no space for them. The saddest thing is seeing animals – like black cats – rejected for their appearance. Around 6.5 million dogs and cats are given to US shelters every year; that is equivalent to one in every twenty-eight dogs and cats. The causes range from problematic behaviour to changes in the owners' lifestyle. There are good shelters: in San Francisco's branch of the SPCA, the cats' rooms have miniature models of the city's landmarks, a sure sign of too much money and human enthusiasm. Anyone who has been to a shelter knows the contradictory mix of power and powerlessness that they in-duce – you can change one animal's life, but you can never change enough. There will always be some left behind, and they will probably be rejected for the very same reasons you rejected them. We shouldn't kid ourselves that all shelters are good, or that the experience of being transferred between homes is not intensely disturbing. Although the number of dogs and cats euthanised has been falling, only one state, Delaware, has achieved 'no kill' status, meaning that no healthy ani-mals are put down in shelters. In California, the number is now 100,000 a year and the state aims to bring it down to zero by spaying and neu-tering animals. But full shelters across the world are a sad by-product of our desire for pets.

There are other pets so good that we want to create them twice. Since the 1990s, companies have been offering to create genetic copies of pets. The technology was developed for livestock – where promoting certain traits had a business purpose – but, to the dismay of some of its developers, was soon marketed to pet-owners too. In 2018 Barbra Strei-sand revealed that she had cloned her curly-haired Coton de Tulear dog, Samantha, and now has genetically identical twins. She posted a photo of the two perched on Samantha's grave, 'honoring their mom'; she brought them on stage at Hyde Park.

Cloning is the logical extension of a mindset where we see our-selves controlling other animals. It involves the expectation that one individual – with their own upbringing and influences – will just be a replica of another. Creating the first clone dog involved the impregna-tion of 123 surrogates, and although the process has improved, it still requires multiple dogs compelled to undergo invasive procedures. Sur-rogates seem more likely to undergo complications, while some cloned dogs may need to be put down shortly after birth. ViaGen, the Texas company that cloned Streisand's Coton de Tulear, says it has only pro-duced 'a few hundred puppies'. Cost is one factor – cloning comes in at $50,000 for dogs, $35,000 for cats. An English woman who won a competition to have her dachshund cloned in South Korea has written a children's story about cloned dogs. My daughters will read it over my own cryogenically frozen body. With cloning, as with breeding, we put our own needs well before the animal's.

Our control of dogs' lives presents us with other double-edged swords. I was coming to the end of my time in San Francisco when I heard about John Honchariw, a former Google engineer. Honchariw had been helping to design Google's voice assistant, when he'd come to a realisation. It would be many years before a computer would be sophisticated enough to have a deep conversation with a human. So maybe it would be better to start with a different species: dogs.

Honchariw founded a start-up, and spent hours training machines to analyse dogs' postures and movements. Three years later, his company, Companion Labs, launched an automated box capable of training dogs. The device monitors the dog with camera footage, motion and infrared sensors, it recognises whether the dog has obeyed a command, and if the answer is yes, the box dispenses a treat.

In true Silicon Valley style, the robot dog trainer is now advertised as making the world a better place. If more dogs are trained, then more might be adopted from shelters, says the San Francisco SPCA, which has helped to develop the technology. But Companion Labs's big market are the 60 million American homes with dogs, many of whom leave their animals at home or in day care for eight hours or more a day. Soon these homes will be able to train and entertain their dogs without a human present. The bonding process between human and dog will be circumvented. Companion Labs struck me as a clever feat of animal communication (assuming it works). But the risk is robot-trained dogs receive less human companionship. Wouldn't it be smarter for some people to concede that they are too busy to have dogs?

*

Our world is finite. If we choose to allocate land to one set of animals, we generally squeeze another set of animals. Our appetites limit the amount of space available to wild species, and so do our pets' appetites. Cats can't digest anything but meat. Dogs are omnivores. They don't need meat but are served it in ever improving quality. Today America's dogs and cats eat as many calories in a year as 62 million American people, according to UCLA geography professor Gregory Okin. America's carbon footprint is also a pawprint. Dogs and cats do eat some animal products that humans do not – such as bone. But that is becoming less true, as loving pet-owners try to please their animals.

It's not just what we feed our pets. Cats are born predators. In the US they have been estimated to kill between 1.3 billion and 4 billion birds a year, and between 6.3 billion and 22.3 billion mammals each year. In Australia, where birds did not evolve alongside land-based predators, and have limited defences, a study put the annual number killed at over 300 million. It's not clear how big a chunk of the bird population this represents, or whether the cats are taking mainly weaker birds who wouldn't have survived anyway. But with such big numbers, it's implausible that the cats have little impact on bird populations. They certainly cause pain to individual birds. This isn't natural, it's a consequence of us increasing the number of predators. It's not just whether cats kill birds, it's the disease and fear they spread. Even placing a taxidermy cat near a blackbird nest reduces the amount that chicks eat – and makes them more vulnerable to being eaten by other birds, because they call out from fear of the cat. (No, this wasn't my experiment.)

We think of cats as cheekily invading our personal space, but they are *really* invading the space of other animals. Scott Loss and Peter Marra, biologists at Oklahoma State and Georgetown universities respectively, put cats among the 'most ubiquitous and environmentally damaging invasive predators on earth'. I find this tricky: I love cats and birds. Having shared more nights on the sofa watching Netflix with cats, I value their individual existence over most birds. I also recognise that cat and dog populations are doing well, while those of birds are not, and that this puts our ecosystems off balance. I don't want to restrain my cat from going outside, and she has rarely brought anything back into the house, but I have to admit that our garden is not full of birds.

Are dogs better? They are predators too, and they impact wildlife. Birds and other mammals flee when they arrive in an area; one study found that two out of five dogs on a Santa Barbara beach disturbed birds. In nature, such disturbances, and the energy they consume, can determine whether an animal survives. It's hardly surprising that dogs have this impact: part of the reason that they were accepted as human companions was because they proved so useful at killing other animals. Dogs rule the parks near my home in London, and they rule elsewhere too.

Dogs and cats haven't been great for their wild relatives either. Threatened wild dogs include Ethiopian wolves, of whom fewer than 440 remain, because their habitat is now grazing land and because of the spread of disease such as rabies. This is a feature of domestication. The wild ancestors of cattle, horses and dromedary camels are extinct. Frederick Zeuner, a pioneer of environmental archaeology, has included the extirpation of wild relatives as the final stage of the domestication process. Today there are 800 million dogs worldwide, including roughly 300 million street dogs. Meanwhile, the global population of grey wolves is estimated at 200,000–250,000. Since wolves were reintroduced to Yellowstone National Park in 1995, their numbers in the lower forty-eight states have grown to around 5,700. Over the same period, the population of dogs in the US has grown by around 24 million. There's a political debate over whether there is space for the wolves – Colorado voters narrowly backed reintroduction of the animals in a ballot measure in November 2020 – but hardly anyone questions if we have room for the dogs. Wildcats, the closest relatives of the domestic cat, started disappearing in Britain as soon as domestic cats were introduced in the Roman period. There are now only a few hundred Scottish wildcats left, and many of those are hybrids of domestic cats. Pets are not just bonus animals to all the wild creatures in the world: they are, to some extent, substitutes.

So-called exotic pets are even more problematic. These are animals who have not been domesticated over thousands of years. Their clash with human needs is even more apparent. They are more likely to suffer welfare problems, and more likely to be released to the wild.

Drug traffickers have a history of capturing big cats, and ripping their teeth and claws out, in order to make them plausible pets. Orangutans are sold in cages. Otters have also been taken from the wild, and taken to homes far removed from the water that they are used to. There are estimated to be more tigers in Texas than in the wild. Flicking through one website selling exotic pets, I found fruit bats, hedgehogs, coatis and kangaroos for sale in places like Florida and New York. There was a rhesus monkey in Texas ('bottle and diaper trained') and a week-old baby zebra in Mississippi ('We are socializing him all throughout the day ... We'll start halter and lead training tomorrow'). The chances of such animals receiving the right care and companionship seem slim.

California prevents many exotic and native species from being kept as pets, plus the only dogs, cats and rabbits that can be sold in pet shops are those from shelters. Still, you can buy parrots. Parrots are brilliant: colourful, intelligent and loyal. The annual 'divorce' rate among one parrot species was estimated at 1–2 per cent, lower than among English and Welsh people. I've kept my distance from parrots since, on an old Colombian coffee farm, one pet parrot stepped calmly onto my outstretched hand and then bit me between my thumb and forefinger – with as much interspecies companionship as an industrial stapler. But I can still understand why people want to get close to them.

The problem is the huge cost of humans' desire for parrots. Between 1980 and 2016, when the international trade was banned, more than a million African grey parrots were taken from the wild and sold overseas. African greys are still illegally taken from the wild: in Cameroon, poachers coat palm leaves with glue, and then tie up decoy birds, which lure other African greys to the spot. The World Parrot Trust, a charity, estimates that there are now as many parrots in cages globally as in the wild. One-quarter of parrot species, although not the African grey, are threatened with extinction. Meanwhile, in Indonesia, hundreds of thousands of songbirds are trapped each year, and sold at markets. The buildings have birdsong, but the forests are being silenced.

I walked into San Francisco's largest and best-loved pet shop, Animal Connection, and found a small room of parrots. Most of them were budgies, were happy to be held, and all of them had presumably been bred by pet-owners. Whether parrots are bred in captivity or taken from the forest, they are not easily kept in confined spaces. To simulate their wild environment, large parrots would need, in the words of two experts, 'an outdoor aviary the size of an airplane hangar'. Parrots don't expect to be kept alone either, and scream more if they are. Sadly, most US parrot-owners keep their birds alone and, on average, only interact with their bird for fifteen minutes a day. In some cases, owners want the bird to be their partner, rather than to give the parrot a companion of their own species.

In London, when you walk through parks, you quite often see flocks of parakeets flying overhead. The flocks were almost certainly started by pet-owners who released their birds. We've managed to re-locate parakeets from their homes in Asia, Africa and South America to London parks. But it amuses me how little interest the birds apparently have in returning to people's homes. If you love something, let it go; if it returns, it's yours. The parakeets didn't return. They're not ours. And the best thing would be not to keep them, or any parrots, as pets.

Other animals don't seem to fit either. We want to cuddle rabbits, who don't enjoy it; we might do better to keep pet rats, who make lovely companions and enjoy tickling, for the few humans willing to question their own perceptions. (Rats – the assistant at Animal Connection informed me, as one ran around her hand – are popular with people who themselves feel misunderstood.) Mediterranean tortoises are staples of British gardens, but they have evolved for the warm climate and high-fibre diet of the Mediterranean, which owners elsewhere will struggle to replicate. Moreover, according to animal welfare experts, the tortoises 'display no affinity or need for human company. In the wild, being picked up or moved is likely to be associated with predators.' What's the justification of keeping an animal who isn't interested in being kept? On a spectrum from partnership to kidnapping, it's closer to the latter.

It's estimated that 9–10 million marine fish are imported to the United States every year. Four in every five travel from the Philippines or Indonesia – some are bred in captivity, but others are taken from coral reefs. They are placed in bags smaller than a Coke can, and not fed for a couple of days while they're transported. The journeys are likely to be stressful, and quite a lot of fish probably die en route. In some cases the fish may have been caught by injecting cyanide onto a reef, temporarily paralysing them so that they are easy to capture but devastating the coral in the process. In other cases more benign methods are used, mortality is low, and the money paid by pet-owners gives local people in the Pacific an incentive to protect the reefs. The problem is that transparency is almost non-existent, and little official data is collated: when you buy a pet fish, you have almost no idea what practices you are supporting. We also have no evidence that fish value our companionship (although some fish may be able to recognise their owners). Ornamental fish tanks have an aesthetic appeal. But we can't claim that pet fish have much to do with the individual animals' best interests. Goldfish can live up to thirty years, but are rarely kept that long.

London's escaped pet parakeets seem to have caused relatively little damage to native birds. If only the same could be said of reptiles. Reptiles have become more popular pets, but it takes only a small percentage of owners to get bored, frustrated or simply scared, and release their reptiles into sewers, lakes and wild spaces – and you have major environmental problems. Florida has suffered the brunt of this. Some pet-owners have predictably grown tired of their Burmese pythons, which reach up to 5.5 metres long and can survive more than twenty years in captivity. The pythons have been released into the Everglades for decades, where they are the first snakes for at least 16 million years big enough to eat small mammals. Between 2003 and 2011, as the population of pythons grew, observations of raccoons and opossums fell 99 per cent. Even white-tailed deer all but disappeared.

Green iguanas also became so popular that, in 2000, the handbook *Iguanas for Dummies* was published. But they can live up to twenty years (in the wild), and many bored pet-owners released them. The iguanas love Florida almost as much as retirees do. Free from predators, they are multiplying. One resident complained to the *Miami Herald* that the iguanas were pooping in her pool so much that she could hardly swim in it; Zoo Miami complained the iguanas were bothering its gorillas. In 2019 the state authorities urged residents to kill the iguanas humanely, but after protests from animal rights groups, refused to give further instructions. Florida has now banned the sale of pythons and green iguanas. It might have been easier not to allow them to be kept as pets in the first place. Of course people could make the most of the situation, and eat the iguanas and their eggs, as has been the case in Central and South America, where the iguanas are known as 'chickens of the trees' on account of their taste. But that would require us to break our mental compartments. For these species, the benefits of human companionship exist only in our minds. Exotic pets flunk the animal test.

There is one potential benefit of pet-owning – that it can act as a gateway drug. Owning dogs and cats might directly harm biodiversity, through hunting and demand for food, but it might also make us more willing to support conservation and veganism, even while feeding our pets meat. There is a bit of evidence that pet-owners are more likely to join wildlife organisations and support wildlife causes. But the causation isn't entirely clear: are people more likely to care for wildlife because they have a pet, or are they more likely to acquire a pet if they care about wildlife? Susie and I adopted a cat because we liked animals, rather than vice versa.

Most evidence is anecdotal. Before she studied chimpanzees in Tanzania, Jane Goodall said she had already learnt about animal emotions from her dog. Other animal thinkers have not been pet-lovers – Peter Singer, who came up with the idea of animal liberation in the 1970s, is driven by justice, not sentimentality. In her novel *We Are Completely Beside Ourselves*, Karen Joy Fowler gives a fictionalised account of (spoiler alert) a real-life experiment in which a chimpanzee was brought up with human children. Fowler's father was a psychologist who experimented on rats and monkeys and, she implies, not in a particularly good way. 'In my family, we had a house full of beloved pets and a lab full of research subjects,' she recalled. The pets sensitised her but not her father.

Pets *can* sensitise us. But they are primarily substitutes. Substitutes for wild animals. Substitutes for company of other humans. They may even be substitutes for God – one US study found that cat-ownership was lower among regular churchgoers. Two-thirds of US households own a pet, but only one in twenty Americans is vegetarian. If our aim is happy companionship with the wider animal kingdom, keeping dogs and cats is a roundabout way of getting there. It's like arguing that eating a bag of crisps will make you lose weight, because it'll convince you to go on a diet.

I went to the Blessing of the Animals at San Francisco's Catholic cathedral. The Church hasn't always welcomed animals. In sixteenth-century England, many churches paid 'dog-whippers' to stop dogs from following their owners to services. Here all was forgiven. An amiable Franciscan friar blessed each animal and their owner, and posed merrily for photos with them while not minding the paw marks on his cassock. He praised the love that people had for their pets but he also wondered aloud how we might 'translate that love' more widely. It was in vain. None of the dog-owners seemed remotely interested in that message, they just loved their dogs.

Our love for dogs and cats comes with more complications than we are prepared to admit. But the love itself is undoubted. I wondered if there was a way of writing wild animals into our hearts and our society as efficiently.

*

I hired a car and drove up the Pacific Coast Highway. I left behind the liberal world of San Francisco techies, puppuccinos and chief love officers, and a few hours later the road was flanked by glorious redwood forests. This was Yurok Country.

The Yurok are California's largest federally recognised tribe with more than 6,000 members. Their official headquarters, Klamath, CA, features a breathtaking landscape, a money-taking Holiday Inn and casino, and a disused brick Catholic church. What brought me here was the Yurok's relationship with animals, and in particular the tribe's efforts to reintroduce the California condor which had disappeared from its skies more than a century before.

Western animal-lovers have wrestled with how Native Americans interact with nature. One school of thought paints tribes as the first environmentalists, who took only what nature could provide, at least until their cultures were disrupted by the arrival of white settlers from the sixteenth century. Others have objected that this is a romanticised picture. They argue that tribes cleared forests, and hunted and fished in ways likely to have depleted animal populations; if the tribes didn't have catastrophic impacts, it was largely because their populations were small and their weapons unsophisticated. Some indigenous people today support mining and infrastructure projects that environmentalists loathe.

What is less controversial, however, is that Native American traditions reflect a deep understanding of ecology, including how animals behave and what functions they fulfil in the environment.

'Being naturalized to place means to live as if this is the land that feeds you, as if these are the streams from which you drink, that build your body and fill your spirit. To become naturalized is to know that your ancestors lie in this ground,' as Robin Wall Kimmerer, a scientist and member of the Citizen Potawatomi Nation, wrote in her memoir *Braiding Sweetgrass*. 'In the indigenous view, humans are viewed as somewhat lesser beings in the democracy of species ... Plants were here first and have had a long time to figure things out.'

Before the arrival of Europeans, few animals were domesticated – probably because previous extinctions had left few species that were suitable. Native Americans focused on domesticating plants. Their meat came from hunting wild animals and harvesting fish.

The only animals domesticated in north-eastern America, before European settlers arrived, were dogs. As in Europe, they were used as watchdogs, in hunting and presumably for company. We show our respect for dogs by not eating them and by feeding them well. The Iroquois, whose territory covered what is now central New York state, didn't eat dogs either. But they showed their respect for other animals by not feeding them to the dogs. Beavers and moose, for example, were hunted but dogs were not allowed to gnaw their bones. In other words, Native American societies were better able to balance the domestication of dogs, with an appreciation for the wider animal world. Our success in domesticating animals – from cows to dogs – has led us to neglect those animals whom we can't domesticate.

In common with other Native American tribes, the Yurok see themselves as connected with nature in a much stronger way than the western Christian tradition has promoted (and which the Blessing of the Animals is belatedly trying to fix). White settlers tried to extinguish Yurok culture in the nineteenth century, by killing members, taking children to boarding schools and banning tribal ceremonies. There was an underground effort to preserve traditions, but some pieces of Yurok culture now exist only in fragments. Alfred Kroeber, an anthropologist in the nineteenth century, recounted a Yurok belief that people themselves are descended from dogs, although this is seen as dubious by some tribal members today. For the Yurok, salmon and sturgeon are foundational species – the basis for food and barter. The California condor holds particular spiritual significance. 'In most scenarios animals are considered to be a better people than humans are,' said Tiana Claussen, a Yurok tribal member and Harvard biologist who had agreed to show me around.

Condors are magnificent sights. Charles Darwin marvelled at the beauty of the California condor's closest relative, the Andean condor, and observed: 'Except when rising from the ground, I do not recollect ever having seen one of these birds flap its wings.' Being Darwin, he also shot one – no reason is given in his account. Recently scientists calculated that Andean condors flap their wings only about 1 per cent of the time; one bird went five hours, and 107 miles, without flapping.

The California condor is the largest soaring land bird in North America. Its wingspan can reach nine feet. It can glide over forty miles per hour, fly up to 150 miles in a day, forage over a range of 7,000 square kilometres, and live for sixty years. But this isn't why the Yurok esteem them. The condor is the bird that flies highest in the sky. It is believed to be the bird that carries people's prayers to the heavens. By incorporating condor feathers into ceremonies 'we incorporate the spirit of condor himself', said Claussen. 'He dances and he sings along with us.'

Claussen also told me the idea of *pyuech we-son'* – living in balance, living well. The period in which Yurok culture was split apart by white settlers is recalled so painfully by Claussen and other members of the tribe that you might think it was just a few years ago. Even when ceremonies were no longer banned, there were times that they were marred by violence and drunkenness.

For the Yurok, the reintroduction of the condor dovetails with the tribe's attempts to restore its identity. Not until the 1990s did the tribal government receive full federal recognition. By then, the ecology itself had changed. Fish numbers had fallen, likely reflecting climate change, hydroelectric dams and overfishing. The restoration of the condor became an expression of the sovereignty and self-sufficiency that the tribe wish to reclaim.

The birds are scavengers, feeding on the carcasses of large mammals. They once ate whale carcasses, but switched to cattle by the nineteenth century, as whale populations were hunted and cattle-ranching increased. Then as livestock and grasslands were replaced by agriculture later in the nineteenth century, their food supply vanished. Moreover, the remaining ranchers left poison to kill grizzly bears who preyed on their livestock. The condors ate the poison intended for bears.

The story of the condor is legendary in conservation. The condor was listed under the Endangered Species Preservation Act in 1966. By 1982, there were just twenty-two of the birds left in the wild. Conservationists had a choice – to allow the condors to remain in the wild, and probably fall into extinction; or to intervene. At least some environmental groups including the Sierra Club argued that the birds should be left to die out 'with dignity'. Instead the condors were placed in captivity, including at Los Angeles Zoo and San Diego Zoo Safari Park. Within a few years their numbers had spiralled.

My visit to Yurok Country coincided with the birth of the 1,000th condor chick in captivity. This number admittedly felt less impressive when I remembered it was still below the number of dogs at CorgiCon. But the success of captive breeding had allowed the condor to be released back in the wild – first, in southern California and eventually in Yurok Country. Yurok cultural leaders voted for which species to restore. They voted, first and second, for the salmon and the sturgeon, and third for the California condor.

For more than a decade, the Yurok had been preparing for the release of condors on their land. This has been a painstaking, expensive process, which is still not assured. Potential sites have been studied, environmental assessments prepared, community consultations carried out. Biologists tried to estimate the dangers from electricity lines (on which the gliding birds might slice or electrify themselves to death) and lead ammunition (fragments of which the birds might swallow). Condors can die if they ingest a piece of lead the size of a pinhead, so the tribe asked hunters to switch to copper ammunition. The state power company agreed to dig certain lines into the ground.

Although the reintroduction testifies to the breeding abilities of zoos, it also demonstrates why zoos struggle to reintroduce many animals. Some of the first birds released elsewhere died of lead poisoning; others were altered by their time in captivity and gravitated towards humans (one group in southern California spent weekends flying alongside hang-gliders). The birds are now established in California, Arizona and Utah, but only with intensive human intervention stretching several decades. The US Fish and Wildlife Service says the project has cost at least $40 million. The true total is likely to be far higher, because the programme started before the service used computers, and had involved various partners including zoos.

For Claussen, there was no question that reintroducing the birds to Yurok Country will be worth it. 'My daughter is going to grow up with condors. She's never going to live in a world where there's no condors. And that's super-exciting to me. You've just got to think intergenerationally.' Pet-owners are excited about having *their* animal – but Claussen's excitement was different. It was caught up in an attachment to the land, the community, and to wildness itself.

The absence of the condor had been noted. The bird had become, in Claussen's words, 'a mythological creature, rather than something that lives and breathes and you have a relationship with.' The Yurok did not see the birds in the sky; they could not find feathers to use in their regalia. The old regalia had been placed in museums, and treated with chemicals to preserve them, so that, from the Yurok's point of view, they had effectively been poisoned.

'We consider regalia to be a living thing. For us to have our regalia on some museum shelves, or even worse in some museum drawer that nobody looks at – I mean, we say that it cries,' said Claussen. To collect enough feathers for a whole regalia would take generations, especially for those who, like her family, did not believe in hunting the condor under any circumstances – only picking up feathers. Because of the Yurok's recent history, traditions are often uncertain. 'Something I've struggled a lot with growing up is not necessarily knowing a traditional way of thinking. I was never taught. And there's still a lot of gaps in my knowledge,' said Claussen.

She and I drove through the forest to a clearing of the kind where the condor might one day be released. 'I always grew up with a lot of pride in being Yurok, a very solid foundation in a sense of place. Even when I was kid, I didn't know what I wanted to be when I grew up but I knew I wanted to do something to serve my tribe, because it's so fundamental to who I am,' she said.

'I probably consider myself a Yurok woman before I consider myself an American ... American [identity] is very individualist – not necessarily in a selfish way, but there's this idea of pull yourself up by your own bootstraps, move across the country and you'll succeed. And to me that's very foreign. You don't do things without community. I don't understand how people just move away from their family. Who watches your kids, and who do you go to church with?'

Together with the National Park Service and the Fish and Wildlife Service, the Yurok's plan would be to release six birds a year for twenty years. The birds breed slowly – couples generally mate for life, and have a chick only every other year – but before long there would hopefully be a self-sustaining population. It would return one piece in the Yurok jigsaw.

'Bringing condor back, making him an active part of our lives again, it's going to heal us as a people in a very big way. It's going to strengthen our ceremony, our prayers. It's going to allow us to bring the world back into balance, to renew it in a much more powerful way than we have been able to since condor disappeared.'

A remaining stage in the federal environmental approval process is a FONSI – a Finding of No Significant Impact on the human environment. 'Man, I hope we don't keel over dead when we get our FONSI. I can just imagine it,' says Claussen. 'They let us know that we can finally do this, after eleven and a half years it might be too much for us.'

At times, I wondered if she was loading more hope on the condor than a wild bird could possibly bear. I thought it was unlikely that all members of the tribe shared the strength of her commitment. The following evening we went to a brush dance, a ceremony of the kind where the condor feathers were historically used. Now, due to the condor's absence, eagle feathers are more common. A hundred or so cars were parked on a piece of flat ground by the mouth of the river.

As the sun set, male and female dancers shuffled and skipped round an earth pit. There were chants that sounded somewhere between hiccups and gargles, interspersed with sharp cries. Some of the dancers wore shells and feathers, and were stripped half naked; others wore sports clothes. It was a stew of the American and the Yurok, the sacred and the informal, the communal and the individual. It went through the night till 7 a.m., a vast pile of brush having been reduced to smoke and ashes.

There were parts of the Yurok ceremony that sat less easily with me – for example, the girls are told to show no expression during the dance, while the boys are free to joke. The future of the Yurok depends on much more than the return of the condor; 80 per cent of residents on the reservation, which runs both sides of the river, live below the poverty line.

The condor may also be a one-off. In many ways, it is an exceptionally suitable species for reintroduction – the birds don't kill livestock or require huge habitat restoration. (By comparison reintroducing the grizzly bear would be a harder challenge – the subspecies that lived in California now survives only on the state flag.) The reintroduction programme involved more intensive breeding than any pedigree dog. And the birds have returned to the skies thanks partly to the tax dollars paid by residents of cities such as San Francisco.

I found the Yurok's narrative – of the condor taking their prayers to the heavens – hard to take literally. But I realised the condor's return would not be possible without the cultural importance attached to it. The Yurok do not treat the condor as we treat our pets – as individuals, with personalities to be owned and adored. They have a place for the birds in their society, which respects the birds' wildness.

I also realised that non-tribal members have their own stories about animals, which are equally hard to take literally. Barbra Streisand insisted that her dog Samantha spoke English; many people think that their dogs and cats have similarly human abilities. These stories encourage us to find a role for domesticated animals in our workplaces and parks. The Yurok have dogs, but they have something more powerful – stories that bind them to the natural world and that encourage them to safeguard wild animals. Animals can be our companions, even if we don't own them, domesticate them or breed them to our aesthetic demands. The question is how to place that within our culture.

*

I love the company of dogs, and I had fun at CorgiCon. I love my cat Crumble. But here's the blunt reality: the Yurok have a better relationship with condor than many people have with their pets. Breeding animals so that they can thrive in the wild is infinitely preferable to breeding them so that they have stroke-able coats.

Like zookeepers, pet-owners are filled with good intentions, but our impact on animals is not as benign as we would like. The premise of pet-keeping is that we treat animals fairly by taking control of them.

We decide much of our pets' lives – including what they eat, which other animals they see, whether they have sex organs, and whether they have sex. We often decide when they die.

At one dog training session in San Francisco, I met a woman with a rescue dog from Guatemala. They had come together in strange circumstances: the woman had been holding out for a particular breed, but suffered concussion from a car accident and ended up accepting a mongrel. 'My brain wasn't working properly,' is how she explained it. So the Guatemalan rescue dog arrived in San Francisco, to a life of beaches and treats and unconditional love. I suggested that the dog must think she has arrived in heaven. 'She frickin' has,' her owner replied. 'Her life is better than mine. We've been to the beach this morning, she's played with three of her friends.' Then the woman paused. Technically the Guatemalan dog was the one being rescued. But 'in a way, I say she's rescuing me'. I almost yelped with agreement. She was right: our pets are rescuing us, not vice versa.

It was San Francisco where, in the 1990s, an animal activist (appropriately named Elliot Katz) first proposed that the authorities should refer to pets as 'companion animals' and pet-owners as 'animal guardians' – in a move designed to end the oppression of animals. I'm too cynically English to refer to myself as an animal guardian. But the idea of guardianship pushes us in the right direction – of considering our animals' interests, and of curbing our own desires, whether it be for ugly-cute breeds or cloning or a dog that we don't have the time to take care of. If we see ourselves as safeguarding our dogs through their lives, rather than simply fitting them into our own, then we are more likely to take their well-being seriously. If you love animals, you don't have to spend $499 on prosthetic dog testicles. In fact you probably shouldn't. If we thought harder of other ways to manage dogs' population, you might not even need to desex your dog at all.

Guardianship might mean our lives keep converging, for example bringing dogs to the office, or it might not. It would certainly mean the phasing out of breeds, and letting dogs return to healthy shapes. Scientists have identified sets of genes that influence dogs' personalities; breeding may be justified to promote personality traits that are suited to the modern world, rather than aesthetics. We should also leave fewer dogs at home during the day. Swedish law recommends dog-owners walk their dog every six hours. Some rescue centres in Britain won't let you adopt a dog unless you work from home at least one day a week (a more demanding ask pre-coronavirus). We should stop seeing dogs as must-have accessories, and start asking whether we can really fit them into our lives.

A lot of people who do think about pets understand the environmental impact. 'At some point, we have to go, how many predators can a plot of land hold?' Francis, a dog trainer, told me. 'You'll have to think about slowing down – about doing more with our individual dogs, and not just having more dogs.'

Brian Hare, an anthropologist who has done fascinating studies on dog behaviour, says, only half-jokingly: 'I would not raise children without a dog.' But, given the environmental impact this would have, I agreed with Francis – that we needed to have fewer pets. Not every apartment or every lifestyle is right. Not every family needs to have their animal fix in the form of their own animal. (Not every family wants one either. Some Muslims see the saliva of the dog as impure. The ratio of dogs to people is estimated at 1 or 2 per 1,000 in the Arabian peninsula, compared to 240 per 1,000 in North America.)

We need to think of other animals too. In cognition experiments, dogs are often treated well – researchers play with them, give them treats and take them home (not to mention the fact that the dogs, as domesticated animals, are at ease in the human world). Perhaps we could make equivalent allowances for other animals, and perhaps we would understand their abilities better. The American activist Henry Spira said that taking care of his friend's cat pushed him to become interested in animal rights: 'I began to wonder about the appropriateness of cuddling one animal while sticking a knife and fork into another.'

The link between pet-owning and veganism is interesting. On the one hand, pet-owners should surely be vegans. The emotional lives of dogs and livestock are not vastly different. Faced with the choice, two in five people say they would save their pet ahead of a foreign tourist. If you think a dog's life is worth more than a stranger's, how can you not conclude that a pig's life is worth more than your tastebuds? If you're willing to spend thousands of dollars on vet bills for a dog, how can you not spend a few hours investigating factory farming? On the other hand, dog- and cat-owning households struggle to be vegan households, because the pets themselves demand meat. There are now vegan dog foods trying to emulate the success of Impossible Foods and Beyond Meat. That still leaves cat-owners, and owners of dogs who don't go for vegan dog food, having to accept a contradiction.

Telling people not to adopt dogs and cats is almost as futile, and as mean-spirited, as telling them not to have children. There are lots of good things about pets (and even about children). But we should at least compensate the downsides. One of the interesting conclusions of the bird-kill surveys is that most of the damage is not done by cats who live in people's homes. In the US study, two-thirds of the kills were attributed to 'unowned' cats, including feral cats and community cats who roam free but are fed by multiple people. In Australia, four-fifths of the killings were by feral cats. Similarly, a large proportion, possibly more than half, of the world's domesticated dogs live unrestrained – for example, as street dogs. (They can scavenge plenty of food; in rural Zimbabwe, about one-fifth of their diet is human faeces.) If pet-ownership really were to inspire us to take care of animals more generally, we might start by working out what to do with feral dogs and cats – who have, after all, the same genetic make-up as our pets.

Recently a group of academics suggested that Australia could place a levy of, say, 0.6 per cent on the price of dog food to support the conservation of wild-living dingoes (themselves originally domesticated dogs), who are currently killed because of the damage they cause to livestock. A tax would remind us that pets have a cost, and that pets do not represent the whole animal kingdom.

We've been here before. In the eighteenth century, some politicians thought Britain had too many dogs. They complained that the dogs were a danger to health (in the form of rabies), a waste of food (at a time of failing harvests), and a source of poaching (with poor dog-owners killing the rich's game). There were different opinions on which dogs were the problems – dogs belonging to poor people, who (MPs said) should be spending their money on themselves, or those belonging to rich people, who (other MPs said) were indulging in the luxurious sport of hunting. In 1796 Britain did introduce a tax on dogs, which charged hunting dogs at a higher rate and exempted poor households. It never raised that much money, and didn't stop the increase in dogs, presumably because no politician dared to set it high enough. By the time it was abolished in 1987, it was just 37p per dog, and cost more to enforce than it raised in taxes.

A modern-day dog tax would be hugely unpopular (even more than a meat tax), and it probably wouldn't reduce the number of dogs (because dog-owners seem willing to pay any cost). But how about this: what if for every pound pet-owners spent on their animal, they spent a pound helping wild species? How about dog-owners support wolf reintroduction, and cat-owners support wildcat, lynx and tiger conservation? Owners could pay the extra alongside their pet insurance.

We need to think of our pets as part of a system. The philosopher Clare Palmer suggests that everyone who has benefited from pet-keeping has a duty to remedy some of its downsides. By allowing dogs to be kept as pets, we accept that some dogs will be badly treated. Even if we personally use only the best breeders, the overall human demand for dogs leads others to use puppy mills. Palmer gives the example of a cat-owner who finds abandoned kittens in a dumpster – that person may have a duty to intervene, because they have benefited from cats. I would expand this idea further: as dog- and cat-owners, we have a duty to improve biodiversity.

We can start by looking around us. By appreciating the animals on our doorsteps, we can start to undo what Robert Michael Pyle called 'the extinction of experience': the spiral by which each generation engages less with the natural world and therefore condemns more of it to oblivion. London's streets were once alive with pigs, chickens, cows and horses. Now those domesticated animals have largely disappeared, and the past century has seen the arrival of wild foxes. The foxes' presence – while not without the downsides such as scattered rubbish bins and loud sex noises – is faintly magical. Cities hold amazing amounts of biodiversity, if we know where to look. In Melbourne, Australia, 239 species of bird, including some nationally threatened species, and more than 1,500 species of insects have been recorded in parks over the last twenty years. The city is working to bring nature to people, in line with the principles of the people of Kulin Nation, who occupied the land before European settlers arrived. (Of course its strategy for doing so doesn't mention the negative impact of dogs and cats.)

Cities are novel environments, ones for which even humans have not evolved. For all the noise and traffic, they also offer animals plenty of food, and often a lower density of their predators. Burrowing owls have spread from grasslands of the Americas to urban areas; those living in cities are less fearful of humans than those in the countryside. The species that adapt best don't seem to be the tamest species – i.e. those least likely to flee from humans – but those with the greater variability of individuals in how readily they flee. This variability means that at least some individuals may be suited to the environment. A bigger brain relative to body size also seems to help (although urban foxes seem to have smaller brains than rural foxes, perhaps because feeding out of bins is less challenging than hunting prey).

Let's stop tailoring cities to dogs, and make them work for all wildlife. Our gardens hold many insects if we don't spray them with pesticides and stop mowing our lawns shorter than a US Navy recruit's hair. When I saw swarms of flying ants in our garden, my instinctive reaction – learnt from childhood – used to be to boil the kettle and get rid of them. (The swarms are so big that they are picked up from space on the Met Office radar.) Loving animals means accepting the messy presence of other lives.

After cats, the biggest human-related killers of birds in the United States and Canada may be ... buildings. Hundreds of millions of birds die in collisions with buildings each year – among them hummingbirds, warblers and many endangered migratory birds. It works out as at least eleven birds every second. Architects see glass as the quintessential modern building material; birds don't see it at all. They die of brain haemorrhages, or often their beak or wing is injured, making them easy prey for a passing cat or a fox.

Almost nobody in cities cares about this. Michael Mesure has a theory why. In the spring of 1989 Mesure owned an art gallery and antiques shop in Ontario, Canada, when a friend told him about birds colliding with buildings in Toronto's financial district. Mesure went down at dawn to look. 'The sidewalks were blanketed with dead birds,' he recalls. But by the time the workers arrived, gulls, rats and human cleaners had swept the streets – so hardly anyone noticed. He suspects that many birds assumed to be cat victims were in fact stunned by collisions with buildings first. 'Our buildings weren't designed with the intention to kill birds. It doesn't mean that we don't have a role in reversing that threat.'

Mesure founded an organisation, Fatal Light Awareness Program (FLAP), and eventually gave up his job to campaign for bird-friendly buildings. FLAP's volunteers have collected dead birds from 172 species, including Mesure's favourite species, Blackburnian warblers, who have orange foreheads and a fondness for treetops. 'When you look at all the different wildlife out there, birds tend to get the most amount of attention but the least amount of action. Birds aren't cute and cuddly,' Mesure says. 'People honestly believe they are disease-ridden animals, which is not true.' Even birdwatchers are more focused on populating their lists of species than helping the species. 'They're the ones who invest themselves the least in issues like this.'

FLAP took building-owners to court, and in 2013 the lawyers found an improbable argument: Ontario law lists radiation as a contaminant; windows produce radiation when they reflect daylight; so windows are creating pollution. We can only assume the judge was an ornithologist, because the argument worked. In theory building-owners in Ontario are now liable for killing migratory birds. In practice nobody has been prosecuted. 'The Ministry of Natural Resources and Forestry doesn't want to enforce a law that everybody's breaking,' Mesure says. Nonetheless, Toronto is the first city in the world to introduce bird-friendly construction standards. Mesure has no regrets about devoting his life to the cause: 'I'll be doing this to my dying day.'

Pets play to humans' hero complex, our desire to be needed. Even the publisher The Dodo, whose viral videos try to emphasise animal agency, often finds the most successful stories are ones like '85-Pound Dog Just Wants A Lifetime Of Snuggles' and 'World's Smallest Alpaca Lives In A House'. Migratory birds can't make us feel so needed. They are not substitute companions for dogs and cats. But if we claim to love animals, we need to balance both. One result of lockdown is that home-owners started to hear more of the thuds of birds crashing into their windows, and wondered what was happening. Feather Friendly, one of several companies that make bird-deterrent films for windows, said its sales had multiplied.

One morning, my daughters and I came down to breakfast to find a baby blackbird dead by the catflap. The bird would have fitted snugly in the palm of my hand – he or she must have been barely a fledging. Almost their entire body seemed on display – the thin white feather bones, the yellow intestines, the red torn flesh. Only the eyes, being hidden behind yellow eyelids, could not be seen. 'Why did Crumble bite the little bird?' asked Eliza.

I didn't know what to say. I suspected this bird had died a horrid death. There was bloodied skin by the bird's head. There were tufts of feathers across the kitchen and the hall. A few whole feathers were no longer than the width of my thumb. At what moment did their eyes close shut? Was it right at the end, or near the beginning? I placed the bird in the garden, where wasps homed in almost immediately. Eliza gave Crumble a spoonful of cat biscuits. I resolved to train Crumble in the hope of satisfying her desire to hunt. I thought that donating to conservation would make me feel less guilty.

I'd never really looked closely at a blackbird before. To take care of a dog or a cat in the modern world takes effort and money. It sucks our attention. We spend so much time looking inwards, towards our pets, that we neglect the broader world of animal wonder. We act as if do-mesticated animals are the highest form, and in the process we just increase the strain that we are placing on natural systems. We need to find ways to engage with animals, without making them our own.

My daughters grew up with Crumble, and quickly learnt to include her name when listing the members of our family. But I hope they will also learn that pets are not enough. The number of species that benefit from being pets is vanishingly small. Owning animals risks unleashing our own selfishness. We need to find companionship without owner-ship. We need a sense of the wider ecology, the wider community of animals. We have to make sure our pets are the beginning of our love for other animals, not the end.

9. PLAYING GOD

The Sapiens regime on earth has so far produced little that we can be proud of ... did we decrease the amount of suffering in the world?

Yuval Noah Harari

Loving animals makes sense only in the context of what is possible. Hunting whales seems repugnant to most westerners because we know it's possible to live without it. We don't need whale oil and meat. Now we don't need cow's meat and leather either. Future technology may change more of our calculations. I'm in my late thirties: when I was born, meat alternatives were terrible, soya milk often came in powder, and climate change was not an emergency. Changes in technology and scientific understanding lead to changes in what we can reasonably expect of people. There are no climate-friendly passenger jets at the moment, but there might be one day and there will be no need for what Swedish environmentalists call *flygskam* – flight shame. Our relationship with animals has never been static. So I started thinking how developments during my daughters' lifetimes might affect what it means to treat animals fairly.

*

From her home in the hills near Los Angeles, Carol Gurney communicates with dogs. Actually, not just dogs – also horses, cats, whales and recently an African elephant.

'I don't think, Henry, I was aware of my feelings until I met animals,' she says. 'It's like I wanted to *think* my feelings rather than *feel* my feelings. The animals helped me become a whole person.'

Gurney is a taut, stylish woman in her early seventies. She is sitting on a pink sofa, surrounded by miniature Buddhas and a coffee table with a framed picture of a deceased dog called Spirit. You might jump to conclusions. But Gurney insists that she didn't start life as an 'airy-fairy person'. She was raised by nuns, and once worked in the human resources department of an advertising agency. 'I'm from New York, I'm a Type A personality!'

Gurney might still work for an ad agency, if her pet cat hadn't started soiling the house. An 'animal communicator' diagnosed the cat's soiling as a sign of problems in Gurney's marriage; Gurney ended up getting divorced. She herself then turned communicator. She was introduced to a pet horse called Timmy, who had developed narcolepsy. Timmy's owner wanted to put him down. Gurney took Timmy aside, and discovered that the horse was heartbroken by the disappearance of another horse who lived in the same field. This other horse had been euthanised, and on the vet's advice, Timmy had been kept well away from the scene.

'I apologised to him, "I'm so sorry that nobody told you, and I'm so sorry that you didn't have a chance to say goodbye" ... He really taught me how to connect with animals. I've never had that sense of connection – or love – with another human being.' Enough said about the ex-husband.

There's a long tradition of people who say they have a special ability to communicate with other animals. Temple Grandin, a scientist at Colorado State University, has pioneered more humane designs for livestock facilities. Grandin argues that her autism helps her to communicate with animals, because they, like her, think visually; her designs strive to see the world from other animals' point of view. Californian horse-whisperer Monty Roberts vowed to treat horses better than his father, who beat them (and him). He says that, by reading horses' body language, he does not just make them perform tasks – he makes them want to perform tasks.

For Gurney, animals can talk to us telepathically. They can tell us when they are ready to be euthanised; they can tell us how they are feeling from beyond the grave. The Gurney Institute of Animal Communication, which she runs from her home, is branded the only institute in the world to train professional animal communicators. 'Animals are absolutely no different to us. They experience the same emotions. They just happen to be in a different body. That's it,' says Gurney, as if it were common sense.

She believes that you can communicate with any animal – within reason. One of the most famous animal communicators, Penelope Smith, once tried talking to fleas. 'All she got was, "eat, eat, eat". So that was the consciousness of the flea.'

I wonder about Crumble, several thousand miles away. 'Whatever you are thinking about your cat in your head, just say it to her,' says Gurney. But if animals are telepathic, shouldn't she already know what I'm thinking? 'You think animals are tuned into us 24/7? If they were, they'd be exhausted!'

I left the Los Angeles hills unconvinced by telepathy; when I tried to communicate with Crumble that evening, I got nothing back. But multiple clients and indeed vets say that animal communicators often diagnose problems that the vets themselves can't. Scientific research may eventually explain why this is the case, or why it's a mirage.

For me, Gurney's work was important for a different reason. One of our first instincts with our pets is to get inside their heads; one of our first frustrations is that we can't. Throughout my reporting on animals – whether pets, livestock, zoo animals or wild animals – I had come up against a wall. What do animals really feel? In most cases, most of us still don't know. There's a Gary Larson *Far Side* cartoon in which a professor has invented a canine decoder that makes him the first person ever to hear what barking dogs are actually saying. The machine tells him: 'Hey! Hey!'

But the idea of decoding animal language is worth taking seriously. Diana Reiss, a psychologist at Hunter College, has spent decades trying to decode dolphin and elephant sounds, and to create interfaces through which different species might understand each other. Over the past decade, she has come together with other researchers into animal communication, technology experts and the former Genesis singer Peter Gabriel, who once had a moving experience playing keyboards with Panbanisha, a bonobo with no musical training. Their proposal is grandly called the 'interspecies Internet'.

Currently our communication with animals is largely intuitive, fragmentary and unscientific. 'We are already communicating with other animals. But it's at a certain level and it's completely subjective,' says Reiss. That makes it easy for us to attribute emotions in those animals whom we know well, namely our pets, and ignore them in animals whom we want to treat less kindly, such as livestock and zoo residents.

There are humans who train other animals – dolphins, dogs, horses. That isn't what interests Reiss. Through the interspecies Internet, she doesn't want to give other animals instructions – she wants to give them *control*. 'We're giving them a voice to say what it is they want,' she says.

Reiss has designed a system so that dolphins in an aquarium can press their nose on a glass touchscreen to request fish, a ball or a rub; they can also play a game of 'whack-a-fish'. Other researchers have built an interface where horses pull a lever to indicate if they want to be covered by a blanket. What would happen if an octopus were given a touchscreen? Or if isolated elephants in zoos were connected to elephants elsewhere? Such a device – obviously nicknamed an Elephone – is ethically trickier: there is no guarantee that elephants would want or benefit from that interaction. If we were stuck in a US hospital bed, would it help us to have a phone call with a stranger in South Africa?

All this has been a slow process. Reiss's research started in the early 1980s. Gabriel played keyboards with Panbanisha in 2000 (their best combination was, in Gabriel's words, 'a sort of sad piece in A minor'). Researchers now at least have the computer processing power to find patterns in recordings of whale, dolphin and bird noises more meaningful than the professor in the *Far Side* cartoon. But the field still relies on a few pioneers, such as Reiss and the parrot expert Irene Pepperberg, some of whom are reaching the end of their careers.

Knowledge may not be passed on: Pepperberg, whose African grey parrot Alex could describe fifty objects including their colour and material, lost most of her video recordings in a flood in her basement.

The hope, however, is that, if large enough sets of recordings can be assembled, researchers will be able to find patterns of language and reproduce those patterns to communicate with other species. It will be a Rosetta stone, a Google Translate for the animal world. 'I don't see any reason why we shouldn't be able to discuss fish with humpback whales, except we have to meet them where they are,' says Laurance R. Doyle, an astrophysicist who has studied humpback songs, as part of an effort to prepare for detecting extraterrestrial intelligence. One problem is separating the noises made by different animals: around half the time African elephants are vocalising, they overlap with other elephants. As at a crowded cocktail party, it's hard to pick out an individual thread.

If animals could express their wants in a way we could understand, then we should be able to improve the way we treat them in captivity. We could offer painkillers, food and stimulation; we could change the temperature, and remove sources of fear. Factory farms might become nicer places, so might zoos. The interspecies Internet would push more people to reject industrial farming and zoos altogether.

Or maybe not. Slave-owners spoke the same language as their slaves; it didn't stop them from appalling cruelty. With non-human animals, there is a conceptual gap. You won't be able to ask captive dolphins whether they'd rather live in the wild, or ask a pig whether they have a good life. They don't have a notion of the alternative. Even if we can hear animals, we will never be certain about what is best for them. We will have to make leaps of compassion. We can already say with some confidence that elephants would be better off outside zoos, and that salmon have poor lives on fish farms. Why wait before doing something about it?

Bringing technology to animals does raise fundamental ethical questions. Are captive primates and dolphins stimulated by computer games? Apparently so. Should we offer wild primates and dolphins such games? Should we invite them to demand things of us? Biologists like Reiss would suggest no – improving captive conditions is one thing;

altering wild spaces is another. I am not so sure. Technology has enriched our lives; I can envisage a distant time when we offer it to wild animals too. We also know that wild animals experience pain. That has led to an even more ambitious technological proposal.

*

David Pearce is keen to make two things clear: he isn't on hallucinogenic drugs and he doesn't want all life on earth to end. Most people I'd met hadn't felt the need to point these things out. But Pearce's ideas are so left-field that he wants to make himself appear as normal as possible. Pearce has taken the animal test perhaps to its furthest logical conclusion.

He has been plotting the path to a world free of pain – for wild animals. He argues, with some justification, that life for most creatures in the wild is 'nasty, brutish and short'. 'A lot of nature is starvation,' says Pearce, when we meet for a vegan lunch in Brighton. Gazelles are torn to pieces by lions, baby penguins die of cold, even predators fight over scarce food. Many animals are covered in parasites – if nothing else, they might be incredibly itchy. Evolution selects for the species' survival, not mental well-being. Natural selection does not guarantee that wild animals live happy lives.

Even when you know nature is cruel, seeing it still shocks you. One day, Eliza and I spotted some goslings by the lake in the park. I lined her up for a photo with them in the background. As I went to press the white spot on my iPhone, a crow flew in from the left side of the picture and plucked one of the goslings. I was horrified. Eliza saw nothing – she was facing towards me. I didn't tell her what had happened, but almost for the first time, I needed my daughter to console me. Suddenly the photo didn't seem so happy. Similarly, tourists often want to see predators killing their prey on the African savannah, but then are repelled when they see how drawn-out the deaths are. In the early years of London Zoo, visitors, including Charles Dickens, complained about snakes being fed live birds and rodents.

This creates one of the hardest problems in animal ethics. Humans treat animals brutally, but isn't nature worse? Jeremy Bentham – the philosopher who posed the key question about animals, 'Can they *suffer*?' – concluded that meat-eating was ethical on the basis that animals would suffer a more painful fate in the wild. Most animal thinkers today don't worry about the suffering of wild animals. Critics of factory farming and medical research, such as Peter Singer, have largely steered clear of the subject. Conservationists, such as those who support the Half-Earth movement, see a focus on wild suffering as preposterous. As long as we leave other species alone, in forests and oceans, we have done enough.

In his writing, Pearce has at least made a plausible case for taking the suffering of wild animals seriously. If we care about the pain suffered by animals on farms and in zoos, can we really ignore the pain they face in the wild? And if we could lessen it, might we one day decide to? Pearce is not completely on his own. Jeff McMahan, an Oxford philosophy professor, has also prodded humans to consider how to reduce suffering. 'If you've ever watched a wounded animal writhing, it's horrible,' McMahan told me. 'Suffering is really bad. When suffering is extreme and protracted, and we could prevent it at little cost, then certainly we should do it.'

McMahan's thinking is largely theoretical: tempered by the fact that there is nothing obvious we can do, certainly not at little cost, to prevent wild animal suffering. Pearce, however, has already written one paper on how humans could create a welfare state for African elephants, offering cradle-to-grave healthcare for $2–3 billion a year. And that's just the start. In his imagined future, there would be a 'pan-species welfare state'. 'It's not a choice between turning the world into a zoo or today's savagery,' he says. 'In tomorrow's wildlife parks, you can have all the nature and the wild animals of today – but you don't need to have the suffering too.'

Pearce wants to gene-edit virtually every species, so that animals do not eat each other and do not starve. He insists it is within reach – probably by the end of the century – thanks to super-computers and nano-robots. He describes it as 'Buddhism plus biotech'. And the fact that gene-editing kits for bacteria are now available online for under $200 has encouraged him further. Gene drives, pieces of DNA inserted into animal chromosomes, can spread edited genes through the entire population of a species. 'We are going to be able to choose the level of suffering in the world, which has never happened before in history,' he says. 'Long-term, I think the aim is to civilise the biosphere. Essentially every cubic metre of the biosphere is going to be accessible to surveillance, micromanagement and control ... We're going to have to decide how we are going to use our power.'

This is an outlandish claim, given that today there are still places that humans have never been, let alone understood well enough to control. I'm not sure who the best messenger for it would be. Probably a billionaire genius like Elon Musk, or a wise aunt like Jane Goodall. Pearce, by his own admission, falls into neither camp. He is an awkward, apologetic figure, whose eyebrows and mouth contort strangely as if guided by rather basic animation software. 'I have a village-idiot grin,' he tells me, apropos of nothing. 'But it's more of the low-status chimpanzee – "please don't hurt me" – not the inner serenity.'

Pearce started thinking about these ideas as a child. His grandparents and parents were all vegetarians. 'One of my earliest memories was watching a blackbird pecking at a worm. I was upset – all life was sacred, and this was terrible, and I clapped and then the blackbird flew off. But then I remember thinking if the blackbird can't eat the worm then her chicks starve. Yes, at that age, one can clearly envisage reprogramming the biosphere.' A few years later, he picked up a beginner's guide to philosophy, *Philosophy Made Simple*, and decided that he was a utilitarian, committed to minimising suffering wherever it may occur. He suffered from depression, which led him to think about artificially stimulating the brain to induce happiness, a process known as wireheading. ('For most people, wireheading is quite degrading. But for someone of quite a melancholic temperament, this struck me as wonderful.') He took drugs: he wrote a tract suggesting MDMA may offer 'a tantalising glimpse of what true mental health may be like in centuries to come'. (These days Pearce makes do with 'ten or eleven cups of coffee a day, together with a couple of cans of Red Bull'. Which doesn't sound much healthier.) He now spends his days running a web-hosting business, and playing *Mortal Combat* on his iPad. He admits violent video games are a strange hobby for a man dedicated to eliminating violence, although he does at least go by the username 'veganpacifist'.

Pearce's philosophy has rather ruined his ability to enjoy the outdoors. 'I see a cat from a mouse's point of view,' he says. 'If I go out into nature, I'm thinking of all the terrible things that go on.' What about wildlife documentaries, I ask? 'I enjoy in some sense the mindless spectacle, but I'm also thinking pain. Showing a starving emperor penguin for five seconds and then cutting away. It's a lie – it's as deceptive as anything you'll get on North Korean propaganda.'

Documentary-makers have a rule that they do not intervene. As a society, we are under no obligation to keep to that. In practice, Pearce's proposals for animals would work something like this. Humans would edit the genes of carnivores to turn them into herbivores; gene drives would spread the change through the population. Gene-editing would also be used to reduce fertility and eliminate all diseases. His 'back of the envelope' calculation is that this would cost billions of dollars to get started, plus 'several hundred million dollars' a year to maintain. If it all seems a bit vague, it's partly deliberate. 'One needs to go into enough detail that one can show what one is talking about, but not so much that it becomes fanciful,' says Pearce.

Won't people still object? Pearce realises that most people think nature is rather beautiful, albeit red in tooth and claw. He puts this down to 'status quo bias'. 'Not many people know it now, but when general anaesthesia was introduced in the mid-nineteenth century, for about fifteen years there was quite fierce opposition to this newfangled innovation. It was completely utopian this idea of pain-free surgery.' (Some surgeons saw pain as a useful medical indicator, particularly in childbirth.) 'But people came around to the idea.'

Pearce asks me to imagine that we discover a civilisation that has abolished suffering; animals would exist only in wildlife parks, leading harmonious lives. 'Would we urge this advanced civilisation to reintroduce predation, parasitism, disease, starvation and all the horrors of the Darwinian past? Some people might say yes, but most people would agree this would be a crazy thing to do.'

I take the train back to London. When I arrive home, I try to summarise Pearce's ideas to Susie. 'You mean, off-the-wall bananas?' she says, keeping both eyes on the TV. My head tells me that she is right. Pearce's ideas are bananas. But I remember his own defence: 'One of the reasons to put forward crazy ideas is that it makes it easier for others.'

A few months later, I stumbled across the Wild Animal Initiative, a group of activists who are trying to make wild animals' lives better by seeing them as individuals rather than 'as mere parts of ecosystems'. The group is barely concerned about endangered species: because these species are rare, the sum total of their suffering is much less than, say, gulls or grasshoppers. Instead one of its first ideas for reducing suffering is to manage animals' fertility: for species that are currently culled by humans, but also for species where offspring compete against one another for resources. Controlling fertility would increase each baby's survival chances. To me, this sounds invasive and ecologically problematic. But I can't rule out that in two centuries people will be quoting their website just as today activists quote Jeremy Bentham's 'Can they *suffer*?' In practice, we do try to act as Good Samaritans for a few chosen wild animals: near San Francisco, the Marine Mammal Center takes in 600 seals, sea lions, otters and other animals a year, including ones who have been injured by shark bites.

How can we love animals, yet accept wild-animal suffering? It's possible that at least some of the pain that we cause – through factory farming, medical research and pedigree pet breeding – is more intense and prolonged than what wild animals might experience. There is no scenario in the wild where a boar cannot turn around for months or years. We may assume that those animals that show play-like behaviour, including wild sheep and seals, take enjoyment from life. In other words, suffering may not define wild-animal lives.

More fundamentally, we may simply have more responsibility for the pain that we cause. The caveat is that it's increasingly difficult to say what suffering is natural. What about wild-animal suffering related to our own actions? We have exposed animals to new dangers – a whale washes up full of plastics in Indonesia, a bobcat is burnt in Californian forest fires, African penguins can't find enough fish off Cape Horn.

Jaguars in the Brazilian Pantanal, possibly including the ones I paid to see as a tourist, were burnt to death by climate-change-fuelled fires in 2020.

After the *Exxon Valdez* oil spill off Alaska in 1989, humans felt a moral duty to help affected sea otters. Some otters died, some couldn't be returned to the wild, and so it worked out as $123,000 – in 1990 dollars – for each one successfully reintroduced. In 2020, billions of Australian animals burnt to death in wildfires, which were intensified by human-caused climate change. Should we have invested money in saving those animals? If so, how much? The philosopher Clare Palmer gives the dilemma of whether to feed polar bears, who are expected to starve because the Arctic ice from which they hunt seals is disappearing. We could save the bears, in a semi-wild state, by providing alternative food. But would we do so by killing seals, whose own lives matter and whose own populations are falling, or wild-caught fish and farmed animals, with all the ethical issues that might involve? To feed 900 bears would require 3.6 tonnes of chow, made of fish and pigs, *each day*. There are no pain-free answers.

Pearce's ideas kept nagging me. Maybe one day we will look back on our disregard of wild animals in the way that we look back at past generations' disregard of farm animals. Our responsibility is at least to consider wild animals' pain, and whether we can address it.

The simplest reason for tolerating wild suffering now is that we can't do much about it. We might be able to rescue some animals from wildfires, but there is no alternative to predator–prey relationships. If we stop lions from eating gazelles, we save the gazelle but harm the lion. Peter Singer's view is that, if prey animals' lives were found to be largely made up of suffering, the most immediate challenge would be rewilding programmes, where humans introduce predators to new areas. But even these schemes could still be justified by the ecological benefits. Healthy ecosystems rely on death and competition. It stretches belief that we will find a way of editing animals while also keeping the earth in balance. Animal genomes are vastly complex; you can't just punch out a carnivore gene.

Gene-editing is often billed as a moonshot – but the current reality is more akin to a single firework. I mention David Pearce's idea of gene-editing all predators to Alison Van Eenennaam, an Australian animal scientist at the University of California, Davis. 'We're so far away from making an omnivore out of carnivore,' she says. 'Every biological process in that animal is going to be built into being a carnivore. You'd have to literally change thousands of genes. We're so far away from that – it's not even funny.'

It's easy to think that humans are on the brink of being able to re-make nature deliberately and intelligently, not accidentally and stupidly like we're currently doing. Van Eenennaam is the illustration of the technological and regulatory limits to gene-editing. Her story began with a stroke of luck. Many physical traits are the product of multiple genes. But she identified that a single gene was responsible for the horns in Hereford cattle. As anyone who wanders into a field of cows quickly realises, horns are potentially hazardous; farmers therefore generally remove them when the cows are young, often without anaesthetic. Making a breed polled, or hornless, should therefore benefit both the cows and the farmers.

Van Eenennaam and her partner company Recombinetic managed to produce two generations of hornless cattle. It seemed a demonstration of the potential of synthetic biology. But in January 2017, in the final days of the Barack Obama administration, the US Food and Drug Administration (FDA) issued a draft rule that gene-edited cattle would be regulated as drugs. Van Eenennaam's work collapsed.

'At that stage, we had six pregnant cows,' she says, in an office that is a rainforest of conference lanyards and marathon medallions. 'They went from one day being polled animals to being a new animal drug – an unapproved animal drug.' Even years later, her anger at the FDA is undimmed. 'They didn't speak to us for ten years, and just dropped that big turd a day before Trump took office.'

I ask if the ruling had placed Van Eenennaam's work on ice. 'Or maybe on fire,' she says. 'Literally, I've got a mass of pictures of a cow getting incinerated if you'd like to see those.' She turns to her PC and brings up photos of a 1,963-pound cow being killed and placed in a furnace. 'I paid to feed him up and I paid to burn him.' To add to the gruesomeness, the cow was too large to be disposed of whole. 'The incinerator can only cope with so many pounds of flesh – I don't know how to put that nicely.

'I eat animals, I'm fine with these animals getting eaten, but I'm not fine with a perfectly edible animal getting burnt in an incinerator. Just about everything about that is wrong. It's disrespectful to the animal itself, it creates greenhouse gas emissions, and then we get nothing.'

In theory the hornless cattle could be used in the food supply of Brazil, Canada and Argentina – all major dairy producers. But the FDA's ruling came with a stigma: 'To suddenly say because we use gene-editing it's a drug puts us in this really awkward category.' And the livestock trade is global. 'If you can't use it in Europe and America, then that's really problematic. So as it relates to animals, we've probably lost it.'

Van Eenennaam argues that gene-editing is a route to making animals less susceptible to disease. The genes for hornlessness that she introduced were present in other cattle; she was not creating a hybrid animal. Humans have been breeding animals for specific traits for thousands of years. But our squeamishness remains. Van Eenennaam notes that even a largely favourable cover story in *Wired* magazine depicted one of her edited cows in a sinister, darkened photo, and depicted her as almost Dr Frankenstein, with a dark coat and the sun behind her.

At the start of her career, she trained in how to genetically engineer plants – and the expectation among her colleagues was that genetic engineering in animals would be the next step. 'And we haven't been able to use it for twenty years,' sighs Van Eenennaam.

There is one approved, genetically engineered animal – an Atlantic salmon, edited with genetic material from the Pacific Chinook salmon and ocean pout, to be faster-growing. It was developed in 1989, started its regulatory process in 1995, and was approved as safe by the FDA in 2015. Even then the fish are not allowed to grow in ocean pens, in case they escape into the wild; only sterile female fish are used. The salmon are slightly more prone to deformities. Farms in Indiana and Florida started 'harvesting' the fish in 2020, but at a tiny scale. It took thirty years and $120 million to get started. 'That's not a viable option. We had a chance to rethink things and say, have there been any unique harms from GMOs [genetically modified organisms]? No, not even a sneeze,' says Van Eenennaam. 'People don't appreciate how important the regulatory piece is to basically blocking innovation.' Our opposition to editing animals – at least those animals we can recognise – is that strong.

In many people's minds, gene-editing will create new super-breeds of livestock, immune to disease and able to generate more meat and milk than ever. Van Eenennaam's expectations are lower. 'It's the cherry on top.' And then tapping a breeding catalogue, she adds: '*This* is the ice-cream sundae. You've never going to get rid of this.'

Progress is now even more distant than Van Eenennaam realised. A few weeks after we met, the FDA, to whom she had appealed for an exemption, revealed that the editing of the hornless cattle had not been as seamless as Van Eenennaam and her partners hoped: some of the cows had some DNA from the bacteria used in the editing process.

Editing animals sits uncomfortably with loving them, if love means accepting them how they are. So long as we farm animals and control their breeding, we will be changing their genetics in some way. Gene-editing, even introducing genetic material from a different species, does not in itself cause suffering. It may do the opposite, by reducing livestock's susceptibility to disease and increasing their efficiency, so fewer are needed in farming. But it also brings the discomforting prospect that we humans, too, could become manipulated, or divided into genetically engineered haves and have-nots. For the foreseeable future, it will be a process at the margin. We're not ready to allow the process to transform fundamentally animals and our relationship with them.

So what will we allow technology to do?

*

'My relationship with mosquitoes has gone from normal dislike to full-on hatred. It is the perfect invasive species.'

Pete Massaro is the director of automation at Verily Life Science, the part of Google that thinks about the whole human body, not just eyeballs that can be sold to advertisers. The mosquito he hates is *Aedes aegypti*. Labelled 'arguably the worst animal in the world' by *Atlantic* magazine, it feeds on humans, and spreads deadly viruses including Zika, dengue fever, and chikungunya. It is originally from Africa, but has spread across the United States – from Virginia, to Texas and now California. It has come to rely on humans, and we have allowed it to. We manipulate water so easily, leaving pools whenever we water our gardens, that a tropical mosquito can now thrive in the American desert, and the semi-arid areas such as those near the city of Fresno, California.

'It takes a bottle cap of water to establish a colony of mosquitoes. In Fresno, they had no *Aedes aegypti* in 2013. Now they're infested,' says Massaro. 'The US doesn't have a disease problem – yet. They have a lit fuse. They have all the right mosquitoes in very high numbers in some places. There hasn't been a spread of dengue yet. But I know there are places – in the warmer, more tropical places in the US – where they are very, very, very worried. And they would tell you it's a matter of time.' In 2016, there were more than 200 cases of Zika in Florida. 'I think that's a warning shot.'

Humans have always felt that certain animals are pests. While some of those animals – wolves, bears, rabbits and sharks – have had defenders, mosquitoes have few, and invasive mosquitoes have none at all. The only question is, are we capable of getting rid of them?

Verily's work in south San Francisco was a test case of how far our powers have come. In the 1930s, American scientists started looking for a way to control screw-worm flies, parasites that feed on wounds in cattle and cause huge suffering. They worked out that they could sterilise huge numbers of the flies using radiation, then drop the males from the air. As wild female flies bred with the sterile males, the population would dwindle. By 1966, the screw-worm was eliminated from the US and has been eliminated from Mexico and much of Central America since. To kill screw-worms, you have to breed millions of (sterile) screw-worms.

This approach struggled to work for mosquitoes, because male mosquitoes sterilised with radiation did not fare well in the real world. So other methods were found, including infecting the male mosquitoes (which do not bite humans) with a bacterium, Wolbachia, that means a female who mates with an infected male will lay unviable eggs. Wolbachia occurs naturally, lowering the risks of disrupting the ecosystem.

But this method has a complication: if female mosquitoes are infected with Wolbachia, they could go on to lay viable eggs. You do not want to release infected females, because doing so risks making the problem worse. So you have to separate females from males before you release them. Female mosquitoes are slightly bigger than males, and one laborious way to sort them is through a form of sieve. What Verily has done is to automate the process: taking millions of images to hone down what a female mosquito looks like, and using machine learning to distinguish the sexes. The mosquitoes are funnelled towards a tiny camera, which analyses whether they are a male or female, and tries to screen out females. The team estimates that perhaps 1 in 100,000 females that approach the cameras will make it through.

To eradicate screw-worm fly, the US had to breed sterile screw-worm flies. And to eradicate mosquitoes, Verily is breeding mosquitoes. We pass into a small room with a few crates. There is a hum of what sounds like an air-conditioner. Then I realise the sound is coming from the crates, which contain 800,000, maybe 900,000 mosquitoes. I haven't been this close to so many mosquitoes since I went camping on Colombia's Caribbean coast and zipped open the tent to let some air in. 'We're producing 7.5 million mosquitoes a week right now, which is a lot,' says Massaro. 'It's nowhere near where I would like to be, but it's a very big number.' Mosquitoes are 'weirdly fragile, considering they're the number-four cause of death in the world'.

Verily aspires to supply the world with Wolbachia-tainted mosquitoes. 'We might have a factory one day that produces 100 million mosquitoes a week,' says Massaro. By producing millions of mosquitoes, they might eliminate millions more.

There seems to be no downside to eliminating *Aedes aegypti* from the US. It is not essential to the food chain. It is invasive. Linus Upson, Verily's head of engineering, is entirely unsentimental. 'The ecological change of removing the mosquito is spectacularly less than the ecological change we brought about by building a city.' Has he ever felt like he is playing God? 'I view it more as just cleaning up the mess that we made.'

Killing off dangerous mosquitoes at precision – this is what our technology can do. In its three-year pilot project in Fresno, Verily released 48 million sterile mosquitoes, causing declines of biting female mosquitoes by up to 84 per cent in peak mosquito season. Other groups have trialled using genetically engineered *Aedes aegypti* in countries like Brazil. It seems likely that at least one of these methods, and probably more, will be adopted widely. Governments will be able to choose how to fight *Aedes aegypti*, depending on their budget and other factors. I left Verily's offices wondering which species might be next for the high-tech firing squad. Maybe another species of mosquito, *Aedes albopictus*, the Asian tiger mosquito, which is also present in the US. In the case of invasive mosquitoes, whose ecological role is small and whose potential to cause suffering is large, it's an easy decision. It may even pave the way for genetic engineering on other species.

As our powers grow, our temptation to kill other invaders will grow. Gene drives could allow entire species to be wiped out deliberately. Alternatively if scientists can find a way to curb the spread of mutations, the effect could be limited to certain populations or a certain number of generations.

Killing could become automated in other ways too. On the Great Barrier Reef, researchers (also part-funded by Google) have developed robots able to identify crown-of-thorns starfish, an invasive species, and inject them with fatal poison. For now, a human would press the trigger, but it's not hard to imagine a scenario where we become redundant.

I once visited S'Albufera national park on the Spanish island of Majorca, where the waterways had become overrun with common carp. (The authorities' best guess is that someone released carp fifteen years ago, with the hope of later fishing them.) The carp, carnivores that grow up to ten kilos, have unbalanced ecosystems in many parts of the world, including the US where they were introduced for sport fishing in the nineteenth century. In S'Albufera, they are a nuisance of an invasive species: they root up the canals, turn the water muddy and prevent plant life from growing. Each year, using nets, hooks and cages, the park authorities extract hundreds of carp from the waterways. It's never enough, and there's no better solution.

Perhaps Google could succeed in controlling invasive species, and bringing down deer populations where hunters have failed. Or perhaps it would backfire. Our attempts to tweak nature have often spun out of control. Stoats were introduced to New Zealand in the 1980s to control rabbit populations; together with rats, they have contributed to the extinction of at least five bird species there. On Marion Island, South Africa, albatross chicks have no evolved defence against the mice who arrived on the island in the past 200 years. In a truly disturbing spectacle, the baby birds just sit in their nests, while the mice gnaw off the skin on their head, leaving their bloodied skulls.

Animal activists do not like the culling of invasive species, arguing that sentient animals are still sentient wherever they are found. Conservationists disagree. But experiences of backfiring interventions have made the conservation industry, well, conservative. Radical ideas are not welcomed. This is why extreme forms of rewilding – such as trying to restore some of the features of the Late Pleistocene, by releasing in North America animals such as Bactrian camels, African cheetahs, and 16,000 domesticated Asian elephants (to preserve the grasslands) – have not gone down well. Conservationists are wary of the ecosystem's unknown unknowns.

Or take a proposal to help the world's most trafficked mammals. Pangolins are rather adorable, often tree-climbers, who are smuggled from Asia and Africa to be cut up for meat and supposedly medicinal scales. 'They're cool, endearing creatures. They're otherworldly,' says Dan Challender, a zoologist at the University of Oxford, who studies them. At least 900,000 have been taken from the wild since 2000. Pangolins curl into balls when threatened. They are often injured when captured. They are thrown into sacks, and left to defecate and urinate on each other while they are transported to market, where they are pulled out, dead or alive. All eight pangolin species are now threatened with extinction – three are critically endangered. One proposal is to farm pangolins, so that poachers stop taking the animals from the wild. But conservationists mainly hate the idea. They worry that a legal trade will just make consumers want more pangolins. Poaching pangolins would still be cheaper than farming them, so wild animals could be passed off as farmed using fake documentation. And of course, if domesticated cows and chickens suffer on farms, good luck to wild pangolins, which seem stressed out by captivity. A similar proposal to legalise the trade in rhino horn has also gone nowhere: one South African farmer, who has bred 1,500 rhinos in the hope the trade would be legalised, is fast going out of business. A group of scientists have come up with a different solution – creating fake rhino horn out of horsehair. Overall conservationists would rather fight invasive species and trafficking through regulation rather than innovation. They are on the same side as animal activists, who don't want to see animals trafficked or farmed.

But the combination of advancing technology and environmental collapse will leave us with decisions to take, where the lives of individual animals could be risked to benefit their species. With climate change, animals no longer 'belong' in a particular place. They are losing their ecological niches. As we've seen, the best way to prevent this is to create protected areas, and to cut carbon emissions drastically. But some species would still have to overcome huge obstacles to find new homes. Australia's golden bowerbirds, bright yellow birds who can build their displays of twigs in the same place for up to thirty years, are limited to cool mountains in Queensland. Those mountains are warming, and to get to cooler mountains further south, the bowerbirds would have to cross hot low-lying areas, for which they are not adapted. Other species simply won't be able to move fast enough. Do we admit we can't save them? Or do we try to help move them?

In the summers of 1999 and 2000, scientists in England caught 500 marbled white butterflies, and 600 small skipper butterflies in nets. They drove the butterflies at least thirty-five kilometres outside their species' then ranges, and, the day after they had captured them, released them. On their own, the butterflies had been only expanding their range by less than a kilometre a year, while the isotherms of northern Britain were moving northwards at 4.5 kilometres a year. The new habitat had been selected as being similar in climate to their previous habitat. Several years later, when the scientists went back, they found that the butterflies had survived. The entire effort for one species took the equivalent of one person working full-time for eight months, plus less than £5,000 in expenses.

Such experiments are known as 'assisted migration'. Scientists also debate the merits of 'assisted evolution', where animals would be selectively bred like livestock for a hotter climate and then released into the wild. Together these methods promise a way for us to help the animals whose ecosystems we are disrupting.

Assisted evolution and assisted migration have had a cool reception from conservationists. The fundamental problem is that they require a detailed understanding of a species and its environment. The Red List shows just how difficult this would be. In nearly half a century, it has surveyed fewer than 2 per cent of the 8 million plant and animal species that might plausibly exist. 'You are rolling a rock up a hill, and it rolls back down and crushes you. But you start rolling it back up again!' says Craig Hilton-Taylor, the unassuming head of the Red List.

Hilton-Taylor is frank about the difficulties involved in keeping track of species. 'When I go to a workshop, I say to the experts, what's the population of this snake? And they'll say – I don't know. And I say, OK, is it more than 10,000? Oh no, it's less than that. Is it more than 2,500? You just try to get them then to narrow it down. The whole time you're trying to take into account people's attitudes to uncertainty, and those vary enormously.'

The Red List is hardly up to date either. The giant armadillo, which is rated vulnerable to extinction, has not been assessed for seven years. The number of mature individuals in the wild is rated decreasing but unknown. Camera traps suggest that, in their native habitat in South American rainforest, there are only six or so giant armadillos in a hundred square kilometres.

The Red List lacks the funding to assess the same groups of animals regularly. It relies on donations from private companies – such as Toyota – and the work of volunteers – such as an orthopaedic surgeon who in his spare time is a world expert on turtles. At the moment, modelling the impact of climate change on species is 'often beyond the technical capabilities of our assessors'.

In Colombia, I worked at a research agency, which was tasked by the government with mapping the country's biodiversity. On first glance, this seemed doable – to map the natural world, just as the Spanish had once mapped Colombia's mountains and rivers. But it was an impossible job, particularly in a country that has coasts on the Pacific and Atlantic, stretches of the Amazon and Orinoco basins, and chunks of the Andes.

Relocating species would be laced with uncertainties, about how species are doing and what ecosystems might look like in the future. Scientists don't know enough about species like the golden bowerbird. If we try to relocate bumblebees struggling with the heat, we risk wiping out native species of bumblebees – and spreading disease, a problem seen among the almond and fruit farmers of California, who use bees on an industrial scale to pollinate their trees.

Overall assisted migration is 'almost impossible to roll out at scale', says Alex Pigot, of University College London. 'On its own, a species focus isn't enough. We can't save them one by one. And that's not how ecosystems work.' If we try to regrow entire ecosystems, our efforts are likely to be expensive and small-scale.

Curbing invasive species is ingenious, but it may be an exception. Micromanaging nature seems beyond our abilities. Instead we can stick to the principles of rewilding, and give nature the chance to play out. We can focus on relocating those extirpated animals like wolves, bears and jaguars, who bind ecosystems.

The simplest way to facilitate the migration of species is to create natural corridors. As well as protecting large areas, governments need to ensure that wildlife can travel between them. Even Yellowstone National Park is not big enough to stop its grizzly bear population – numbering several hundred – being considered genetically isolated; it may have to import bears from Montana's Glacier National Park, 150 miles away, unless another way of connecting the populations can be found. In China pandas cannot meet to breed if large roads carve up their territory. Tigers, who have been well protected in India recently, won't spread across their former range unless there is habitat for them along the way. Migratory species need staging posts; all kinds of species need to be able to move when drought hits. Green crossings can be built across roads; fences can be removed; staging posts – lakes and forests – can be maintained along migration routes. If we create protected areas, and link them, then animals and plants that are displaced by climate change have a chance to find new places where they can thrive. 'It's about making the world a bit more connected again,' says Pigot. Corridors will not save every species or every population, but, in a world where there is limited money for conservation, they still make more sense than assisted migration.

*

If anyone represents the belief that technology can enhance our relationship with the natural world, it is Stewart Brand. Caring for animals can sometimes seem a primitive pursuit. It forces us to see the world from the perspective of beings who generally lack our level of cognitive function, so strips us down from the technological prowess of modern society. Brand views things differently.

In 1968, he published a compendium, *The Whole Earth Catalog*, which proclaimed: 'We are as gods and might as well get used to it.' These days he has tweaked the motto to give more urgency: 'We are as gods and have to get good at it.' He now leads a think tank, the Break-through Institute, whose band of so-called 'eco-modernists' convene in lush surroundings near San Francisco each summer for a high-minded 'dialogue'. They aspire to filter the environmental urgency of Greta Thunberg through the tech evangelism of Mark Zuckerberg.

Brand likes to think long-term. One of his favoured complaints is that the lines on charts don't stretch out far enough. I encountered him at one Breakthrough talk on human population growth, where he complained that the X axis stopped at the year 2100. Perhaps human population would naturally decline rapidly after that, he suggested. The idea of extending the X axis struck me as futile, given how uncertain our projections for 2100 are. But Brand made his point that there's a long view we cannot yet see.

Eco-modernists don't talk about love for the natural world in terms of human restraint and sacrifice. They imagine a world where robotics, machine learning and advanced sensors can keep ecosystems in balance, without us getting our hands dirty. Move over smart cities, here come smart forests, wetlands and grasslands. This is several leaps beyond anything that we are capable of today. But technology is becoming a tool for conservationists, and a way that we interact with wild animals. Drones can count wildlife, machine learning can identify the species caught on camera traps, and soon presumably individual animals too.

Harvard and Cornell universities have been trying to create robotic bees that mimic real bees. Perhaps the bees could act as pollinators. The Harvard–Cornell team hasn't worked out how to co-ordinate the mini-robots to swarm like bees, or to equip them with sufficient power to handle high winds. The RoboBees might be better suited to simpler (if more questionable) tasks, such as surveillance. But if you're an eco-modernist, such experiments are an exciting demonstration of human ingenuity.

Another eco-modernist passion, championed by Brand, is de-extinction. This is not bringing a species back from the grave, but editing a living species so that it replicates the ecological function of an extinct species. Rather than resurrecting the woolly mammoth, the plan is to adapt the Asian elephant to cold climates by editing several genes. The goal is not for the animal's sake, or to satisfy our curiosity: it's to 'restore vital ecological functions', in the words of Ben Novak, who leads Brand's de-extinction initiative. Novak himself is working to bring back the American passenger pigeon, hunted to extinction in the early twentieth century and which, he argues, has a key role in disturbing the forest so that other species can thrive. He plans to gene-edit its closest genetic relative, the band-tailed pigeon, and is hoping to release the first test flocks sometime between 2030 and 2040.

This is all underpinned by the philosophy of the Anthropocene: we control everything anyway, either by our deliberate acts or by our omissions, so why not ensure it's the former? Gene-editing is therefore only turning our power to beneficial purposes. 'There is no species alive today that has not adapted in some way to human activities of the past and thus become changed from its prehuman contact state,' Novak has written. This is evidently true. What's controversial is the response. Novak and others working on de-extinction truly love the natural world. But ultimately their technologies remain dreams. And most geneticists are dubious of de-extinction. Simple descriptions of gene-editing make the process sound like a cut-and-paste, but mimicking a whole species would require multiple, complex changes, perhaps more akin to trying to recreate a rainforest from scratch on a spare piece of land.

What does the prospect of de-extinction mean for animal-lovers? Could we worry less about the extinction of millions of species, if we knew that we could recreate similar creatures? I think not, given the uncertainties involved. De-extinction doesn't affect our responsibility to stop the emptying of animals from earth. There's no point being able to breed animals, if there's nowhere for them to live. Mostly we should be going around raising money for that.

De-extinction is, however, an intriguing possibility where we haven't been able to save certain species. If it might be possible someday, perhaps we have a responsibility not to make it impossible. A few years ago, an American geneticist called Harris Lewin realised his research was hitting a wall: he wanted to map how species had diverged, but there weren't enough sequenced genomes to continue. On a plane across the Atlantic, he ordered a gin and tonic and used the napkin to work out how much it would cost to map the genomes of all eukaryotes – that is, animals, plants, fungi and any other creature whose DNA is found in the nucleus of a cell.

That back-of-the-napkin calculation became the basis for a serious project to create a digital repository of life – the Earth BioGenome Project. For Lewin, the alternative is that we lose species forever. 'We're losing maybe a couple of hundred species on the planet every day and that's accelerating. So if we don't change, you can do the math,' he said. 'We don't know what science will be able to do in the future ... If we have the digital information – if we know the sequence of the whole genome – it may be possible to de-extinct, resurrect, whatever you want to call it. It's science fiction, but so is that cell phone you're holding.'

The process of sequencing genomes might even change our perspective on life. California's redwood trees, for example, have genomes than are ten times bigger than our own. 'It kind of puts us in our place, it humbles us, to say we're your average mammal-sized genome,' says Lewin. 'We're nothing different to a cow.'

Lewin's team has estimated the cost of the BioGenome Project at $4.7 billion, not entirely dissimilar to what he had written on his napkin. It would be like a fire insurance policy. Would it be a better use of money than trying to extinguish the fire, by buying tropical forests for conservation? Probably not, but maybe a billionaire will disagree.

*

There are two types of conservationist: those, like Stewart Brand, who are fundamentally optimistic, and those, like Doug and Kris Tompkins, who think technology got us into this mess and isn't going to get us out. The optimists can point to the fact that, contrary to some predictions in the 1970s, humans have not run out of food and other materials. We have improved agricultural productivity, and started to curb our population growth voluntarily. The pessimists can point to the fact that climate change shows no sign of being controlled, and hundreds of thousands of species may soon go extinct.

If you're an optimist, you can also say that technology will free us to be less cruel to animals. We might produce stem-cell meat instead of livestock. One of Brand's projects is to stop the pharmaceutical industry from using the blood of horseshoe crabs in vaccines. Since the 1970s the crabs' light-blue blood has been the only source of a substance that detects bacterial contaminants. (Drugmakers previously used rabbits, euthanising hundreds of thousands a year.) Today around 500,000 crabs are caught off the east coast of the US, and then bled each year in laboratories. At least 130,000 die afterwards – either because they are sold as bait, or because they die after returning to the water. Atlantic horseshoe crabs have been relatively unchanged for 450 million years, but they are dying out now, because their blood helps to keep us healthy. A synthetic alternative is going through regulatory processes. It is the best bet for the Atlantic horseshoe crab, and the seabirds that rely on it for eggs.

If you're a pessimist, however, technology could jeopardise our relationship with other animals further. We could continue to find new ways to suck up the earth's resources, for example through deep-sea mining. We could spend more time staring at screens, and less in the natural world. We could strengthen ourselves so much, through biological and robotic implants, that we become a new type of being. In 2020 Elon Musk showed the world several pigs with computer chips and electrodes implanted in their brains. The billionaire's ultimate aim isn't to enhance pigs: it's to allow humans to merge with artificial intelligence. What's more, through synthetic biology, we may have the power to create new species that have no evolutionary ancestors. In 2019, a British laboratory announced that it had created the world's first entirely synthetic bacteria. Martin Rees, a brilliant and humane astrophysicist, has speculated that we 'are perhaps near the end of Darwinian evolution'.

This would be a break in a chain, a kicking away of the ladder. There are signs that we have started to see ourselves as separate from our environment. The idea of creating human settlements on the moon and Mars, as promoted by Musk and Jeff Bezos, suggests that humans can be extracted from the climate, the food system and even the companionship that we receive here on earth. Art Harman, an enthusiast for colonising Mars, who had access to the Trump administration, once claimed that the advantages of living in space would include a lack of endangered-species legislation.

Good luck with that. What animal is going to pollinate our food? What organism will break down our waste? What creature will feed on that organism to keep it in check? As Harris Lewin points out, 'We can't go alone. We'll bring plants. And microbes and bacteria – they'll come with us because they're on us.' The pilgrims on the *Mayflower* brought pigs and chickens; rich people going to outer space would surely insist on taking their pet dogs and cats.

I think it's one thing to leave the door open for new technologies, like de-extinction and alternatives to medical research. It's another to expect those technologies to save us from our ethical dilemmas. In the wrong hands, tech optimism and long-term thinking relax us too much. They distract from the decisions we have to take now – before the technologies are available. They make us believe that human ingenuity will fix everything. They make us think cruelty to animals and the sixth extinction are just phases that we will pass through.

As for colonising space, what do we think we're escaping from? As one animal-loving techie put it to me: 'The biggest risk to the planet is not a giant asteroid. It's humans. By putting humans on another planet, that risk will still be there.' And what do we think we're going to find? If we're looking for other intelligent life forms, they are right here on earth. Laurance Doyle, the astrophysicist who studies humpback whales, says, 'There's no reason to stare at the stars, and ask, are we alone?, when there are all these critters [on earth] trying to communicate.'

Over the past century, the push for innovation has given us deformed chickens, cloned dogs and, probably quite soon, farmed octopuses. We didn't need any of it to understand the basis for animal emotions, veganism, ethical hunting and moderating consumption. Those arguments have been around since at least the nineteenth century – we just didn't take them seriously. Similarly our relationship with animals won't suddenly become less problematic if we find ourselves able to understand animal language, create hybrids of existing and extinct species, and build robots that can manage ecosystems. We don't need new technologies; we need to change ourselves. Restraint will take us further than ingenuity.

CONCLUSION
BEAUTY AND THE BEAST

A child's world is fresh and new and beautiful, full of wonder and excitement. It is our misfortune that for most of us, that clear-eyed vision, that true instinct for what is beautiful and awe-inspiring, is dimmed and even lost before we reach adulthood.

Rachel Carson

Often I am asked if I prefer chimpanzees to humans. The answer to that is easy – I prefer some chimpanzees to some humans, some humans to some chimpanzees!

Jane Goodall

There's a small pond in our garden in London. The first time my parents came to visit, they identified it as a drowning risk for children, and insisted that it should be drained. It was a sensible suggestion, but because it came from my parents, I ignored it. The pond stayed. I had no idea how much I would love it.

In the spring frogspawn appeared. Eliza and I would crouch down by the stone edge and look for frogs. Sometimes their eyes would be barely above the surface, other times they would scurry below the water, and just occasionally they would freeze in full view. They were common frogs – but they provoked a strange emotion that I suppose resembled pride, joy and respect, and yet was not exactly any of those things. The pond was a tiny scene of wildness, and I thought it would be the backdrop to my children's lives.

The next year the pond sprung a leak. Every time I filled it up, it emptied as surely as a college student's tequila glass. So I carefully decanted the frogspawn into buckets, with the intention of fixing the pond, and then I carelessly did nothing about it. I went to San Francisco for three months. Needless to say, there were no frogs that year. Eliza took it in her stride: 'Daddy has taken the frogs to America.' I returned from America with a suntan but no frogs, and my daughter made clear her disappointment. 'When are the frogs going to come back?' she would ask plaintively.

In the aftermath of the Second World War, George Orwell published an essay about watching amphibians in London, entitled 'Some Thoughts on the Common Toad'. It reads curiously now. Orwell feels he has to apologise for writing about something so 'sentimental': 'I know by experience that a favourable reference to "Nature" in one of my articles is liable to bring me abusive letters.' He relishes the fact that the joys of spring will be there for as long as humans want to enjoy them: 'The atom bombs are piling up in the factories, the police are prowling through the cities, the lies are streaming from the loudspeakers, but the earth is still going round the sun, and neither the dictators nor the bureaucrats, deeply as they disapprove of the process, are able to prevent it.'

Things feel quite different now. Unlike Orwell, we don't have to apologise for loving nature. We also don't have the certainty to think that nature will survive in its current form. The seasons come round, but their meaning shifts every year. The worst leaders in the world, like Bolsonaro in Brazil, really do seem to change nature itself. It might sound overdramatic, but the disappearance of the frogs from our pond felt to me like a microcosm of what we are doing to the planet. I didn't want my daughters to have to face it.

I'm a clumsy gardener, better at purchasing plants than pruning them. I had tried to find the leak in the pond's rubber lining and failed. Eventually I found two tears, each no bigger than a cat's paw in the lining. I patched them up. The next spring, there was frogspawn again.

I watched the first few tadpoles wriggle free. I felt wildness returning. The tadpoles grew eyes then legs. They clambered up onto the stones then fell over backwards with the weight of their tails. I'm not sure how they learnt or what they learnt. But as I watched copper-brown froglets escape through our overgrown garden, I felt the company of animals again. I started grasping for more.

*

Hens are warmer than I expect. As I place my hands under the cardboard box, I feel the heat of their bodies. I look in the top and see two chickens, both quite brown, big, and not entirely feathered. I can see the bare skin around their tails, reddened and sore.

I umm-ed and ah-ed about adopting chickens. I jumped for a few reasons. First, these were egg-laying hens whose productivity was dropping. They were slated for slaughter, so I felt like the bar for my adopting skills was pretty low. I thought that, if my children were vegetarians rather than vegans, they could at least know what eggs involved. I also thought that, if coronavirus restrictions were going to stretch for months, we would need all the company we could find. I had heard of people falling in love with hens. Most naïvely of all, I thought that maybe if people who came to my house met some chickens, they would be less likely to eat chickens.

So I spend an absurd amount of money on a coop, and I put my name down on a list run by a hen rescue group. I pay a £6 donation for two hens. One Saturday I drive with Eliza and Cleo to a farmhouse north of London. Due to social distancing, we are given a ten-minute slot. When we get there, it's raining so hard that we feel no inclination to stay longer than sixty seconds. I take the cardboard box, place it in the boot, and decline the offer of an extra chicken.

It's only when we arrive home I can take a proper look at the chickens. Their feet are formidable. Someone needs to lift our two hens out and gently onto the ground, so they don't break their fragile bones. I realise it can't be me.

Susie rolls her eyes. 'You could have mentioned you were scared of chickens,' she says, as she places our hens in their new home.

Eliza names one hen Patilda, Cleo calls the other Kakiyaki. The next day, Sunday, it becomes clear that Patilda is not well. She mainly perches sadly. She receives a few, aggressive pecks from Kakiyaki. Her comb shrivels over to one side. Susie tries to get her to drink water, with a plastic syringe that we use for the kids' medicine, but the hen isn't interested.

Patilda's ill health does not escape Eliza's notice. On Monday, before going to nursery, she swaps the names of the birds, so that 'her' hen, the new Patilda, is suddenly the one in better shape. Cleo is too young to notice she's been had. The light relief doesn't last very long. I'd never felt emotional attachment to a chicken, but as Kakiyaki – formerly known as Patilda – huddles on a wooden strut, her body language strikes me as not very different to a sick person's. I spend an hour on the phone trying to find a vet who will look at a chicken. Eventually I get an appointment miles away. But Kakiyaki won't make it.

Susie finds the hen lying on the ground in the coop. She has ceased to be, expired, gone to see her maker. The charity asks if we want £3 of our donation back. But unlike John Cleese in the Monty Python sketch, I don't feel out of pocket. I feel sick, and so does Susie. The indignity of the hen's final hours, our inability to help her. Kakiyaki was an animal, she had a life, and if the cards had fallen differently, she would still be living it. 'Poor little mite, so close to a chance of a happy life out of a cage,' says a nice woman from the British Hen Welfare Trust. 'Sometimes their little bodies just cannot cope and they rather shut down.' I take her body to a vet's, where a dog-owner chuckles at my predicament. I pay £15 for what I grimly realise would in other circumstances be called a barbecue. We tell Eliza and Cleo that Kakiyaki has gone back to the farm.

Patilda thrives. Her feathers grow back, brown and white. She sees off Crumble's forlorn attempts to hunt her. She speeds round the garden like a kid in a playground – digging into this bit, perching on that bit. She dust-bathes in our herbs. Quite soon, it becomes her garden rather than ours. Then she wants to come in the kitchen. All this time I thought chickens wanted to be free range, and now it turns out they want a terraced house too. Patilda waits till the back door is ajar, and then outruns us to the threshold. She feasts on the crumbs beneath the kids' chairs. When I am working on my laptop in the living room, she comes and pecks on the window.

I can't say that Patilda is an ideal pet. She disappoints Eliza and Cleo by not laying any eggs. She disappoints them more by pecking them to the point where their main way of interacting with her is to see how fast they can run away from her coop. When I sit in the garden, Patilda approaches my chair – generally from behind and from below. My eyes twitch. My muscles tighten. Do I wait to be pecked? Or do I move? I move, obviously. Patilda is the hen, but I am the chicken.

Even so, Patilda is a marvel. She is curious, she is determined, she dwarfs any other bird who has been into our garden. How ridiculous to keep animals like this in small spaces, I think. How silly to imagine their brains and feelings could be an afterthought in our own appetite. I become used to picking her up, and I enjoy setting aside the leaves from vegetables for her. We buy her nicer bedding, which she likes, and a mirror, which she doesn't.

And then in the middle of September, Patilda's behaviour changes. She had once put herself to bed around sunset, settling in one of the three nesting boxes. Now she starts hiding around the garden. A couple of nights she sleeps in the large bamboo bush instead of her coop. I try cleaning the nesting boxes, and buy a spray in case she is being afflicted by red mite. One evening I can't find Patilda in the darkness. It's late, and I assume she will be fine, as she had been those previous nights.

In the morning I glance through Eliza's curtains, and see a white and brown splodge on the lawn. I know at once that it is Patilda's flattened body. I always said that I would rather the hens had a free-range life, even if it meant they were at more risk from foxes. Of course I wish that hadn't been necessary. Of course I wish I'd managed to lock her up that night. 'Nest in peace', they say on the hen-lovers' Facebook page.

There comes a point when you don't have to pretend to your kids any more. It's earlier than you think. Kids' books and films are full of animal brutality. Foxes eat pigs and chickens, wolves eat boys and girls. A few weeks before Patilda dies, Susie's grandmother had died. In a modern twist, a death in the family had prepared us for the death of a pet, rather than vice versa. So that morning before breakfast, we tell the girls the truth – that Patilda has been taken by a fox. 'Foxes eat chickens,' says Eliza, and I think she's understood. 'Will she have to live underground because foxes live underground?' she then says, and I'm not so sure. Then Eliza cries, and I hug her, but I am half-hugging Patilda too, the hen who never really wanted to be hugged.

'Is Patilda sad?' Eliza says. I clench my teeth, and think of the head-less hen in a Sainsbury's bag outside the kitchen door. 'I don't think so,' I say. We make porridge, and listen to a children's story. For two months we were a family with a chicken. Now we are not.

Some people will think I was an ignorant, careless adopter. Believe me, I've thought this myself. Although we didn't extend the lives of our two chickens very much, I like to think that Patilda at least had a couple of happy months of liberty in the sun. We gave her freedom, and treats, and space. I was responsible for Patilda's death. But we are all respon-sible for the fates of animals through how we live.

People will find their own ways to connect with other animals; the hens were mine. Patilda was not exactly livestock, or a pet. She was simply a sentient, unique creature. It's easy to love magnificent animals half the world away – the elephants, the jaguars, the koalas. It's harder to recognise the meaning of another life, which is not so filled with beauty and slightly filled with nuisance. We eat chickens now, but we used to eat blackbirds. We don't have to farm livestock forever. We can choose to live differently. Hens are warmer than you expect, and so are humans.

*

To love animals is not just to be amazed by other species. It is to reflect on them and to question ourselves. I see the animal test in three stages. The first is to check whether we do really care about animals. We do. You can go to almost any news website on any day of the year, and find a story about some newly discovered wonder of the natural world. Who isn't amazed to hear that an Arctic fox has travelled from Norway to Canada, 3,506 kilometres in just seventy-six days? Or that lobsters use social distancing, by identifying sick fellow lobsters and shunning them? When I started this book, I knew people who loved pandas, kangaroos, parrots and other charismatic species. Now I know there are people who feel just as strongly about chickens, moths and dragonflies. A large majority of Americans say they want farm animals treated fairly, and a large majority of Europeans say that fish feel pain. A significant minority in the US and the UK don't want animals to be used in medical testing that could benefit humans. We have got one big thing right – we do love animals.

The second step is whether our actions follow through on this. They clearly don't. We are eating our planet, and causing immense suffering to sentient beings as we do so. We are making life impossible for many wild animals, and endangering ourselves. Earth is finite. The more space we take up, the less is left for wild animals. A management consultant from Mars would be entirely baffled by the balance we have struck. Love has limits. You could call it the Meatloaf caveat: I will do anything for love, but I won't do that. When it comes to giving up animal produce, the cost to us is small, but the benefit to animals is immense. So the Meatloaf exemption should not apply to actual meatloaf.

We think of meat-eating as the traditional option, the safe option. Actually it's the risky one. In environmental terms, we are going at full speed, and we are about to go round a corner into the unknown. If we don't cut back on meat and dairy – not just by a little bit, but by a whole lot – we won't be able to control climate change, and we will condemn hundreds of thousands of species to extinction. One vision is that lions and giraffes will be confined to only a few parks. Another is that an ever greater proportion of animals will live in the human orbit, like urban foxes and burrowing owls. 'People tend to think that domestication happened a long time ago. But we're doing it now,' Naomi Sykes, of Exeter University, told me. 'There'll be dogs, cats, foxes, pigeons and nothing else.' That's deliberate hyperbole, but it should make us think.

The hardest part of the animal test was not sweeping up sheep innards in an abattoir, or even reaching into the straw to retrieve suffocated dead piglets, although I wouldn't recommend either. It was confronting the cognitive dissonance of people who love animals and resist facing the obvious implications. Most of us have learnt to categorise animals to justify our treatment of them: some animals are food, some are pets, some are majestic animals worthy of saving. We have so many opportunities to realise that these categories are nonsense, and for the most part, we chicken out.

The third stage of the animal test asks if there is a better way. There obviously is. Changing our food system would open up a new relationship with animals. We should be protecting and restoring wild spaces, and relentlessly fighting climate change. We should realise that we are not clever enough to keep animals happily in zoos, or keep breeding dogs into strange shapes and sizes without compromising their health.

Our love for animals will never quite be rational. With our fellow humans, we aspire to treat everyone fairly – not to discriminate on grounds of gender or race. With other animals, we seem hardwired to discriminate. We are obsessed by pandas, because of their flat faces, large eyes and upright postures. We may have evolved to fear snakes; we should certainly evolve a dislike of mosquitoes. Loving animals does not mean loving all animals equally: this is not an HR department. But we can recognise what different animals have in common – that crows are sentient, intelligent and well adapted, just like cheetahs; that ants matter for the environment, just like otters do. Our love for some species can rub off on the others.

Our tendency for outrage will never quite be rational either. For the foreseeable future, social media will combust more over hunting, even though it's habitat loss that leads to the death of far more animals. If people want to take aim at wasteful holidays, the first on the list should be cruises. Tourists on cruises to Antarctica, many of them environmentally conscious, each emit eight times as much greenhouse gas as the average international tourist. Remarkably, most of them said, in one 2010 study, that they didn't think their trip affected climate change. At least trophy-hunters pay for land conservation.

Some animal rights activists may never be persuaded of the conservation benefits of hunting. But perhaps they can at least accept that there are more urgent ways to reduce animal suffering and to increase animal populations. Since the nineteenth century, animal activism has focused on cruelty – actions where humans are intending to inflict harm on animals. What really threatens animals today is not cruelty, so much as thoughtlessness. We focus on the harm we see in front of us. We underestimate the effect that meat-eating and flying has on climate change.

It's time to put aside our old animal categories, and time to treat animals instead in terms of our values. One value is our desire to not cause suffering. This means that all animals who are likely to suffer pain – from the apes to birds to fish and insects – deserve consideration. They have complex, evolved needs, which we probably don't understand. Just because they survive in very different conditions – farms, zoos, laboratories – does not mean they are thriving. Most people spend less than two hours in a zoo, yet they assume animals are happy to spend two decades there. When we inhibit animals' natural behaviour, when we expose them to strain or sudden death, we must apply a high threshold. The fact that pigs taste nice, or that cow's milk is what we drank as kids, simply doesn't cut it. One day we may have some solid basis to compare the moral value of cows, chickens, salmon and pigs. For now, it's sufficient to say that we should be causing much less suffering to all of them.

Another value is to allow animals to exist. Modern humans are not striving for domination. We are striving for a sense of justice. We need to accommodate animals – in our cities, on our farms, and in wild spaces. The Matsigenka people of the Peruvian Amazon understand that animals need the forest, just as humans need the village. The forest is 'not a natural order, it's a social order', Glenn Shepard, an anthropologist who has studied the Matsigenka, told me. The more we understand that animals have social relationships and consciousness, the more reluctant we will be to deprive them of life. The less we rely on animals for food, clothing and other products, the more we will be able to appreciate their needs.

I started off this book wanting clear answers: does a farm animal have a good life? Would a zoo animal like to be set free? Or even, how many deer are there in the United States? At times there are obvious answers: of course a pregnant pig wants enough space to turn around. Other times the living world is too complex, and funding is too sparse. At best we get partial answers: zebrafish *seem* to have consciousness, caged mink *seem* to become bored, assisted migration *might* work.

In Scotland, on an involuntary visit to one of Donald Trump's golf courses, I met a man who had given up running a fishing shop, because salmon numbers had dropped precipitously. Scientists were trying to ascertain why – but he was scornful. 'They'll still be researching when the last fish dies,' he muttered. I wonder if we'll still be researching the welfare of European zoo elephants when the last member of that population dies. Or whether we'll still be weighing up the health impacts of the Labradoodle by the time that breed falls out of popularity. Without timely scientific research, we would not have grasped the danger that certain pesticides pose to bees or that climate change poses to the whole animal kingdom. But just as often, we are faced with uncertainty. That uncertainty leads us to exercise caution – why farm fish and octopuses if there's at least a good likelihood that they will suffer? It also leads us to humility.

You can't write about animals without recognising yourself as one. This is a disconcerting process. It pierces through education and culture. It forced me to think about myself as a member of a species, adapted for a particular moment in the earth's history, its fate inextricably bound with many others. Each time I thought about the fair way for animals to live and die, there was an implicit subtext: they are all going to die sometime, and we are too. We have long lives compared to octopuses, but not compared to Greenland sharks, who live for perhaps up to five centuries. Either way, we have to accept the reality summed up by Harry Greene, a snake expert and one of the world's wisest conservation biologists: 'the cosmos doesn't turn on individual lives'. There is a theory that, because animals confront us with our own mortality, we become less sympathetic to them the more we think about them. This wasn't my experience. Recognising that we are not on this planet for very long should make us even keener to be kind while we are here, and to safeguard what exists for future generations.

I recognised myself as an animal, but I also recognised humans as very special animals. We are, as the University of Auckland's Alex Taylor puts it, 'amazingly co-operative compared to many animal species' – with unparalleled abilities to plan and to pass on cultural adaptations to our children. Each day I am with my daughters, I see that in action

– not so much the amazingly co-operative bit (I'll give my daughters some time), but the passing on of culture. Yet it's not just one-way. My attempts to teach my daughters how to treat animals have also been about changing my own habits. 'Will the snail be happy or sad?' Eliza asked as I tried to save the beetroot we'd planted together. This whole process has taught me as much as it has taught them.

This book is mostly about what we've got wrong. But I hope for a future where humans recognise what they share with animals – where we put less effort into owning animals, and more into accommodating them alongside us. If I could sum up my desired relationship with animals in one sentence, it would be: deliberate domestication is a dead end, wildness is the path that takes us where we need to go.

*

In the winter of 2019, I met a woman called Amanda Millar, who had turned part of her home into an amateur bat hospital. She believed that wounded wild bats should be given the chance to recover or live out their days. 'If you put yourself in their position, you wouldn't want to be put down just because you've lost an arm,' she told me, adding the caveat that she could never know what the bats were thinking. She spent £1,500 a year on worms to feed her bats. 'Just occasionally if you release one at dawn it will bump into other bats and they'll fly around. That brings tears to your eyes,' she explained.

Bat numbers have fallen in England due to the loss of forests and the decline in insects. Millar put me in touch with a group of bat enthusiasts, who survey local populations, and lobby for adaptations like bat bricks that make the animals' lives a little easier. Such efforts try to remedy humans' failure to make fundamental changes to our cities and our agriculture.

I joined one of the surveys in a railway tunnel in Sussex, south of London. We walked into the semi-darkness, shining torches at the brickwork. The bats were small. Some of them, huddled in crevices, were barely distinguishable as bats. They were present in much smaller numbers too. We saw around a dozen in the tunnel. The volunteers had a few worries – perhaps the winter was a little warm, and too few were hibernating – but overall they went away happy, and so did I. Along the way, we discussed how the public had a negative view of bats, partly because of Dracula, partly because of disease. You could have known that SARS had been hosted by bats, and still felt, in Amanda Millar's bat hospital or in that Sussex tunnel, that the idea of the natural world as a source of disease was remote. Unbeknownst to us, Chinese hospitals were already dealing with the first victims of coronavirus.

Coronavirus is a parable for the absurdity of human practices. If non-human animals could have designed a disease to teach us the error of our ways, they couldn't have come up with anything more effective. We now understand what zoonotic diseases are, and how our disruption of ecosystems, by removing some of the predators that control pathogens, makes them more prevalent. Actually we'd known it all along, we'd just denied it. In May 2010, the Obama administration's National Security Strategy concluded: 'Climate change and pandemic disease threaten the security of regions and the health and safety of the American people.' Exactly ten years after that was published the US reached 100,000 deaths from coronavirus – or to be more grimly precise, its first 100,000 deaths from coronavirus.

At the time of writing, the pandemic's legacy is far from clear. The disruption led to farm animals being inhumanely culled across the world. But it also led China to signal the end of selling wild animals for food (albeit not for medicine), and to reclassify dogs as companion animals, rather than livestock. The Netherlands accelerated a ban on mink fur farming, after finding the animals could spread Covid-19. The pandemic temporarily reduced global greenhouse gas emissions, but in the most socially damaging way possible. The Glasgow climate summit was delayed until 2021, when it made some progress, but only scratched the surface of our broken food system. There were sharp declines in tourism and trophy-hunting that make many protected areas viable. In the quiet days of lockdown, we heard birdsong, and attuned to nature. We wondered if our frenzy of activity was really necessary. The wealth we have created had not made us impregnable; our busy lives could come to a complete halt. If that didn't make us realise our fragility, what would? Many people could finally spend more time with their dogs. Many households adopted pets, albeit often without the wholesale rethink of breeding and environmental impact that is needed. We realised our spiritual reliance on animals: the BBC broadcast a special episode of *Planet Earth* 'to raise our spirits'. Our reliance was bluntly physiological too. All of the drugs used to treat Covid-19 had been tested on animals. Many clinical trials into potential new treatments used cells from a line taken from an African green monkey decades earlier. Mice, pigs and rhesus macaques were used to develop new potential vaccines. Hamsters were fitted with surgical masks, to see whether the face coverings affected the spread and severity of the virus. The race for a vaccine briefly placed attention on the plight of horseshoe crabs, whose blood is drained and used to make medicines safe.

The hope is what endures is humility towards the natural world. That depends on us. Coronavirus showed us that we cannot isolate ourselves from the effects of destroying nature. We must realise, too, that there is no normal to return to, just a set of contradictory, unsustainable practices. There is no reason to think that this will be the worst pandemic we face in our lifetimes. We are seeing more diseases cross from animals. We may have entered an age of pandemics. Climate change will allow pathogens to spread to new parts of the world. Moreover, with extreme weather and rising sea-levels, we worry about our world becoming uninhabitable. But for millions of animals, it has already become uninhabitable. Animals are not just reminders of our evolutionary past. They are reminders of our future. We are the smartest species on earth; why do we insist on being the dumbest too?

Anthony Waldron, the conservationist at the University of Cambridge, talks about people's 'conceptual backyard' – the animals we encounter either in person, or through books, TV and social media. For most of us, it probably includes our pets, a few storybook images of farms, and the delights of wildlife documentaries. The quickest way to improve how we treat animals is to expand our conceptual backyard, while shrinking the number of hectares that we actually tread on. Even in the busiest cities, animals are everywhere.

As a child, I learnt to be amazed by pandas and tigers. With my own daughters, I am now learning to find greater beauty throughout the natural world. As I write these last words, my cat is clambering over the keyboard and a magpie is flying back and forth at the window. A bee has just flown into the windowpane. If we open our eyes and our minds, we realise that we are not alone on this planet. We should stop acting as if we are.

HOW TO LOVE ANIMALS

What you can do

1. Stop eating meat, or start on the journey. Even with the best intentions, it's impossible to eat meat only from good farms. And even good farms push animals' bodies to the limit, and create unnecessary emissions. The system is rotten, and vegan food is not. You don't have to switch overnight: do what feels comfortable, and see where you end up. Change is contagious. By changing what you eat, you can nudge those around you who may have been asking the same questions.

2. Give up dairy. Humans are not baby cows and there is no humane way of producing dairy at scale. Cutting out dairy may well reduce your carbon emissions more than cutting out meat. One way is to start by ordering vegan options in restaurants: eating out is when you have the least control over the origin of animal products.

3. Eat less fish. Try to eat fish caught only by low-impact, small-scale fishing boats. Even better, limit yourself to seafood that is sustainable and doesn't suffer – farmed mussels, oysters and clams.

4. Experience the wild. Go camping. Go birdwatching. Go hunting (for deer, not for released birds). Feel the natural world and become angry that we are destroying it. The creatures around us – frogs, crows, dragonflies, foxes – are just as beautiful and their behaviour, in the wild, is more fascinating than anything in zoos.

5. Or don't. Treating animals justly doesn't mean you have to love them. It just means believing that other creatures' suffering matters. You can do that from your sofa.

6. Offset your pet. For every pound you spend on your pet, spend another helping other species. Donate to conservation organisations. Place stickers on your windows to stop birds dying in collisions. Build habitats for frogs and bees.

7. Shrink your footprint. We're squeezing wild animals off the planet. Ask for second-hand birthday presents. Give up flying. Take pleasure in things that don't arrive in huge boxes; take pleasure in things that aren't things.

8. Tell kids the truth. Let's not pretend that the world has to be like this. Let's not try to explain away the way we treat animals. Let's not acclimatise kids to meat and dairy and mad consumerism. It's their world we're sabotaging. It's their arrival that can push us to change. We have screwed up a lot – let kids embarrass us into doing better.

What we can do together

1. Demand transparency over meat and clothing. People should know how animal products are produced. Milk, leather, chicken and farmed salmon are four areas where consumers are shopping in the dark. Sunlight will bring higher standards. For factory chickens and pigs, it may bring actual sunlight. The goal is the end of the cruelty and waste of factory farming.

2. Promote vegan foods. People eat more meat outside the home, because that is what's on offer. Schools and public buildings should offer as many vegan options as they do meat and fish. Governments should use planning laws and agricultural subsidies to boost the least-polluting, highest-welfare foods.

3. Create national parks and fill them with species. There is time to protect 30 per cent, or even 50 per cent, of our land and sea, but we have to act now. This is the best way to keep animal populations healthy. It promotes mental well-being and tourism. If you're a billionaire, there's no better way to spend your money. If you're not, you can still lobby and donate. We need large reserves, connected by corridors across agricultural land and through urban areas. We should introduce the species that previous generations drove out. But where local people pay the price they must be compensated fairly.

4. Show children the outdoors. We love animals before we go to school, then we have to learn to love them again after we've left. We should let our kids see how nature works, and how unbalanced our relationship with other species is. Our curriculums could do more, including a dedicated natural history syllabus. But most of all, children need to be taken outside, away from concrete – to gardens in schools, to parks and wetlands. They can only fight for what they know.

5. Be more critical of zoos, less critical of ethical hunting. The zoo today is a pastiche of the natural world and a recipe for frustrated animals. Zoos should focus on supporting animal populations in the wild, through breeding programmes and land purchases. There is no point in demonising hunting, when it can provide money for conservation and when populations of deer, wild boar and other animals threaten ecosystems.

6. Cut greenhouse gas emissions. Climate change threatens everything. We need to insulate our homes, phase out coal and gas power stations, electrify our transport system, and more. Our aim should be net zero by 2040. It'll happen only if environmental credentials are at the top of our minds every time we go into the voting booth. The sooner we move away from fossil fuels, the less damage to other species – and ourselves.

ACKNOWLEDGEMENTS

It takes a village to raise a child and another village to write a book, so I am now indebted to some serious urban sprawl. My agent Carrie Plitt, of Felicity Bryan Associates, made me believe that I could write on this subject and provided wisdom along the way. I have been lucky to have two exceptional editors: Bea Hemming at Jonathan Cape in London and Paul Slovak at Viking in New York. Their instincts were invariably better than my own. Thanks also to Anna Redman Aylward, Victoria Murray-Browne, Alice Johnstone and David Milner for their superb support.

My reporting relied on the generosity of many researchers, activists and others, including Dan O'Neill, David MacDonald, Tiana Claussen, Alex Taylor, David Williams, Alex Lockwood, Georgia Mason, Lynne Sneddon, Jonathan Birch, Cwyn Solvi, Luke Steele, Will Travers, Tim Ashton and Yuichiro Kanematsu. Countless other people were kind enough to share stories about how animals had affected their lives.

Thanks to Susannah Gibson, Alexander Lees, Darragh Hare, Hugh Costello, Miles King, James Crabtree, Seb Falk, Ed Wethered, Jonathan Mance, Megan Murray-Pepper, Glen Goodman, Edward Davey and David Hancocks, who read draft chapters and provided valuable feedback. Holly O'Donnell fact-checked the text. Any errors remain my responsibility.

My editors at the *Financial Times*, particularly Alec Russell, gave me the freedom to write this book and restrained their bafflement when they found out that I wanted to work in an abattoir. I hope the text reassures them that I won't be switching careers. Thank you also to all those who work at the British Library. It is one of the greatest places in London, even if, at time of writing, it charges £4.50 for a vegan donut.

I would like to give special thanks to my daughters, Eliza and Cleo, for making me think about animals in unexpected ways, and to our cat Crumble, for agreeing not to lie on my laptop long enough for me to jot some of these thoughts down. Most of all, I am contractually obliged to thank my wife, Susie Braun, without whom this book and so much else would never have happened.

SOURCES

In writing this book, I've drawn from a wide selection of books, academic journals and news reporting, as well as my own interviews. Detailed references are available online at hmance.medium.com. Here are some of the sources that I found most helpful and enjoyable, and some suggestions for further reading.

Introduction

The influence of animals in human history, particularly the European colonisation of North America, is covered in Jared Diamond's *Guns, Germs and Steel*. Frans de Waal's *Mama's Last Hug: Animal Emotions and What They Teach Us About Ourselves* details what we have learnt about other animals' mental and social complexity, as do Jane Goodall's various accounts of her research, such as *Through a Window: My Thirty years with the Chimpanzees of Gombe*. Adam Rutherford's *The Book of Humans* is an entertaining review of what does and doesn't make humans unique. On elephant grief, see Barbara J. King's *How Animals Grieve*. Todd Feinberg and Jon Mallatt's theory on shared vertebrate consciousness is found in their book *The Ancient Origins of Consciousness: How the Brain Created Experience*.

Peter Singer's *Animal Liberation* is an essential, compelling read for anyone interested in animal suffering. Mark Sagoff argued that animal activists and conservationists were doomed to quarrel in his paper, 'Animal Liberation and Environmental Ethics: Bad Marriage, Quick Divorce'. Details about Peter Scott's life are taken from Elspeth Huxley's biography *Peter Scott: Painter and Naturalist*. I have drawn on Janet Browne's two-volume biography of Charles Darwin, *Voyaging* and *The Power of Place*.

The 1977 study on shoppers buying tights was 'Telling more than we can know: Verbal reports on mental processes', by Richard Nisbett and Timothy Wilson. *Why We Love and Exploit Animals: Bridging Insights from Academia and Advocacy*, edited by Kristof Dhont and Gordon Hodson, provides evidence of contradictory human attitudes to animals.

1: A Brief History of Humans and Other Animals

Perhaps the finest book on the west's evolving attitudes to animals is Keith Thomas's *Man and the Natural World: Changing Attitudes in England 1500–1800*. Britain's historic flirtations with vegetarianism are found in Tristram Stuart's *The Bloodless Revolution: A Cultural History of Vegetarianism: From 1600 to Modern Times*. Allegations that vegetarians suffered sexual impotence are found in *The Vegetarian Crusade: The Rise of an American Reform Movement, 1817–1921* by Adam D. Shprintzen.

For dog-breeding and more, see Harriet Ritvo's *The Animal Estate: The English and Other Creatures in the Victorian Age*. John Hostettler's biography of Lord Erskine is *Thomas Erskine and Trial by Jury*. Norm Phelps's *The Longest Struggle: Animal Advocacy from Pythagoras to PETA* covers the major shifts in thinking about other animals.

The story of Alexander von Humboldt, the explorer who inspired Charles Darwin, lay beyond this book, but is covered beautifully in Andrea Wulf's biography, *The Invention of Nature: Alexander von Humboldt's New World*.

2: Slaughterhouse Rules

Yuval Noah Harari's *Sapiens* is the book that turned me vegetarian. Lori Marino wrote on the mental abilities of animals, including in her paper, 'Thinking Chickens: A Literature Review of Cognition, Emotion, and Behavior in the Domestic Chicken', published in *Animal Cognition*. I have drawn on several accounts of livestock farming, including Ingvar Ekesbo's *Farm Animal Behaviour: Characteristics for Assessment of Health and Welfare*. Ramachandra Guha wrote about

Gandhi's promise to his mother in *Gandhi: The Years that Changed the World, 1914–1948*. For easy-access data on how much land livestock use, see: www.ourworldindata.org/global-land-for-agriculture. For the carbon footprint of meat and dairy, see: www.ourworldindata.org/food-choice-vs-eating-local. Agricultural data are generally from the UN's Food and Agricultural Organization databases. The World Resources Institute's 2019 report *Creating a Sustainable Food Future* sketches a pathway to a better future. The Humane Society's ranking of US companies is at: www.humanesociety.org/resources/food-industry-scorecard.

3: The World Without Meat

Anthony Bourdain expressed his disgust for vegetarians in *Kitchen Confidential*, a book that even a vegan can't help but love. Bee Wilson's *First Bite: How We Learn to Eat* explores ways to encourage children to eat well. After throwing out all my old cookbooks (metaphorically), I became indebted to Anna Jones's *A Modern Way to Eat* and Hugh Fearnley-Whittingstall's *River Cottage Much More Veg*.

The statistic that 99 per cent of US farm animals live on factory farms comes from the Sentience Institute, based on the US Census of Agriculture. The predominance of livestock over wild land animals, in terms of biomass carbon, comes from Yinon M. Bar-On, Rob Phillips and Ron Milo's 'The Biomass Distribution on Earth', *PNAS* (2018). The economist Jayson Lusk has written about the 'vote-buy' gap.

4: The Ocean Always Loses

Callum Roberts' *Ocean of Life* outlines the destructive nature of modern fishing. Helen Scales' *Eye of the Shoal* discusses the wonders of fish. Statistics on the global fishing industry come from the FAO's *State of the World Fisheries and Aquaculture*. For the shortcomings of these figures, see Daniel Pauly and Dirk Zeller's paper 'Catch reconstructions reveal that global marine fisheries catches are higher than reported and declining', *Nature Communications* (2015), and Rashid Sumaila et al.'s 'Illicit trade in marine fish catch and its effects on ecosystems and people worldwide', *Science Advances* (2020). ICCAT is the source of some statistics on fish stocks. The IUCN Red List database covers the conservation status of marine animals. Alison Mood's estimates of the number of fish killed for food are at www.fishcount.org.uk. Robert Elwood has a chapter on invertebrates' ability to feel pain in *The Welfare of Invertebrate Animals*, edited by Claudio Carere and Jennifer Mather. Feedback's work on the inefficiency of fish farms is available at: www.feedbackglobal.org. For the wonder of octopuses, see Peter Godfrey-Smith's *Other Minds: The Octopus and the Evolution of Intelligent Life* and Sy Montgomery's *The Soul of an Octopus: A Surprising Exploration into the Wonder of Consciousness*. For the effect of climate change on the oceans, see the Intergovernmental Panel on Climate Change's *Special Report on the Ocean and Cryosphere in a Changing Climate*.

5: Holidays for Psychopaths

WildCRU, the Oxford research group that tracked Cecil the lion, has produced much of the key research on trophy-hunting, some of which is available at www.wildcru.org. For the changing demographics of US hunters, see the *National Survey of Fishing, Hunting & Wildlife-Associated Recreation*.

Aldo Leopold's ethos of conservation has stood the test of time remarkably: see, for example, *The Essential Aldo Leopold*, edited by Curt Meine and Richard L. Knight, and Julianne Lutz Newton's *Aldo Leopold's Odyssey*. Douglas Brinkley's *The Wilderness Warrior: Theodore Roosevelt and the Crusade for America* recounts Roosevelt's brand of hunting conservation, and his run-in with a lassoed bear.

Lorna Marshall's *Nyae Nyae !Kung Beliefs and Rites* and Jacques Lizot's *Tales of the Yanomami: Daily Life in the Venezuelan Forest* give accounts of indigenous societies.

6: The Ark of History

Nigel Rothfels' *Savages and Beasts: The Birth of the Modern Zoo* and Eric Baratay and Elizabeth Hardouin-Fugier, *Zoo: A History of Zoological Gardens in the West* cover the dawn of the modern zoo. For London Zoo in particular, see J. Barrington-Johnson's *The Zoo: The*

Story of London Zoo and Takashi Ito's *London Zoo and the Victorians, 1828–1859*. Ian Jared Miller's *The Nature of the Beasts: Empire and Exhibition at the Tokyo Imperial Zoo* tells the story of the massacre of zoo animals during the Second World War.

Colin Tudge's *Last Animals at the Zoo* depicts the role of zoos a generation ago. For a vision of how much worse zoos were then in welfare terms, Molly Dineen's BBC documentary series *The Ark*, shot at London Zoo in the early 1990s, is eye-opening.

Ros Clubb et al. analysed the longevity of elephants in their paper 'Compromised Survivorship in Zoo Elephants', *Science* (2008). Dalia Conde et al. estimated the conservation impact of zoos in 'An Emerging Role of Zoos to Conserve Biodiversity', *Science* (2011), to which Andrew Balmford et al. responded in 'Zoos and Captive Breeding', *Science* (2011).

For the updated dilemmas of zoos, and estimates of what percentage of revenues US zoos spend on conservation, see Ben A. Minteer, Jane Maienschein, and James Collins (eds), *The Ark and Beyond: The Evolution of Zoo and Aquarium Conservation*.

7: Nothing But Footprints

Living in Colombia, I was entranced by John Hemming's *Tree of Rivers: The Story of the Amazon*. Ciro Guerra's 2015 film *Embrace of the Serpent* conjures up the magic of the forest.

Bill Adams's book *Against Extinction* traces the history of conservation. The IUCN Red List database is publicly available at: www.iucnredlist.org. For statistics on how much of a country's land and sea is protected, see www.protectedplanet.net. Friederike C. Bolam et al. estimated conservationists' role in saving species in 'How many bird and mammal extinctions has recent conservation action prevented?', *Conservation Letters* (2020). WWF's Living Planet Index is available at: www.livingplanetindex.org.

George Monbiot's *Feral* sparked interest in rewilding in Britain. Josh Donlan and colleagues proposed cheetah, lions and elephants being released into the US in 'Re-wilding North America', *Nature* (2005). Douglas Tompkins's story is vividly told by Andrés Azócar in

Tompkins. El millonario verde. For updates on E. O. Wilson's Half-Earth campaign, see: www.half-earthproject.org.

For evidence that land-sparing may do better for biodiversity than land-sharing, see Matthew Scott Luskin et al., 'Study context shapes recommendations of land-sparing and sharing; a quantitative review', *Global Food Security* (2017). The situation may be more nuanced in Europe: see Tom Finch et al., 'Bird conservation and the land sharing-sparing continuum in farmland-dominated landscapes of lowland England', *Conservation Biology*, (2019).

Everyone should realise the depth of our current predicament with nature, summed up in Elizabeth Kolbert's *The Sixth Extinction* and Bill McKibben's *Falter.* Dave Goulson's *A Sting in the Tale* addresses the beauty and precariousness of bees. To see how bees can reduce conflict between humans and elephants in Kenya, see: www.elephant sandbees.com.

8: It's Not About the Dog

There are several excellent books on humans' relationship with pets, including John Bradshaw's *The Animals Among Us*, Alexandra Horowitz's *Our Dogs, Ourselves: The Story of a Singular Bond* and Hal Herzog's *Some We Love, Some We Hate, Some We Eat.* Andrew Rowan has estimated the global dog population: see www.wellbeingintl.org. For the difficulties of keeping certain animals in captivity, see Catherine Toft and Timothy Wright's *Parrots of the Wild: A Natural History of the World's Most Captivating Birds* and *The UFAW Companion Animal Handbook*, edited by James Yeates. Clare Palmer's views are taken from *Animal Ethics in Context.*

9: Playing God

Helen Pilcher's *Life-changing: How Humans are Altering Life on Earth* is a brilliant journey through the myriad ways in which humans are changing animal life, deliberately or not. Ben A. Minteer unwraps some of the philosophical dilemmas involved in his thoughtful book, *The Fall of the Wild: Extinction, De-Extinction and the Ethics of Conservation.* Emma Marris's *Rambunctious Garden* eloquently makes the case that nature is not as static as we sometimes think. Martin Rees's thoughts are from his 2018 book, *On the Future: Prospects for Humanity*; Toby Ord explores the possibility of human extinction in *The Precipice*.

10: Conclusion: Beauty and the Beast

Harry Greene's quote is from his memoir, *Tracks and Shadows: Field Biology as Art*. If ever the task of changing our relationship with nature seems too great, there is Rebecca Solnit's inspirational account of the power of activism, *Hope in the Dark*.

INDEX